ARCANA

Arcana Vol. 8
Created by So-Young Lee

Translation - Ellen Choi
English Adaptation - Barbara Randall Kesel
Copy Editor - Shannon Watters
Retouch and Lettering - Star Print Brokers
Production Artist - Bowen Park
Graphic Designer - James Lee

Editor - Bryce P. Coleman
Digital Imaging Manager - Chris Buford
Pre-Production Supervisor - Erika Terriquez
Production Manager - Elisabeth Brizzi
Managing Editor - Vy Nguyen
Creative Director - Anne Marie Horne
Editor-in-Chief - Rob Tokar
Publisher - Mike Kiley
President and C.O.O. - John Parker
C.E.O. and Chief Creative Officer - Stu Levy

A **TOKYOPOP** Manga

TOKYOPOP Inc.
5900 Wilshire Blvd. Suite 2000
Los Angeles, CA 90036

E-mail: info@TOKYOPOP.com
Come visit us online at www.TOKYOPOP.com

ISBN: 978-1-4278-0166-1

First TOKYOPOP printing: April 2008
10 9 8 7 6 5 4 3 2 1
Printed in the USA

VOLUME 8
SO-YOUNG LEE

HAMBURG // LONDON // LOS ANGELES // TOKYO

THE JOURNEY THUS FAR...

THE TALE OF ENRIL CONTINUES...
AFTER MAKING CONTACT WITH A DRAGON
NEAR HER VILLAGE, ENRIL RETURNS HOME
ONLY TO FIND HER ENTIRE FAMILY MURDERED.
THE HORRIBLE DEED WAS COMMITTED BY ONE
OF THE DARK ELVES, AESHIMA, WHO WOULD
HAVE KILLED THE GIRL AS WELL, IF IT WEREN'T
FOR THE INTERVENTION OF THEIR LEADER,
KYRETTE. UPON LEARNING OF ENRIL'S TIES TO
THE POWERFUL DRAGON, KYRETTE BECOMES
OBSESSED WITH GAINING THE POWER FOR
HIMSELF. AND AS HE MANIPULATES THE YOUNG
HUMAN FOR HIS OWN ENDS, AESHIMA SCHEMES
TO LEARN MORE ABOUT HIS LEADER'S
MOTIVES...

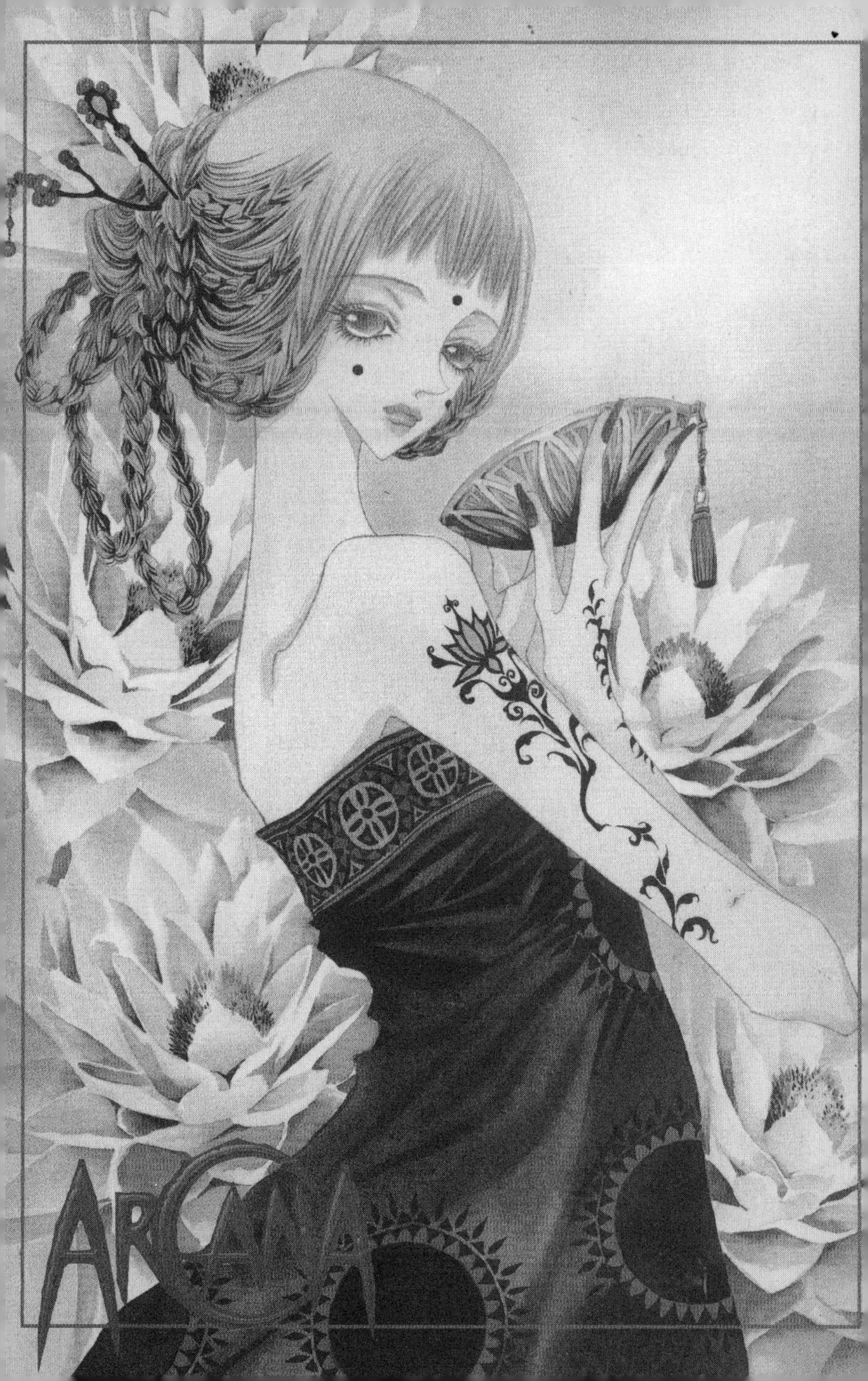

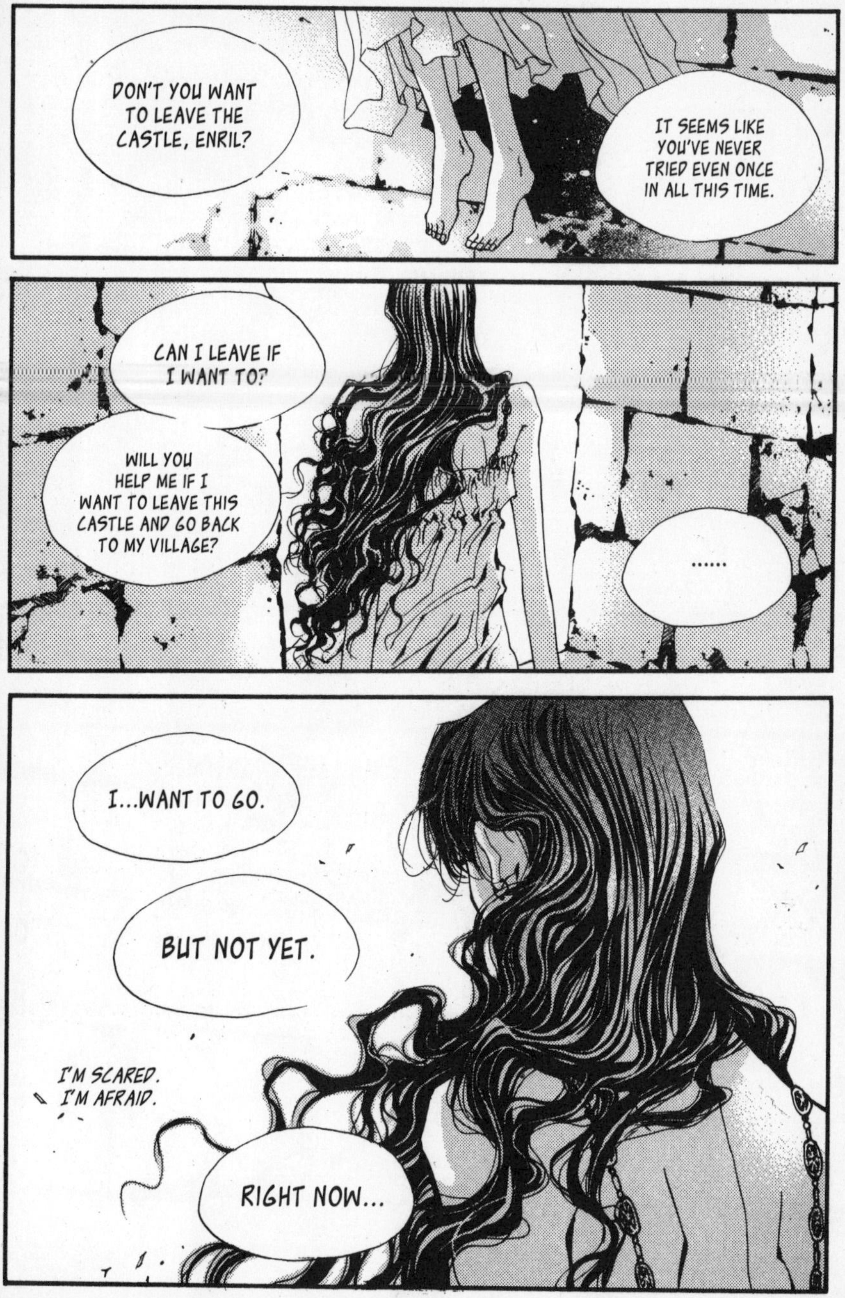
DON'T YOU WANT TO LEAVE THE CASTLE, ENRIL?
IT SEEMS LIKE YOU'VE NEVER TRIED EVEN ONCE IN ALL THIS TIME.
CAN I LEAVE IF I WANT TO?
WILL YOU HELP ME IF I WANT TO LEAVE THIS CASTLE AND GO BACK TO MY VILLAGE?
......
I...WANT TO GO.
BUT NOT YET.
I'M SCARED. I'M AFRAID.
RIGHT NOW...

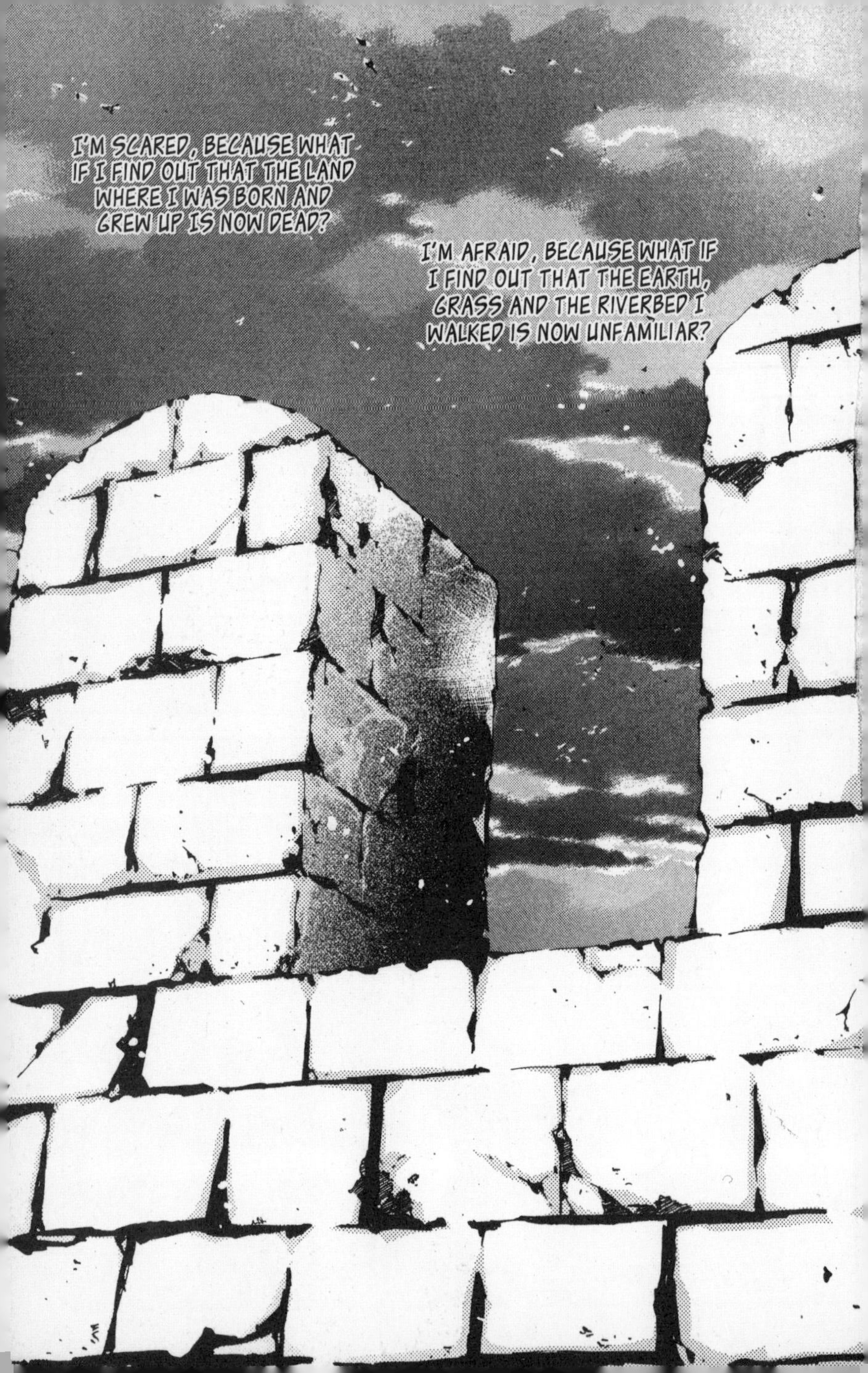
I'M SCARED, BECAUSE WHAT IF I FIND OUT THAT THE LAND WHERE I WAS BORN AND GREW UP IS NOW DEAD?
I'M AFRAID, BECAUSE WHAT IF I FIND OUT THAT THE EARTH, GRASS AND THE RIVERBED I WALKED IS NOW UNFAMILIAR?

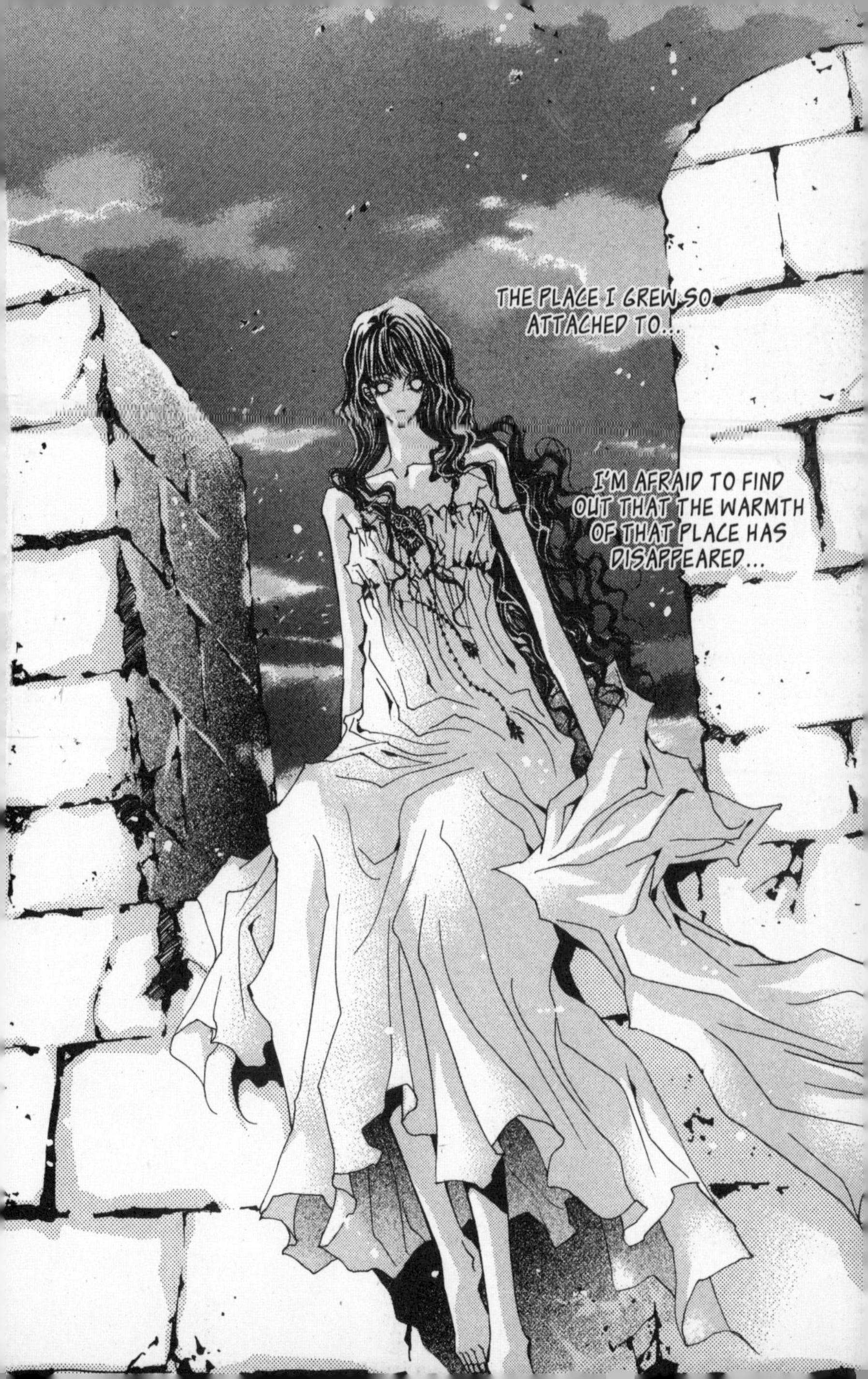
THE PLACE I GREW SO ATTACHED TO...
I'M AFRAID TO FIND OUT THAT THE WARMTH OF THAT PLACE HAS DISAPPEARED...

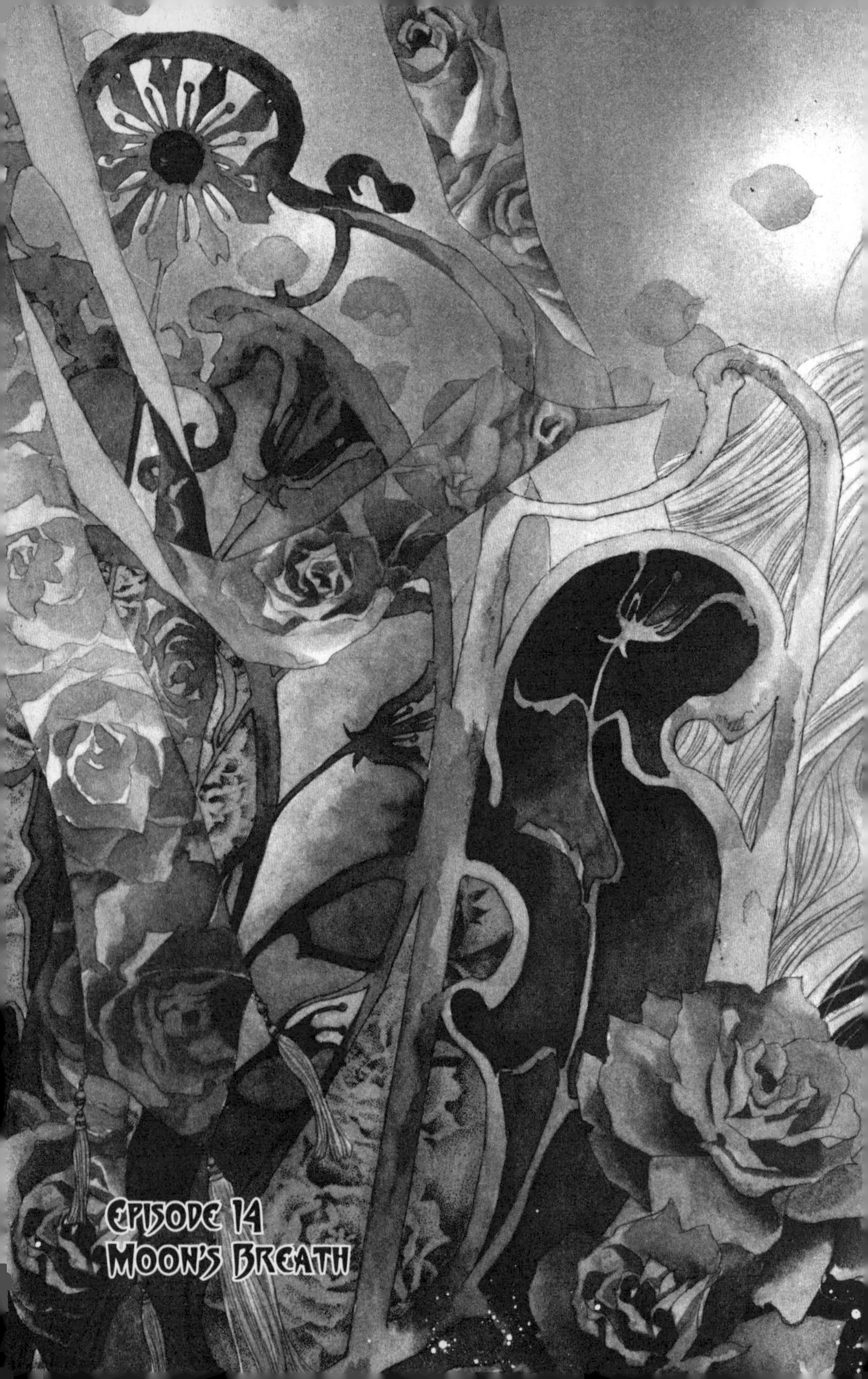
Episode 14
Moon's Breath

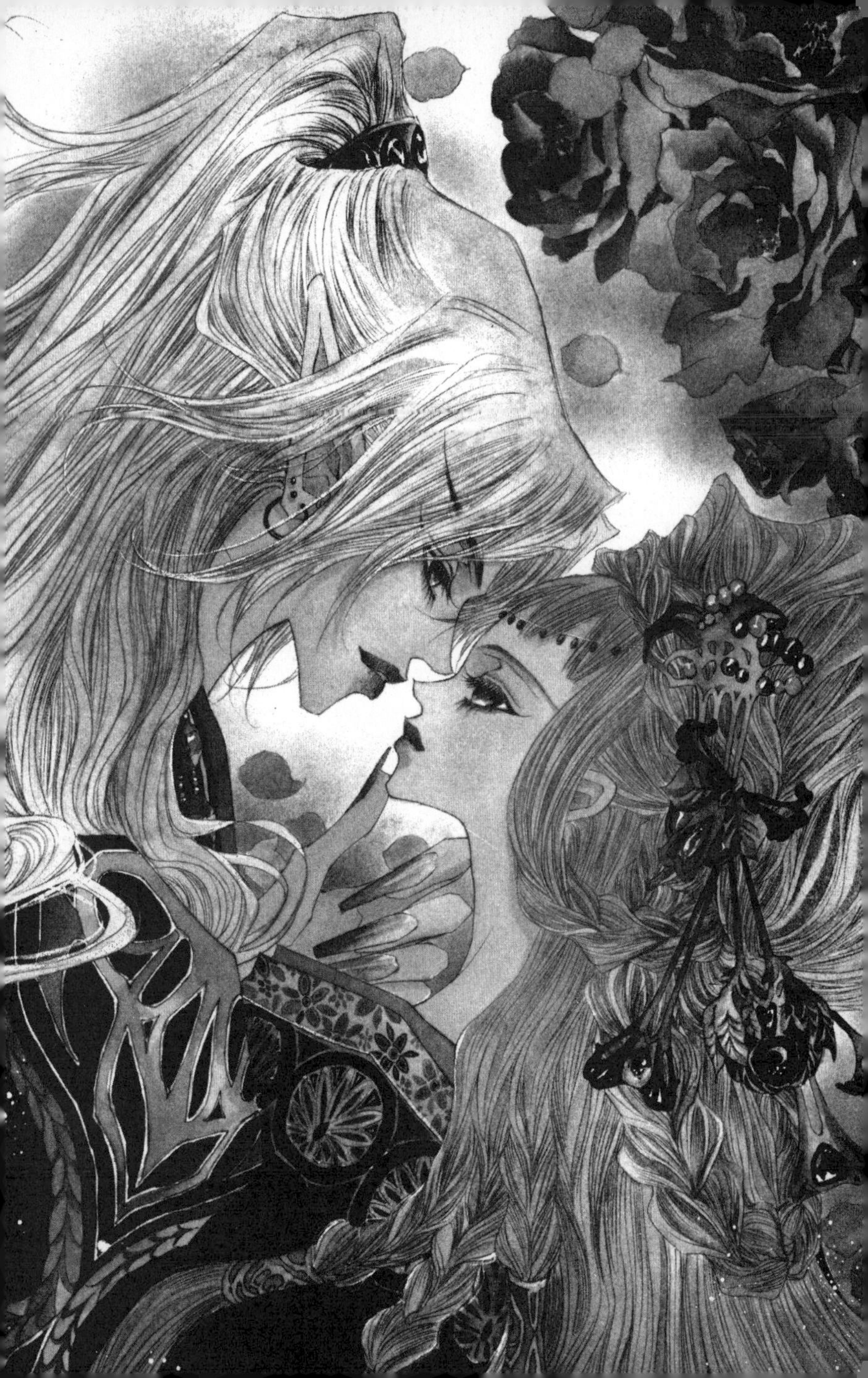

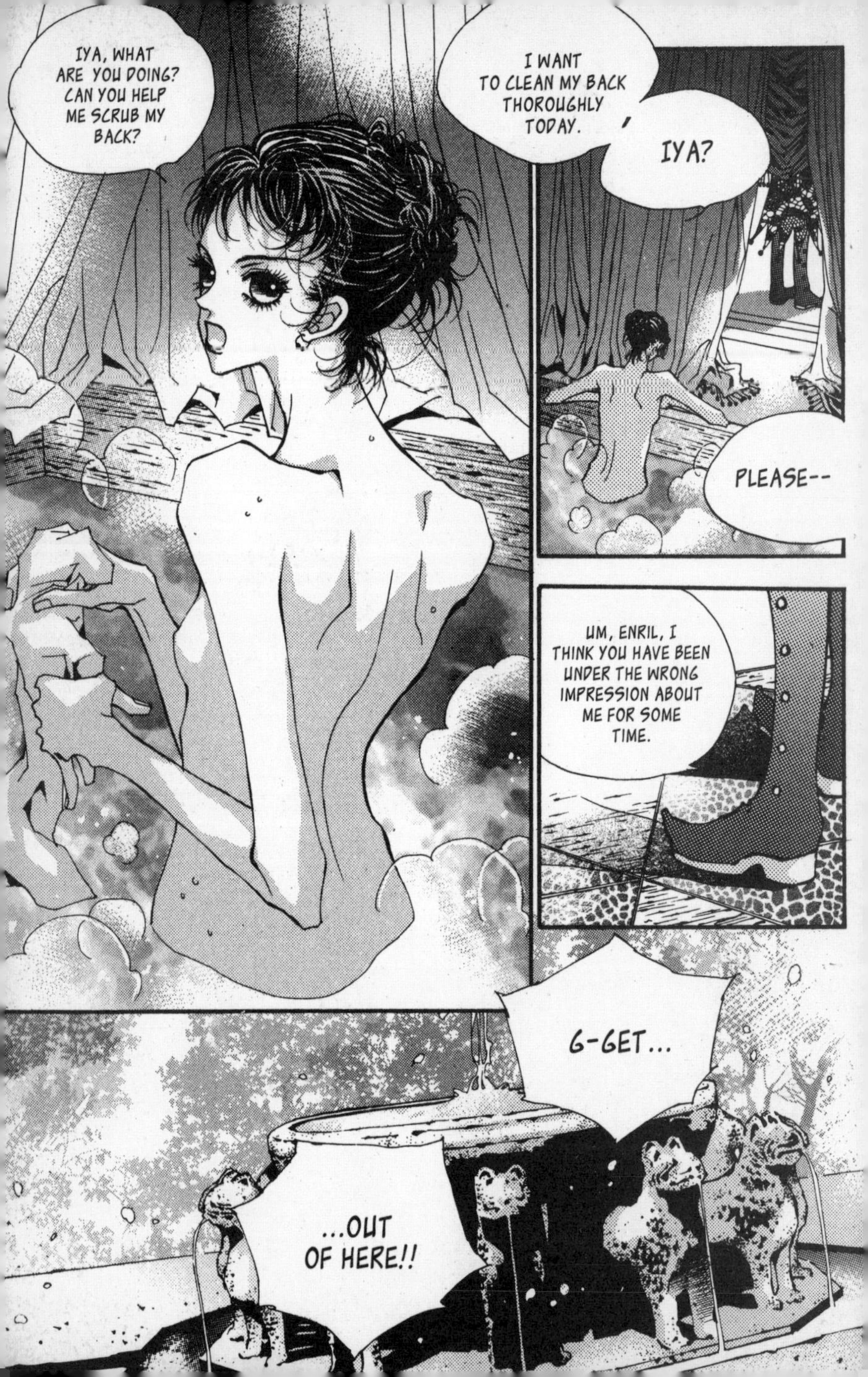
IYA, WHAT ARE YOU DOING? CAN YOU HELP ME SCRUB MY BACK?
I WANT TO CLEAN MY BACK THOROUGHLY TODAY.
IYA?
PLEASE--
UM, ENRIL, I THINK YOU HAVE BEEN UNDER THE WRONG IMPRESSION ABOUT ME FOR SOME TIME.
G-GET...
...OUT OF HERE!!

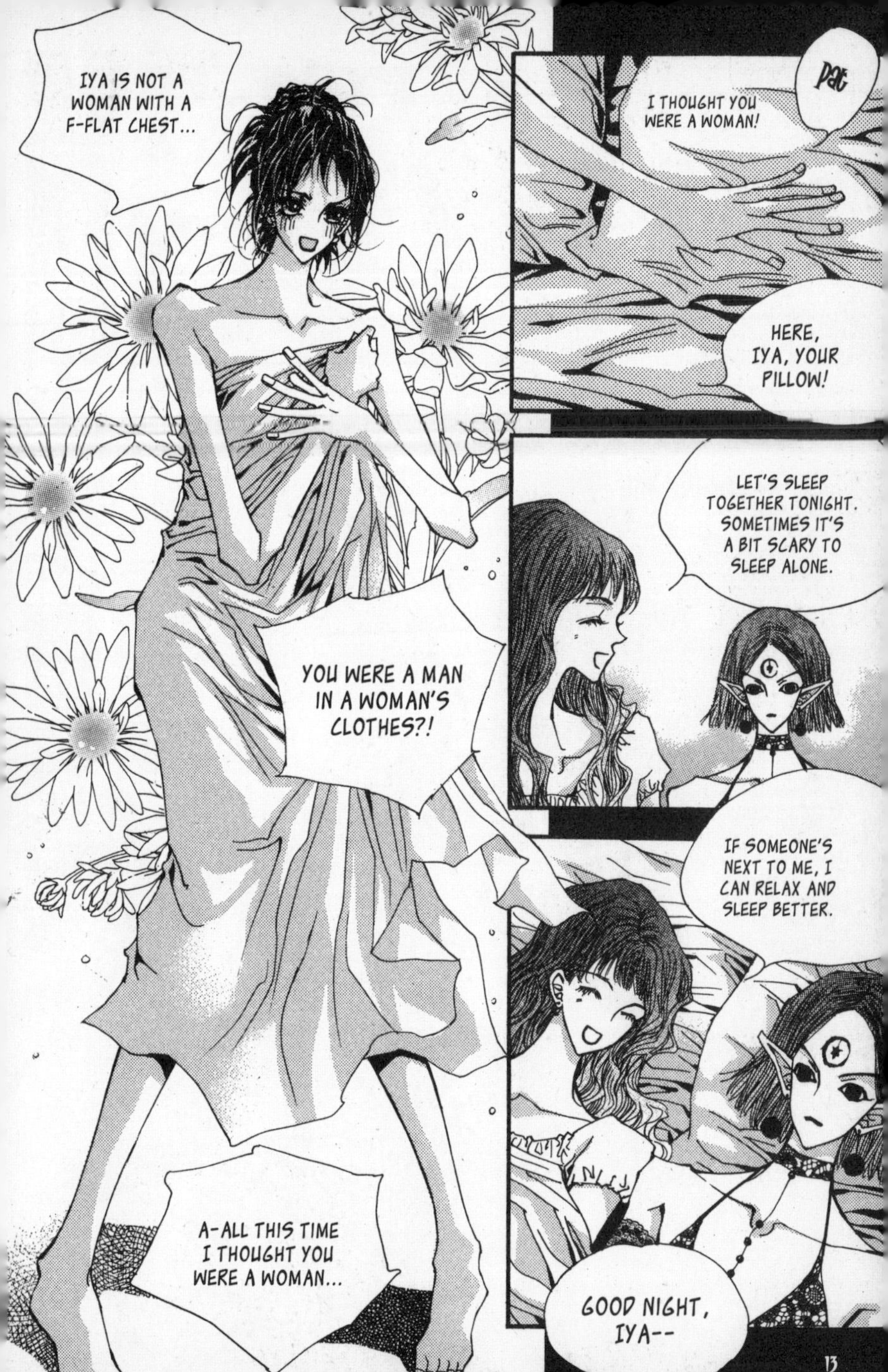

IYA IS NOT A WOMAN WITH A F-FLAT CHEST...
YOU WERE A MAN IN A WOMAN'S CLOTHES?!
A-ALL THIS TIME I THOUGHT YOU WERE A WOMAN...
I THOUGHT YOU WERE A WOMAN!
Pat
HERE, IYA, YOUR PILLOW!
LET'S SLEEP TOGETHER TONIGHT. SOMETIMES IT'S A BIT SCARY TO SLEEP ALONE.
IF SOMEONE'S NEXT TO ME, I CAN RELAX AND SLEEP BETTER.
GOOD NIGHT, IYA--

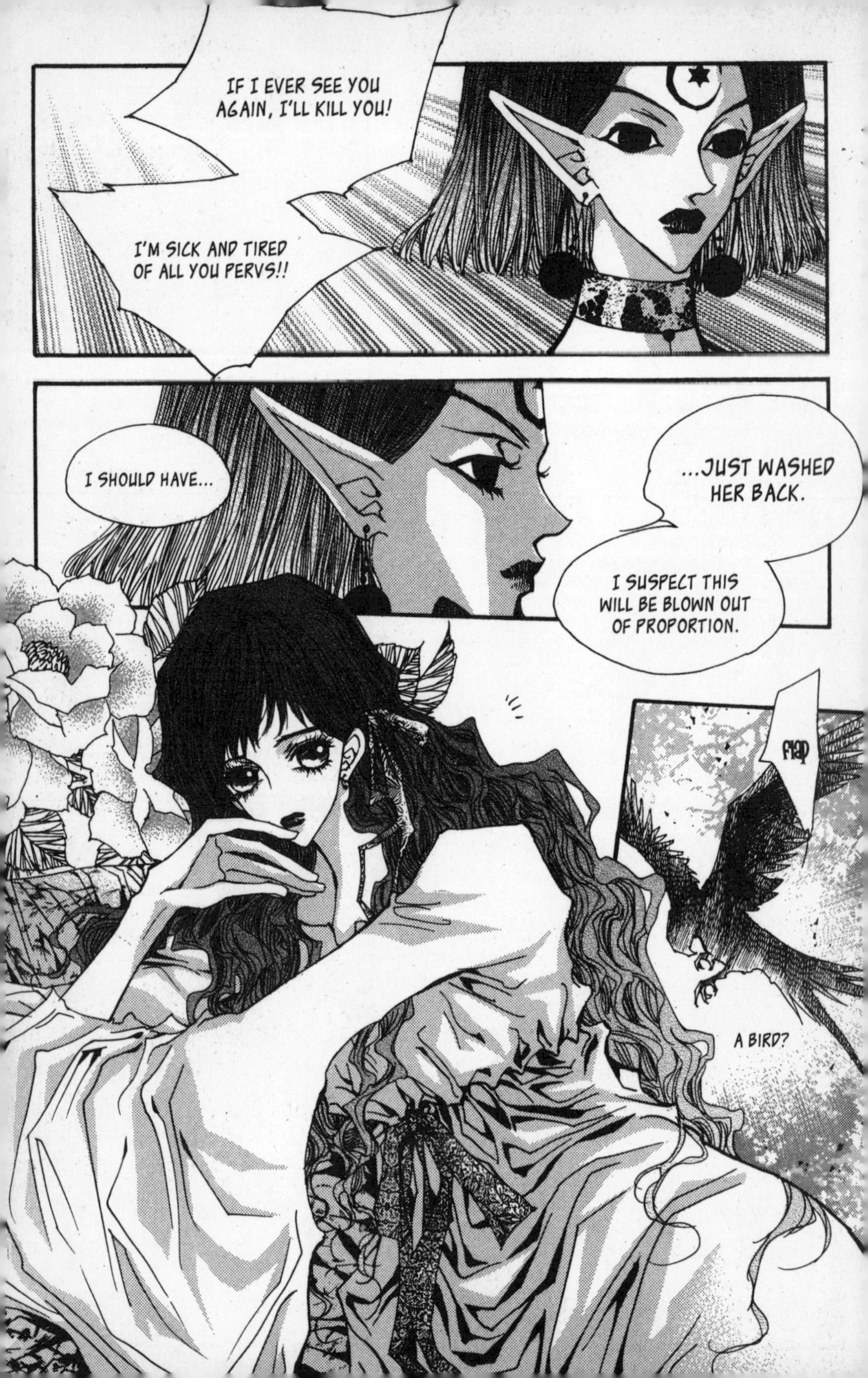
IF I EVER SEE YOU AGAIN, I'LL KILL YOU!
I'M SICK AND TIRED OF ALL YOU PERVS!!
I SHOULD HAVE...
...JUST WASHED HER BACK.
I SUSPECT THIS WILL BE BLOWN OUT OF PROPORTION.
FLAP
A BIRD?

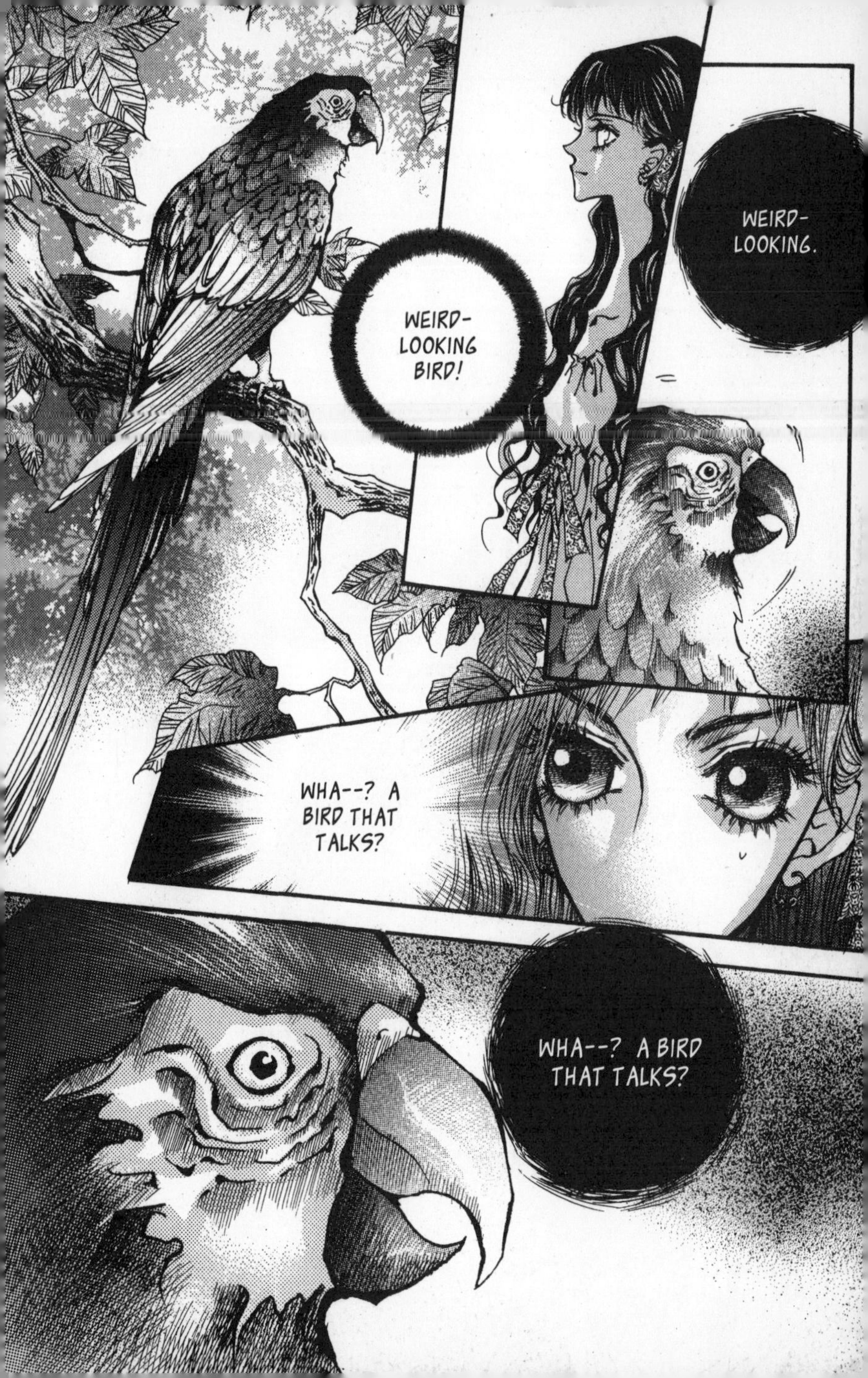
WEIRD-LOOKING BIRD!
WEIRD-LOOKING.
WHA--? A BIRD THAT TALKS?
WHA--? A BIRD THAT TALKS?

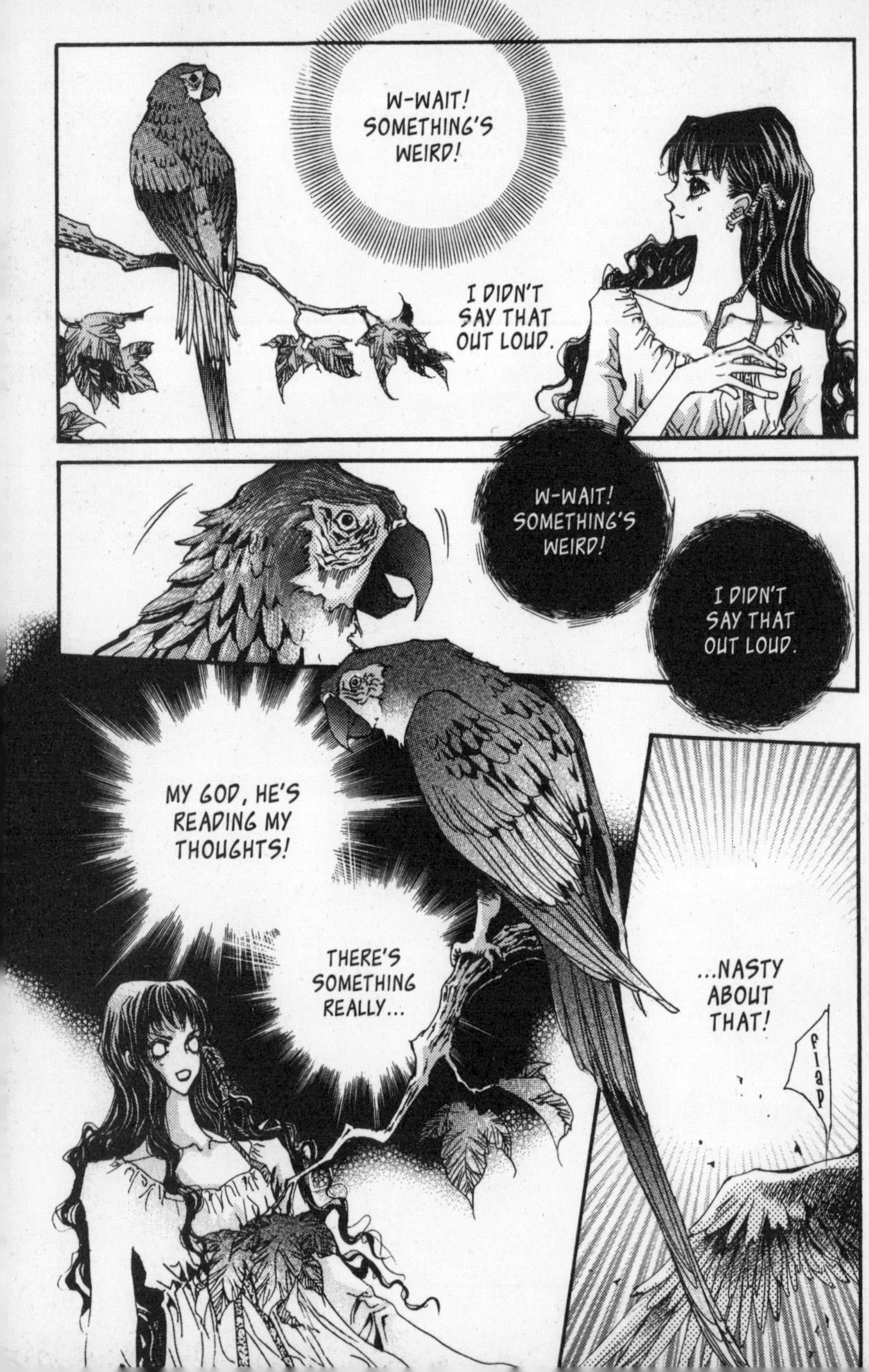
W-WAIT! SOMETHING'S WEIRD!
I DIDN'T SAY THAT OUT LOUD.
W-WAIT! SOMETHING'S WEIRD!
I DIDN'T SAY THAT OUT LOUD.
MY GOD, HE'S READING MY THOUGHTS!
THERE'S SOMETHING REALLY...
...NASTY ABOUT THAT!
flap

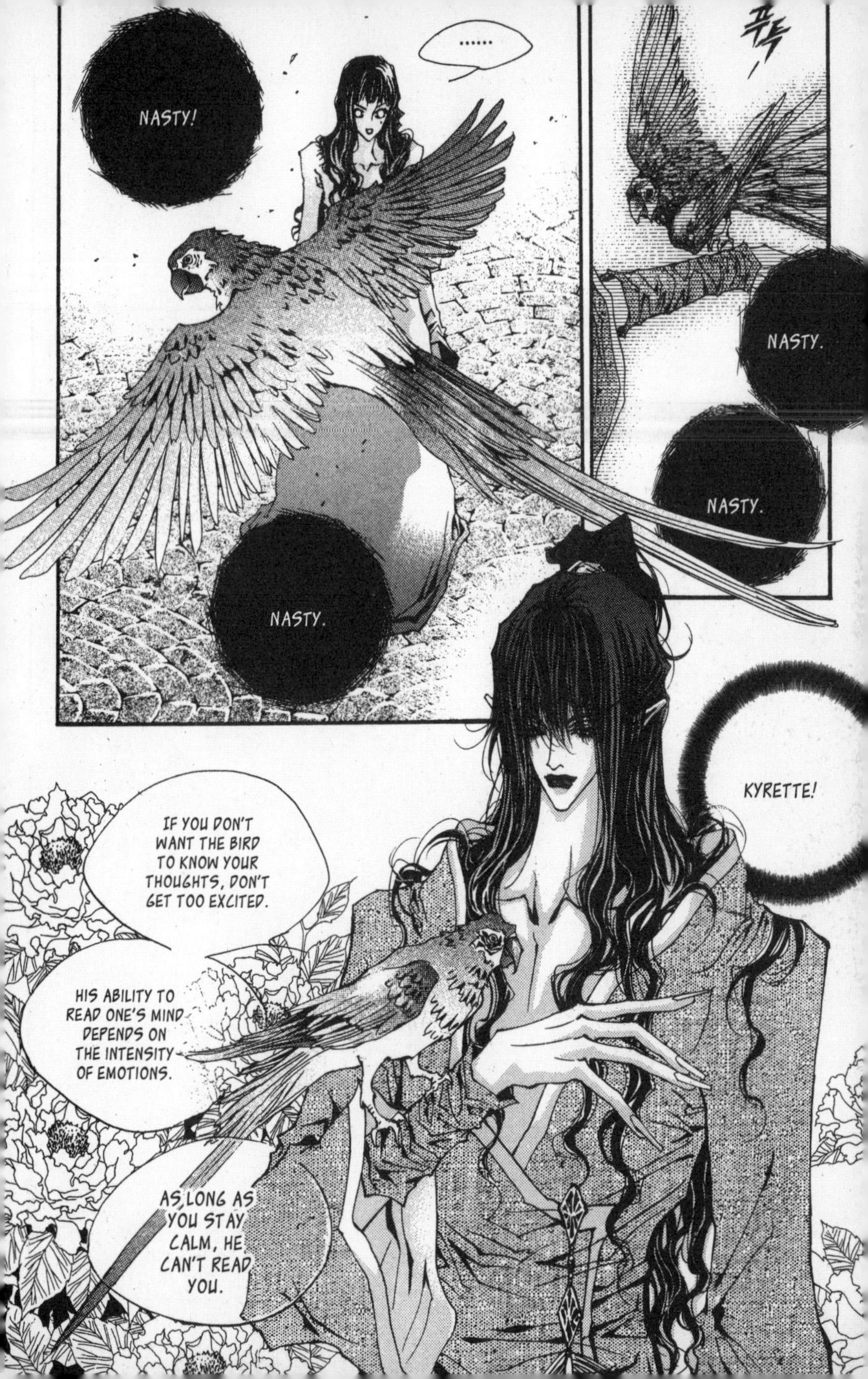

....
NASTY!
NASTY.
푸득!
NASTY.
NASTY.
KYRETTE!
IF YOU DON'T WANT THE BIRD TO KNOW YOUR THOUGHTS, DON'T GET TOO EXCITED.
HIS ABILITY TO READ ONE'S MIND DEPENDS ON THE INTENSITY OF EMOTIONS.
AS LONG AS YOU STAY CALM, HE CAN'T READ YOU.

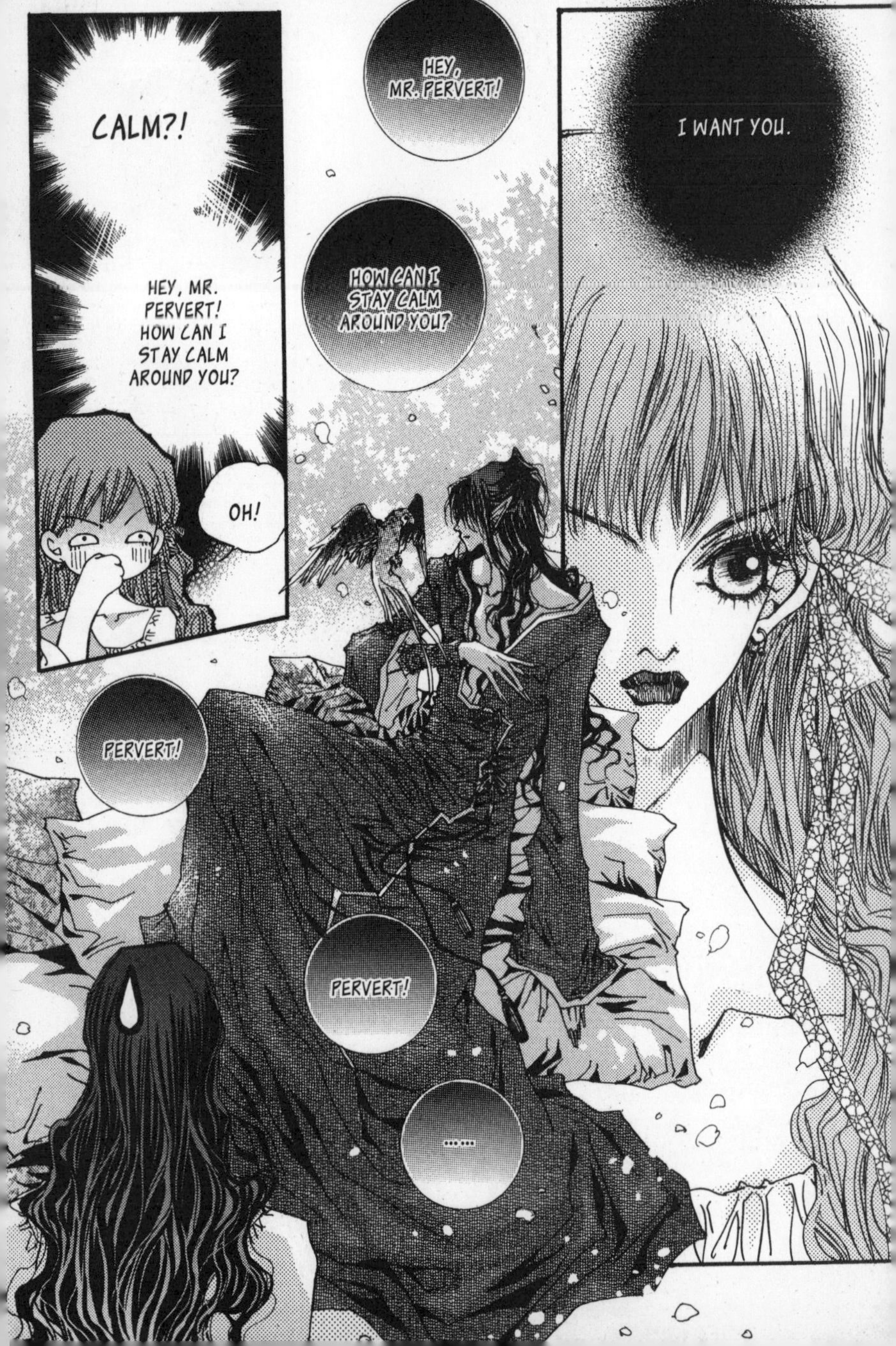
CALM?!
HEY, MR. PERVERT! HOW CAN I STAY CALM AROUND YOU?
OH!
HEY, MR. PERVERT!
HOW CAN I STAY CALM AROUND YOU?
I WANT YOU.
PERVERT!
PERVERT!
……

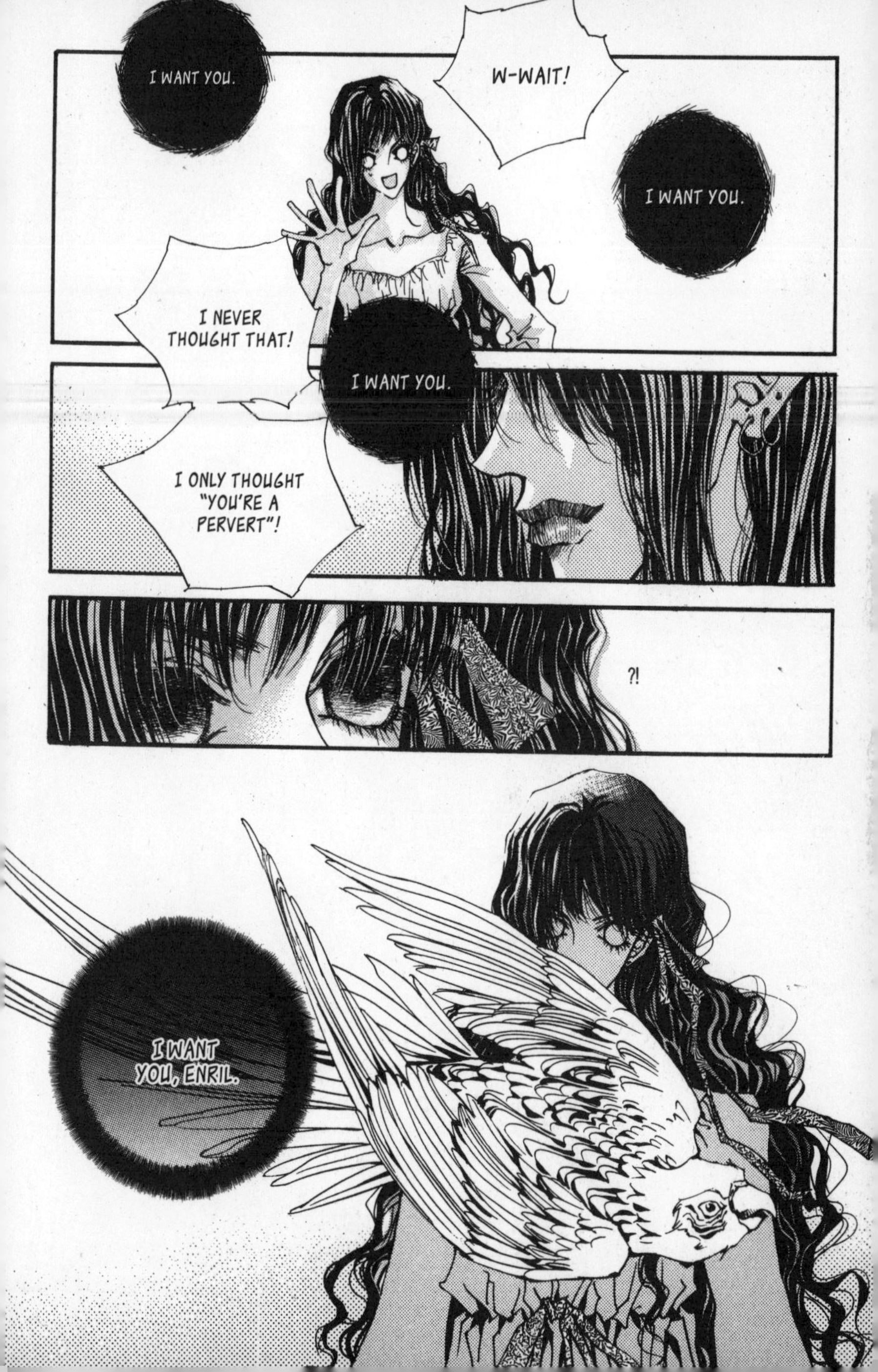
I WANT YOU.
W-WAIT!
I WANT YOU.
I NEVER THOUGHT THAT!
I WANT YOU.
I ONLY THOUGHT "YOU'RE A PERVERT"!
?!
I WANT YOU, ENRIL.

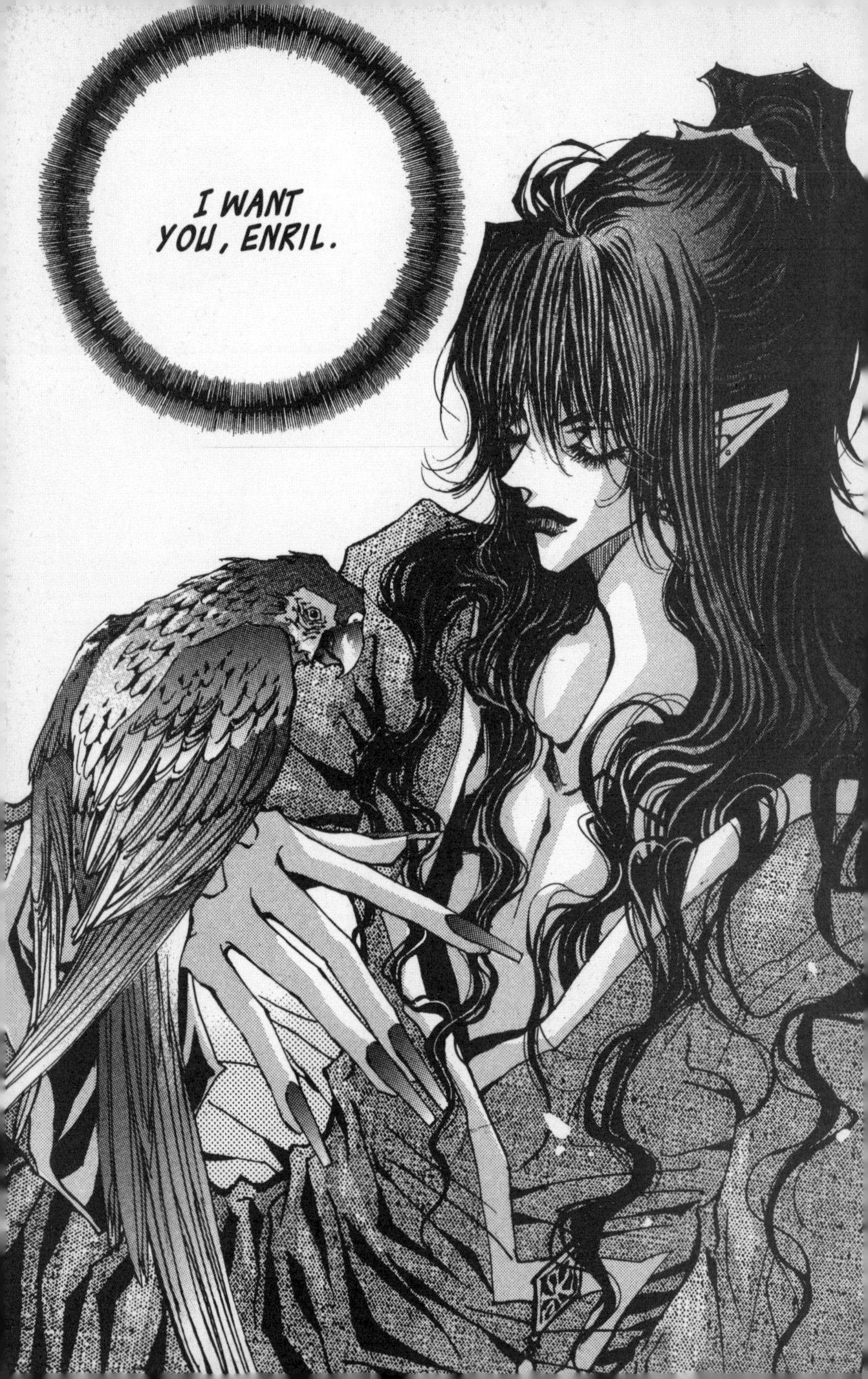
I WANT YOU, ENRIL.

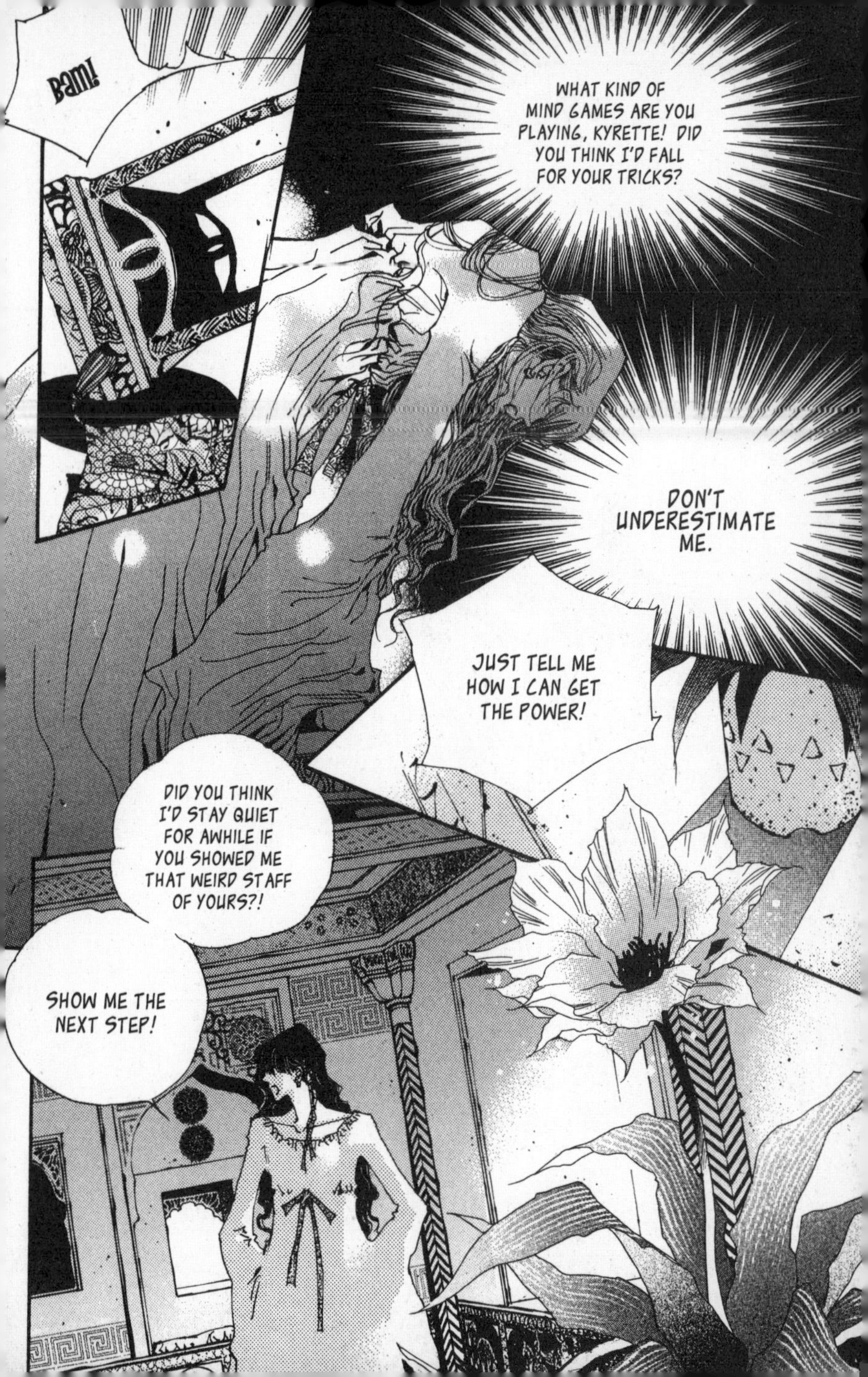
BAM!
WHAT KIND OF MIND GAMES ARE YOU PLAYING, KYRETTE! DID YOU THINK I'D FALL FOR YOUR TRICKS?
DON'T UNDERESTIMATE ME.
JUST TELL ME HOW I CAN GET THE POWER!
DID YOU THINK I'D STAY QUIET FOR AWHILE IF YOU SHOWED ME THAT WEIRD STAFF OF YOURS?!
SHOW ME THE NEXT STEP!

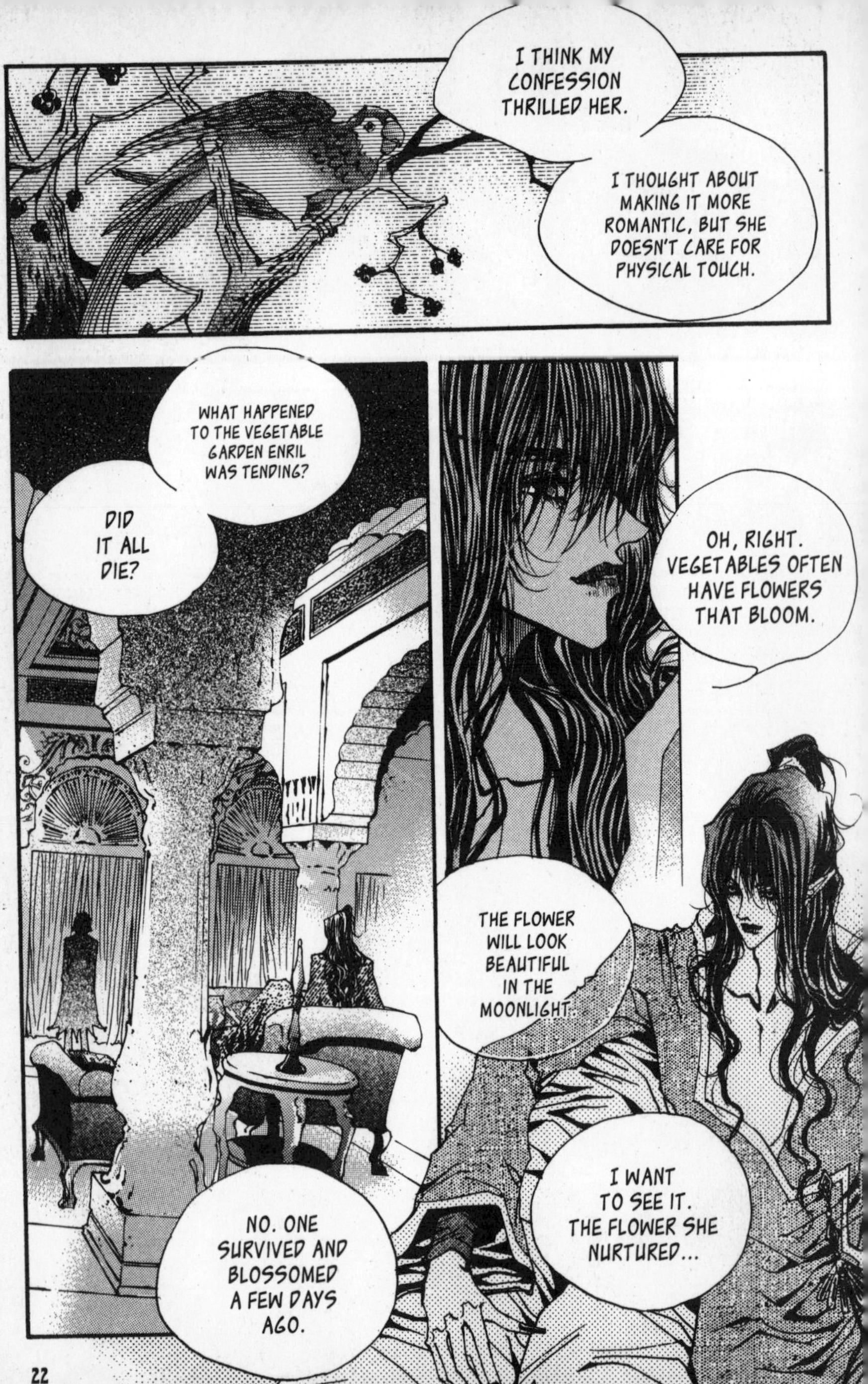

I THINK MY CONFESSION THRILLED HER.
I THOUGHT ABOUT MAKING IT MORE ROMANTIC, BUT SHE DOESN'T CARE FOR PHYSICAL TOUCH.
WHAT HAPPENED TO THE VEGETABLE GARDEN ENRIL WAS TENDING?
DID IT ALL DIE?
OH, RIGHT. VEGETABLES OFTEN HAVE FLOWERS THAT BLOOM.
THE FLOWER WILL LOOK BEAUTIFUL IN THE MOONLIGHT.
NO. ONE SURVIVED AND BLOSSOMED A FEW DAYS AGO.
I WANT TO SEE IT. THE FLOWER SHE NURTURED...

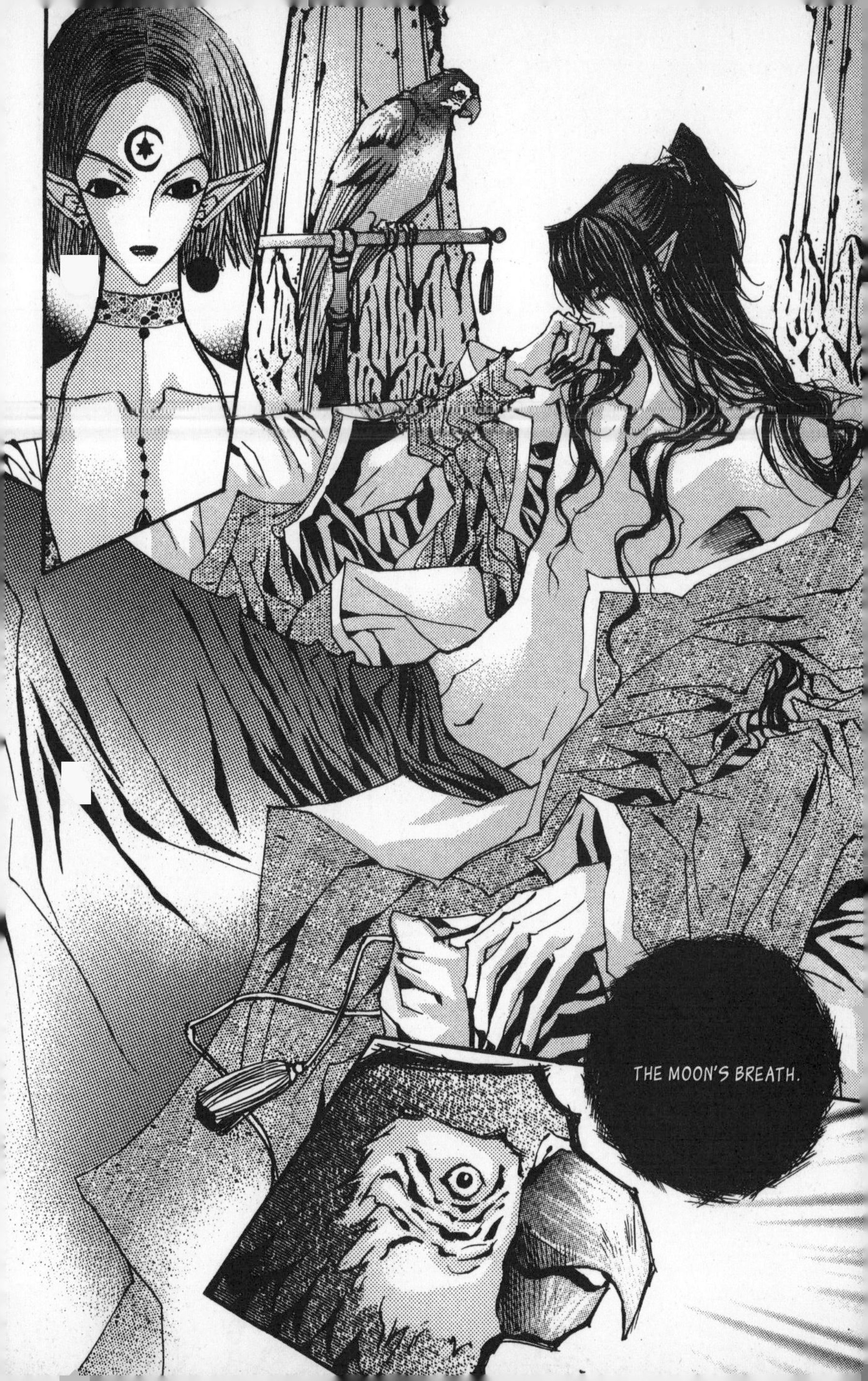
THE MOON'S BREATH.

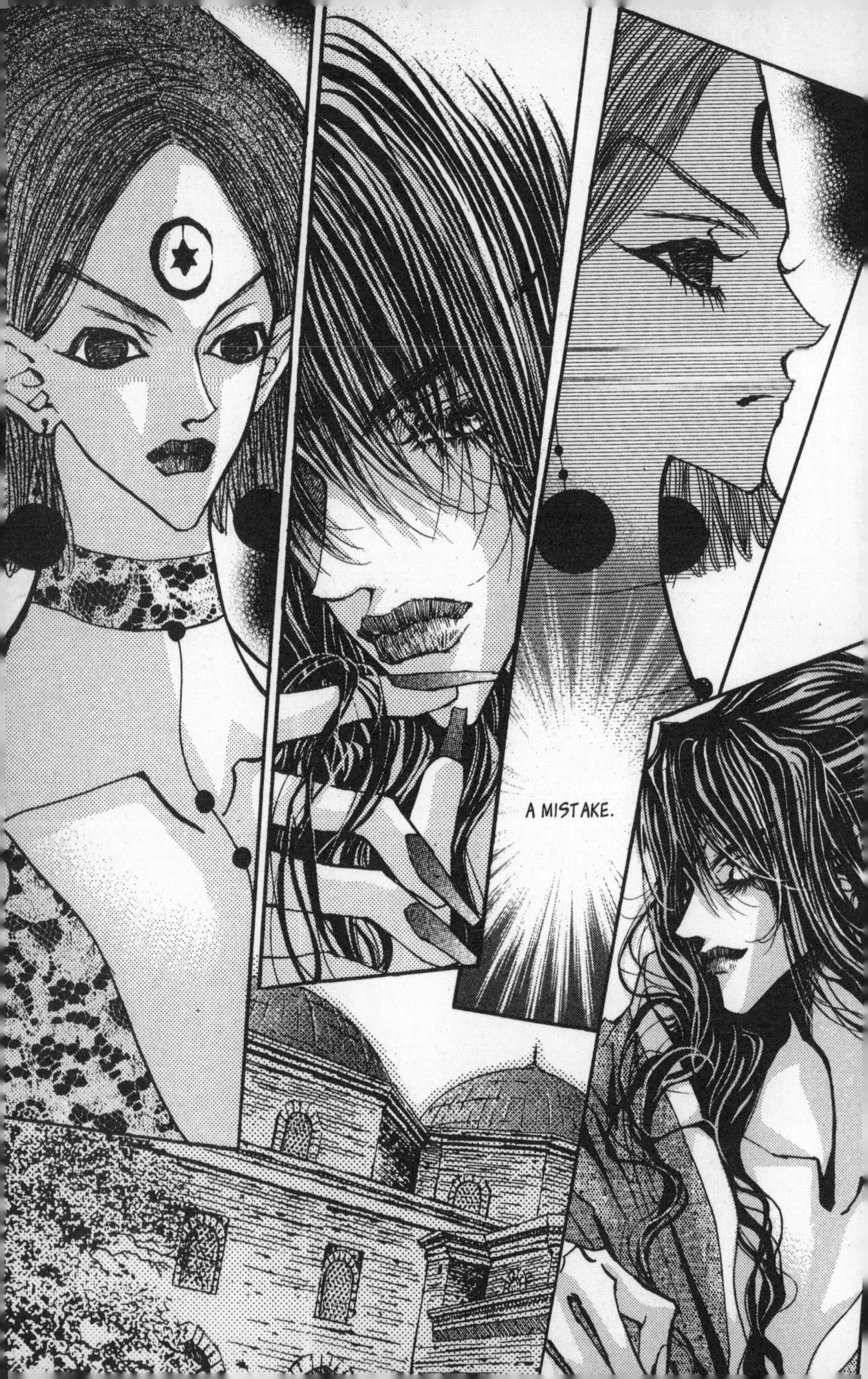
A MISTAKE.

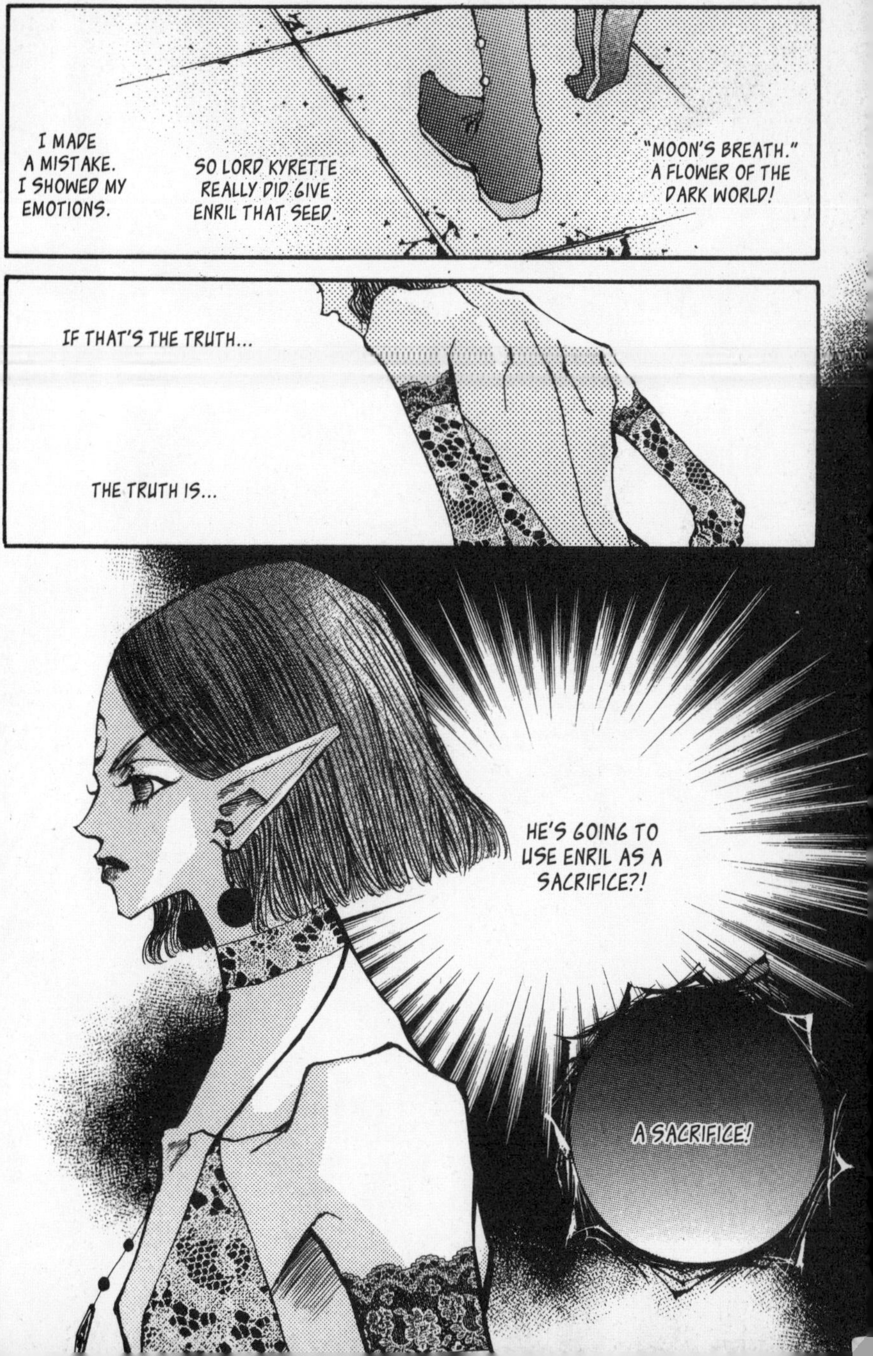
I MADE A MISTAKE. I SHOWED MY EMOTIONS.
SO LORD KYRETTE REALLY DID GIVE ENRIL THAT SEED.
"MOON'S BREATH." A FLOWER OF THE DARK WORLD!
IF THAT'S THE TRUTH...
THE TRUTH IS...
HE'S GOING TO USE ENRIL AS A SACRIFICE?!
A SACRIFICE!

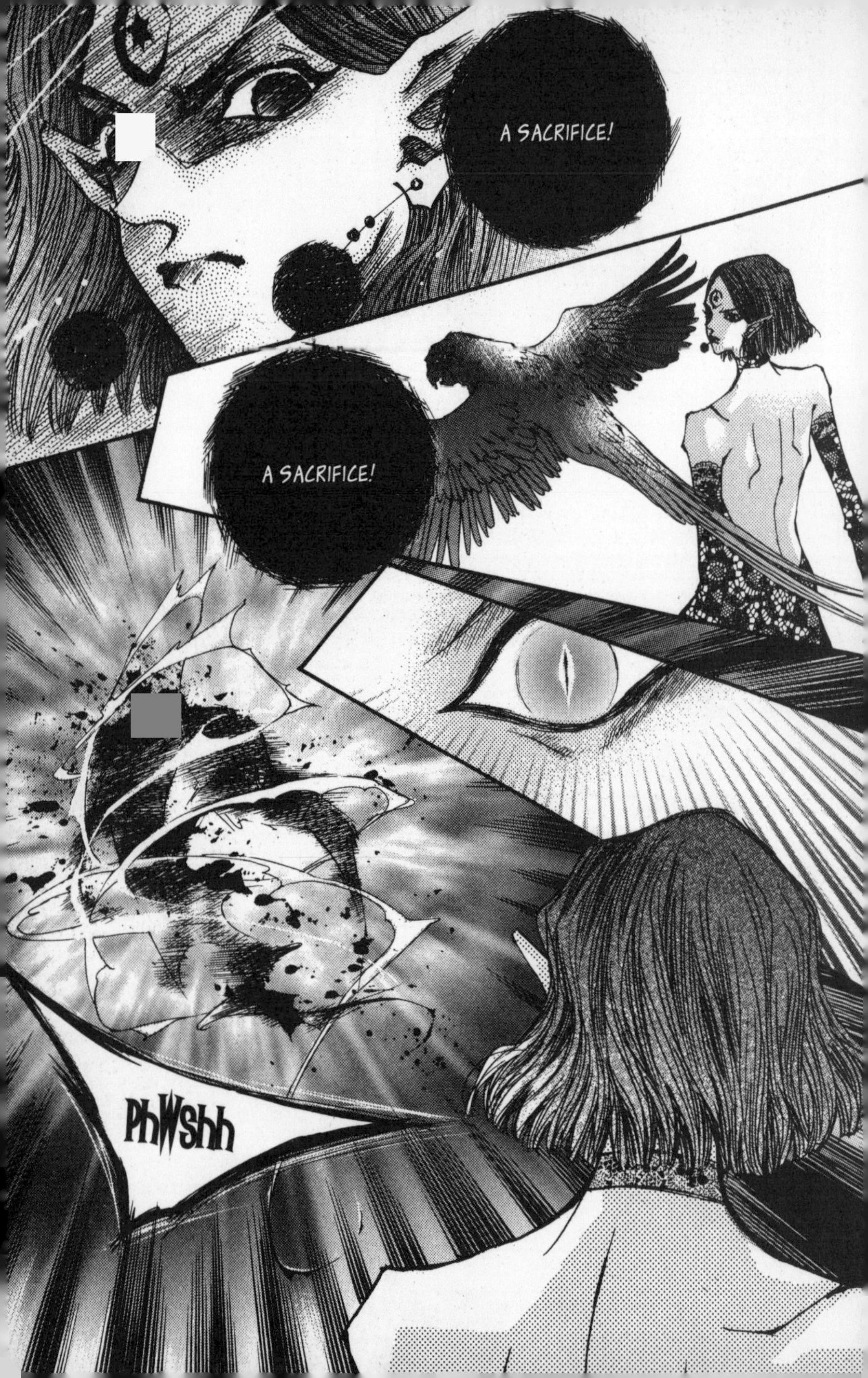
A SACRIFICE!
A SACRIFICE!
PhWshh

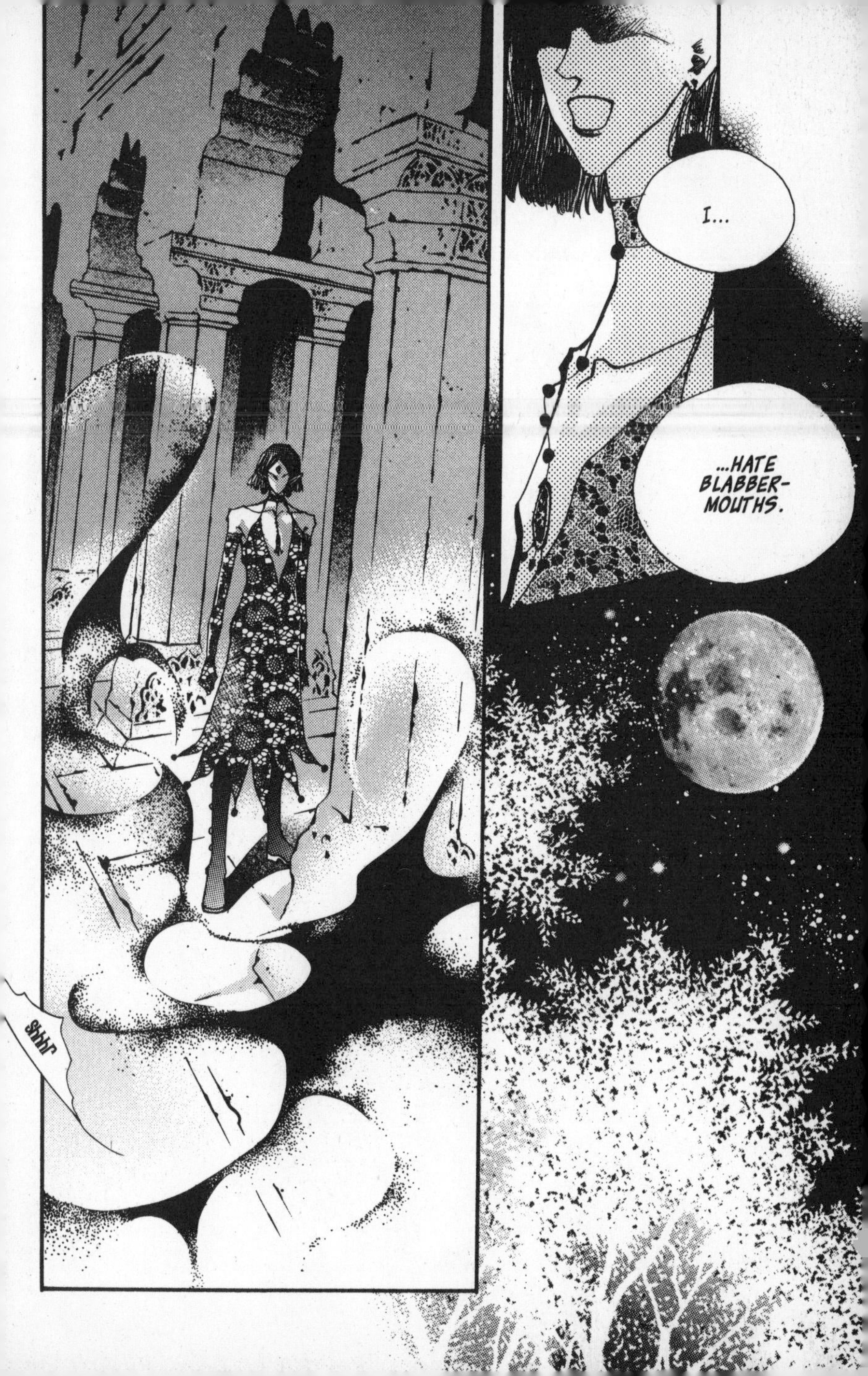
I...
...HATE BLABBER-MOUTHS.

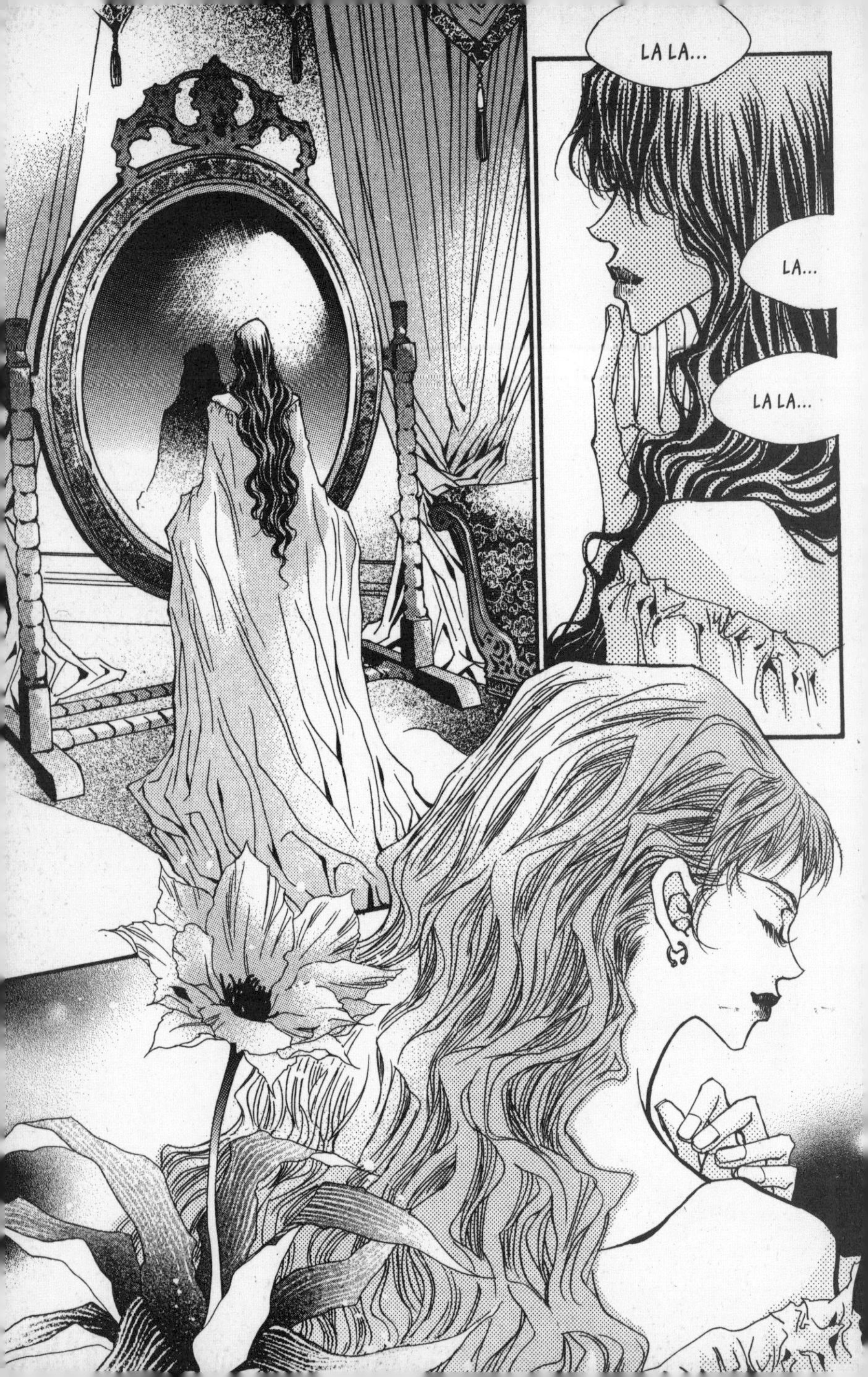
LA LA...
LA...
LA LA...

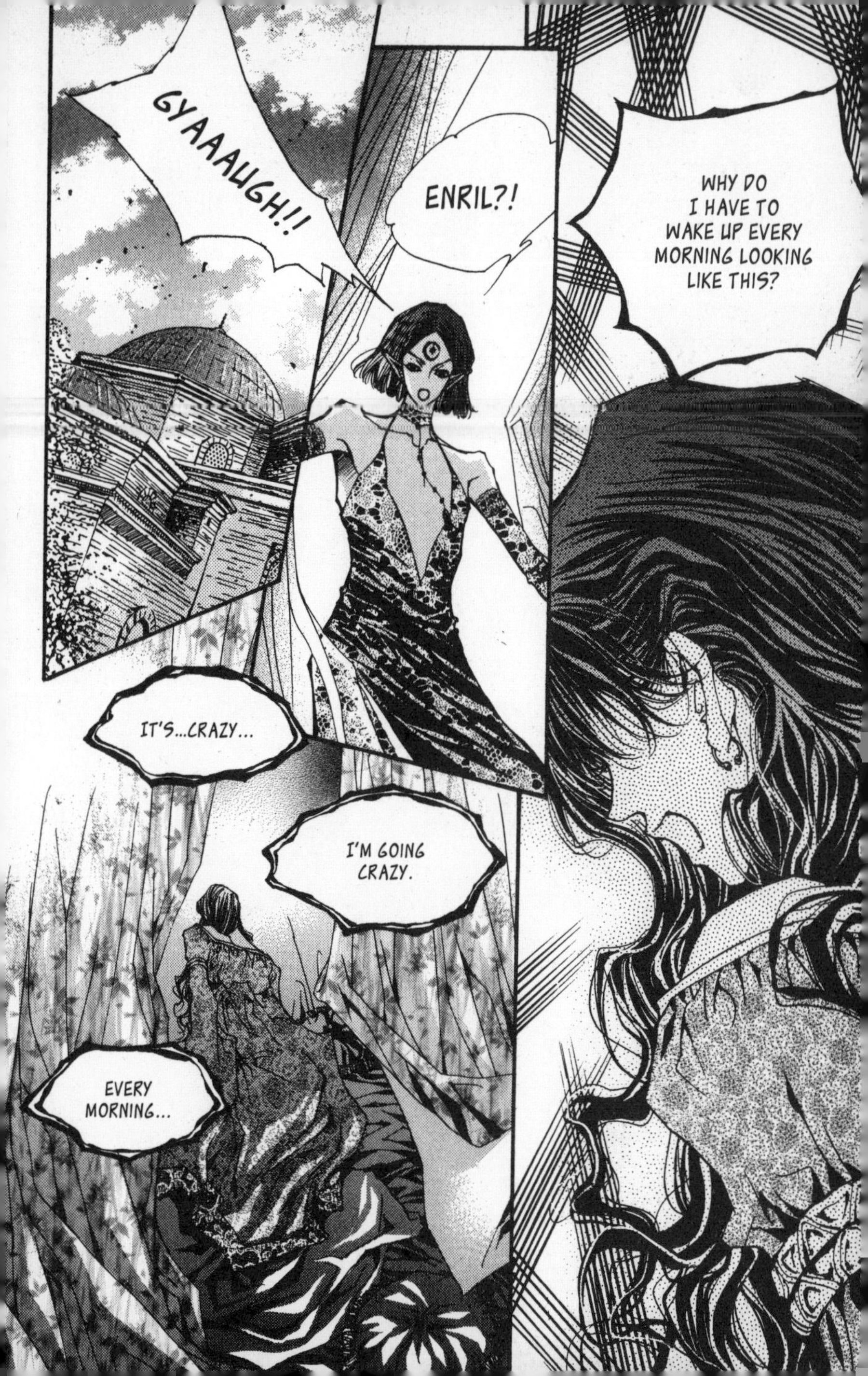
GYAAAUGH!!!
ENRIL?!
IT'S...CRAZY...
I'M GOING CRAZY.
EVERY MORNING...
WHY DO I HAVE TO WAKE UP EVERY MORNING LOOKING LIKE THIS?

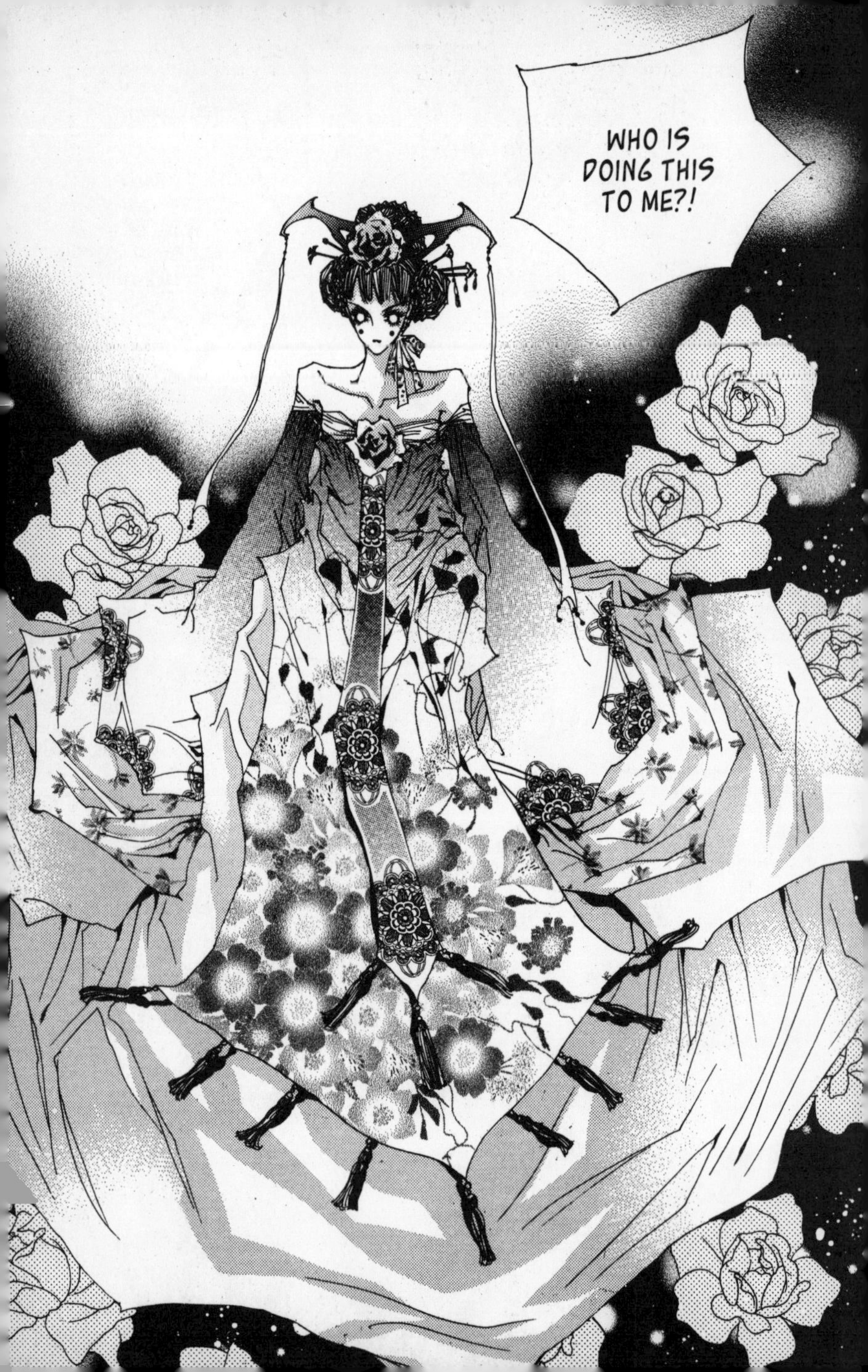
WHO IS DOING THIS TO ME?!

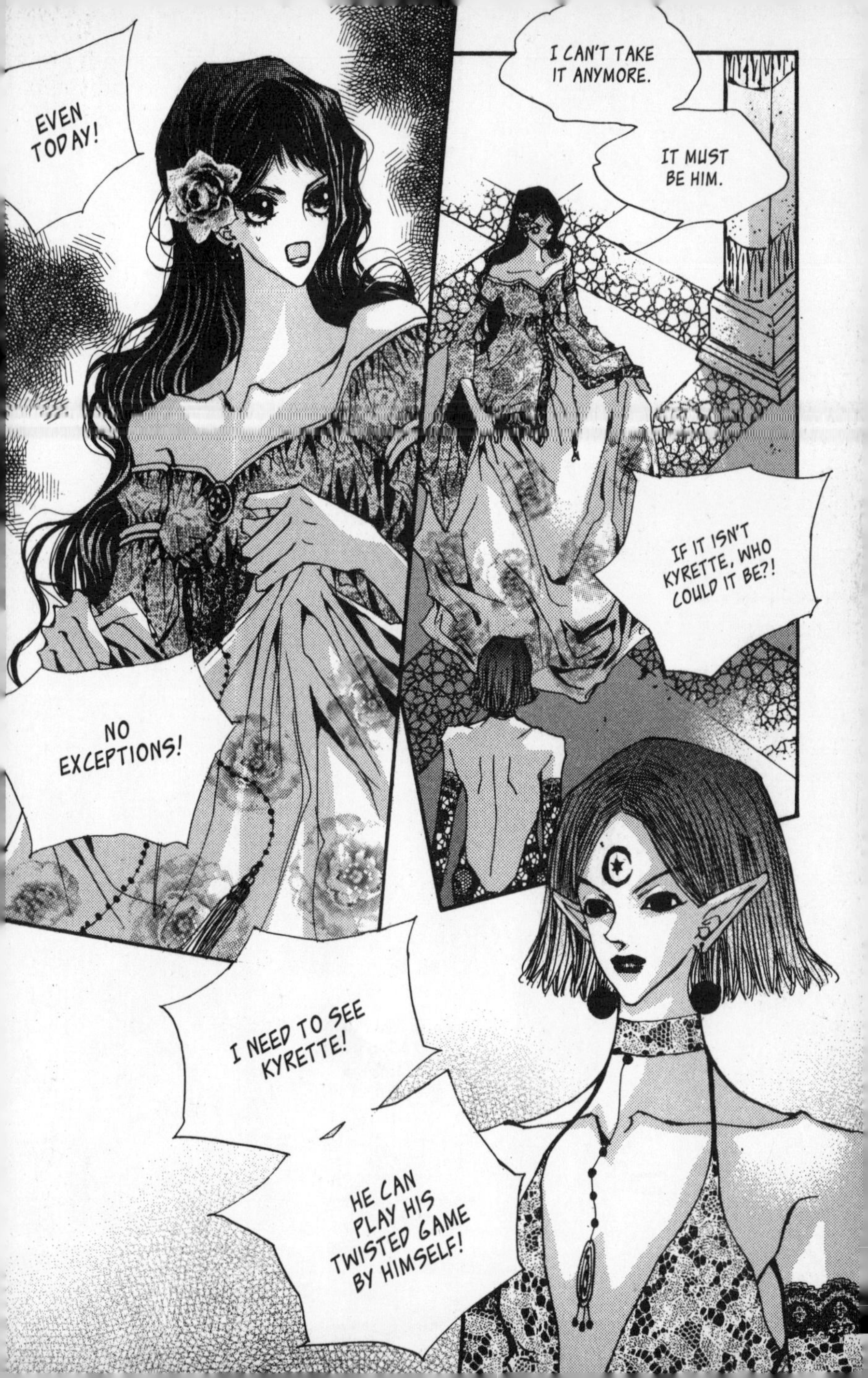

EVEN TODAY!
NO EXCEPTIONS!
I CAN'T TAKE IT ANYMORE.
IT MUST BE HIM.
IF IT ISN'T KYRETTE, WHO COULD IT BE?!
I NEED TO SEE KYRETTE!
HE CAN PLAY HIS TWISTED GAME BY HIMSELF!

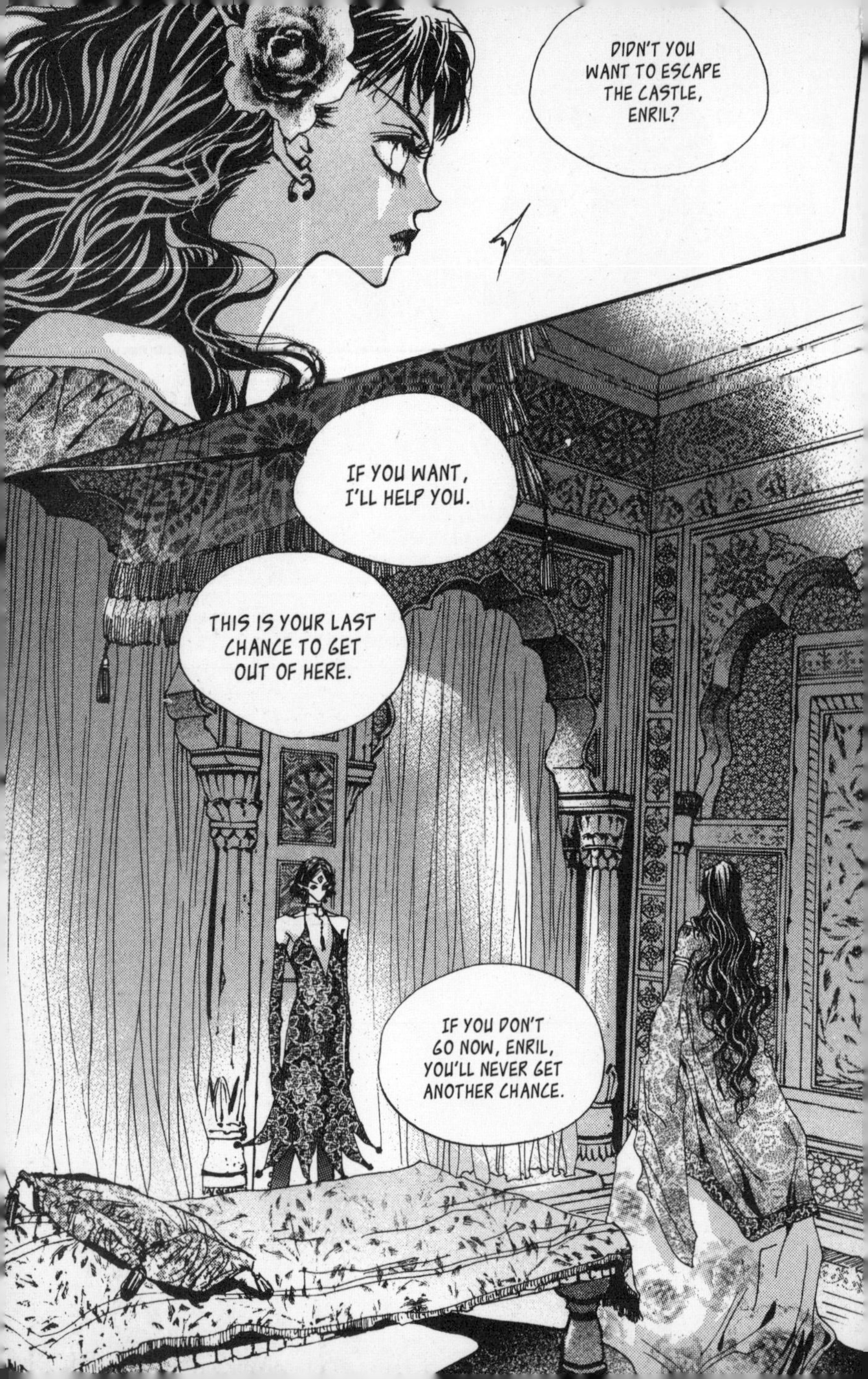
DIDN'T YOU WANT TO ESCAPE THE CASTLE, ENRIL?
IF YOU WANT, I'LL HELP YOU.
THIS IS YOUR LAST CHANCE TO GET OUT OF HERE.
IF YOU DON'T GO NOW, ENRIL, YOU'LL NEVER GET ANOTHER CHANCE.

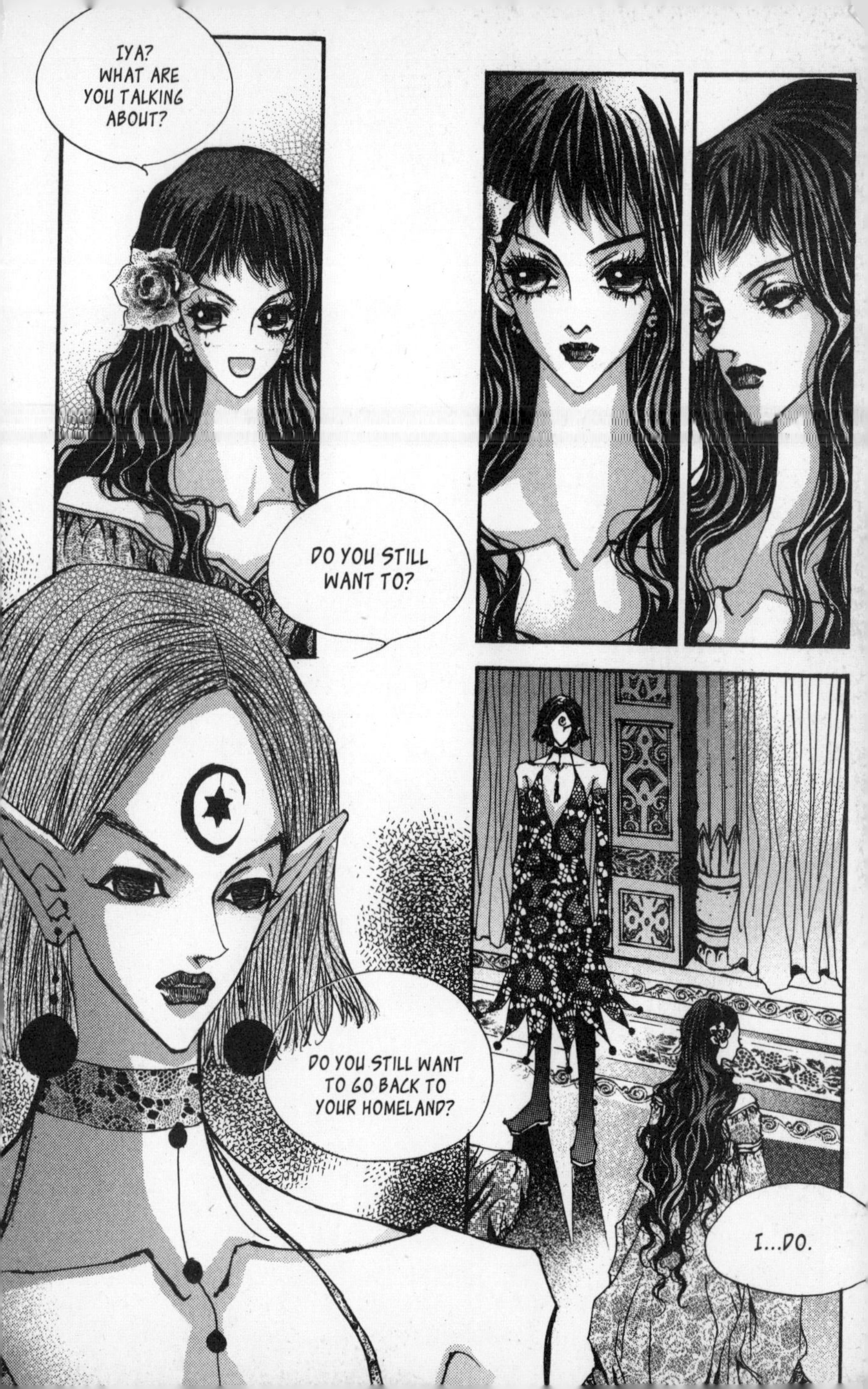
IYA? WHAT ARE YOU TALKING ABOUT?
DO YOU STILL WANT TO?
DO YOU STILL WANT TO GO BACK TO YOUR HOMELAND?
I...DO.

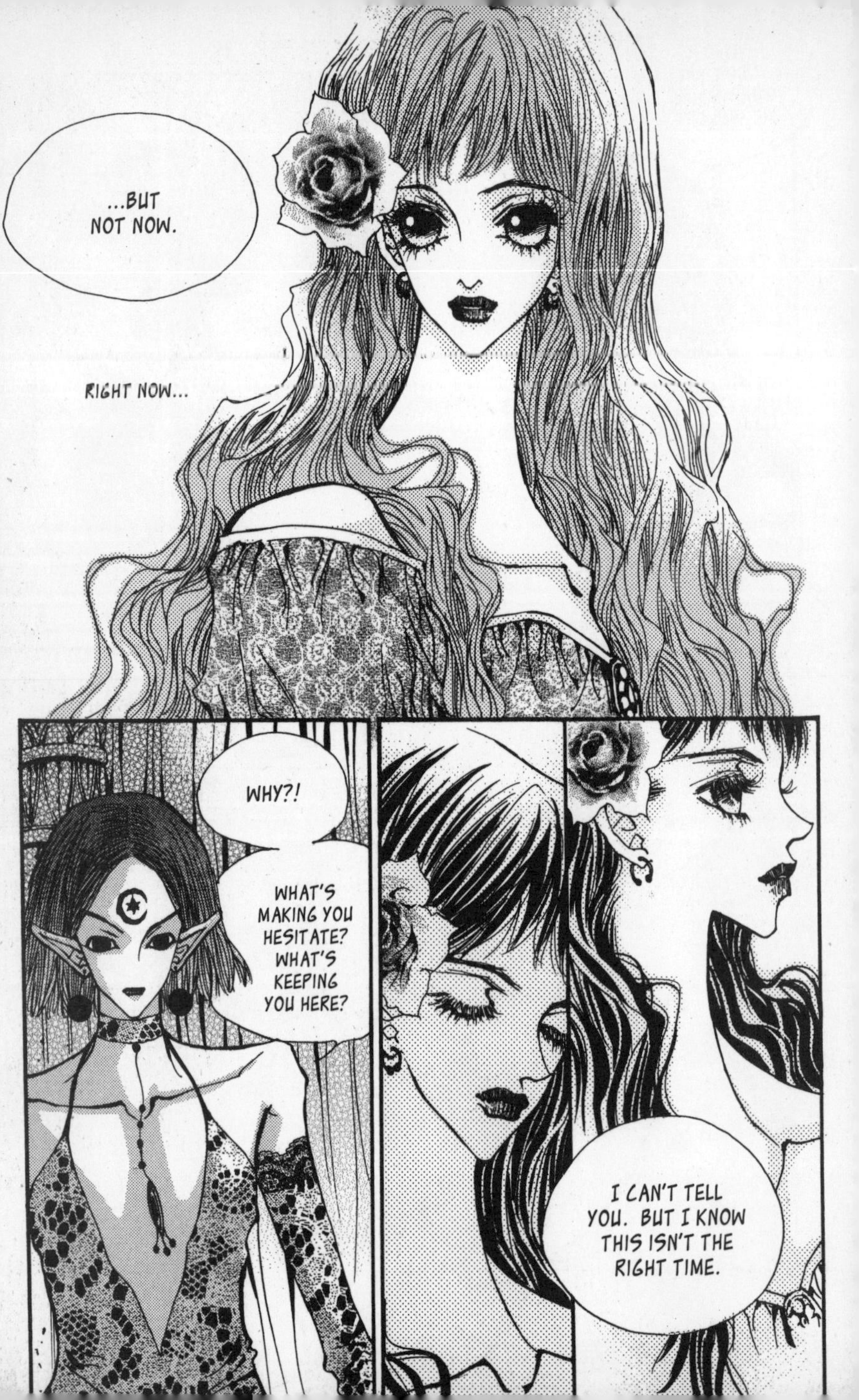
...BUT NOT NOW.
RIGHT NOW...
WHY?!
WHAT'S MAKING YOU HESITATE? WHAT'S KEEPING YOU HERE?
I CAN'T TELL YOU. BUT I KNOW THIS ISN'T THE RIGHT TIME.

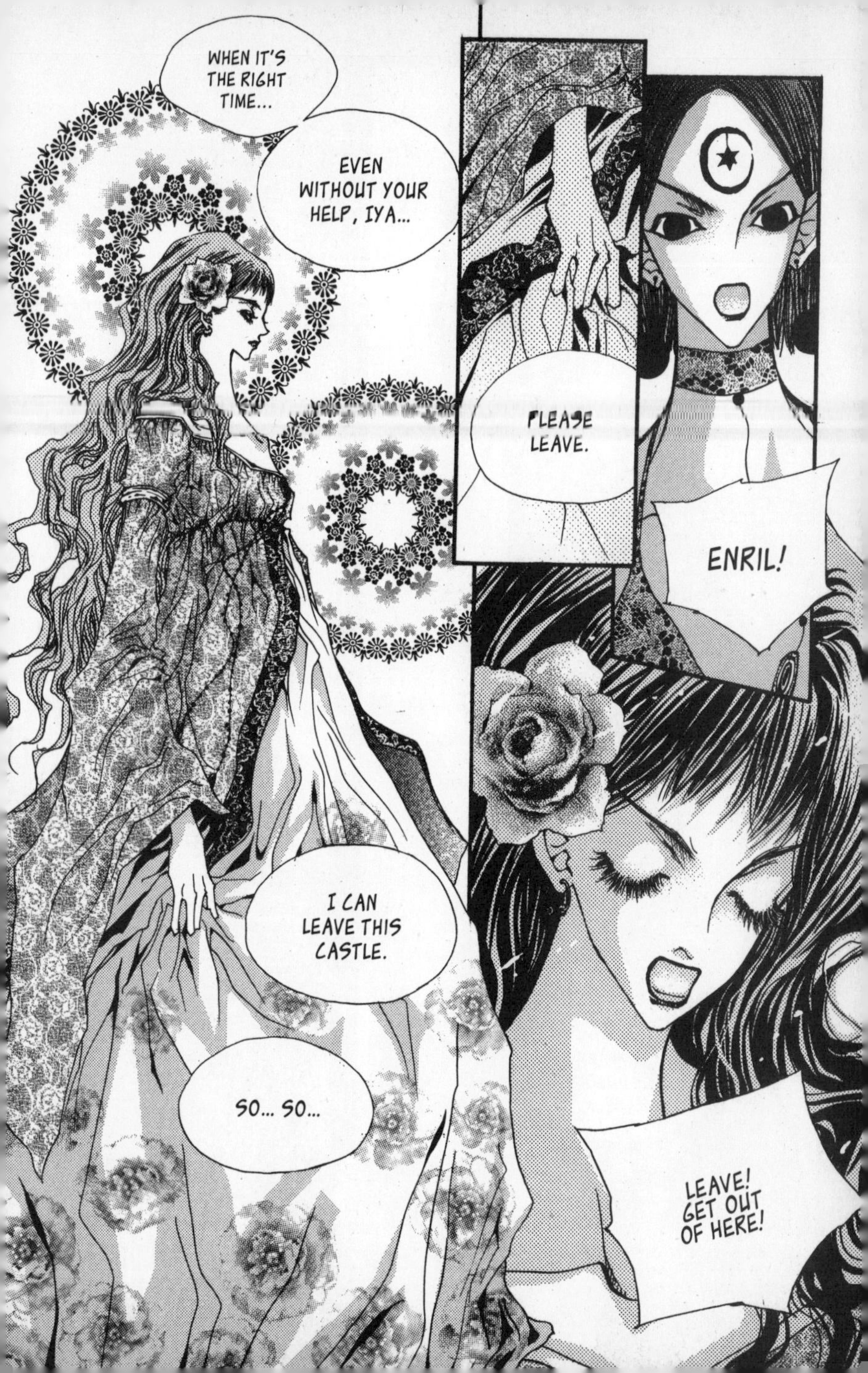
WHEN IT'S THE RIGHT TIME...
EVEN WITHOUT YOUR HELP, IYA...
I CAN LEAVE THIS CASTLE.
SO... SO...
PLEASE LEAVE.
ENRIL!
LEAVE! GET OUT OF HERE!

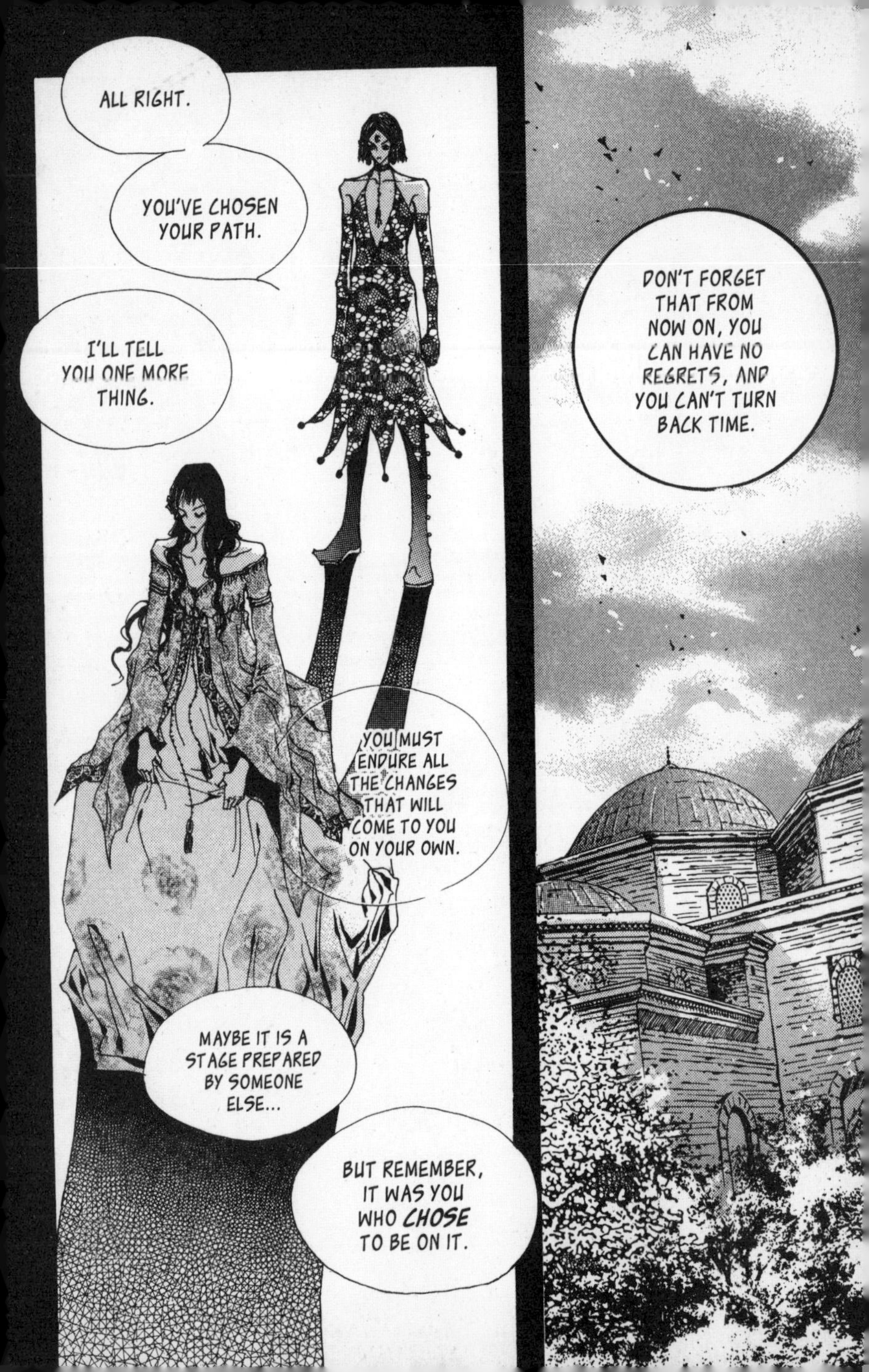
ALL RIGHT.
YOU'VE CHOSEN YOUR PATH.
I'LL TELL YOU ONE MORE THING.
YOU MUST ENDURE ALL THE CHANGES THAT WILL COME TO YOU ON YOUR OWN.
MAYBE IT IS A STAGE PREPARED BY SOMEONE ELSE...
BUT REMEMBER, IT WAS YOU WHO *CHOSE* TO BE ON IT.
DON'T FORGET THAT FROM NOW ON, YOU CAN HAVE NO REGRETS, AND YOU CAN'T TURN BACK TIME.

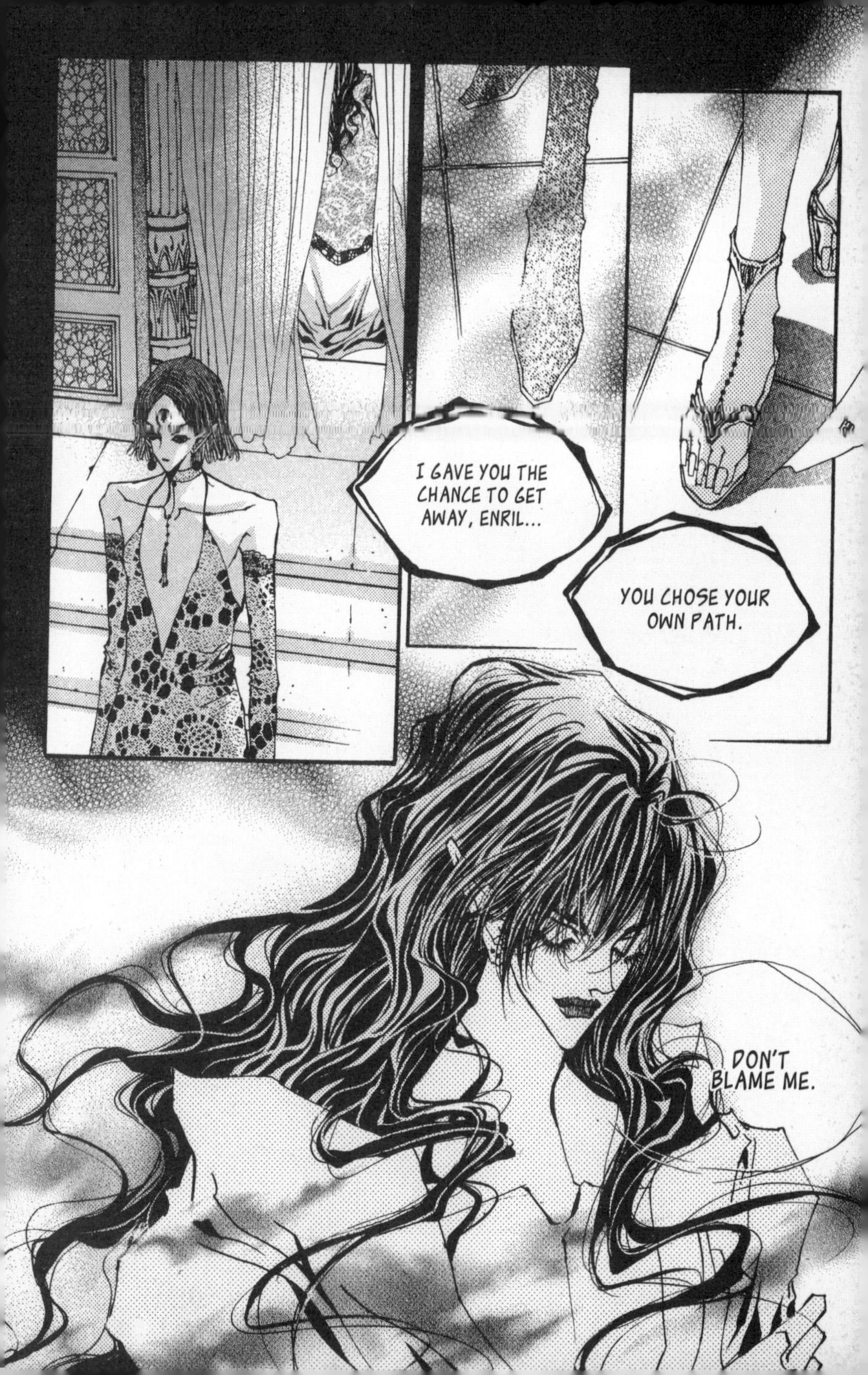
I GAVE YOU THE CHANCE TO GET AWAY, ENRIL...
YOU CHOSE YOUR OWN PATH.
DON'T BLAME ME.

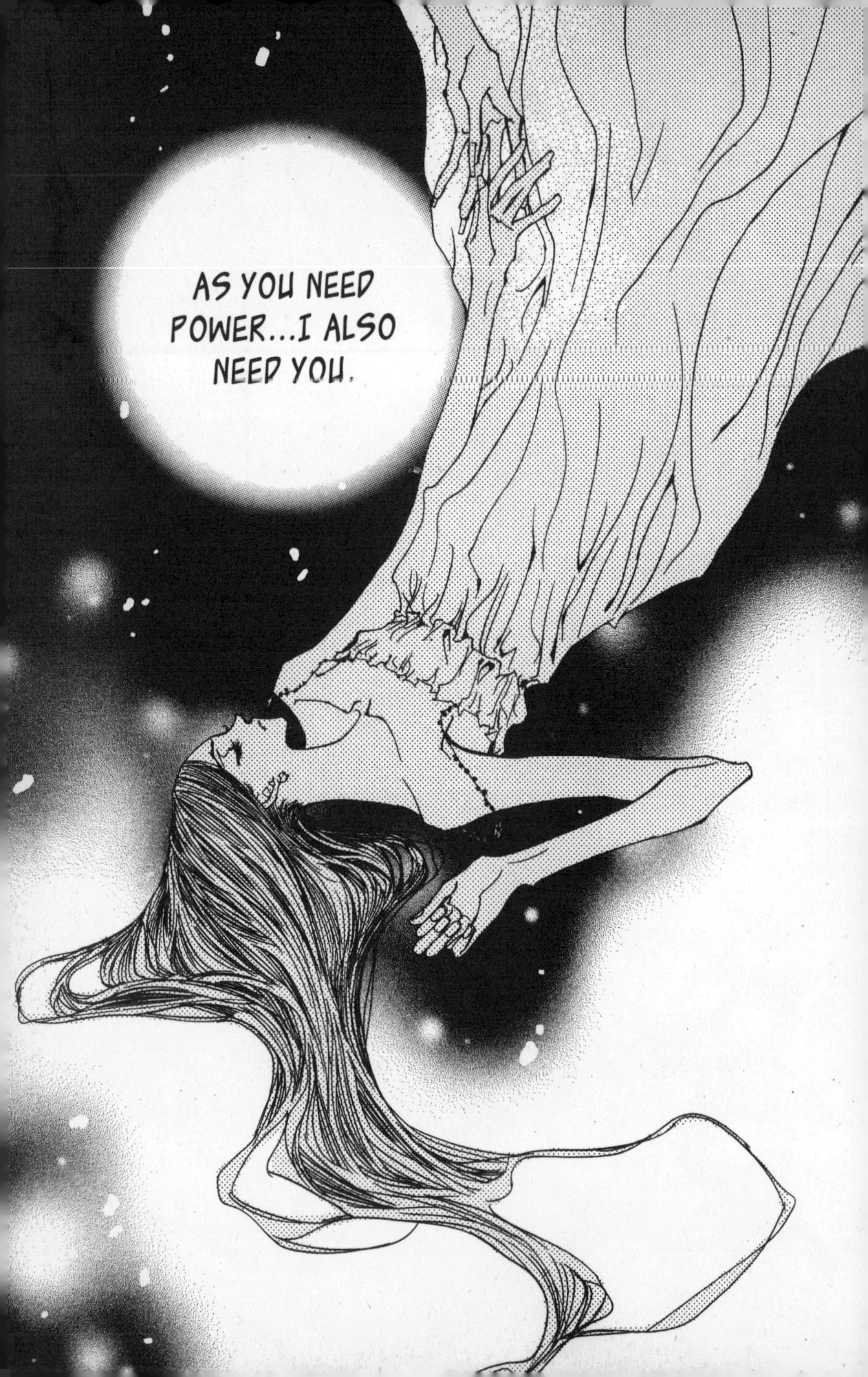
AS YOU NEED POWER...I ALSO NEED YOU.

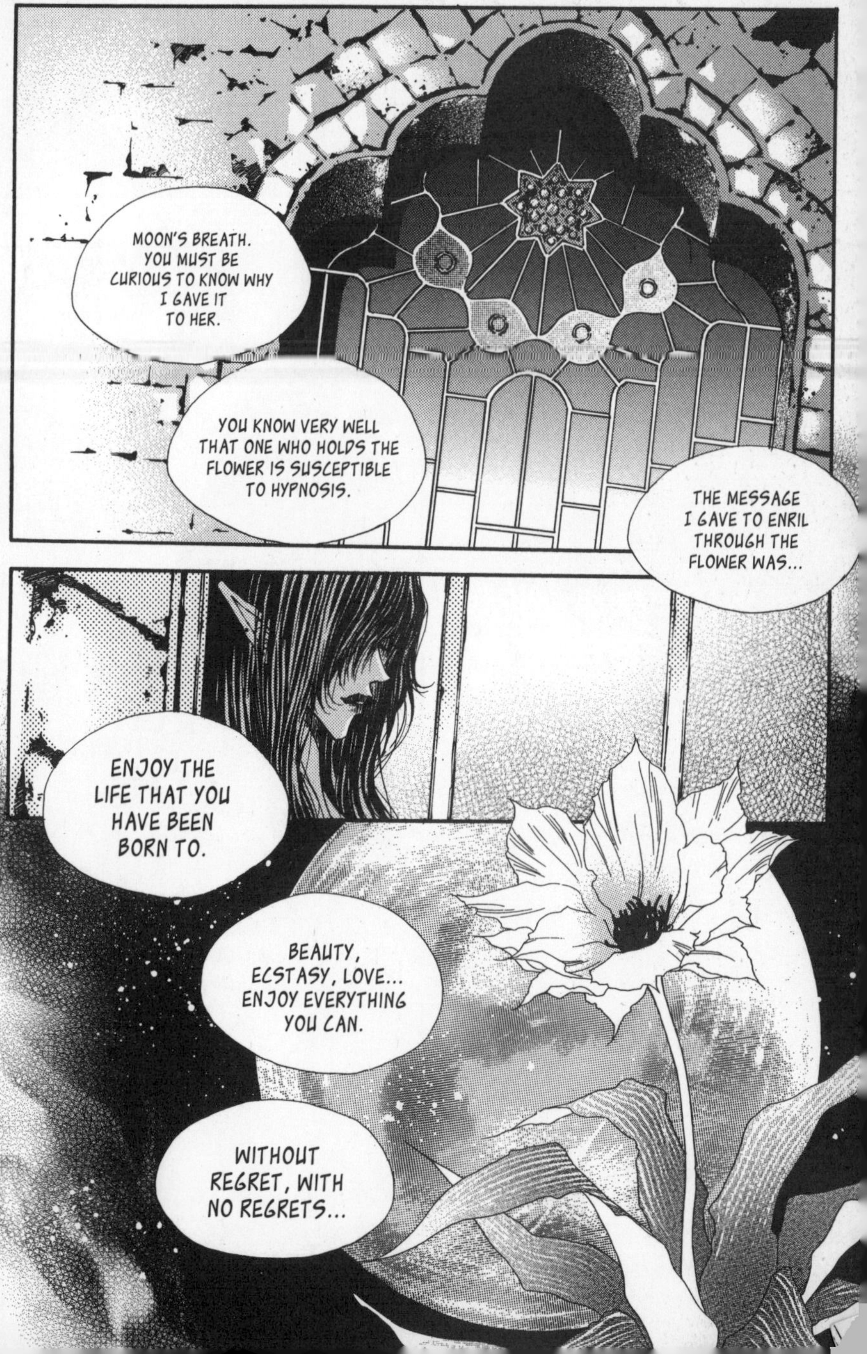
MOON'S BREATH. YOU MUST BE CURIOUS TO KNOW WHY I GAVE IT TO HER.
YOU KNOW VERY WELL THAT ONE WHO HOLDS THE FLOWER IS SUSCEPTIBLE TO HYPNOSIS.
THE MESSAGE I GAVE TO ENRIL THROUGH THE FLOWER WAS...
ENJOY THE LIFE THAT YOU HAVE BEEN BORN TO.
BEAUTY, ECSTASY, LOVE... ENJOY EVERYTHING YOU CAN.
WITHOUT REGRET, WITH NO REGRETS...

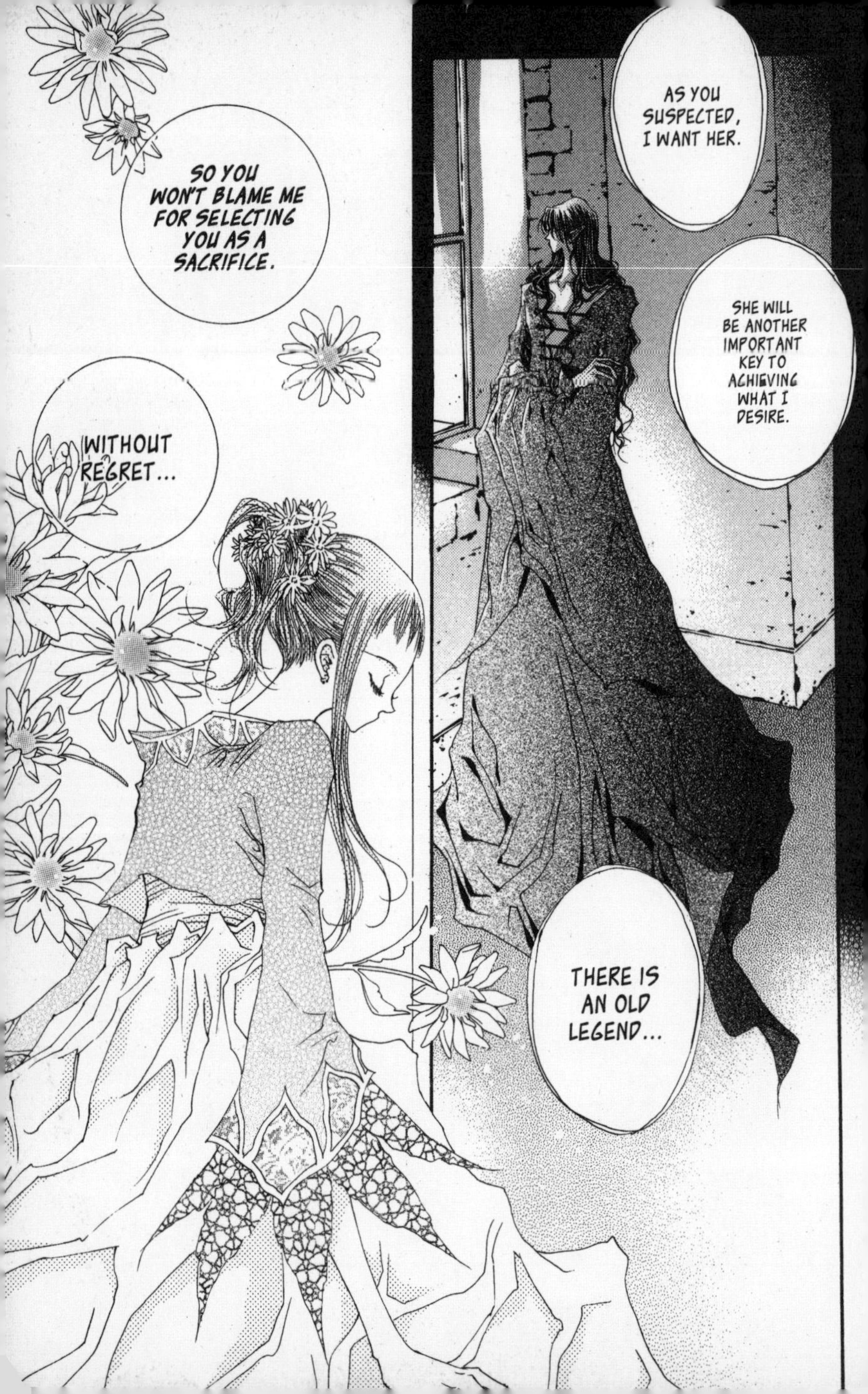
SO YOU WON'T BLAME ME FOR SELECTING YOU AS A SACRIFICE.
WITHOUT REGRET...
AS YOU SUSPECTED, I WANT HER.
SHE WILL BE ANOTHER IMPORTANT KEY TO ACHIEVING WHAT I DESIRE.
THERE IS AN OLD LEGEND...

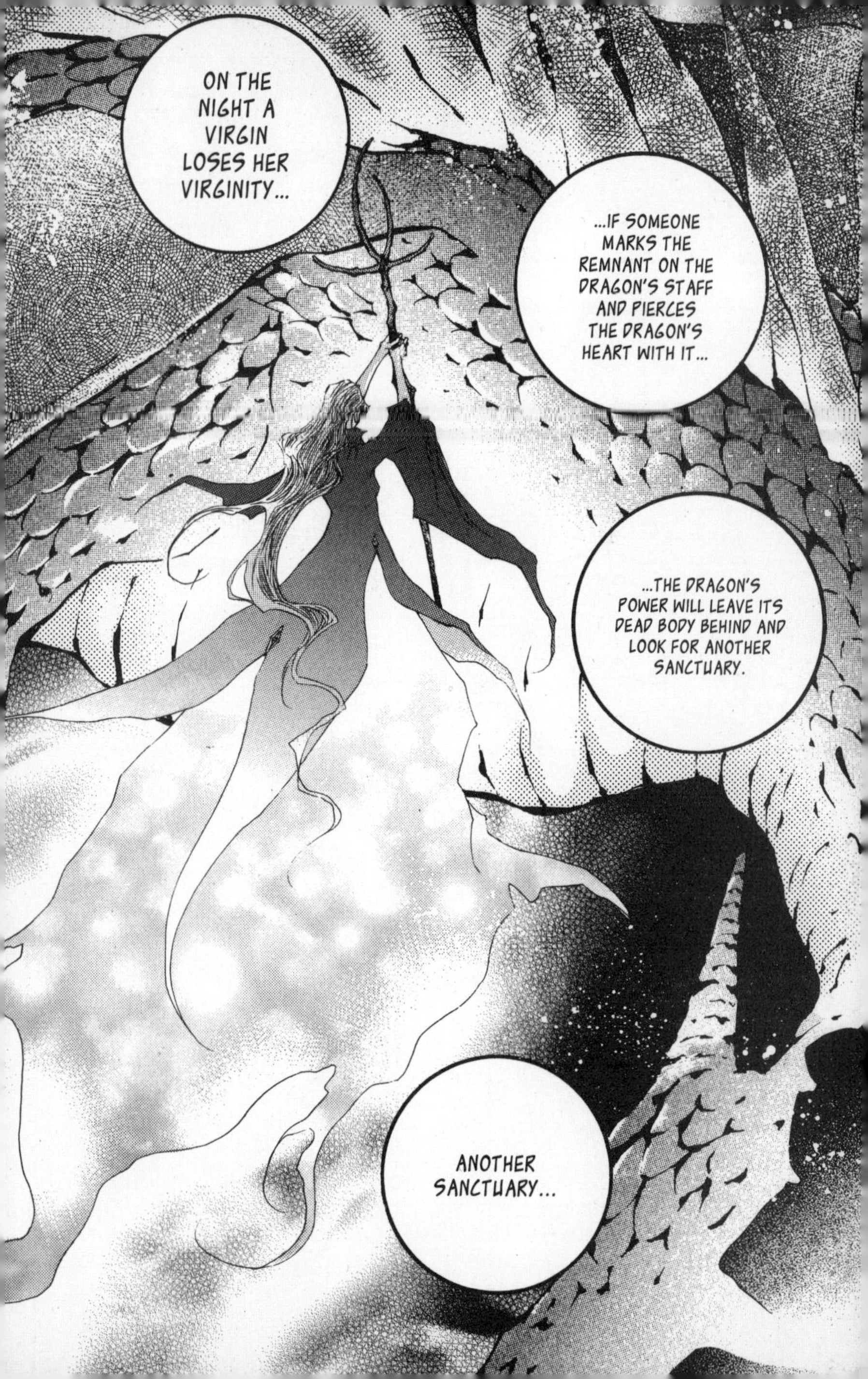
ON THE NIGHT A VIRGIN LOSES HER VIRGINITY...
...IF SOMEONE MARKS THE REMNANT ON THE DRAGON'S STAFF AND PIERCES THE DRAGON'S HEART WITH IT...
...THE DRAGON'S POWER WILL LEAVE ITS DEAD BODY BEHIND AND LOOK FOR ANOTHER SANCTUARY.
ANOTHER SANCTUARY...

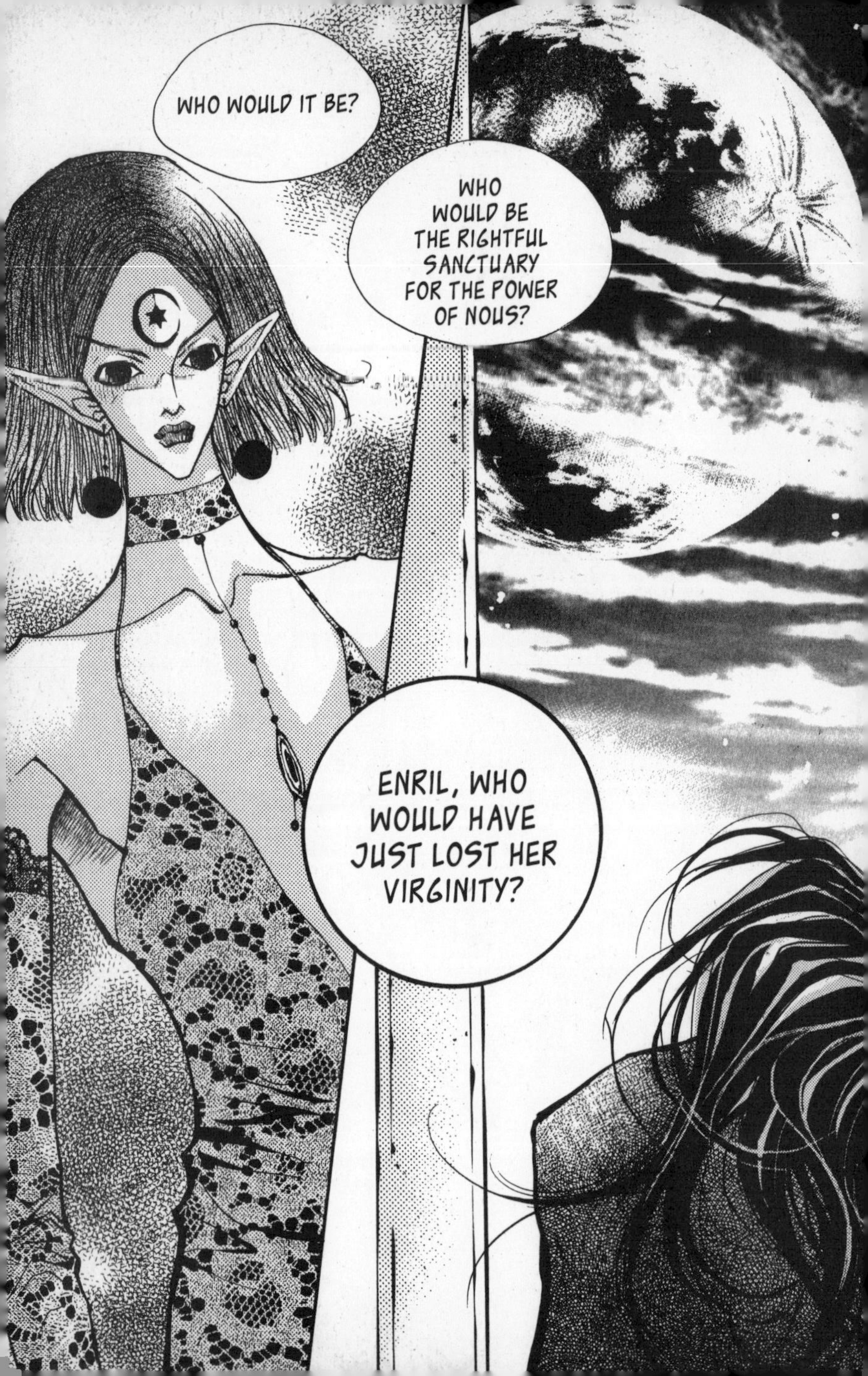
WHO WOULD IT BE?
WHO WOULD BE THE RIGHTFUL SANCTUARY FOR THE POWER OF NOUS?
ENRIL, WHO WOULD HAVE JUST LOST HER VIRGINITY?

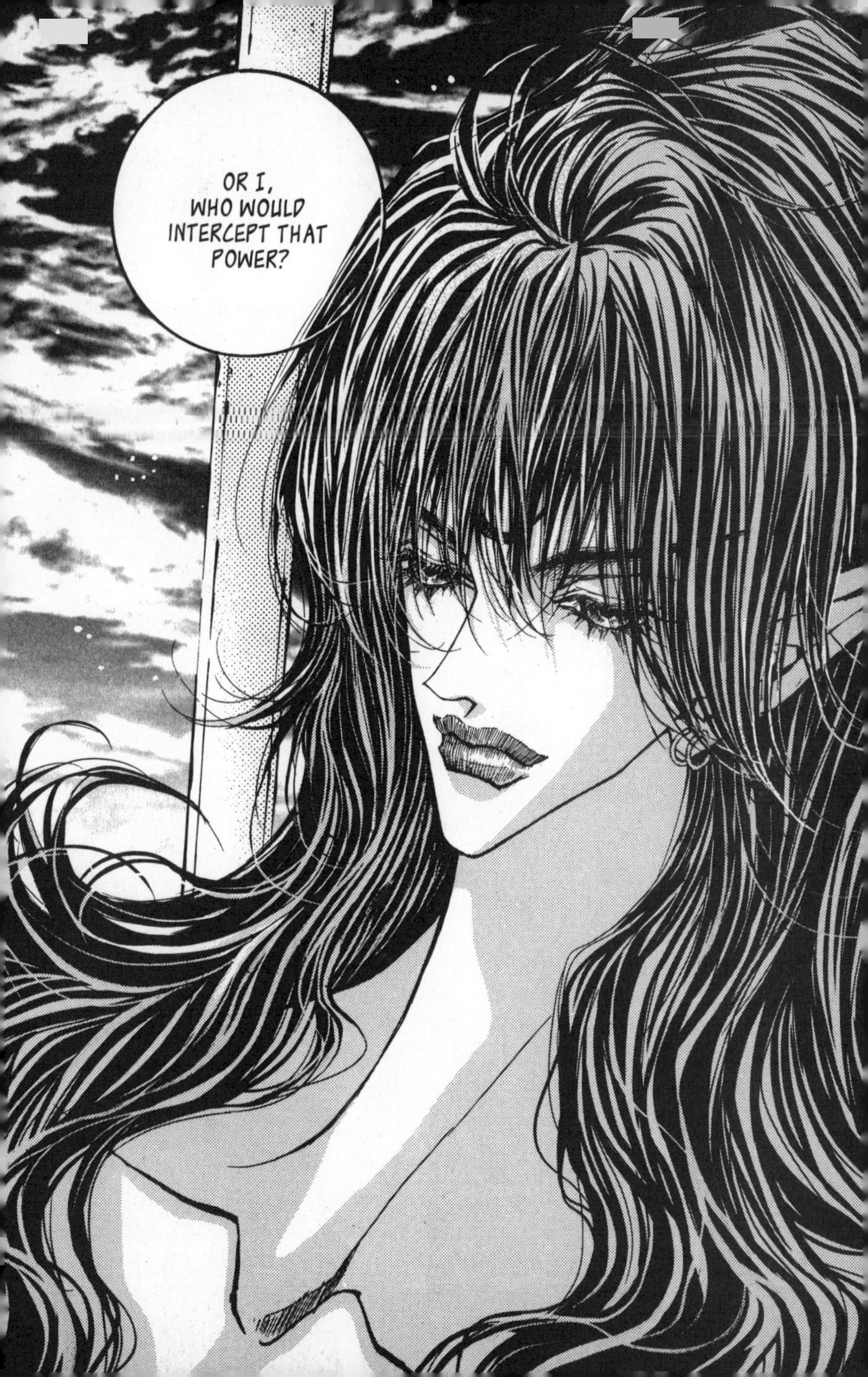
OR I,
WHO WOULD
INTERCEPT THAT
POWER?

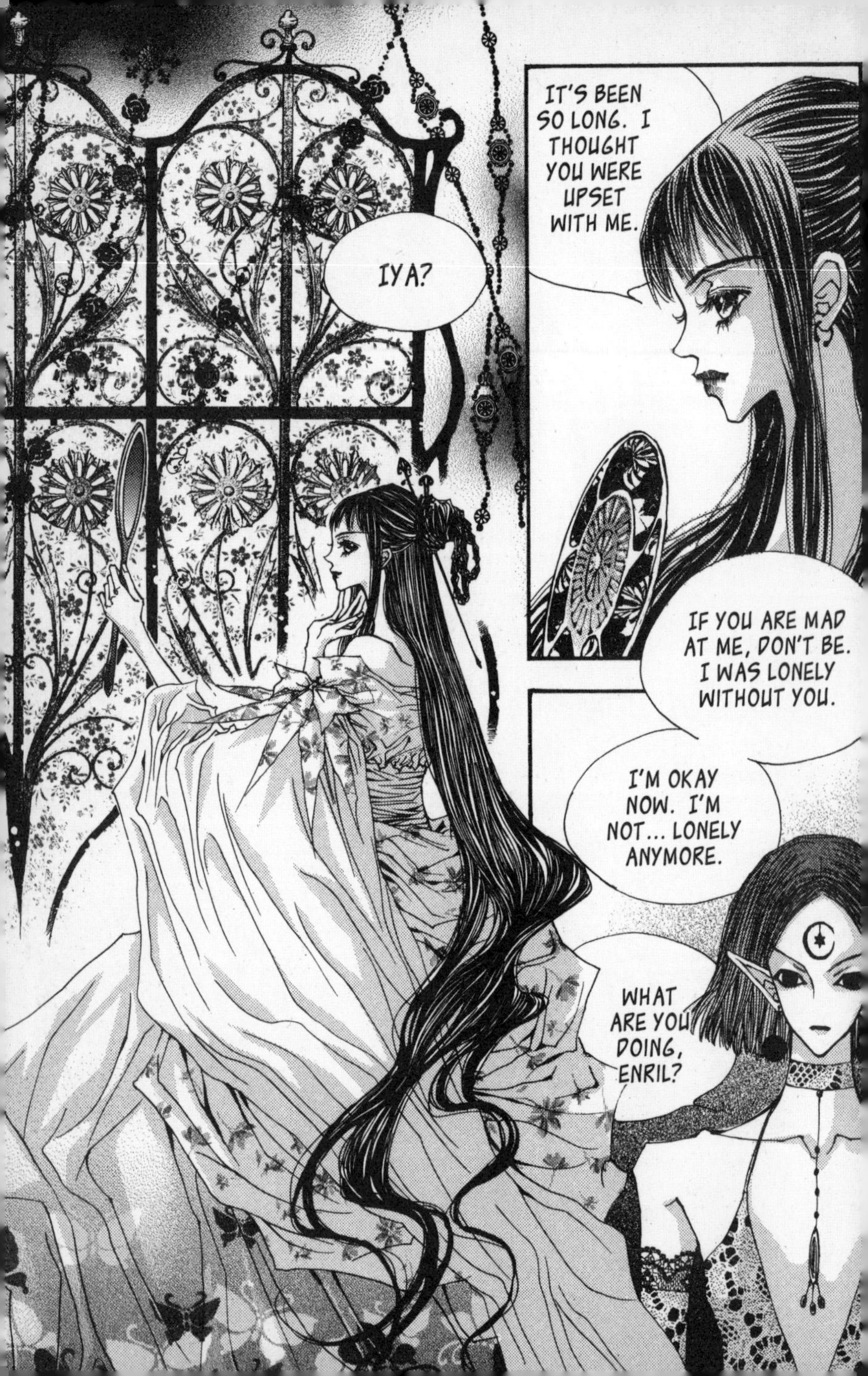
IYA?
IT'S BEEN SO LONG. I THOUGHT YOU WERE UPSET WITH ME.
IF YOU ARE MAD AT ME, DON'T BE. I WAS LONELY WITHOUT YOU.
I'M OKAY NOW. I'M NOT... LONELY ANYMORE.
WHAT ARE YOU DOING, ENRIL?

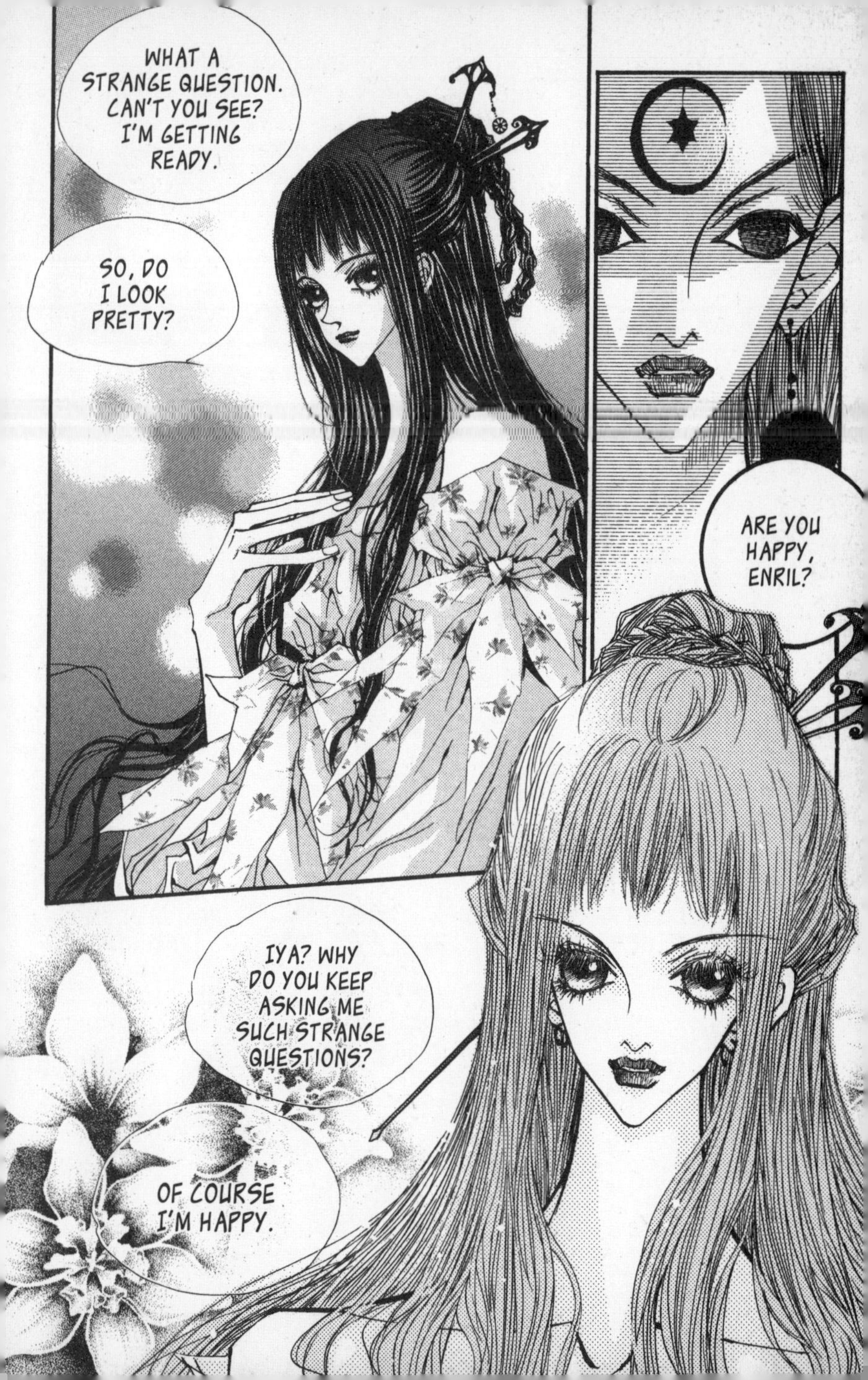
WHAT A STRANGE QUESTION. CAN'T YOU SEE? I'M GETTING READY.
SO, DO I LOOK PRETTY?
ARE YOU HAPPY, ENRIL?
IYA? WHY DO YOU KEEP ASKING ME SUCH STRANGE QUESTIONS?
OF COURSE I'M HAPPY.

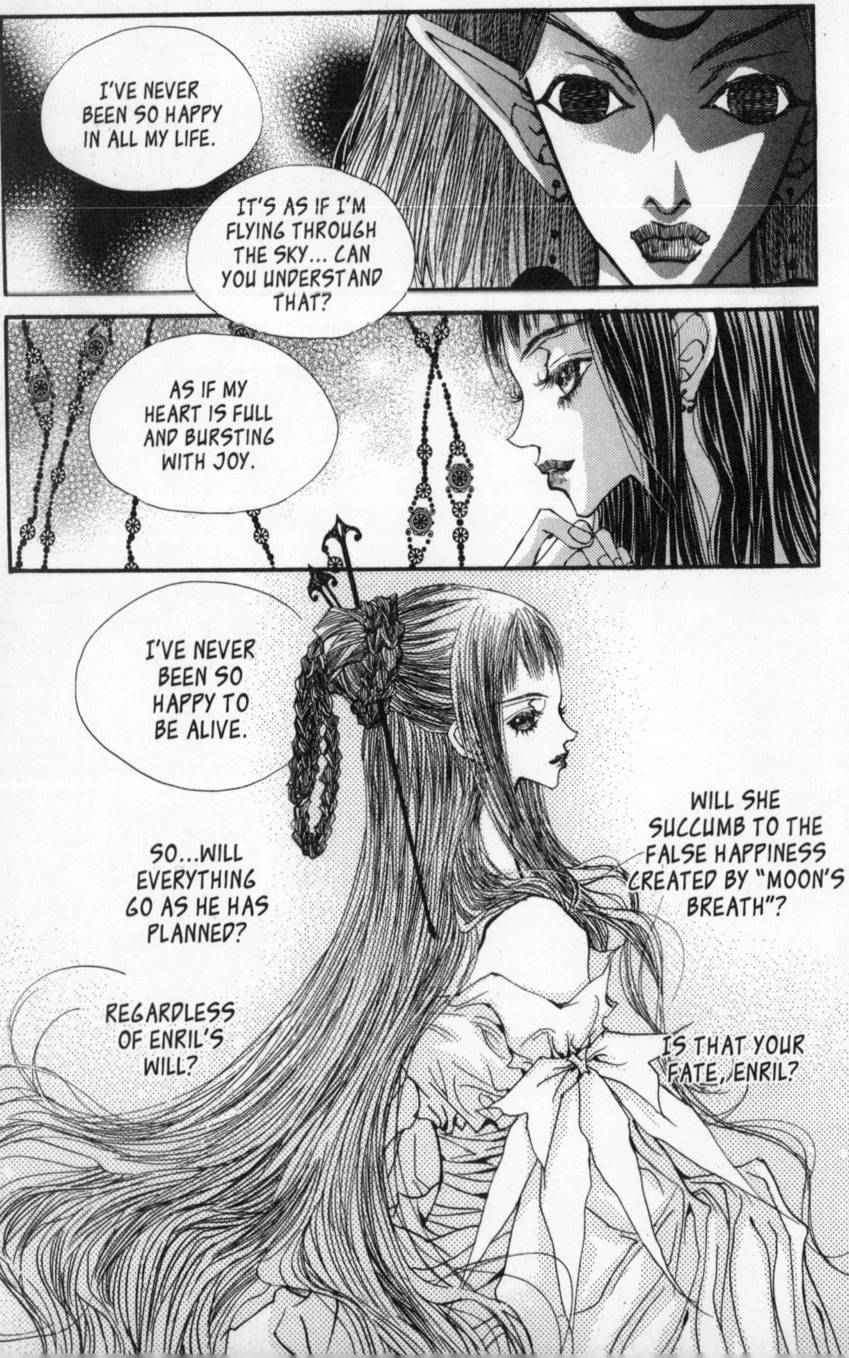
I'VE NEVER BEEN SO HAPPY IN ALL MY LIFE.
IT'S AS IF I'M FLYING THROUGH THE SKY... CAN YOU UNDERSTAND THAT?
AS IF MY HEART IS FULL AND BURSTING WITH JOY.
I'VE NEVER BEEN SO HAPPY TO BE ALIVE.
SO...WILL EVERYTHING GO AS HE HAS PLANNED?
WILL SHE SUCCUMB TO THE FALSE HAPPINESS CREATED BY "MOON'S BREATH"?
REGARDLESS OF ENRIL'S WILL?
IS THAT YOUR FATE, ENRIL?

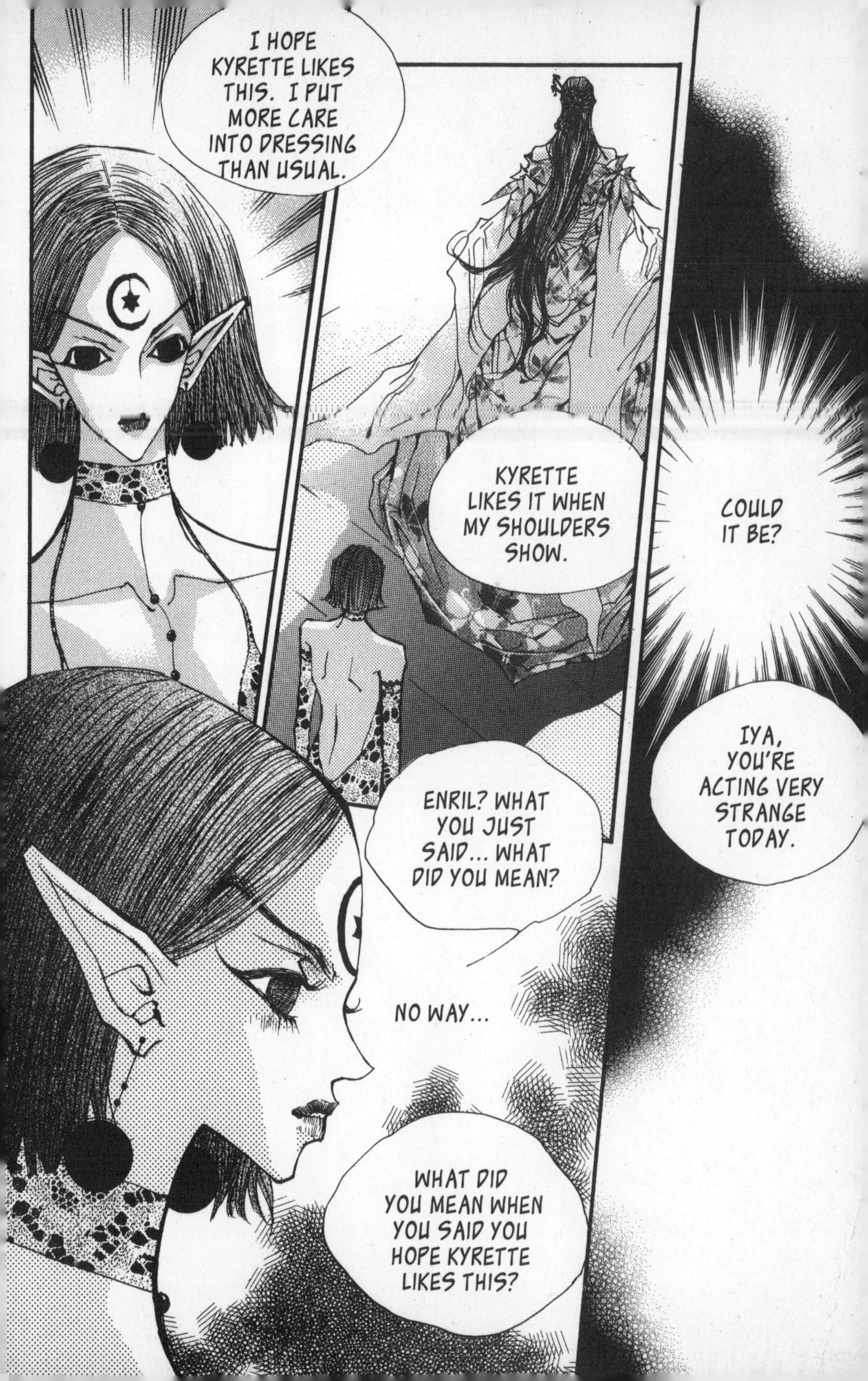
I HOPE KYRETTE LIKES THIS. I PUT MORE CARE INTO DRESSING THAN USUAL.
KYRETTE LIKES IT WHEN MY SHOULDERS SHOW.
COULD IT BE?
IYA, YOU'RE ACTING VERY STRANGE TODAY.
ENRIL? WHAT YOU JUST SAID... WHAT DID YOU MEAN?
NO WAY...
WHAT DID YOU MEAN WHEN YOU SAID YOU HOPE KYRETTE LIKES THIS?

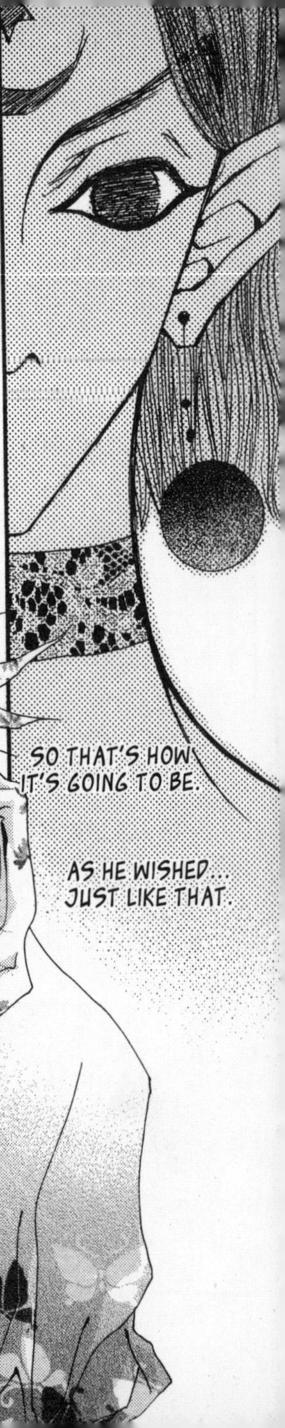
SO THAT'S HOW IT'S GOING TO BE.
AS HE WISHED... JUST LIKE THAT.
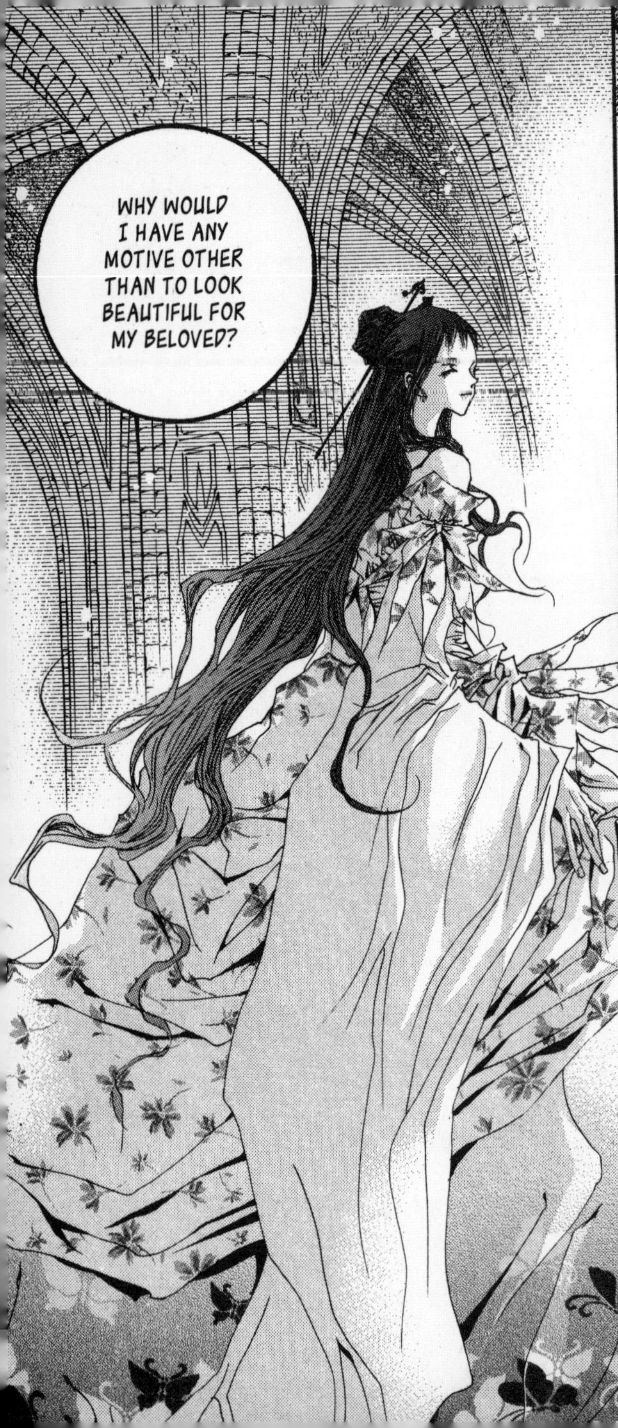
WHY WOULD I HAVE ANY MOTIVE OTHER THAN TO LOOK BEAUTIFUL FOR MY BELOVED?

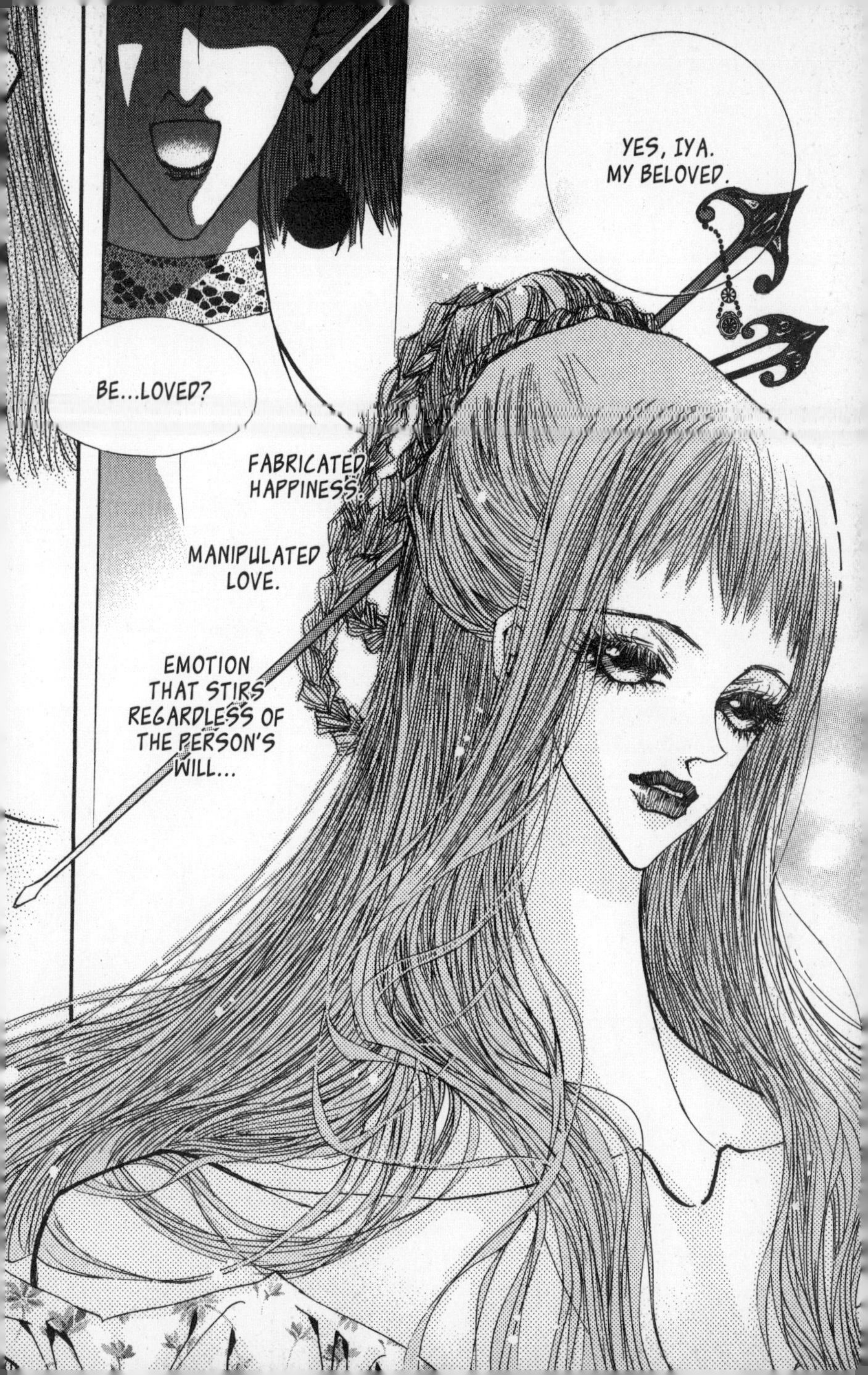
BE...LOVED?
YES, IYA. MY BELOVED.
FABRICATED HAPPINESS.
MANIPULATED LOVE.
EMOTION THAT STIRS REGARDLESS OF THE PERSON'S WILL...

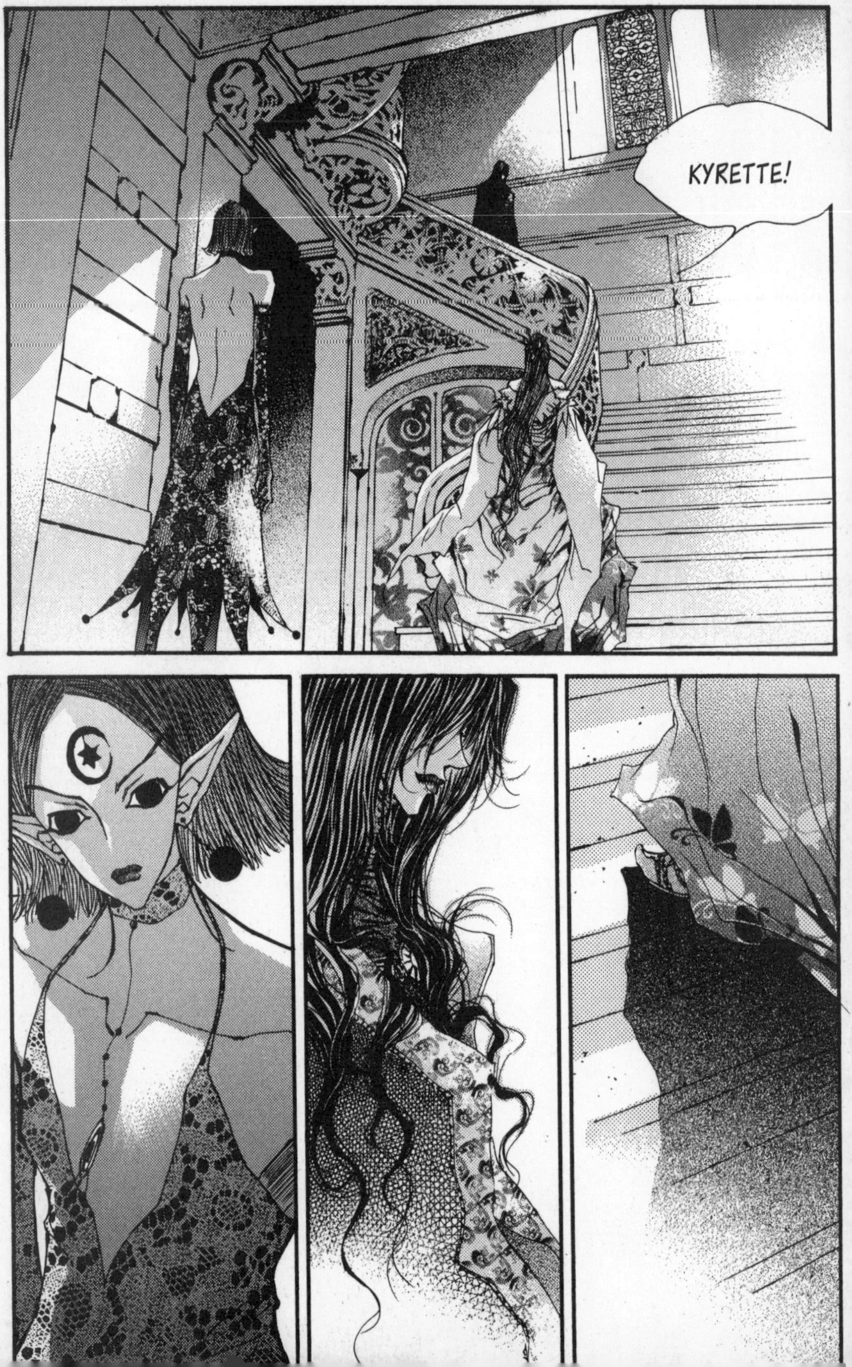
KYRETTE!

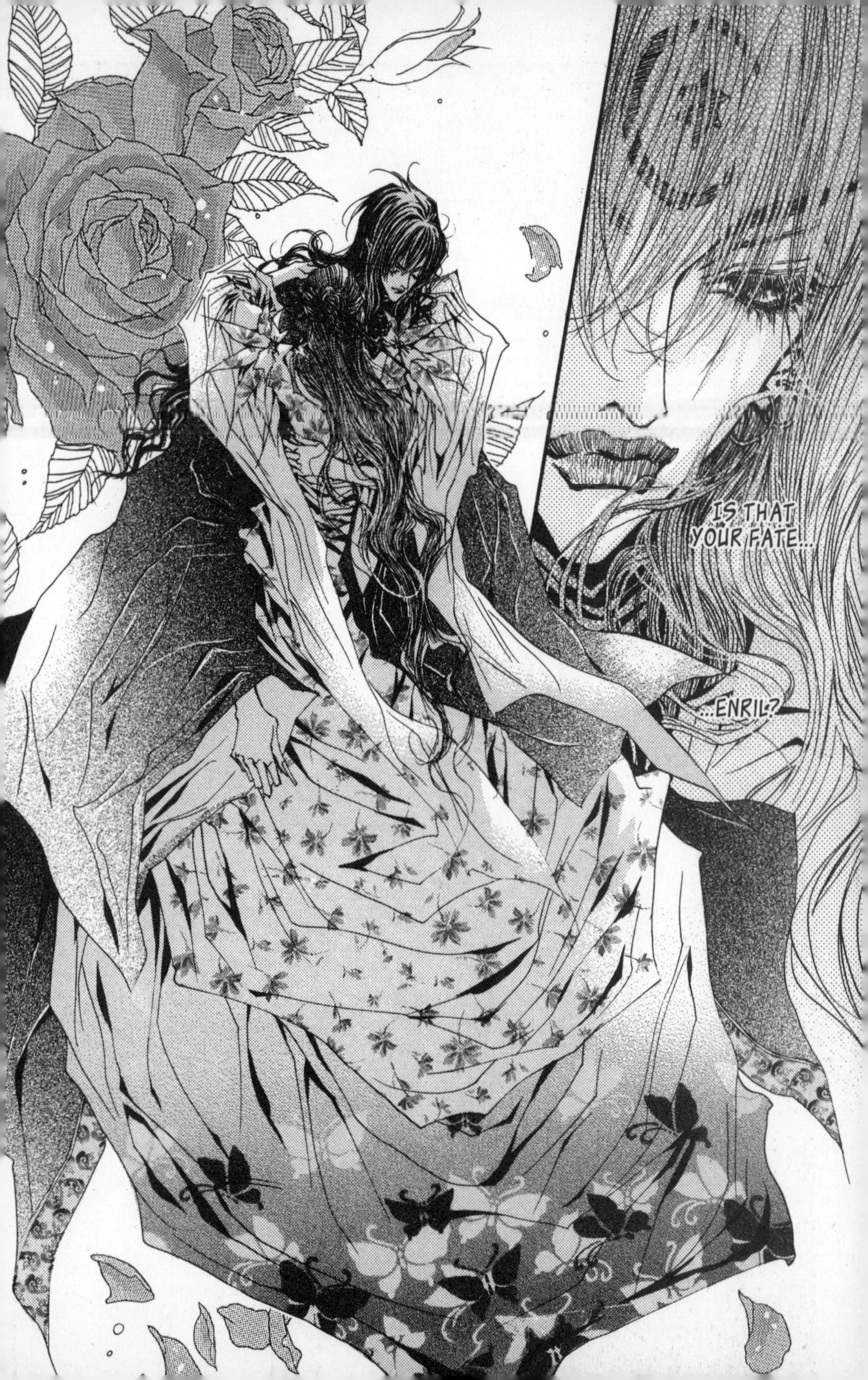
IS THAT YOUR FATE...
...ENRIL?

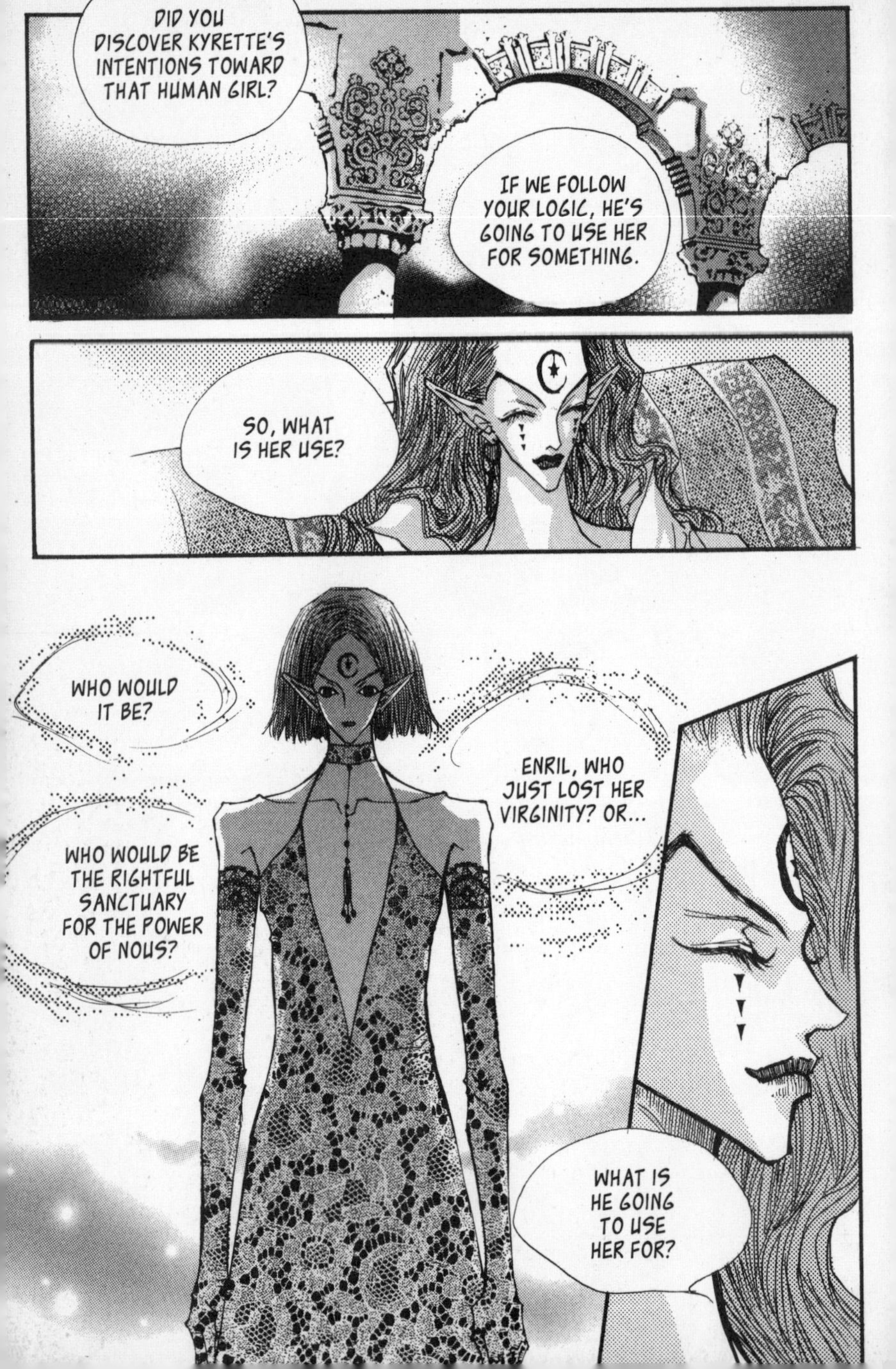
DID YOU DISCOVER KYRETTE'S INTENTIONS TOWARD THAT HUMAN GIRL?
IF WE FOLLOW YOUR LOGIC, HE'S GOING TO USE HER FOR SOMETHING.
SO, WHAT IS HER USE?
WHO WOULD IT BE?
WHO WOULD BE THE RIGHTFUL SANCTUARY FOR THE POWER OF NOUS?
ENRIL, WHO JUST LOST HER VIRGINITY? OR...
WHAT IS HE GOING TO USE HER FOR?

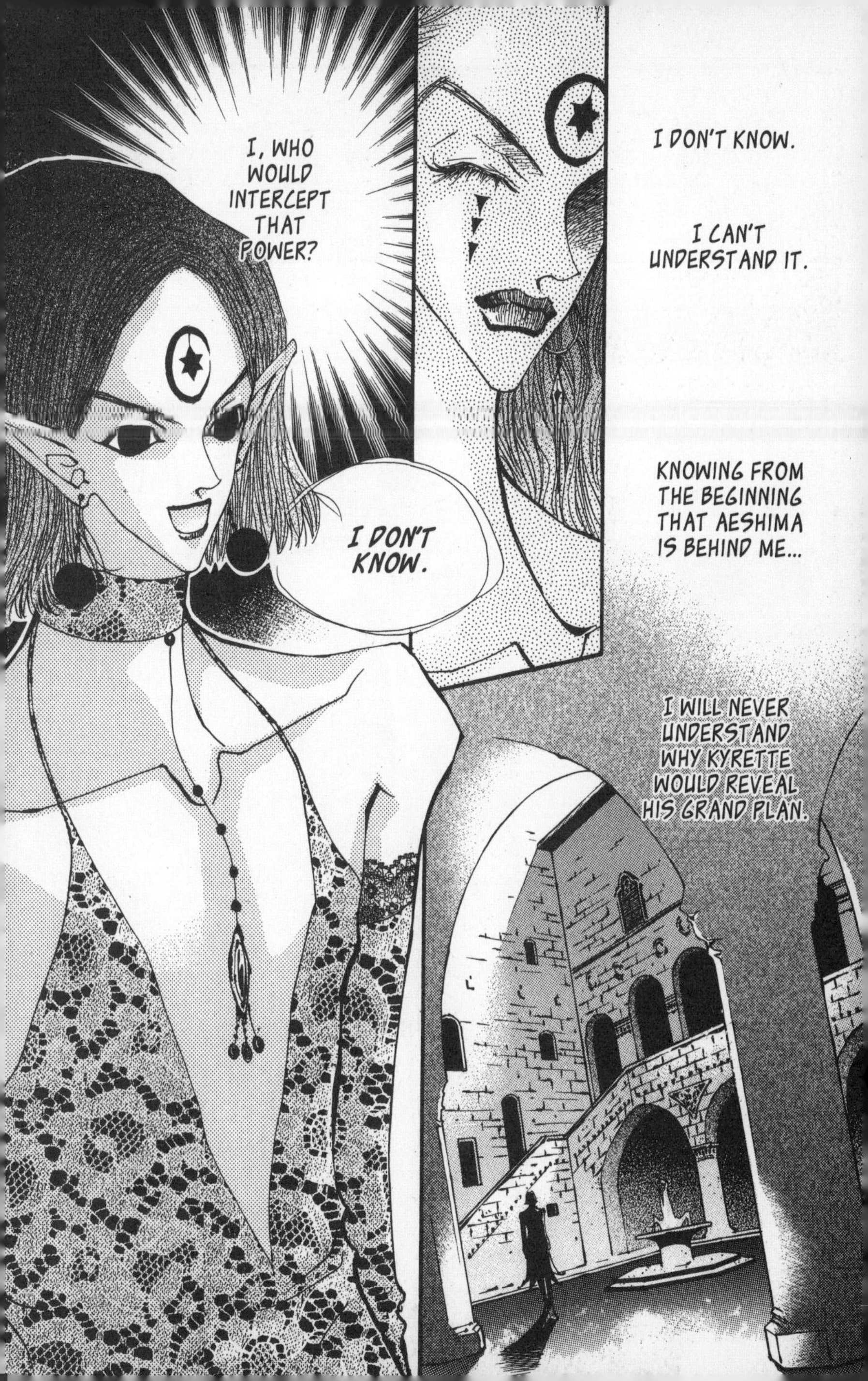
I, WHO WOULD INTERCEPT THAT POWER?
I DON'T KNOW.
I DON'T KNOW.
I CAN'T UNDERSTAND IT.
KNOWING FROM THE BEGINNING THAT AESHIMA IS BEHIND ME...
I WILL NEVER UNDERSTAND WHY KYRETTE WOULD REVEAL HIS GRAND PLAN.

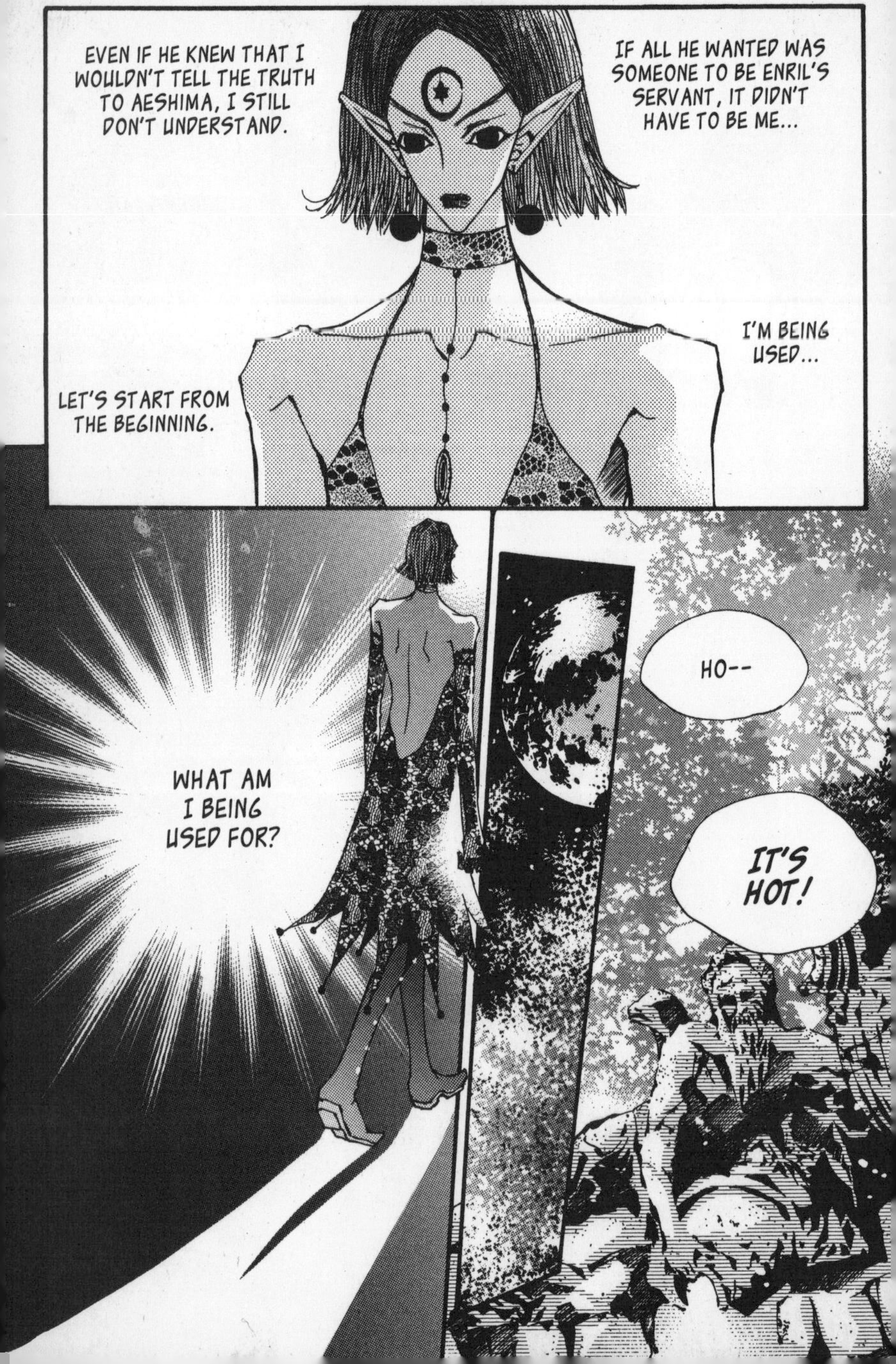

EVEN IF HE KNEW THAT I WOULDN'T TELL THE TRUTH TO AESHIMA, I STILL DON'T UNDERSTAND.
IF ALL HE WANTED WAS SOMEONE TO BE ENRIL'S SERVANT, IT DIDN'T HAVE TO BE ME...
LET'S START FROM THE BEGINNING.
I'M BEING USED...
WHAT AM I BEING USED FOR?
HO--
IT'S HOT!

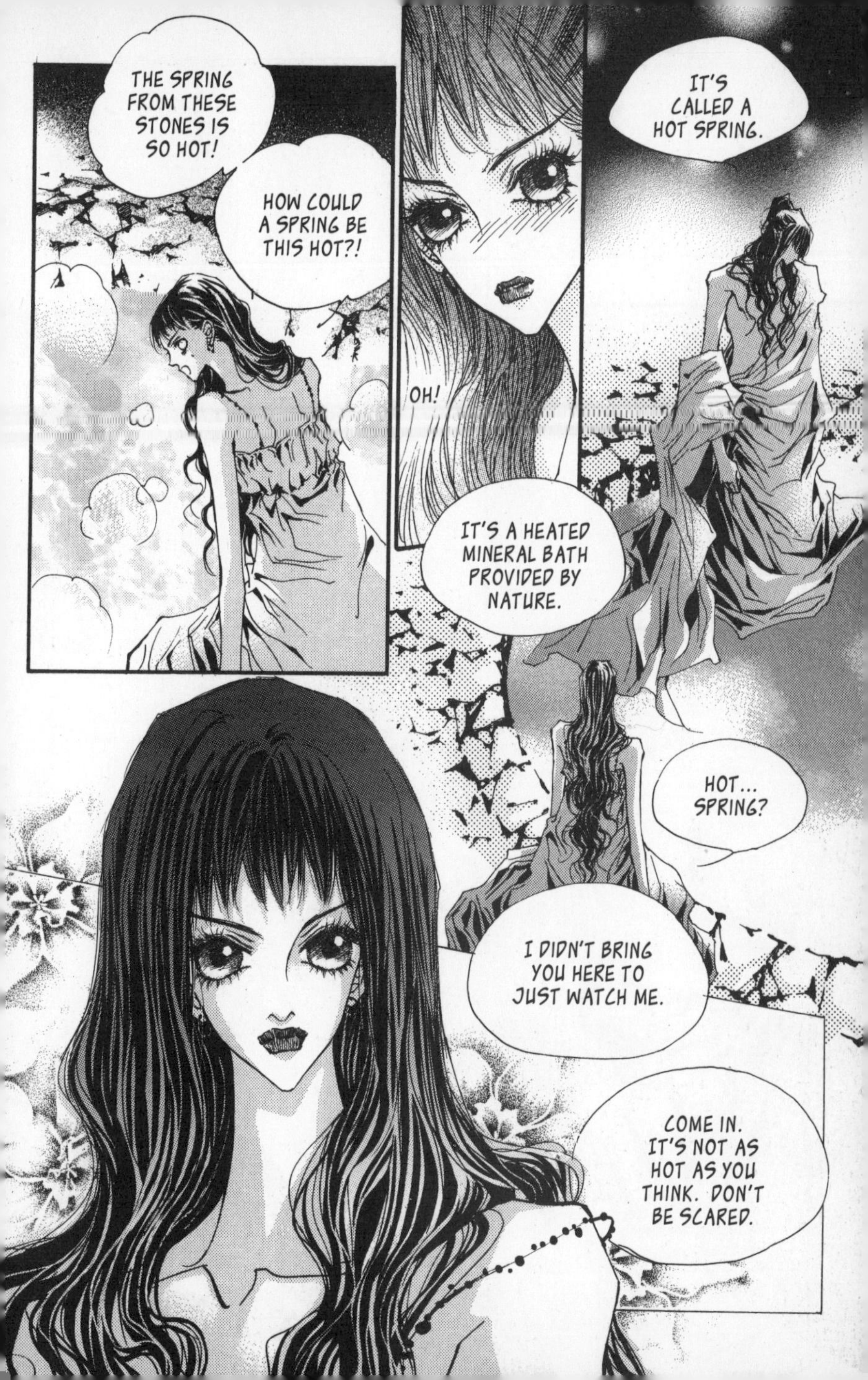
THE SPRING FROM THESE STONES IS SO HOT!
HOW COULD A SPRING BE THIS HOT?!
OH!
IT'S CALLED A HOT SPRING.
IT'S A HEATED MINERAL BATH PROVIDED BY NATURE.
HOT... SPRING?
I DIDN'T BRING YOU HERE TO JUST WATCH ME.
COME IN. IT'S NOT AS HOT AS YOU THINK. DON'T BE SCARED.

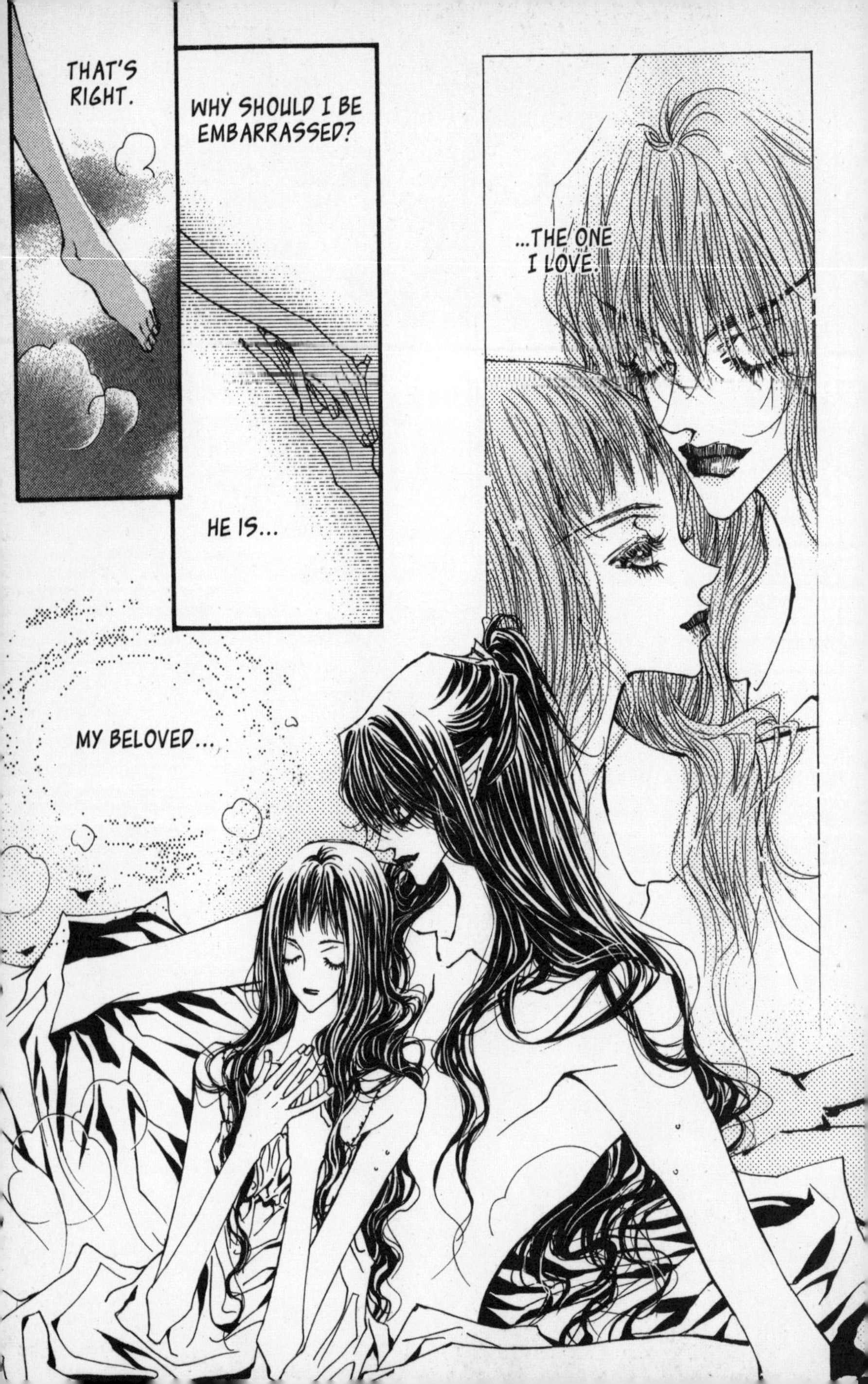
THAT'S RIGHT.
WHY SHOULD I BE EMBARRASSED?
HE IS...
...THE ONE I LOVE.
MY BELOVED...

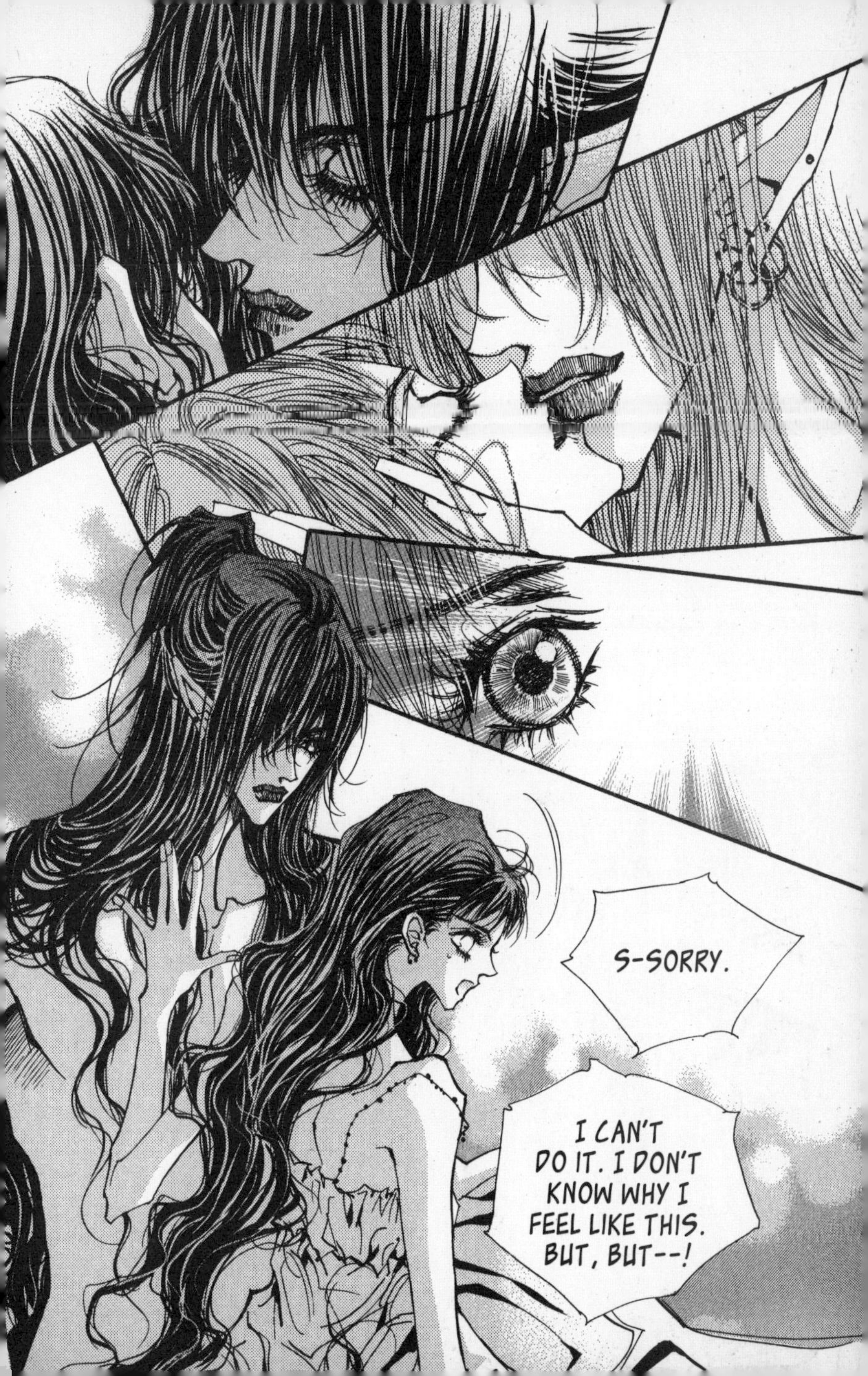
S-SORRY.
I CAN'T DO IT. I DON'T KNOW WHY I FEEL LIKE THIS. BUT, BUT--!

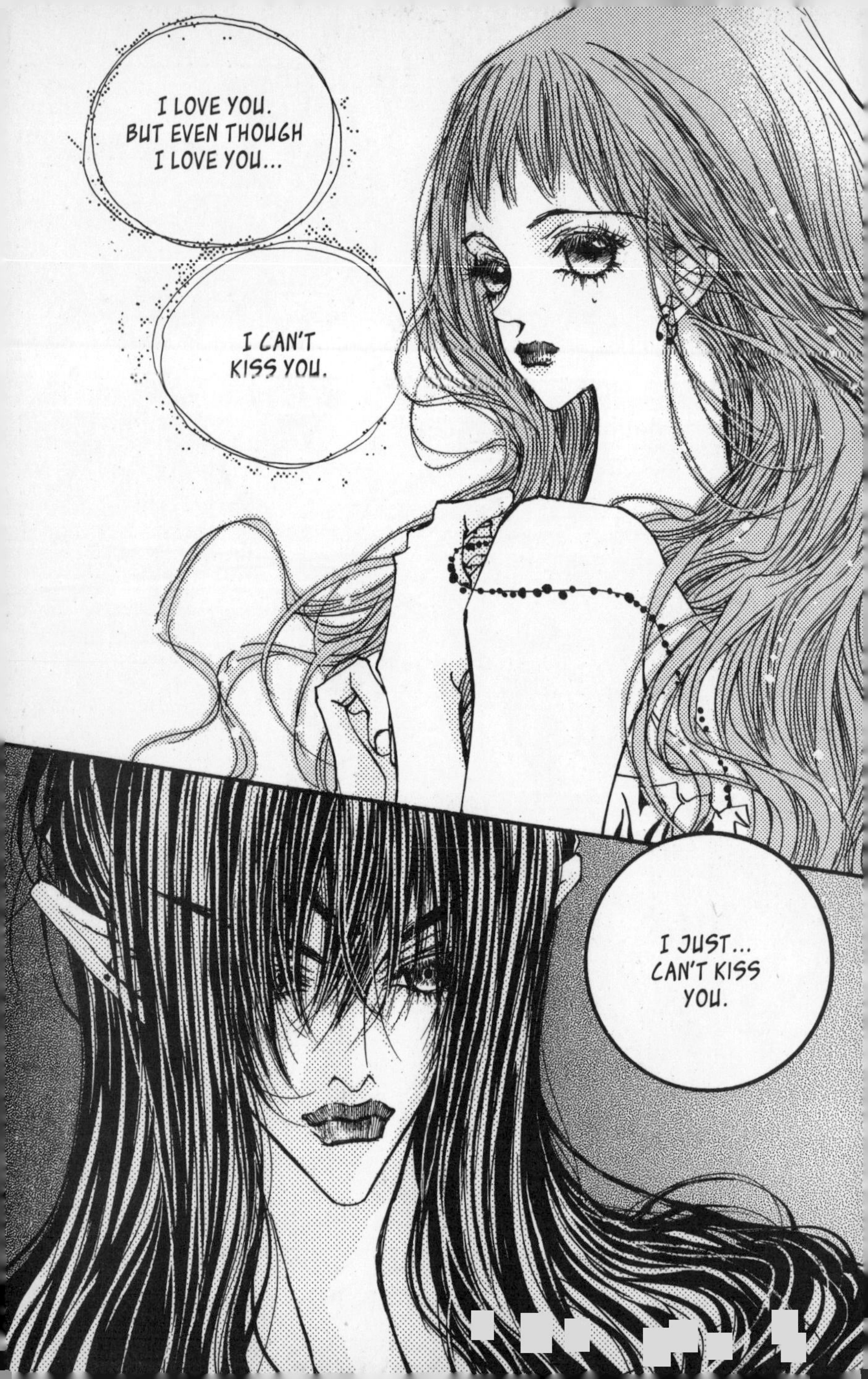
I LOVE YOU. BUT EVEN THOUGH I LOVE YOU...
I CAN'T KISS YOU.
I JUST... CAN'T KISS YOU.

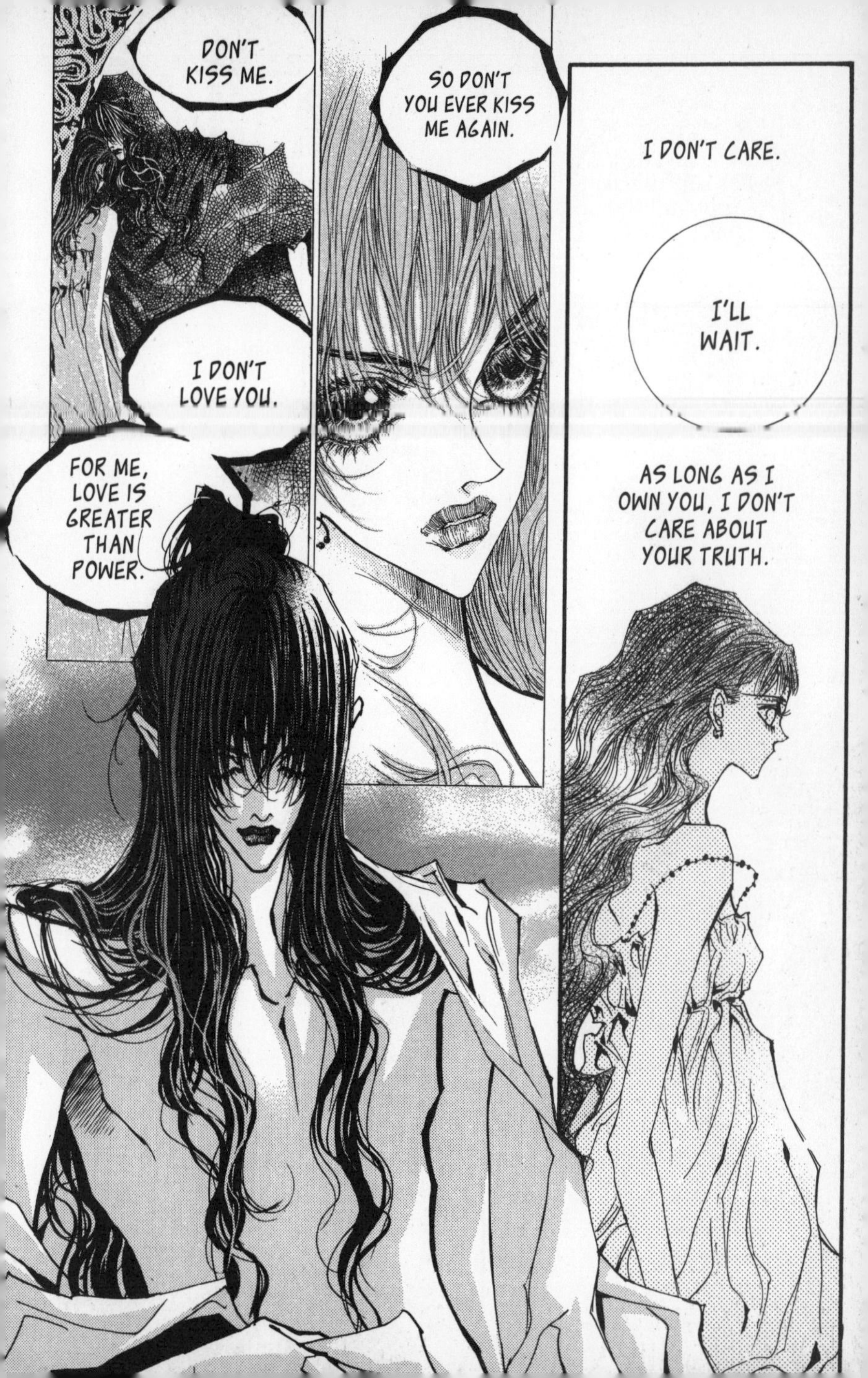
DON'T KISS ME.
I DON'T LOVE YOU.
FOR ME, LOVE IS GREATER THAN POWER.
SO DON'T YOU EVER KISS ME AGAIN.
I DON'T CARE.
I'LL WAIT.
AS LONG AS I OWN YOU, I DON'T CARE ABOUT YOUR TRUTH.

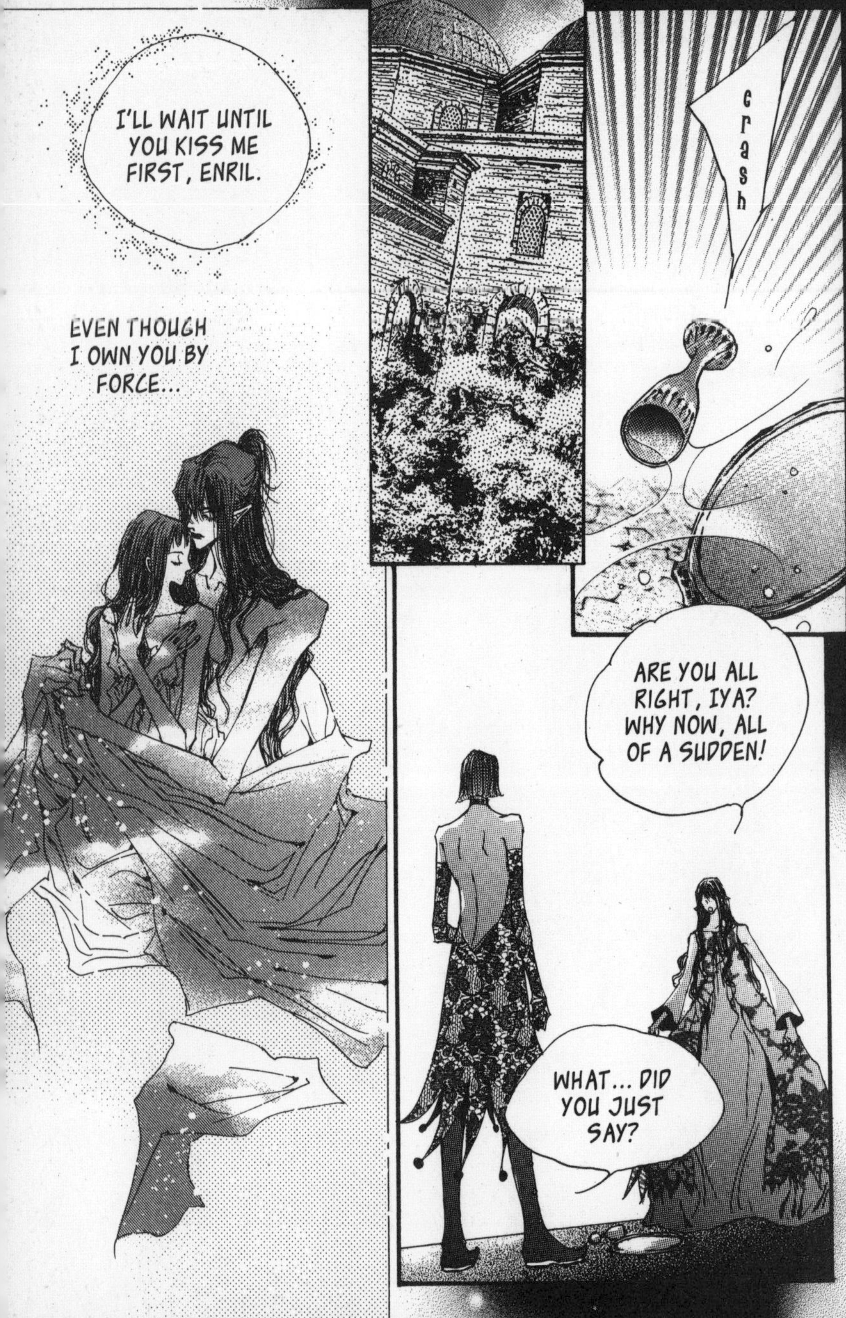
I'LL WAIT UNTIL YOU KISS ME FIRST, ENRIL.
EVEN THOUGH I OWN YOU BY FORCE...
crash
ARE YOU ALL RIGHT, IYA? WHY NOW, ALL OF A SUDDEN!
WHAT... DID YOU JUST SAY?

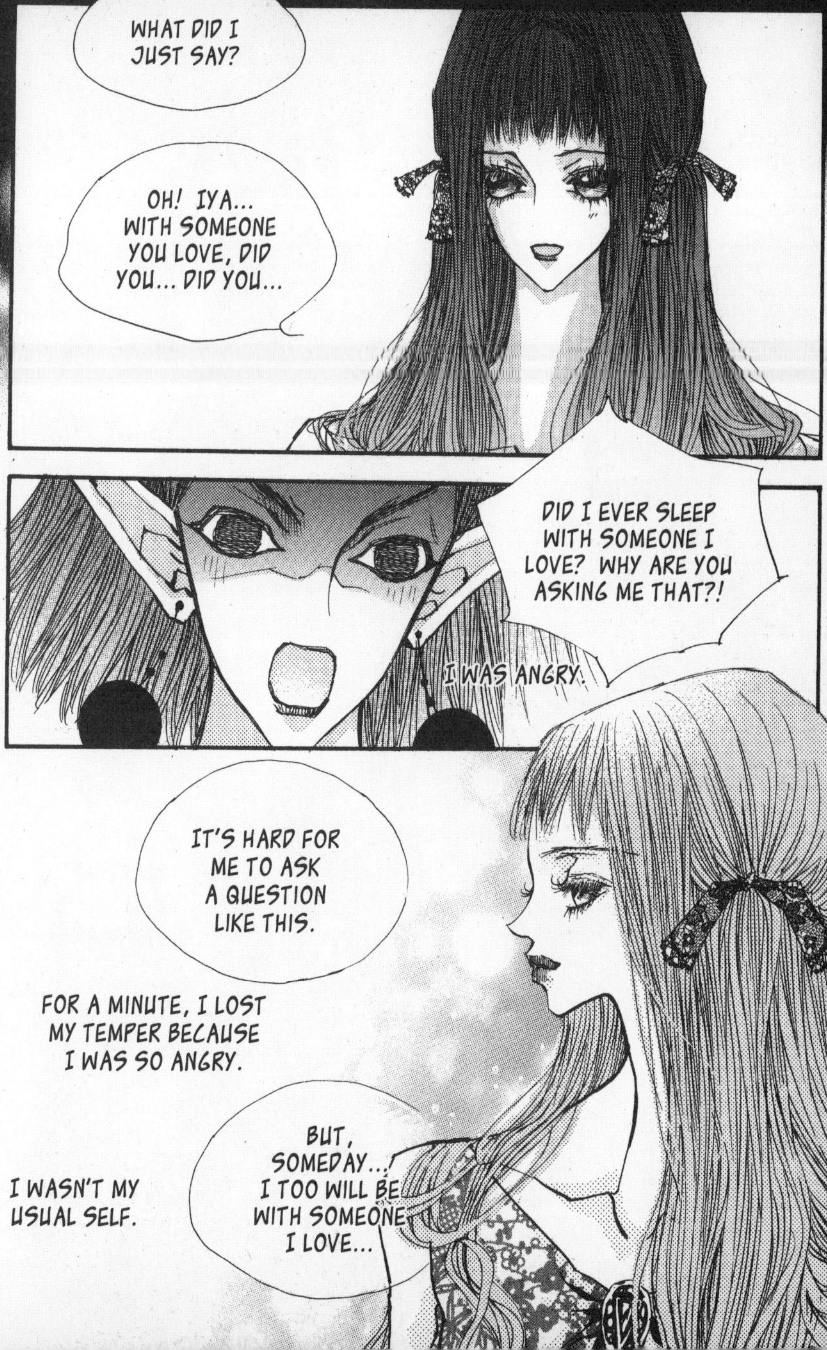
WHAT DID I JUST SAY?
OH! IYA... WITH SOMEONE YOU LOVE, DID YOU... DID YOU...
DID I EVER SLEEP WITH SOMEONE I LOVE? WHY ARE YOU ASKING ME THAT?!
I WAS ANGRY.
IT'S HARD FOR ME TO ASK A QUESTION LIKE THIS.
FOR A MINUTE, I LOST MY TEMPER BECAUSE I WAS SO ANGRY.
I WASN'T MY USUAL SELF.
BUT, SOMEDAY... I TOO WILL BE WITH SOMEONE I LOVE...

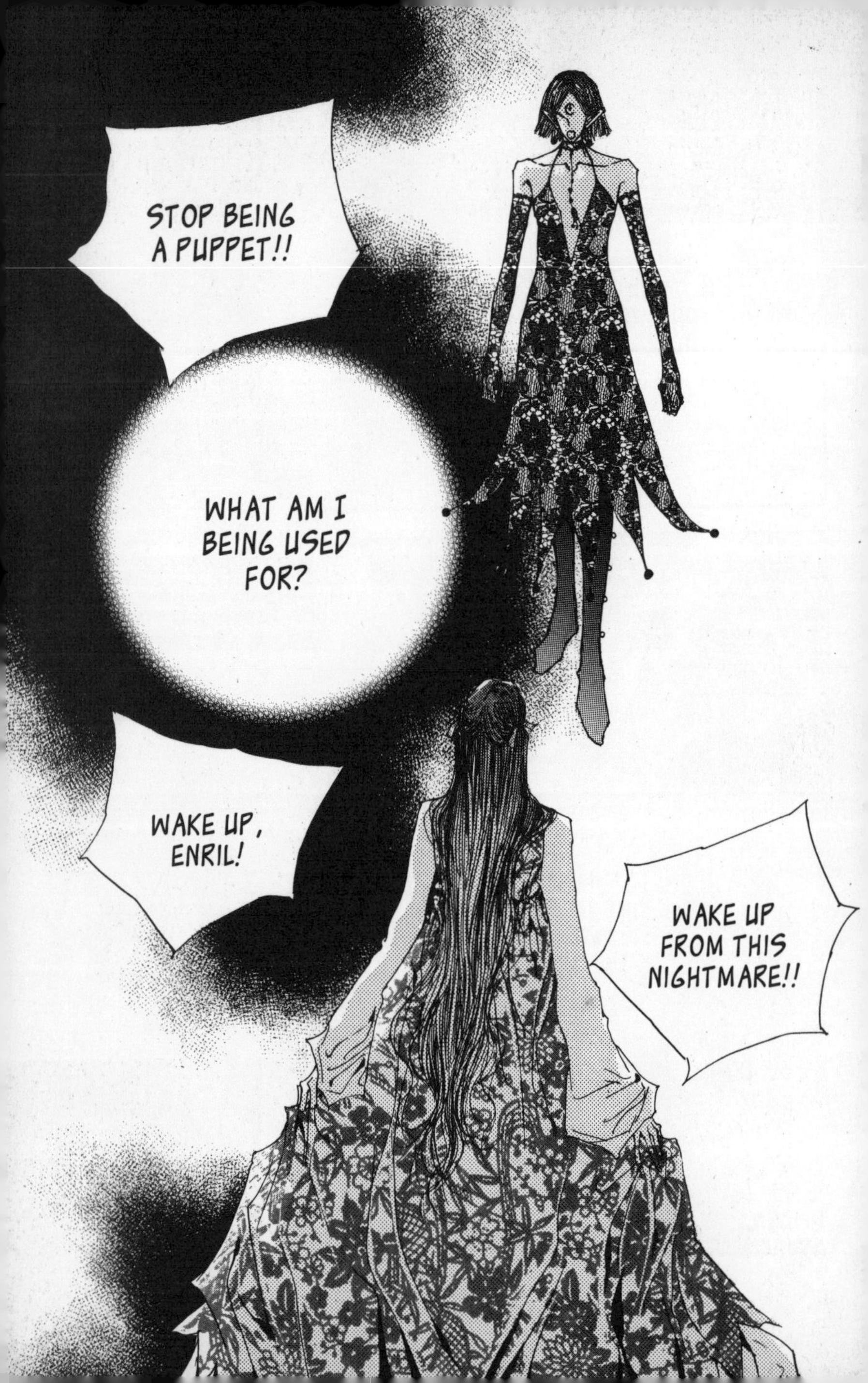
STOP BEING A PUPPET!!
WHAT AM I BEING USED FOR?
WAKE UP, ENRIL!
WAKE UP FROM THIS NIGHTMARE!!

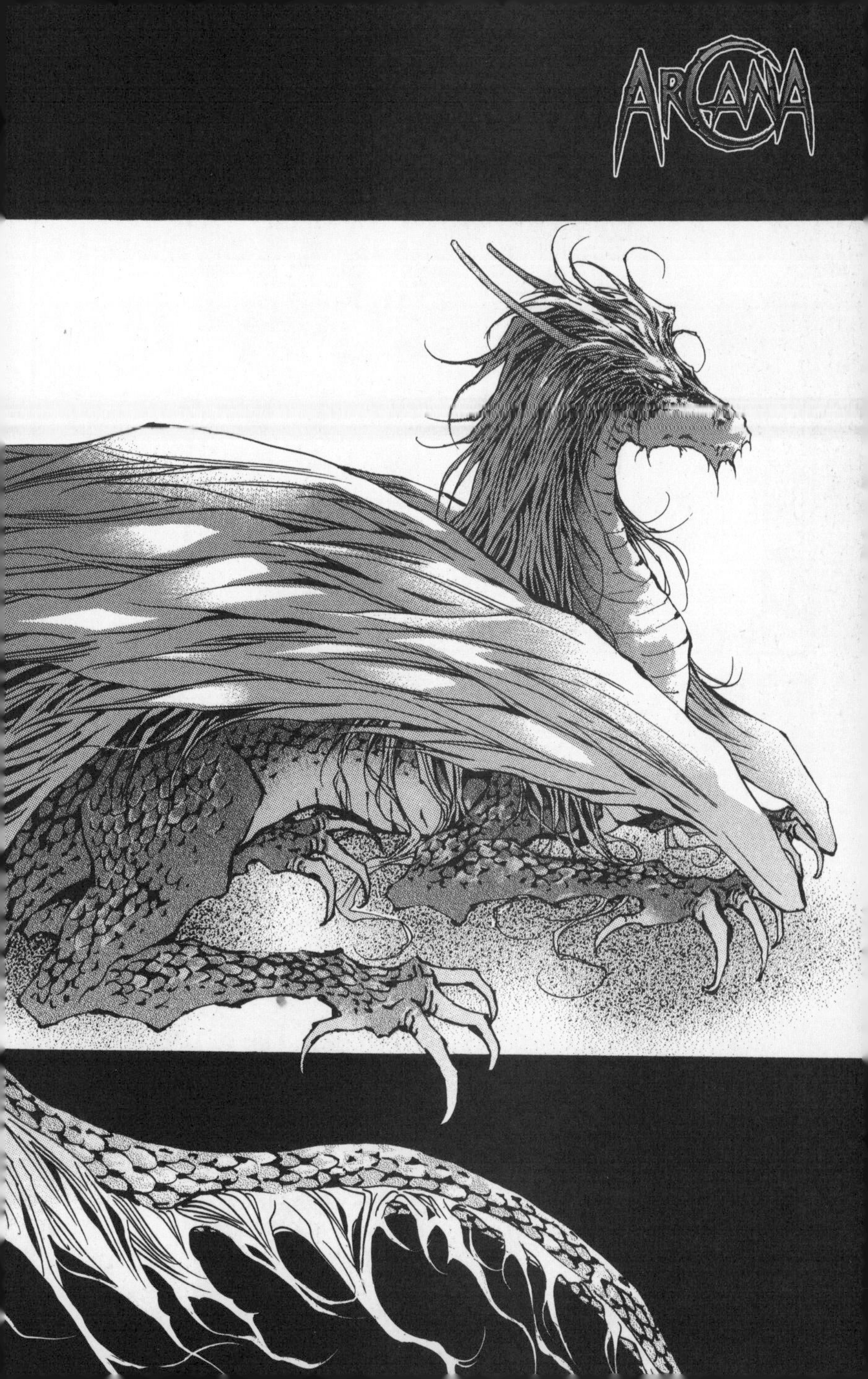
ArCaNa

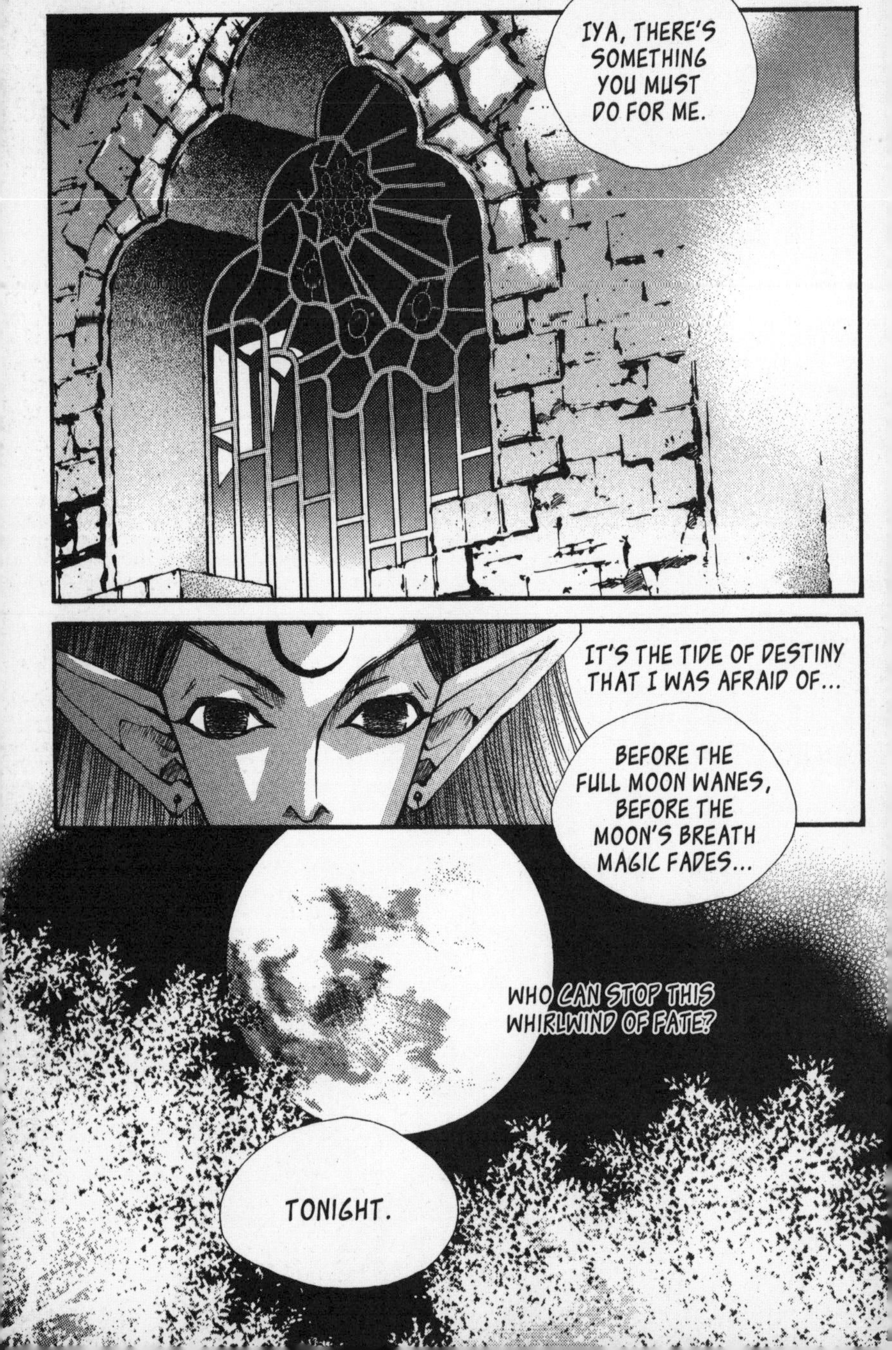
IYA, THERE'S SOMETHING YOU MUST DO FOR ME.
IT'S THE TIDE OF DESTINY THAT I WAS AFRAID OF...
BEFORE THE FULL MOON WANES, BEFORE THE MOON'S BREATH MAGIC FADES...
WHO CAN STOP THIS WHIRLWIND OF FATE?
TONIGHT.

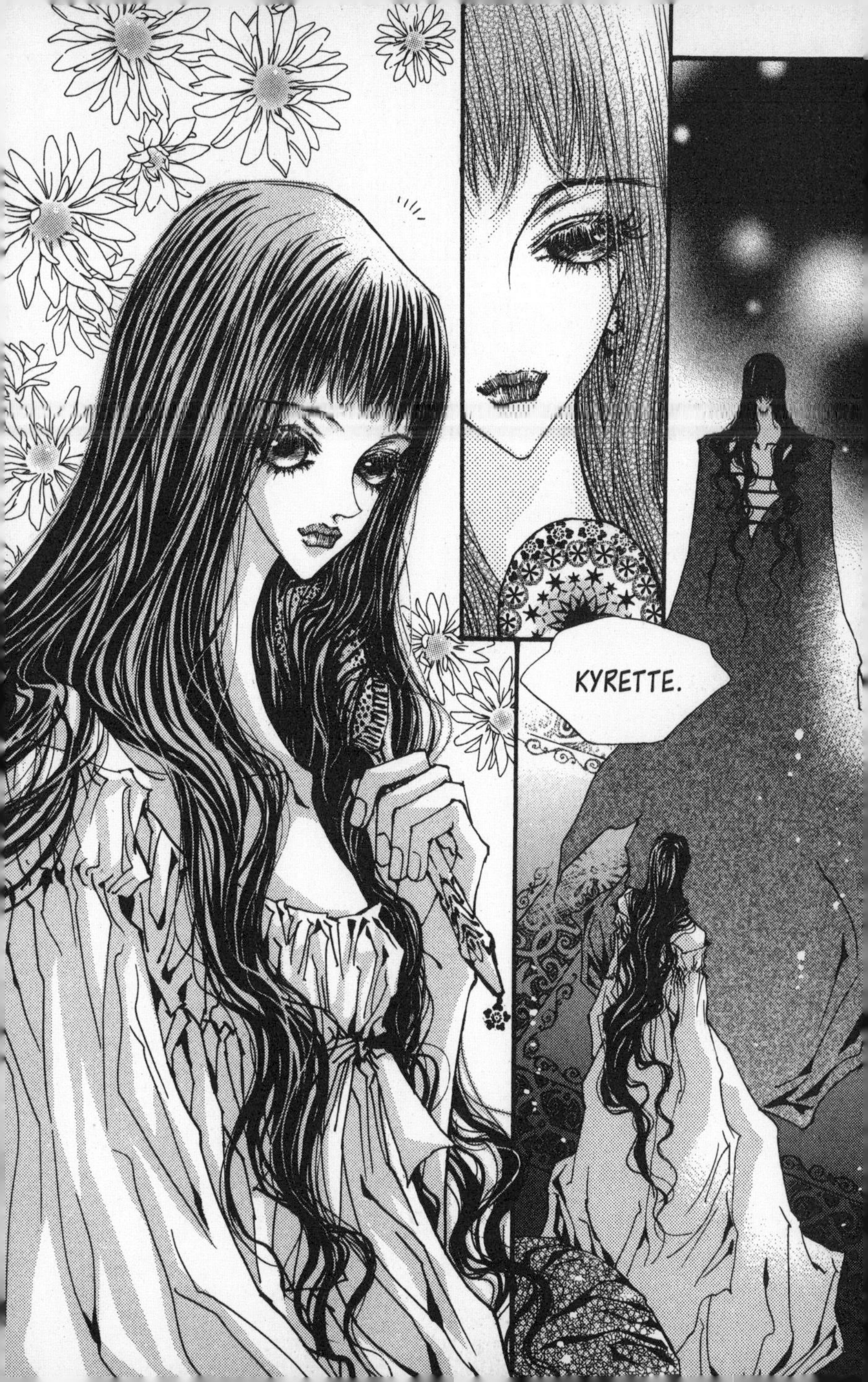
KYRETTE.

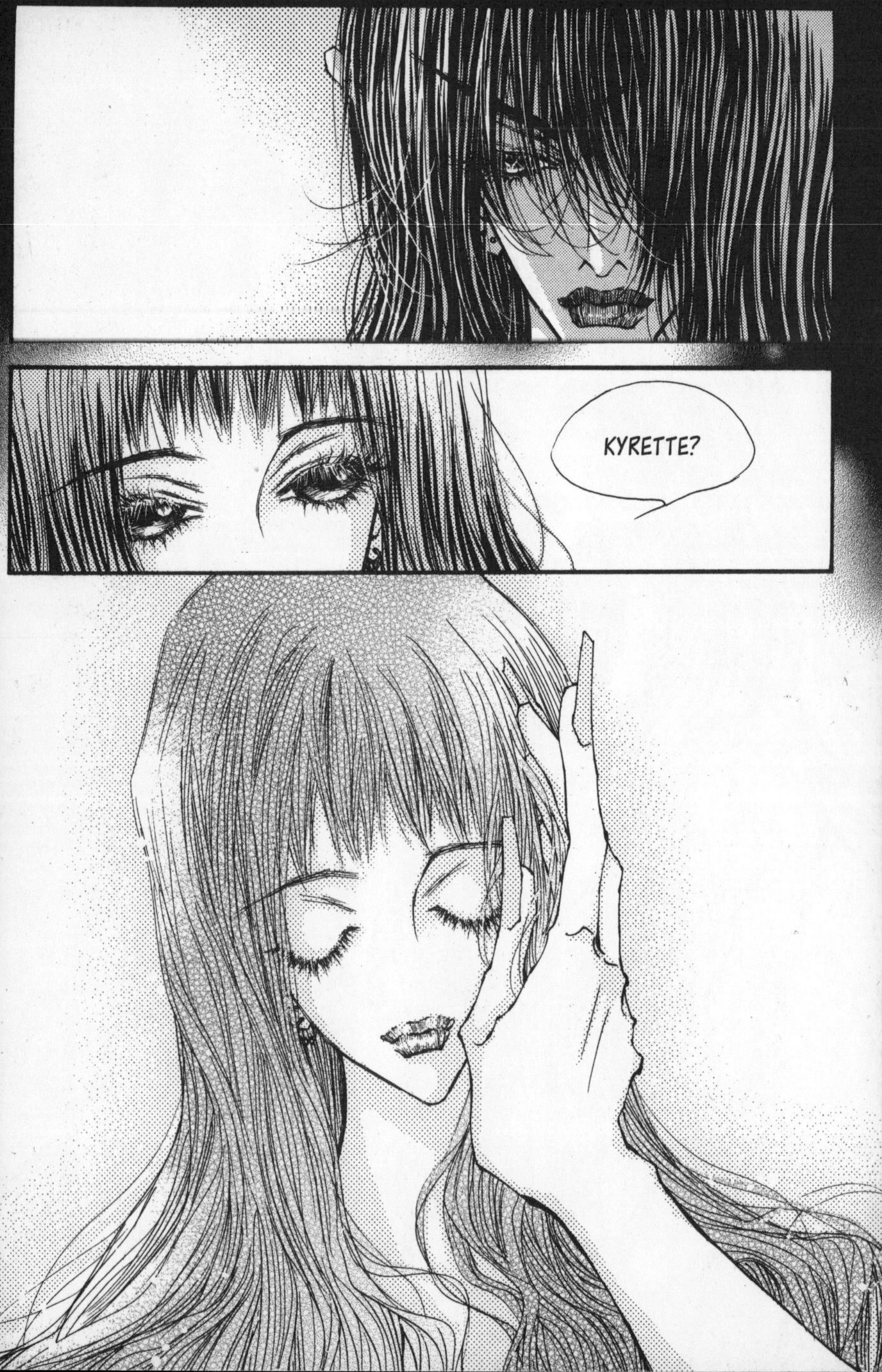
KYRETTE?

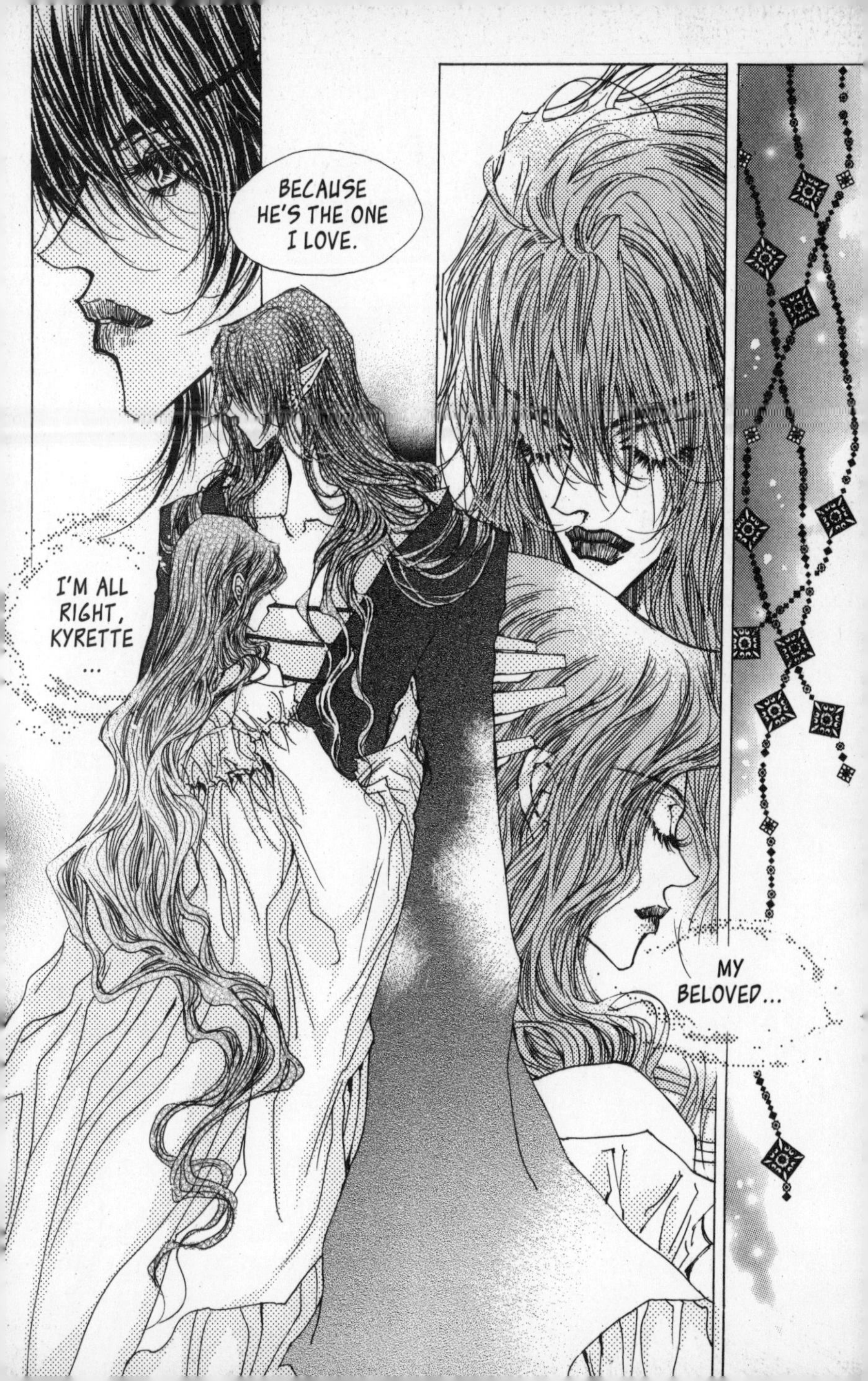
BECAUSE HE'S THE ONE I LOVE.
I'M ALL RIGHT, KYRETTE ...
MY BELOVED...

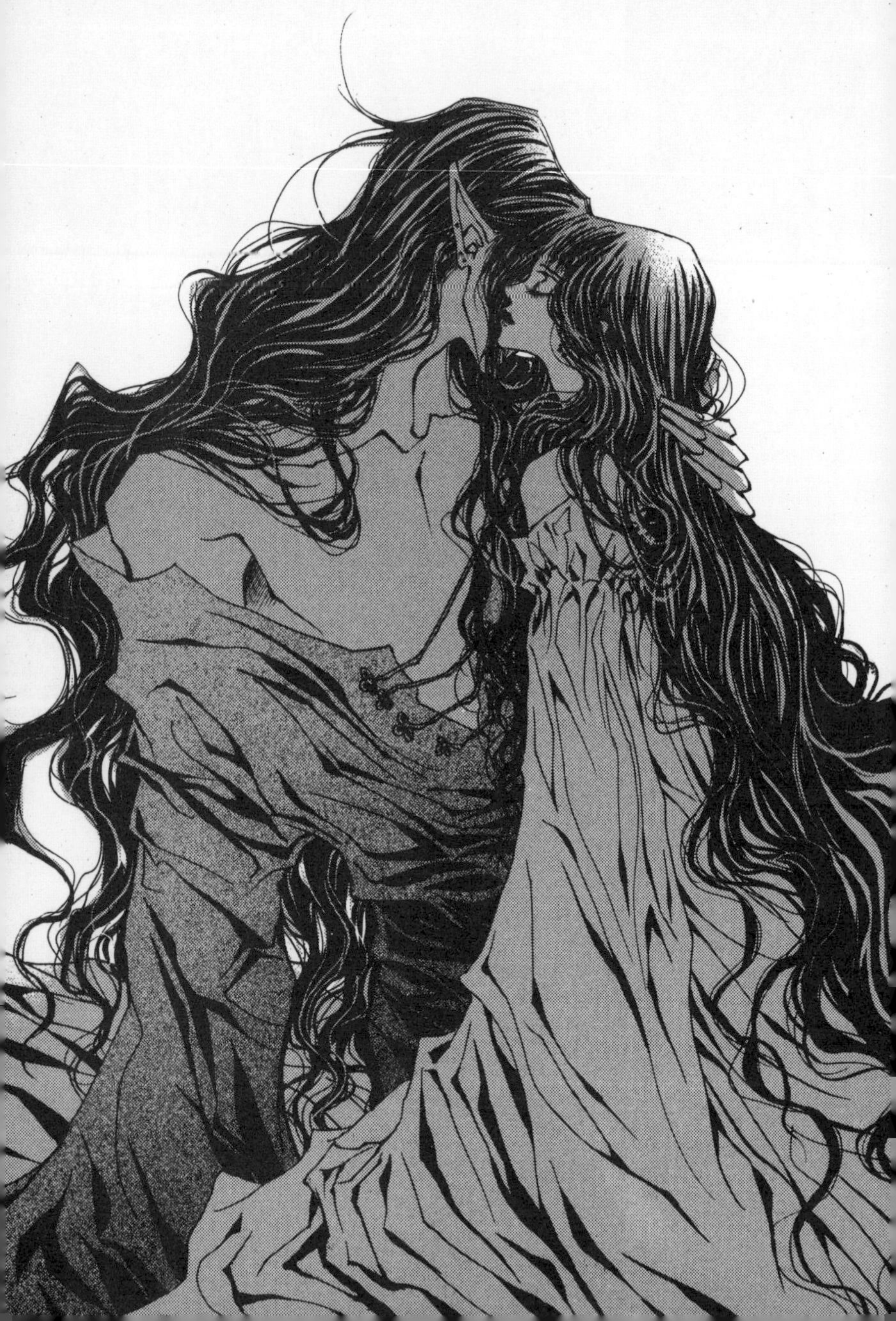

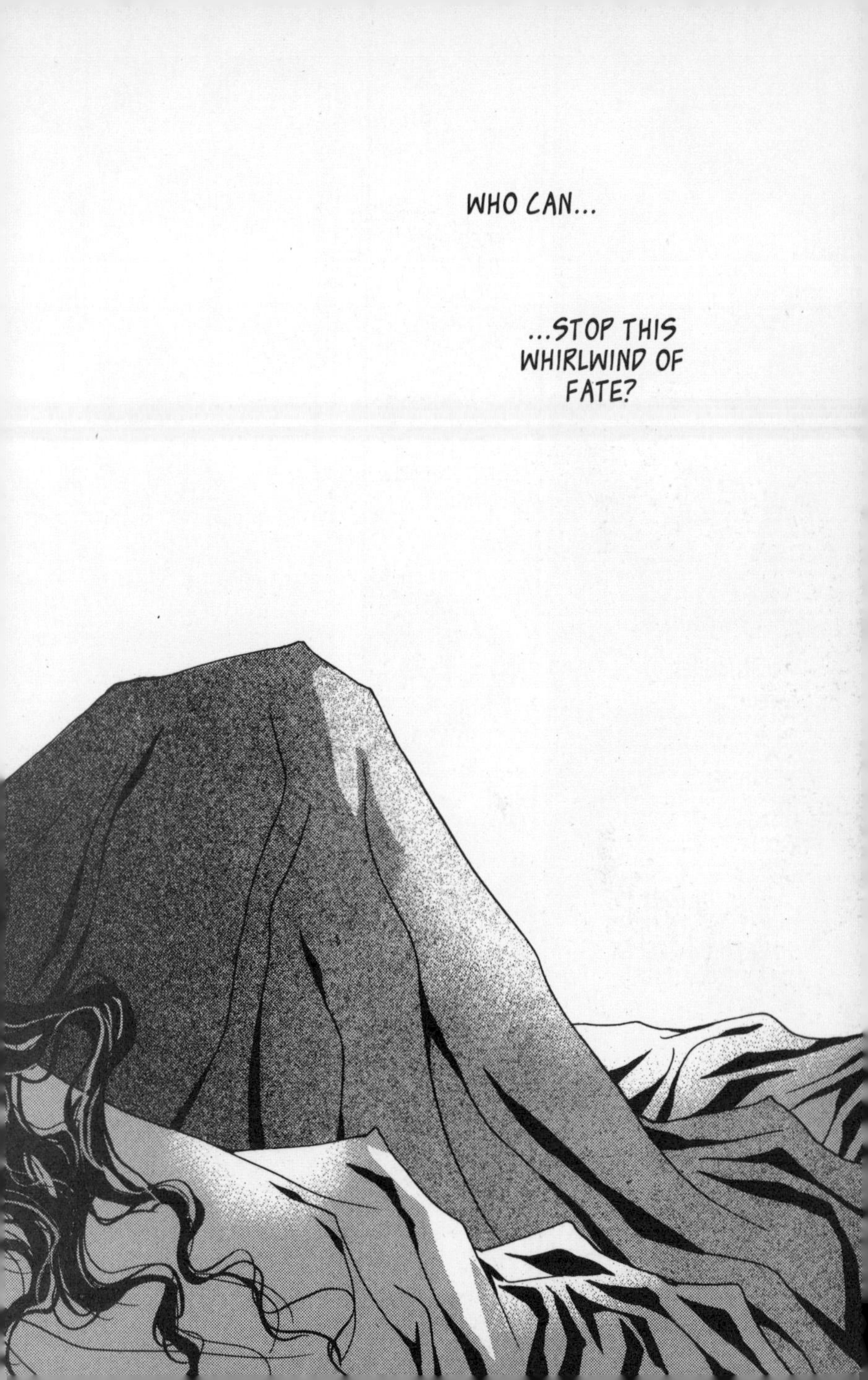
WHO CAN...
...STOP THIS WHIRLWIND OF FATE?

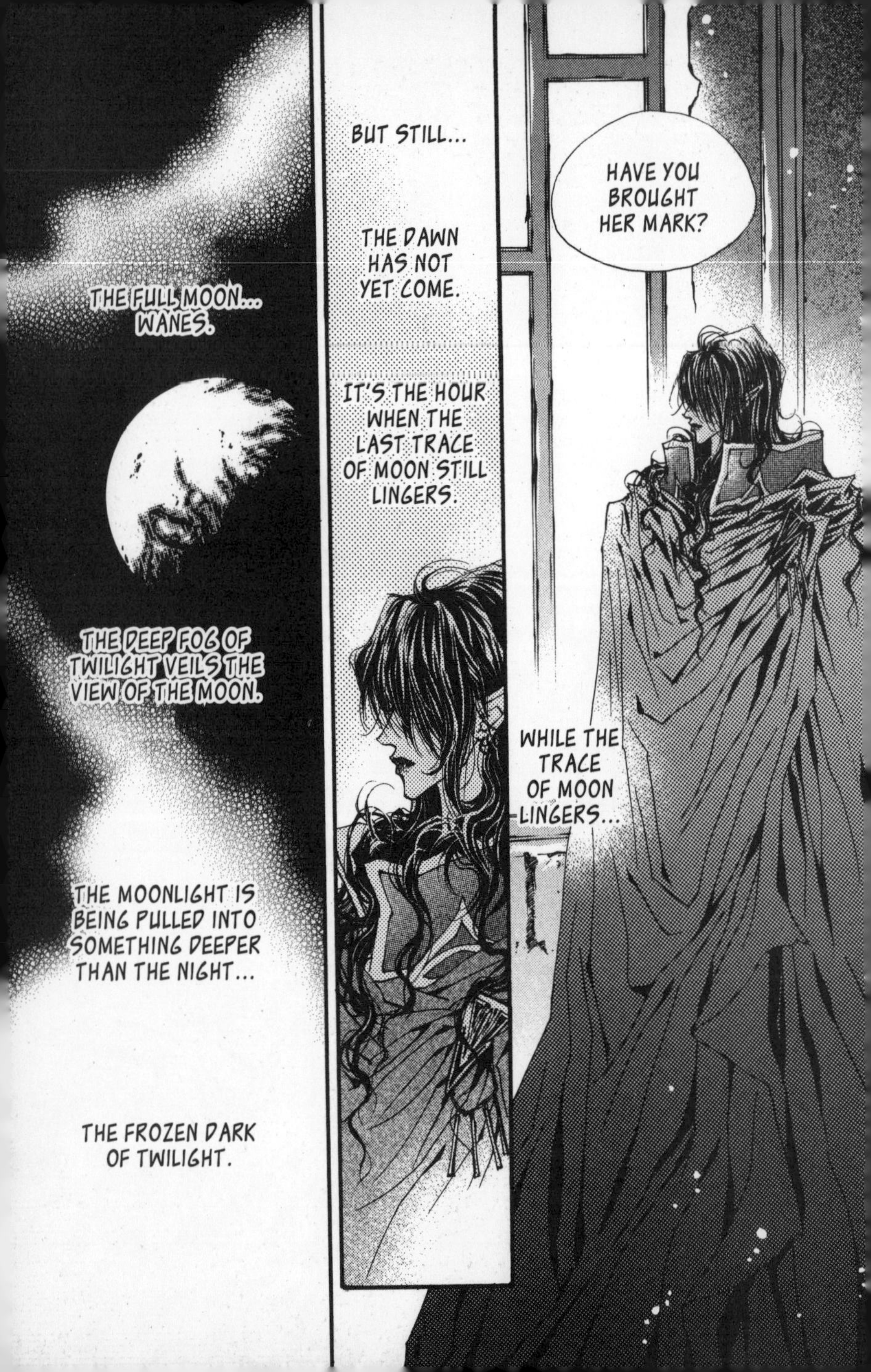
THE FULL MOON... WANES.
THE DEEP FOG OF TWILIGHT VEILS THE VIEW OF THE MOON.
THE MOONLIGHT IS BEING PULLED INTO SOMETHING DEEPER THAN THE NIGHT...
THE FROZEN DARK OF TWILIGHT.
BUT STILL...
THE DAWN HAS NOT YET COME.
IT'S THE HOUR WHEN THE LAST TRACE OF MOON STILL LINGERS.
HAVE YOU BROUGHT HER MARK?
WHILE THE TRACE OF MOON LINGERS...

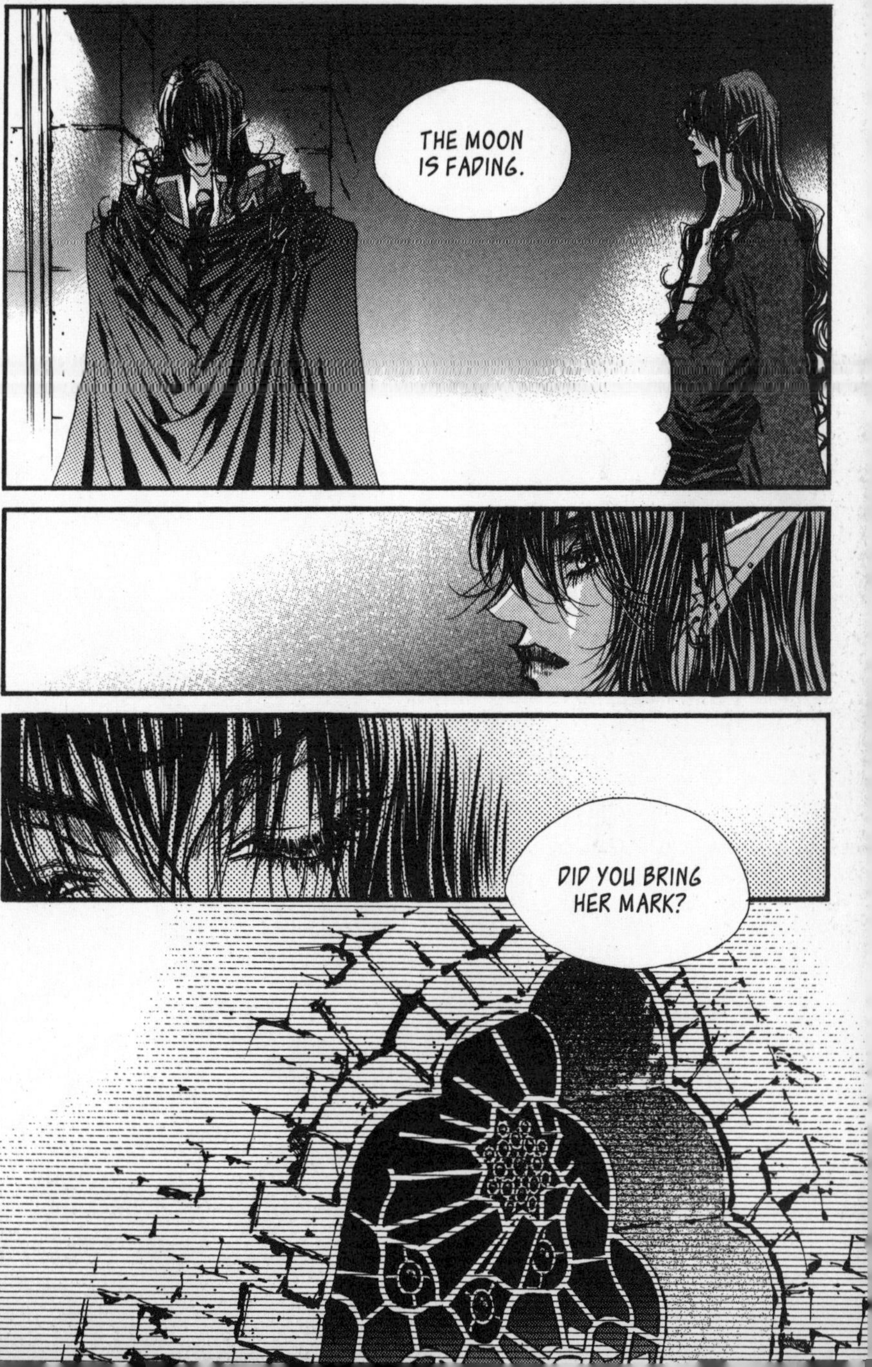
THE MOON IS FADING.
DID YOU BRING HER MARK?

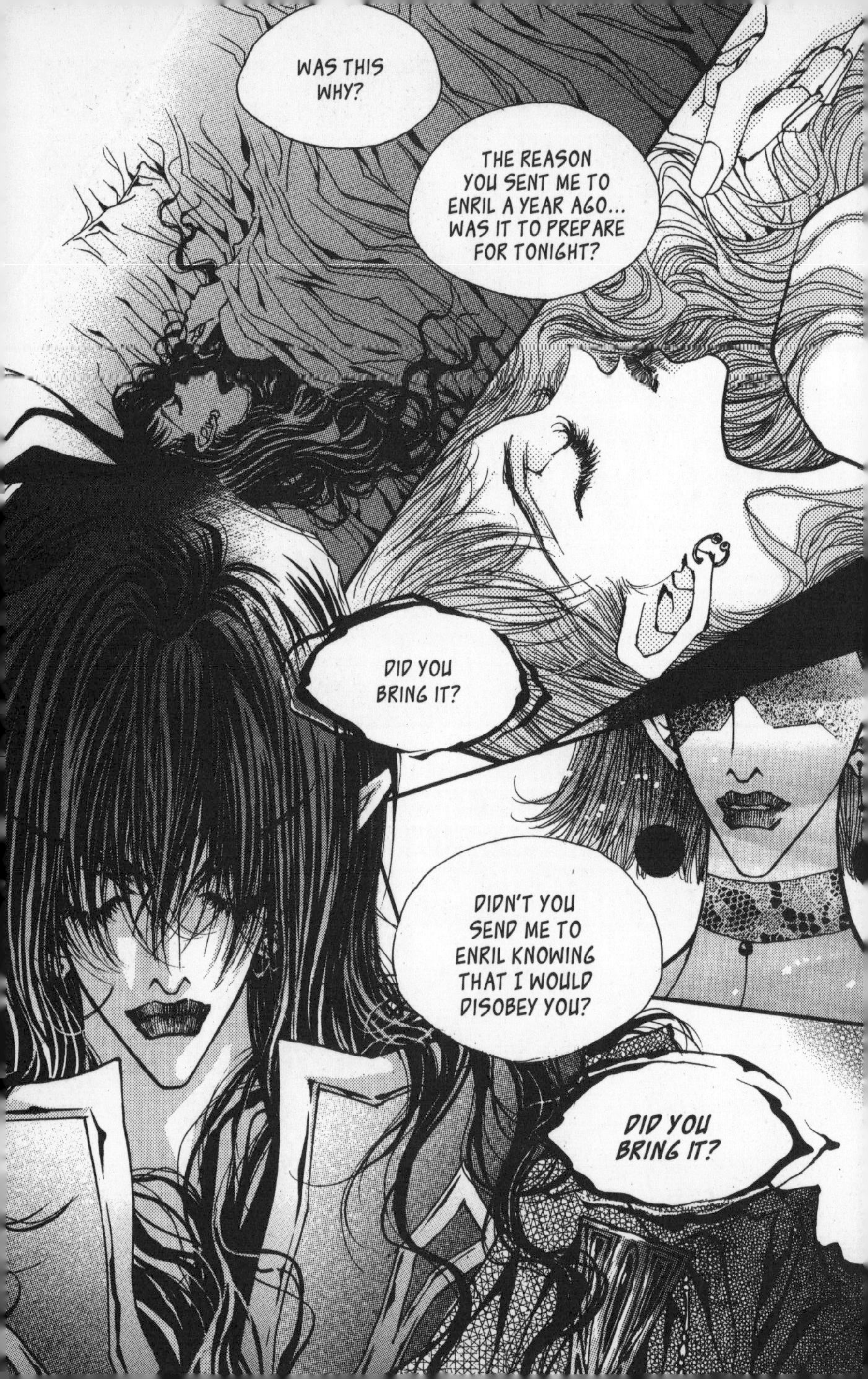
WAS THIS WHY?
THE REASON YOU SENT ME TO ENRIL A YEAR AGO... WAS IT TO PREPARE FOR TONIGHT?
DID YOU BRING IT?
DIDN'T YOU SEND ME TO ENRIL KNOWING THAT I WOULD DISOBEY YOU?
DID YOU BRING IT?

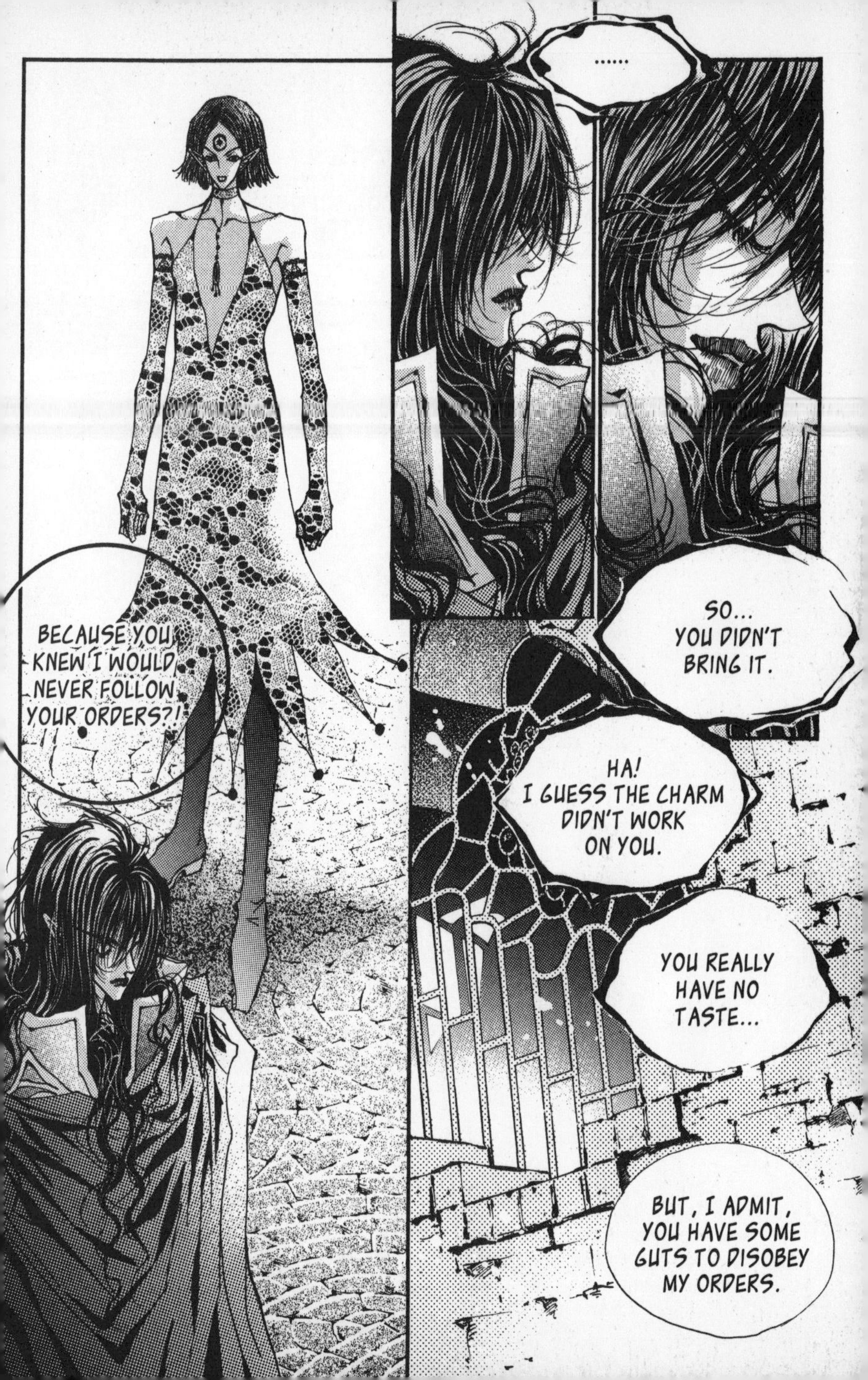
BECAUSE YOU KNEW I WOULD NEVER FOLLOW YOUR ORDERS?!
......
SO... YOU DIDN'T BRING IT.
HA! I GUESS THE CHARM DIDN'T WORK ON YOU.
YOU REALLY HAVE NO TASTE...
BUT, I ADMIT, YOU HAVE SOME GUTS TO DISOBEY MY ORDERS.

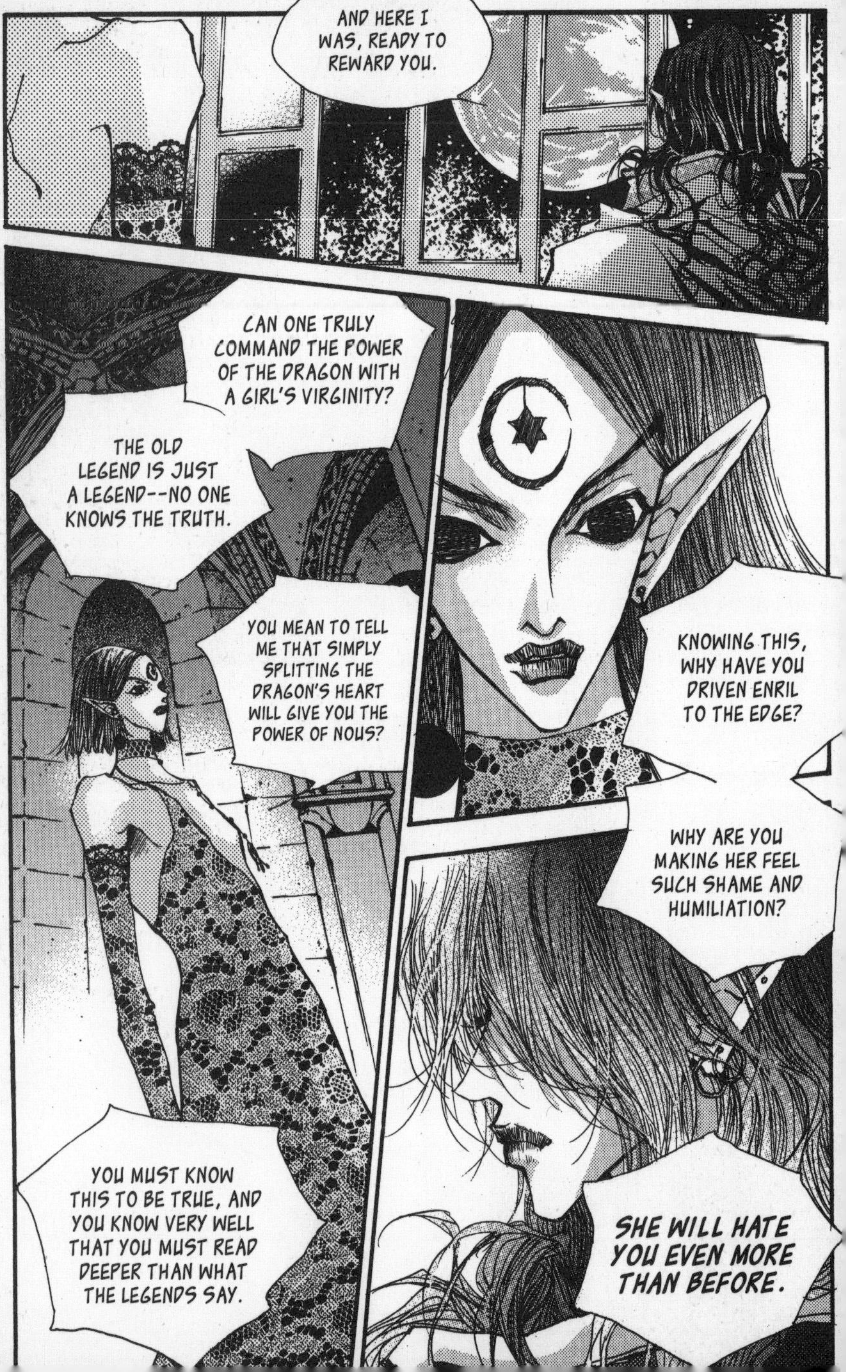
AND HERE I WAS, READY TO REWARD YOU.
CAN ONE TRULY COMMAND THE POWER OF THE DRAGON WITH A GIRL'S VIRGINITY?
THE OLD LEGEND IS JUST A LEGEND--NO ONE KNOWS THE TRUTH.
YOU MEAN TO TELL ME THAT SIMPLY SPLITTING THE DRAGON'S HEART WILL GIVE YOU THE POWER OF NOUS?
YOU MUST KNOW THIS TO BE TRUE, AND YOU KNOW VERY WELL THAT YOU MUST READ DEEPER THAN WHAT THE LEGENDS SAY.
KNOWING THIS, WHY HAVE YOU DRIVEN ENRIL TO THE EDGE?
WHY ARE YOU MAKING HER FEEL SUCH SHAME AND HUMILIATION?
SHE WILL HATE YOU EVEN MORE THAN BEFORE.

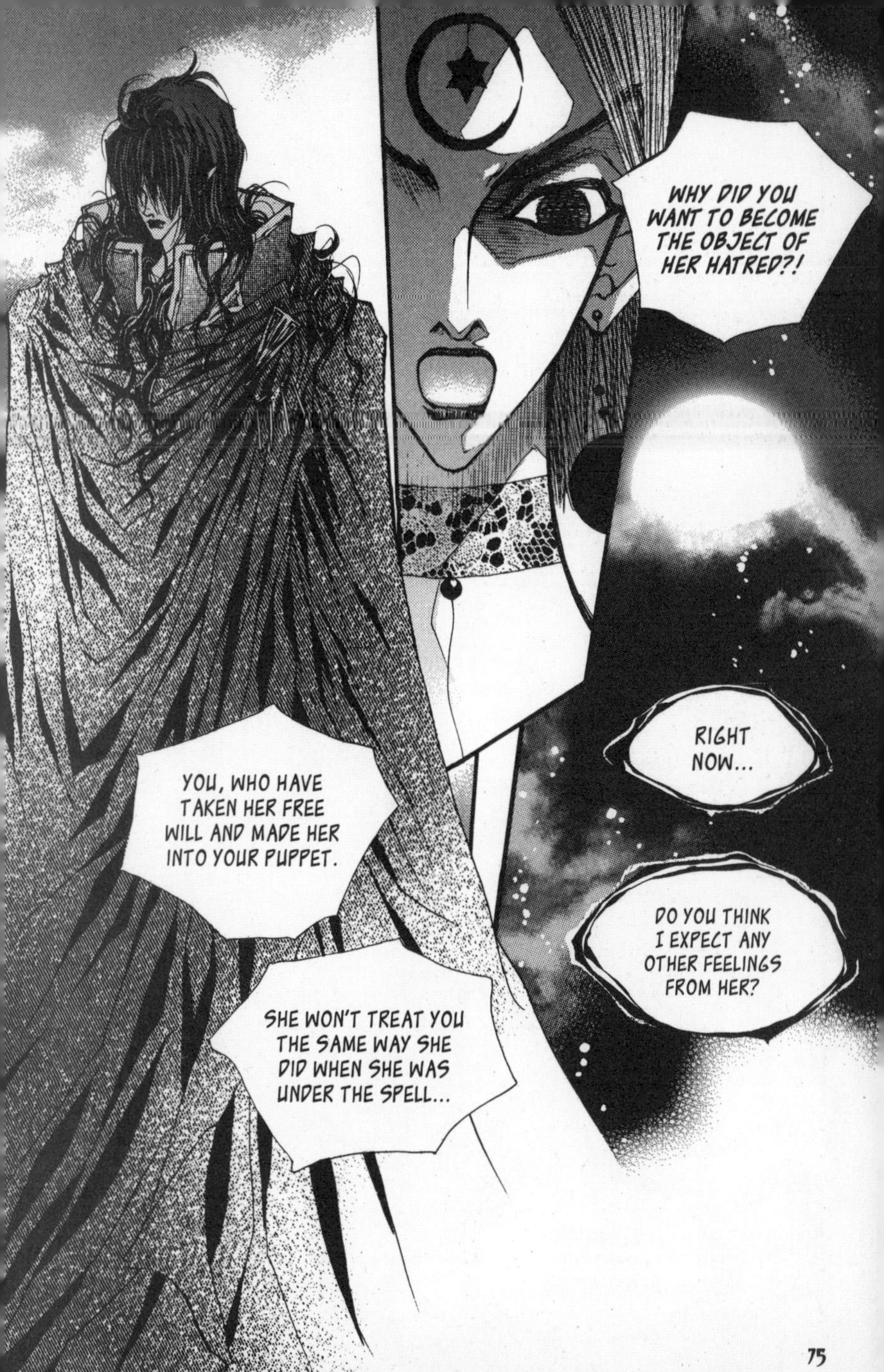
WHY DID YOU WANT TO BECOME THE OBJECT OF HER HATRED?!
YOU, WHO HAVE TAKEN HER FREE WILL AND MADE HER INTO YOUR PUPPET.
SHE WON'T TREAT YOU THE SAME WAY SHE DID WHEN SHE WAS UNDER THE SPELL...
RIGHT NOW...
DO YOU THINK I EXPECT ANY OTHER FEELINGS FROM HER?

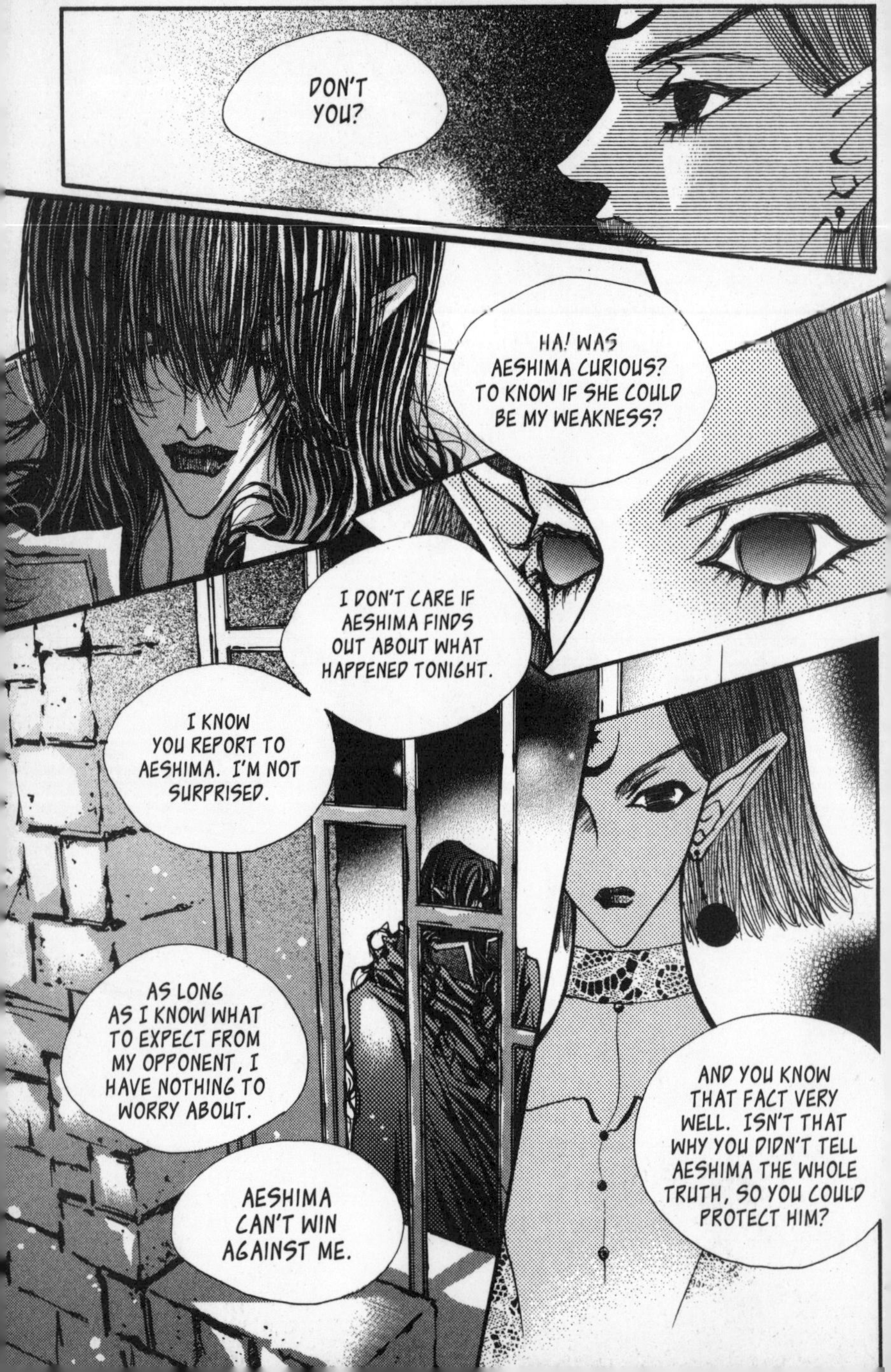
DON'T YOU?
HA! WAS AESHIMA CURIOUS? TO KNOW IF SHE COULD BE MY WEAKNESS?
I DON'T CARE IF AESHIMA FINDS OUT ABOUT WHAT HAPPENED TONIGHT.
I KNOW YOU REPORT TO AESHIMA. I'M NOT SURPRISED.
AS LONG AS I KNOW WHAT TO EXPECT FROM MY OPPONENT, I HAVE NOTHING TO WORRY ABOUT.
AESHIMA CAN'T WIN AGAINST ME.
AND YOU KNOW THAT FACT VERY WELL. ISN'T THAT WHY YOU DIDN'T TELL AESHIMA THE WHOLE TRUTH, SO YOU COULD PROTECT HIM?

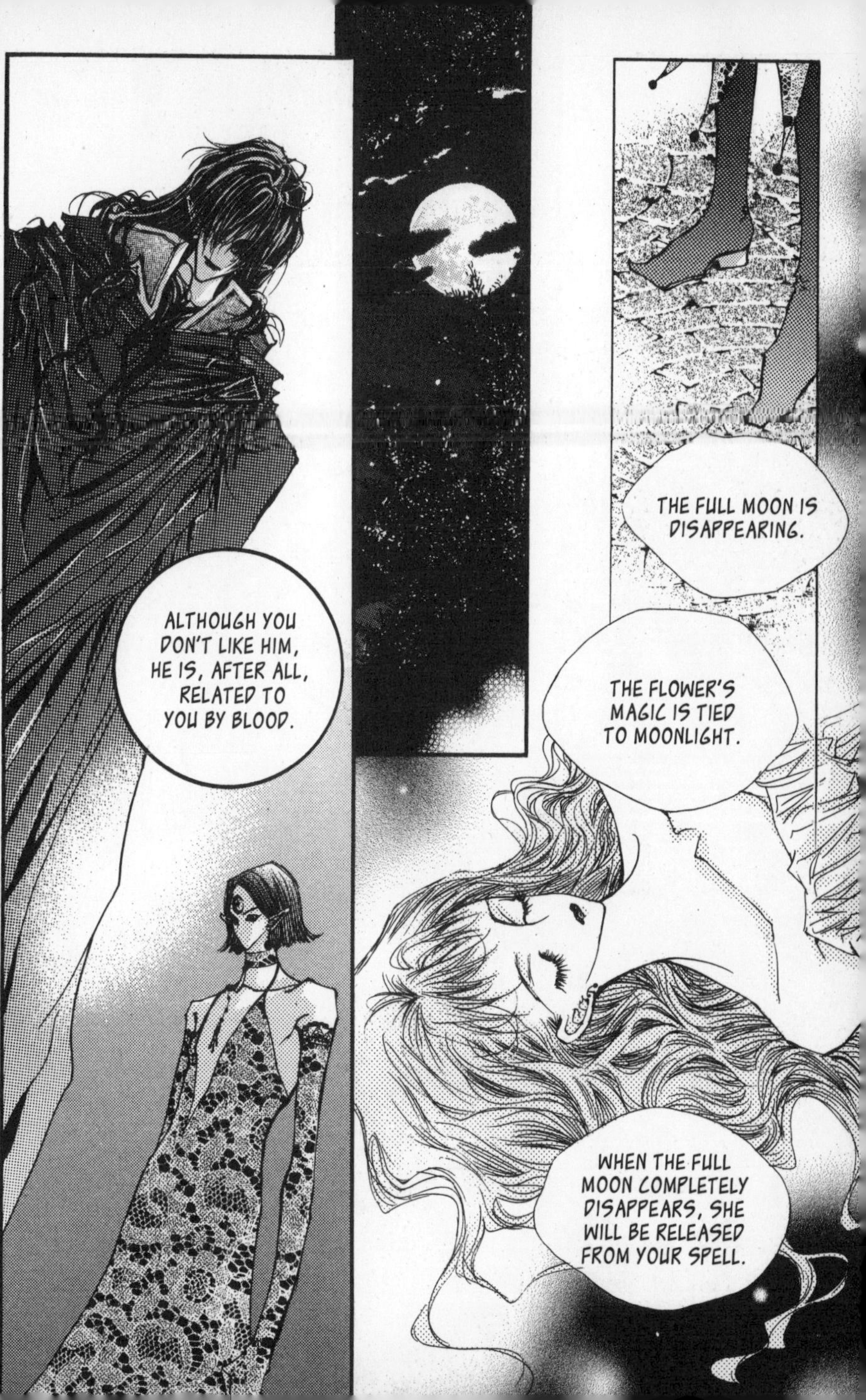
ALTHOUGH YOU DON'T LIKE HIM, HE IS, AFTER ALL, RELATED TO YOU BY BLOOD.
THE FULL MOON IS DISAPPEARING.
THE FLOWER'S MAGIC IS TIED TO MOONLIGHT.
WHEN THE FULL MOON COMPLETELY DISAPPEARS, SHE WILL BE RELEASED FROM YOUR SPELL.

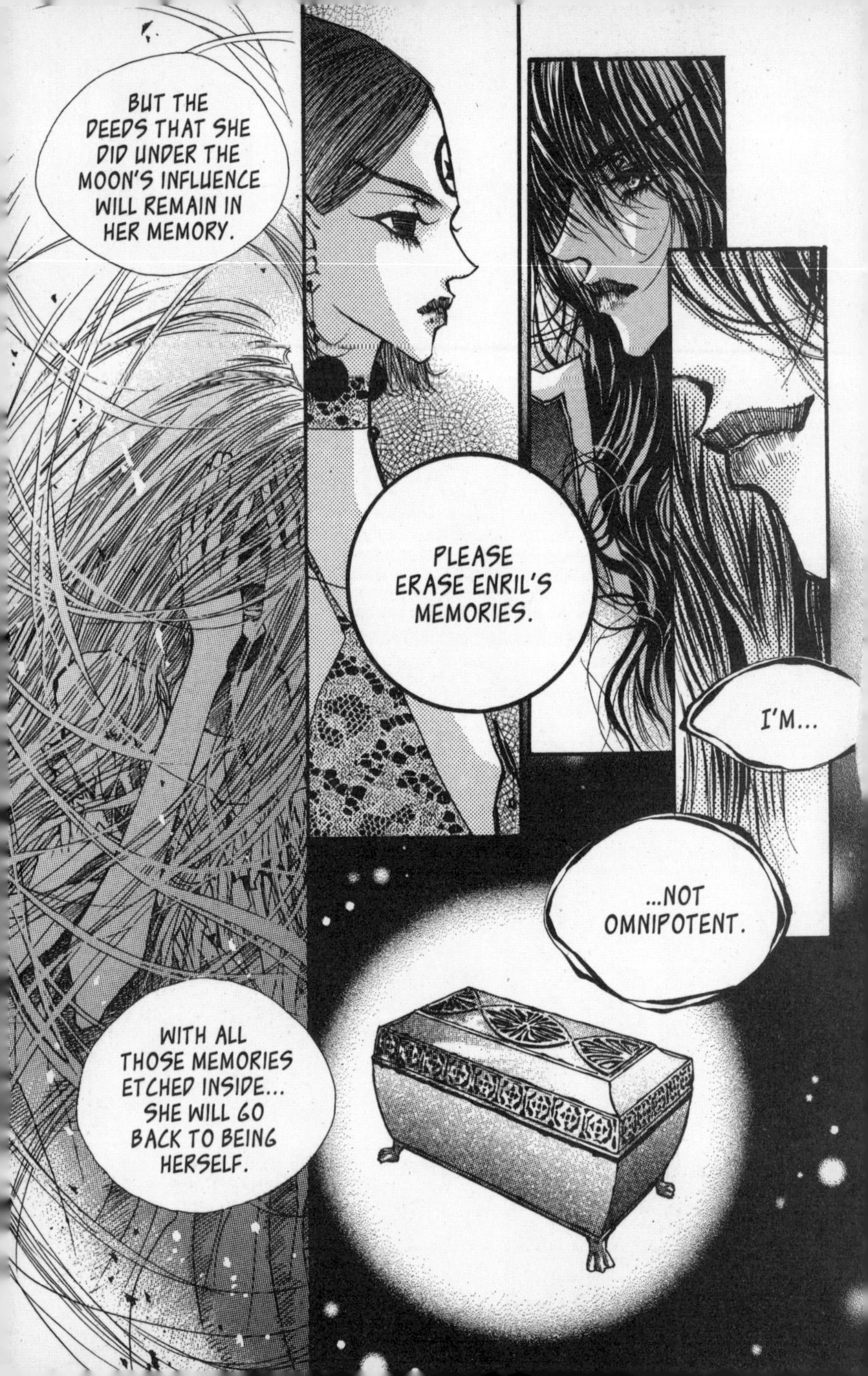

BUT THE DEEDS THAT SHE DID UNDER THE MOON'S INFLUENCE WILL REMAIN IN HER MEMORY.
WITH ALL THOSE MEMORIES ETCHED INSIDE... SHE WILL GO BACK TO BEING HERSELF.
PLEASE ERASE ENRIL'S MEMORIES.
I'M...
...NOT OMNIPOTENT.

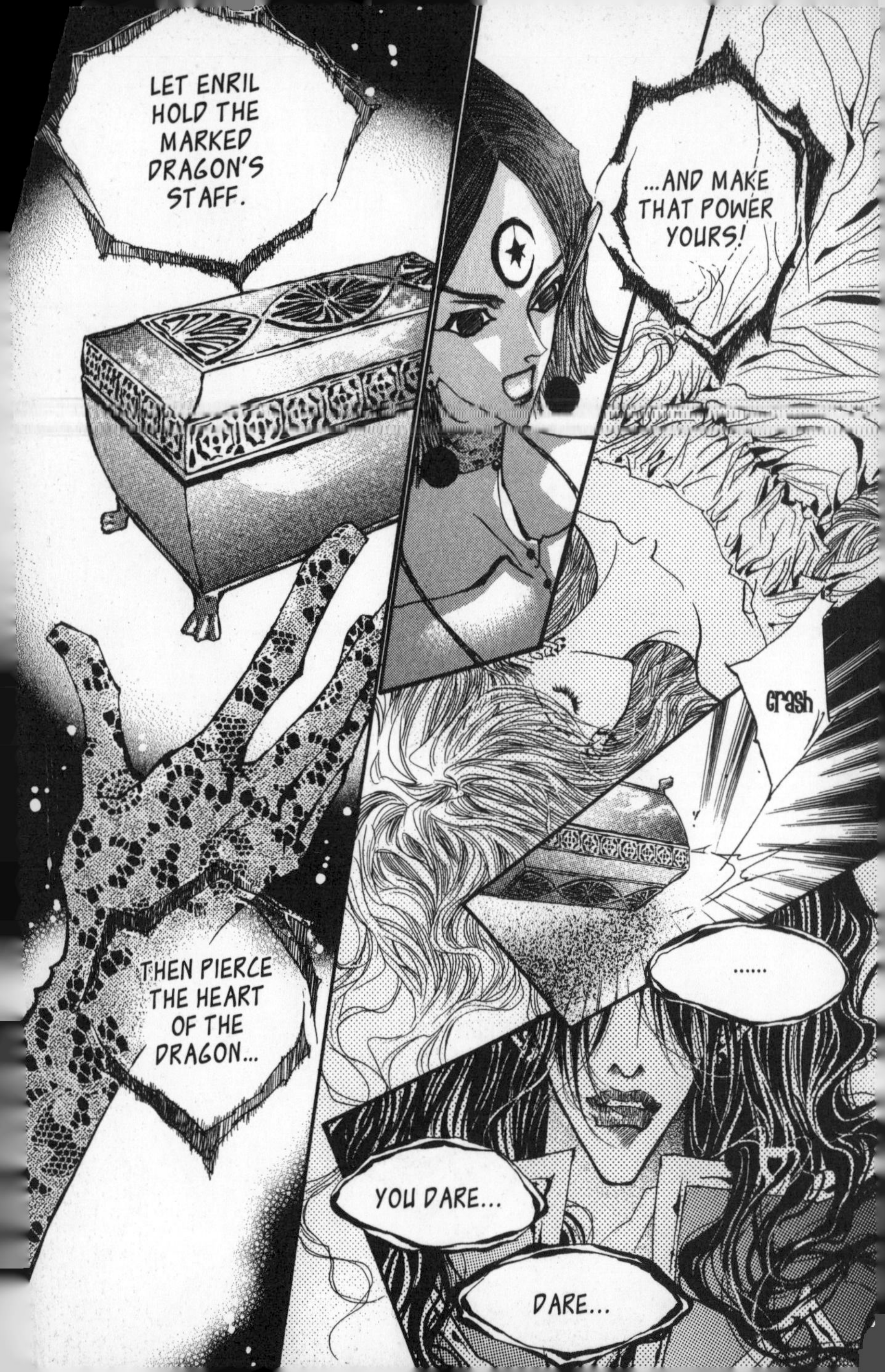
LET ENRIL HOLD THE MARKED DRAGON'S STAFF.
THEN PIERCE THE HEART OF THE DRAGON...
...AND MAKE THAT POWER YOURS!
crash
......
YOU DARE...
DARE...

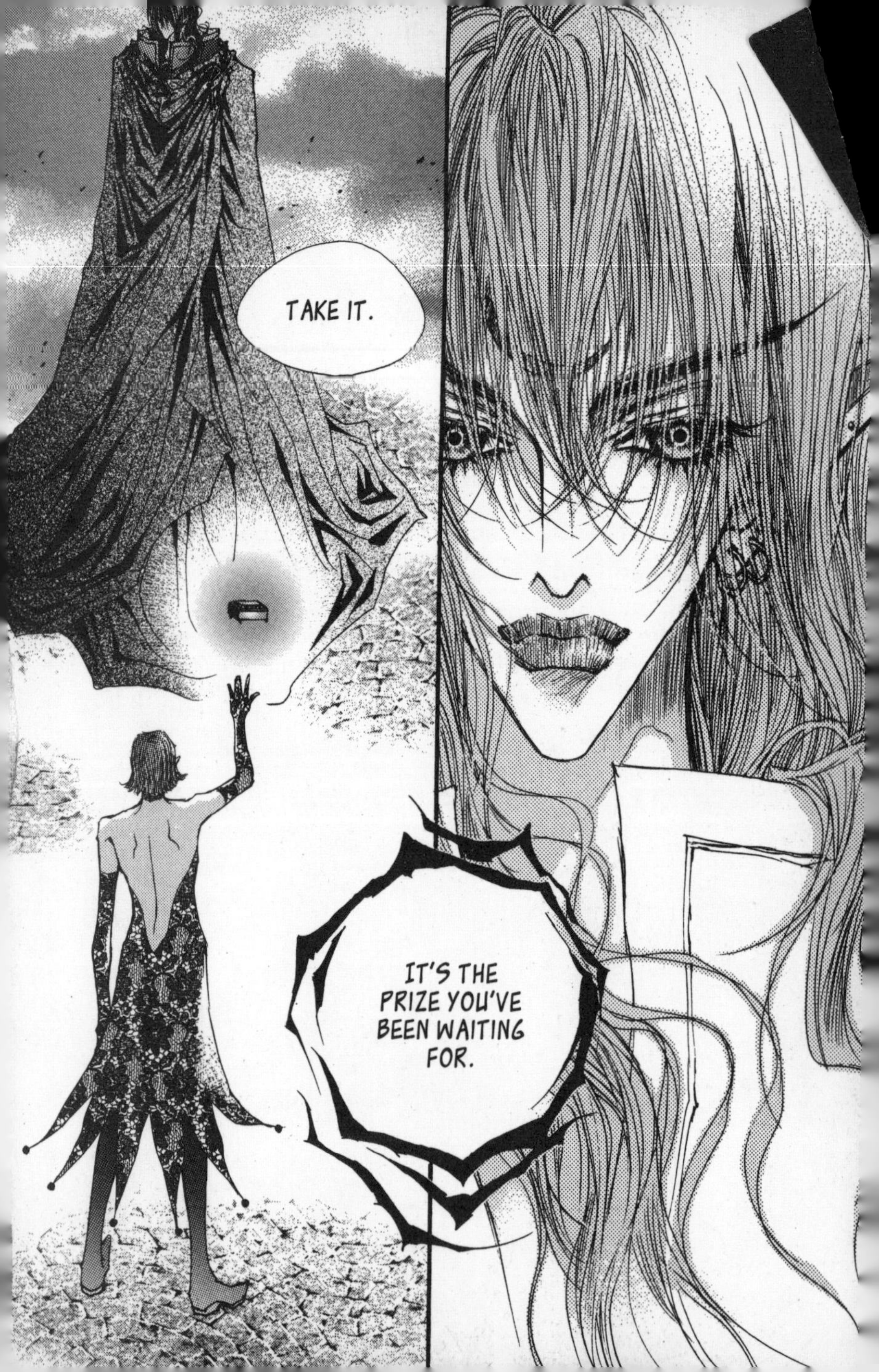
TAKE IT.
IT'S THE PRIZE YOU'VE BEEN WAITING FOR.

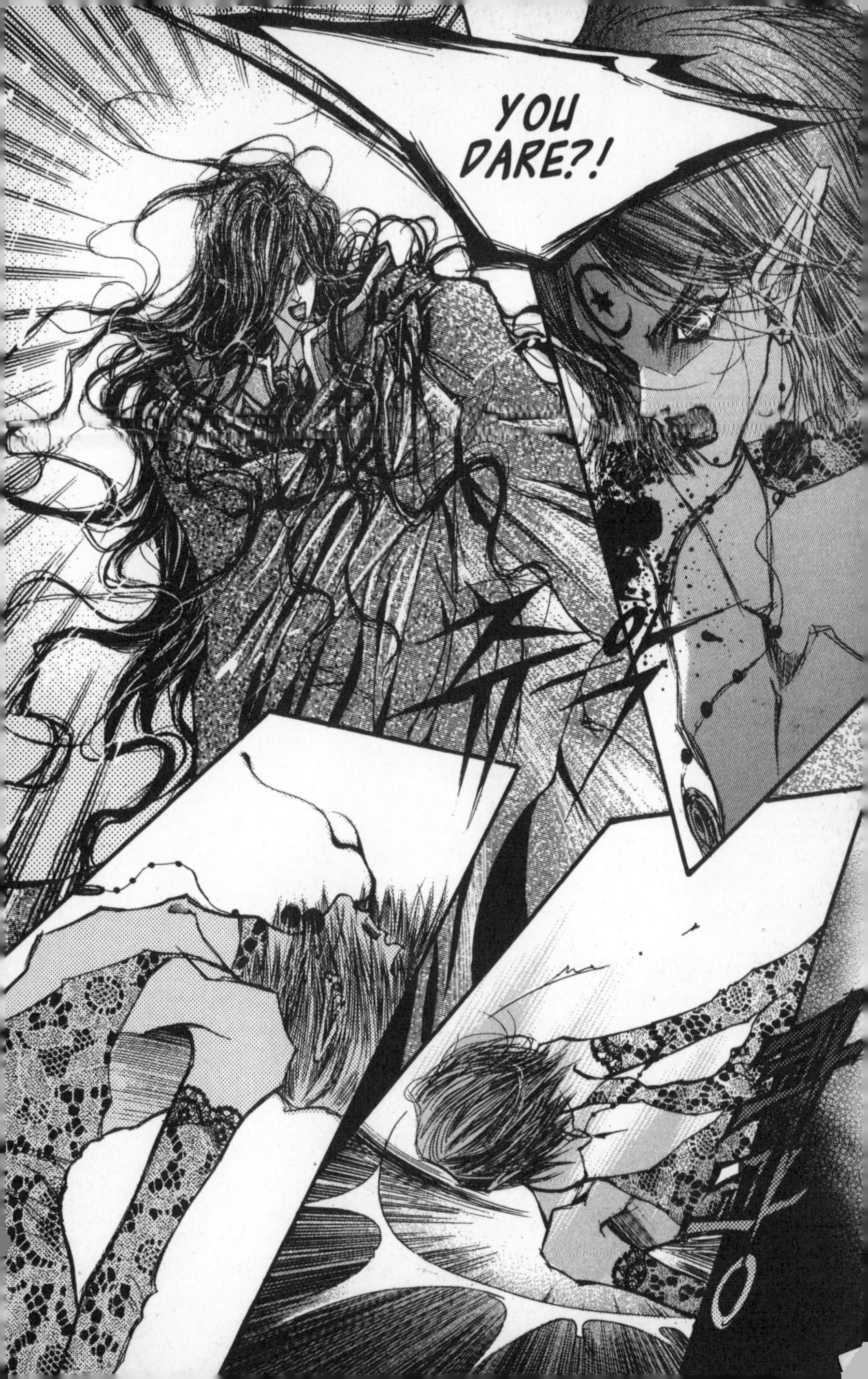
YOU DARE?!

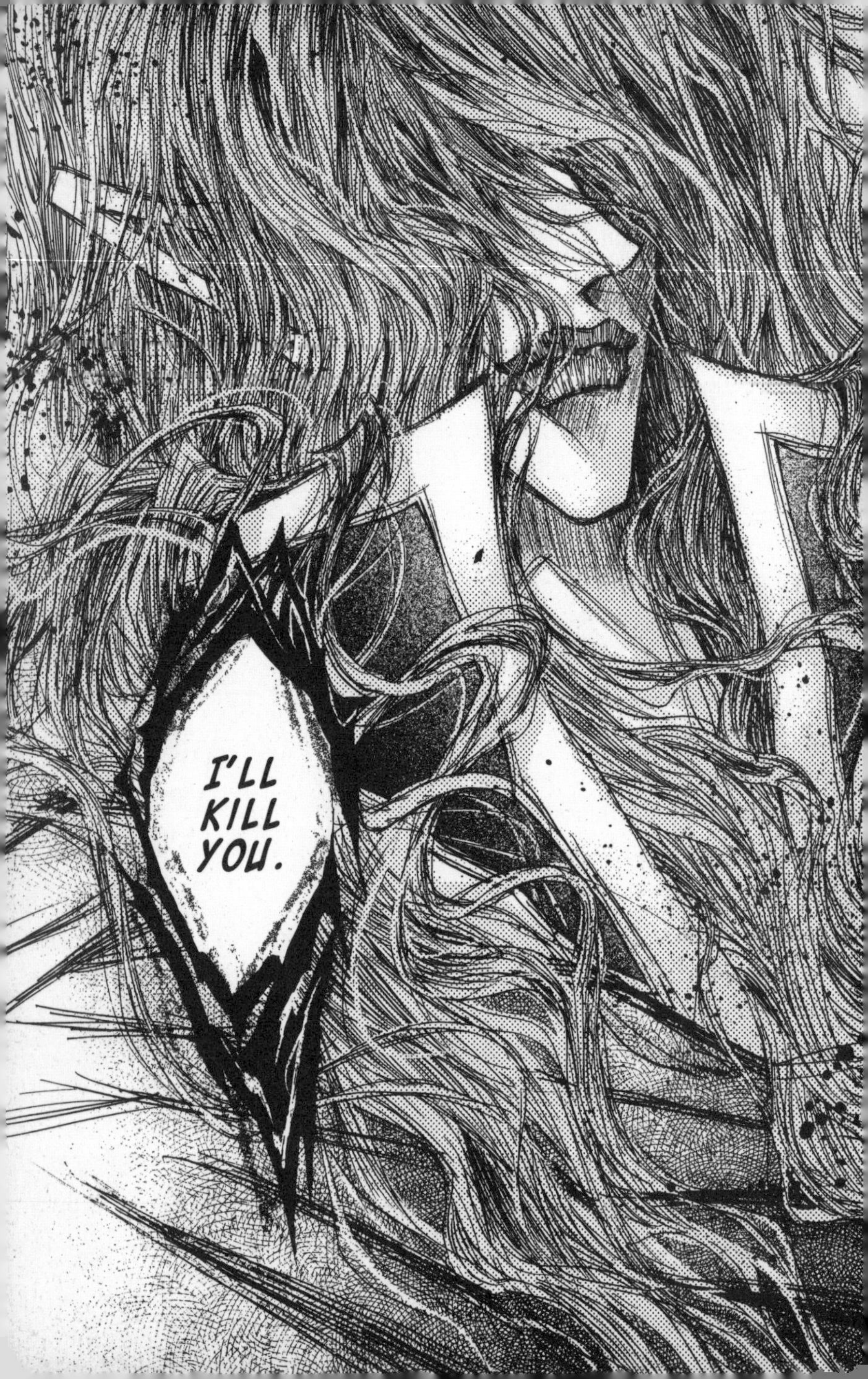
I'LL KILL YOU.

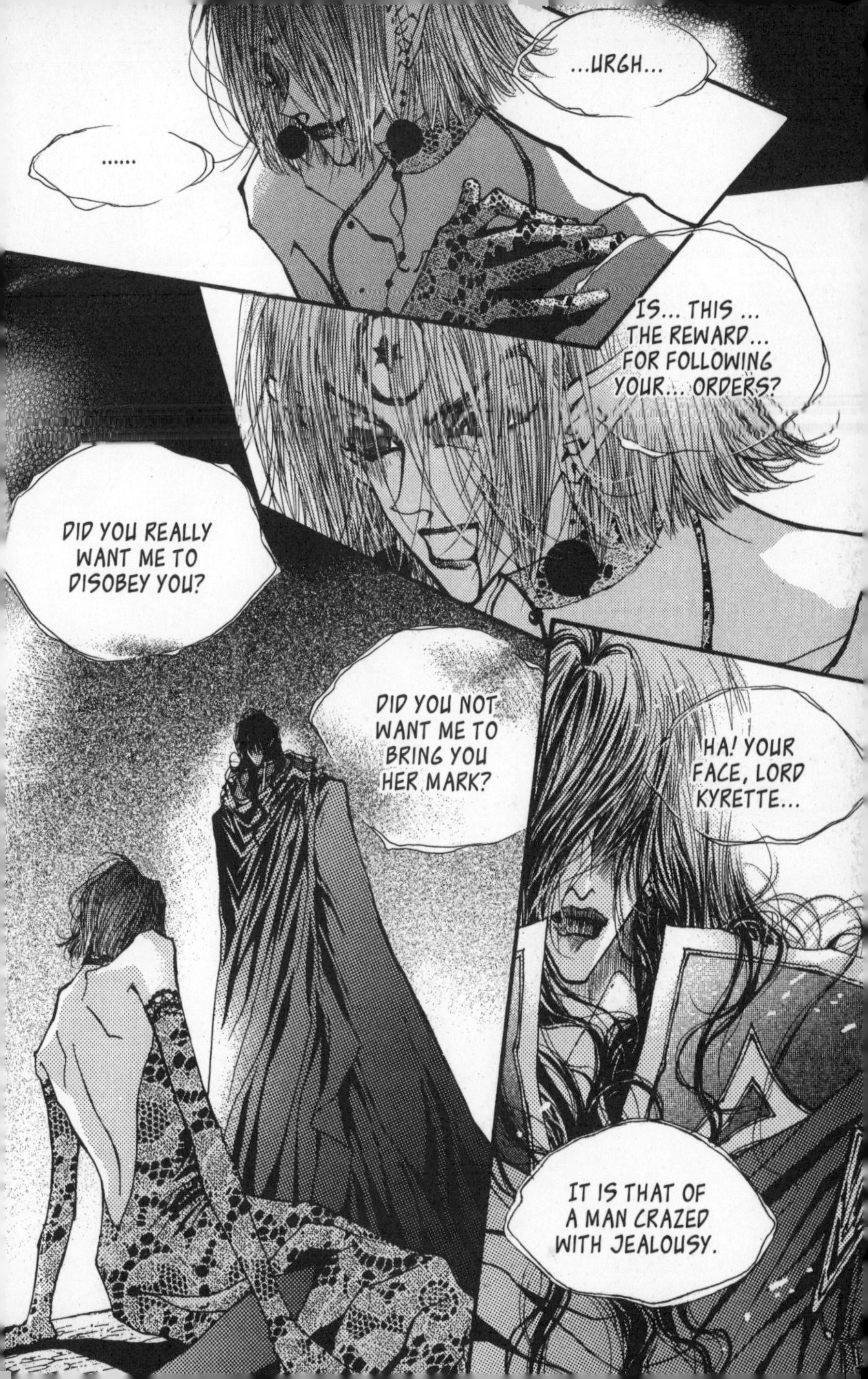
...URGH...
......
IS... THIS ... THE REWARD... FOR FOLLOWING YOUR... ORDERS?
DID YOU REALLY WANT ME TO DISOBEY YOU?
DID YOU NOT WANT ME TO BRING YOU HER MARK?
HA! YOUR FACE, LORD KYRETTE...
IT IS THAT OF A MAN CRAZED WITH JEALOUSY.

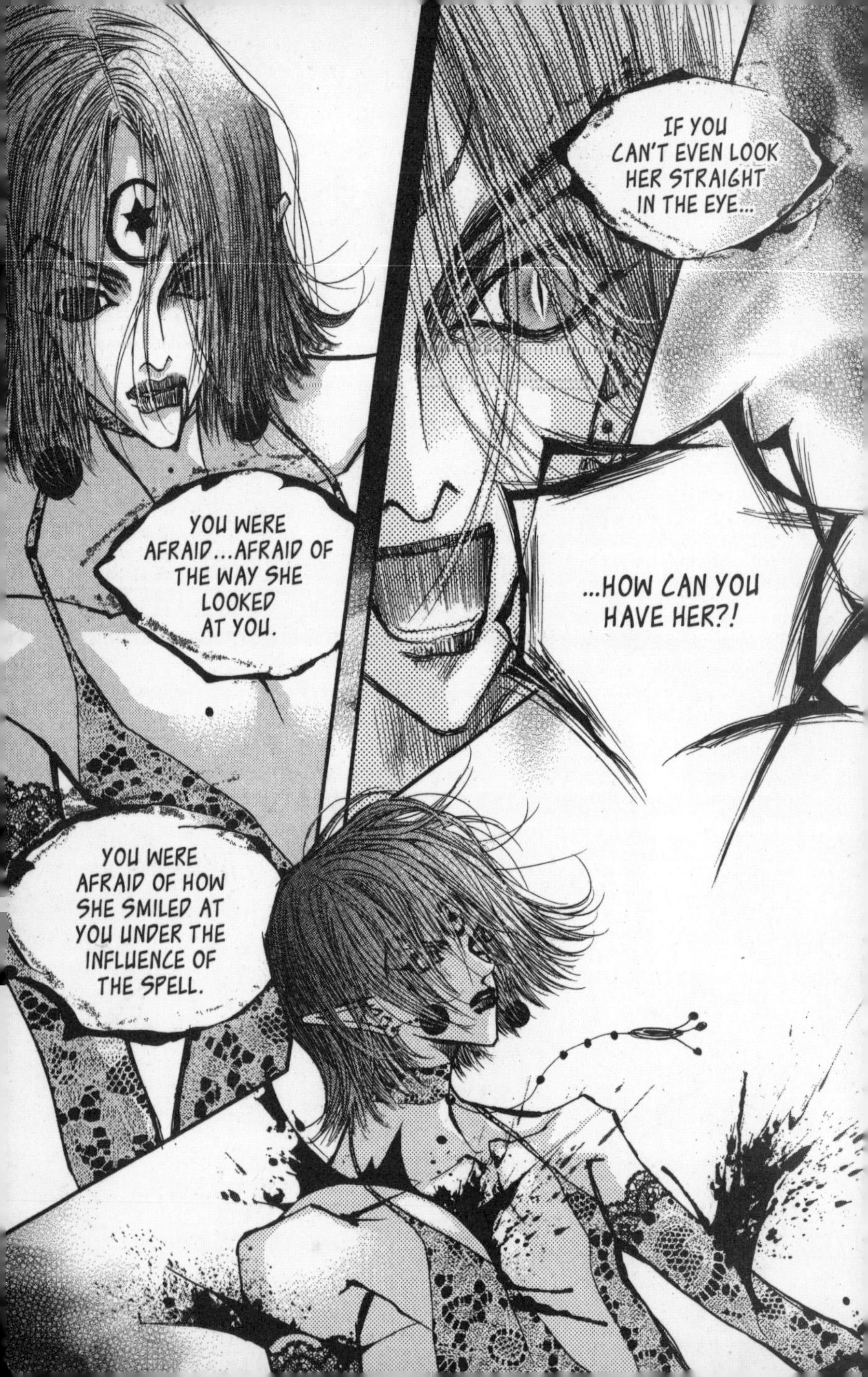
YOU WERE AFRAID...AFRAID OF THE WAY SHE LOOKED AT YOU.
IF YOU CAN'T EVEN LOOK HER STRAIGHT IN THE EYE...
...HOW CAN YOU HAVE HER?!
YOU WERE AFRAID OF HOW SHE SMILED AT YOU UNDER THE INFLUENCE OF THE SPELL.

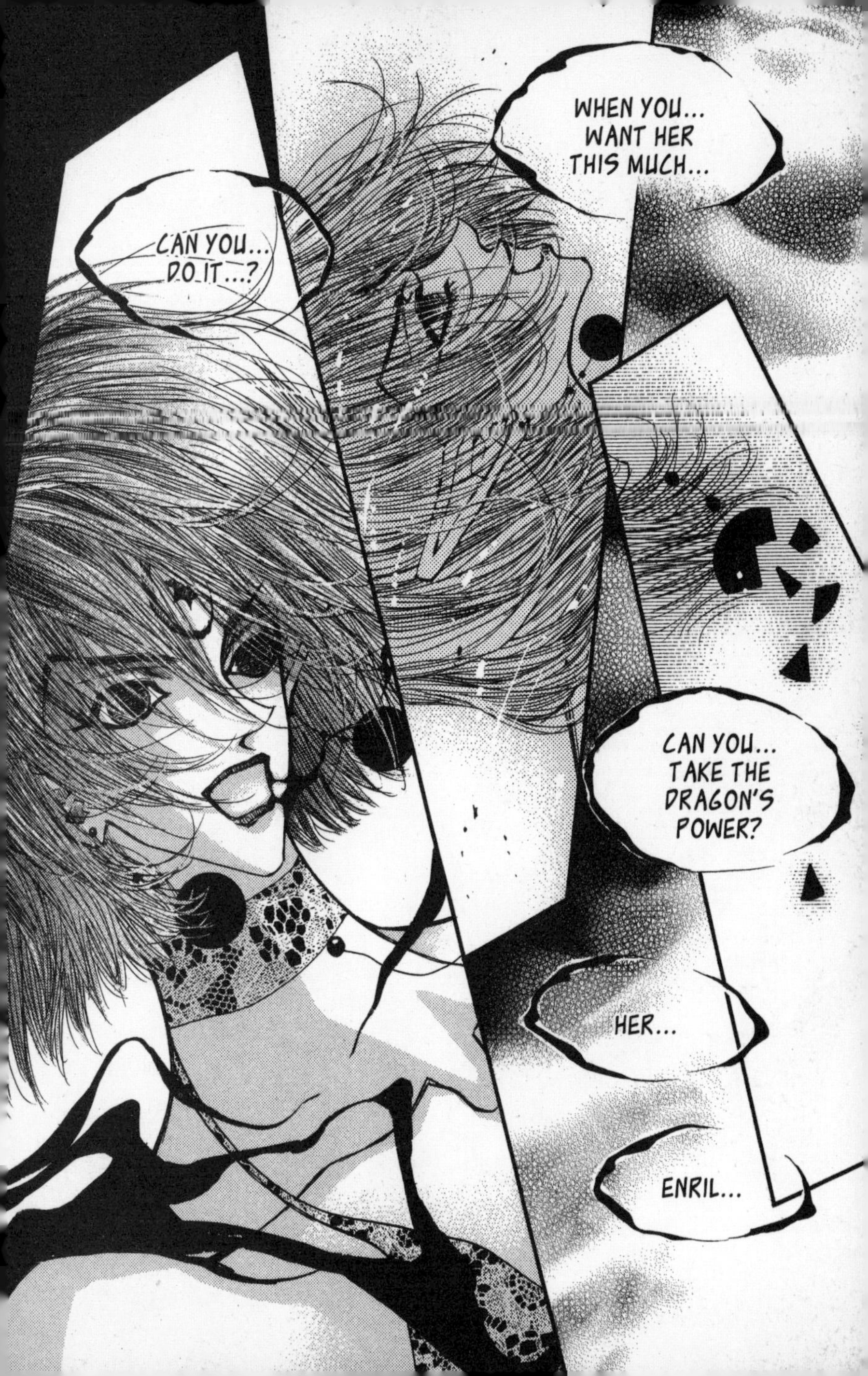
CAN YOU... DO IT...?
WHEN YOU... WANT HER THIS MUCH...
CAN YOU... TAKE THE DRAGON'S POWER?
HER...
ENRIL...

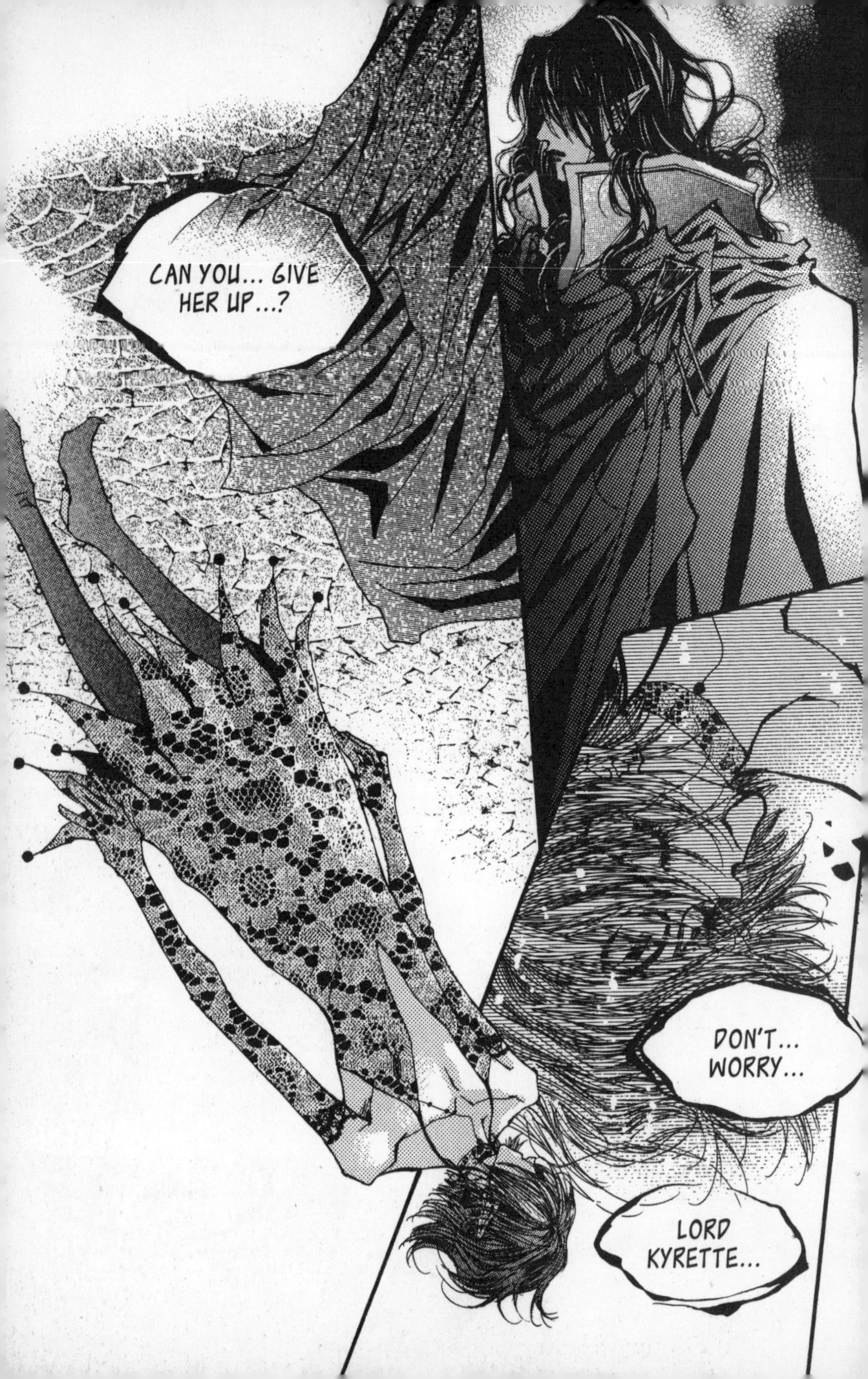
CAN YOU... GIVE HER UP...?
DON'T... WORRY...
LORD KYRETTE...

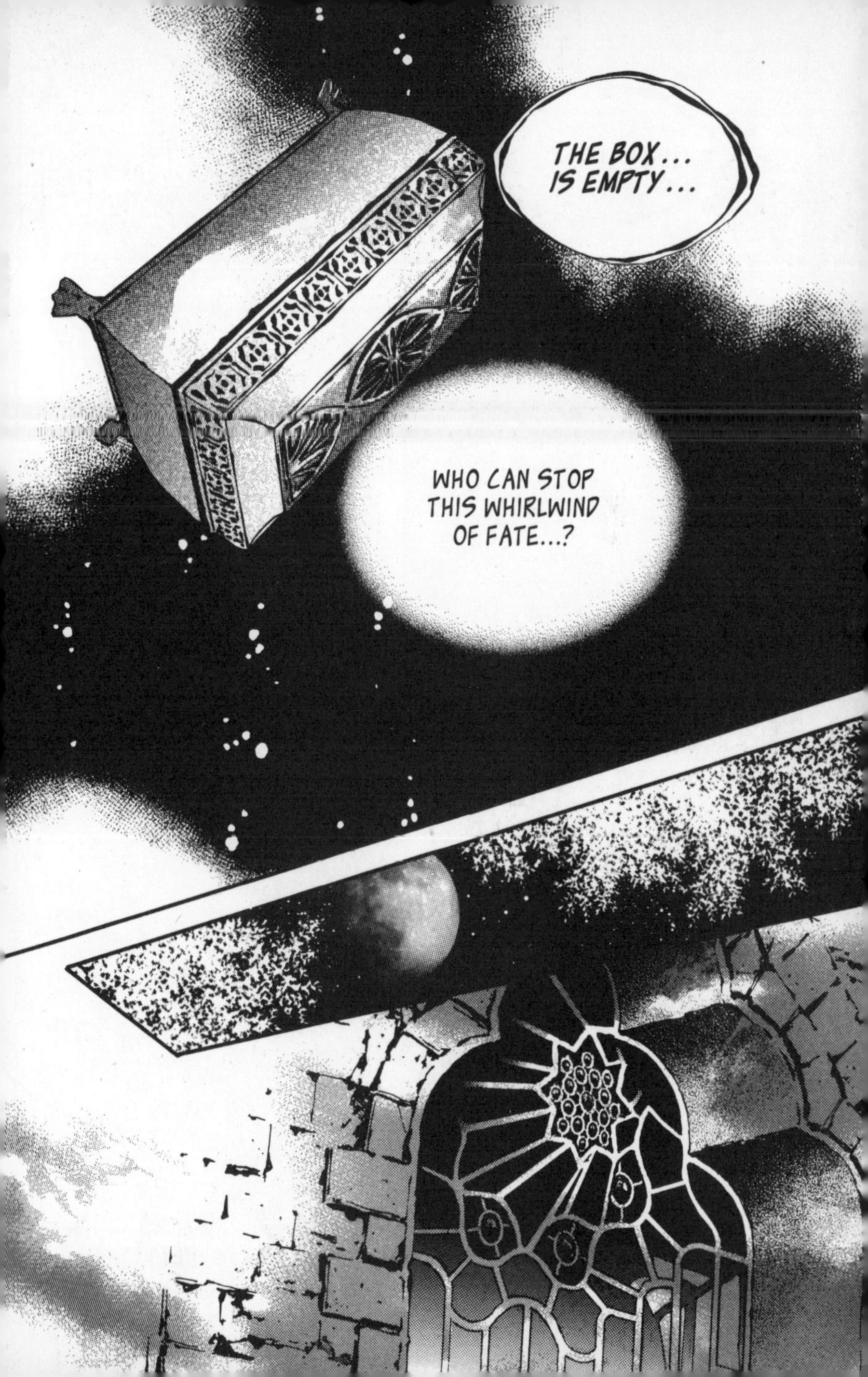
THE BOX... IS EMPTY...
WHO CAN STOP THIS WHIRLWIND OF FATE...?

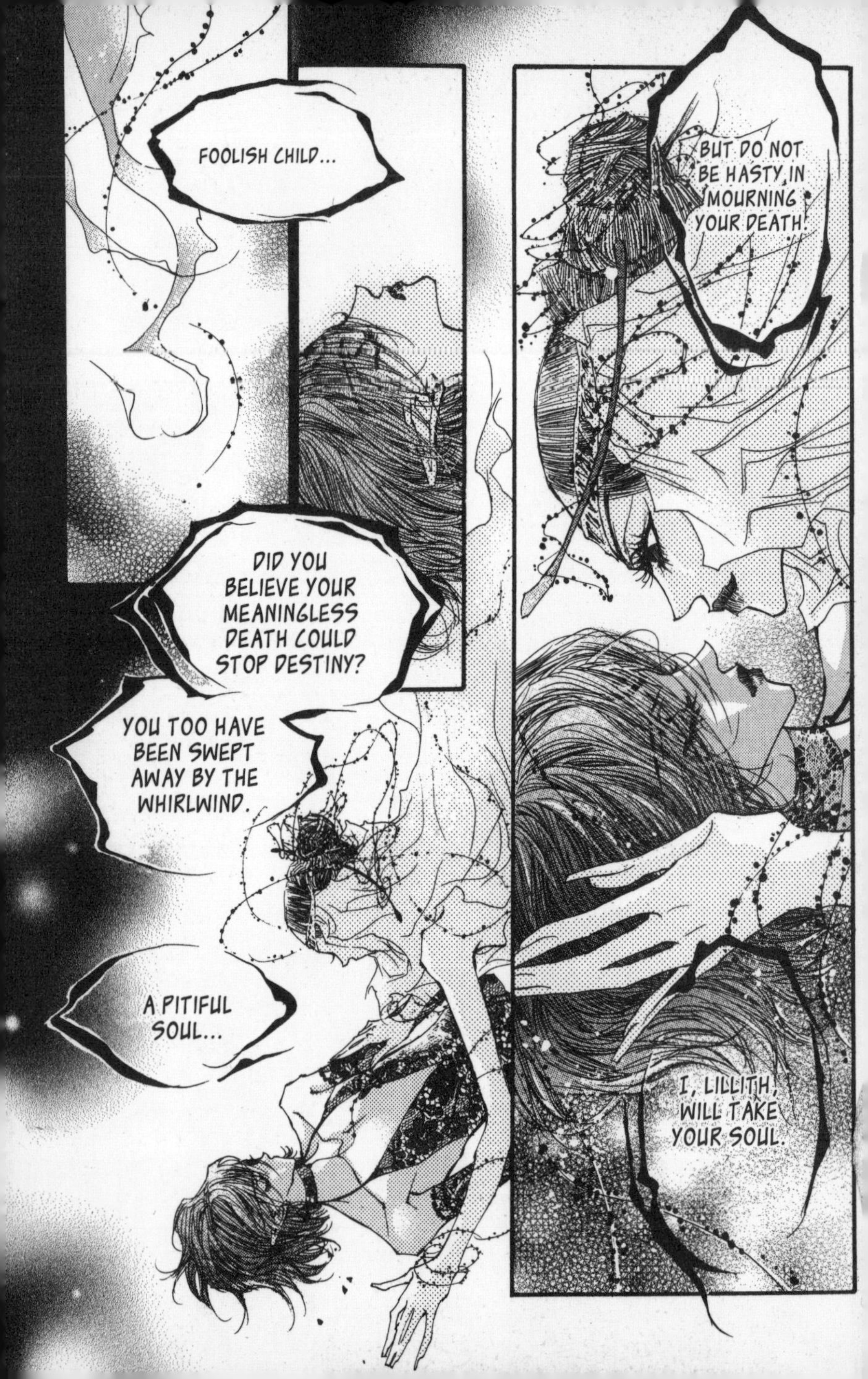
FOOLISH CHILD...
DID YOU BELIEVE YOUR MEANINGLESS DEATH COULD STOP DESTINY?
YOU TOO HAVE BEEN SWEPT AWAY BY THE WHIRLWIND.
A PITIFUL SOUL...
BUT DO NOT BE HASTY IN MOURNING YOUR DEATH.
I, LILLITH, WILL TAKE YOUR SOUL.

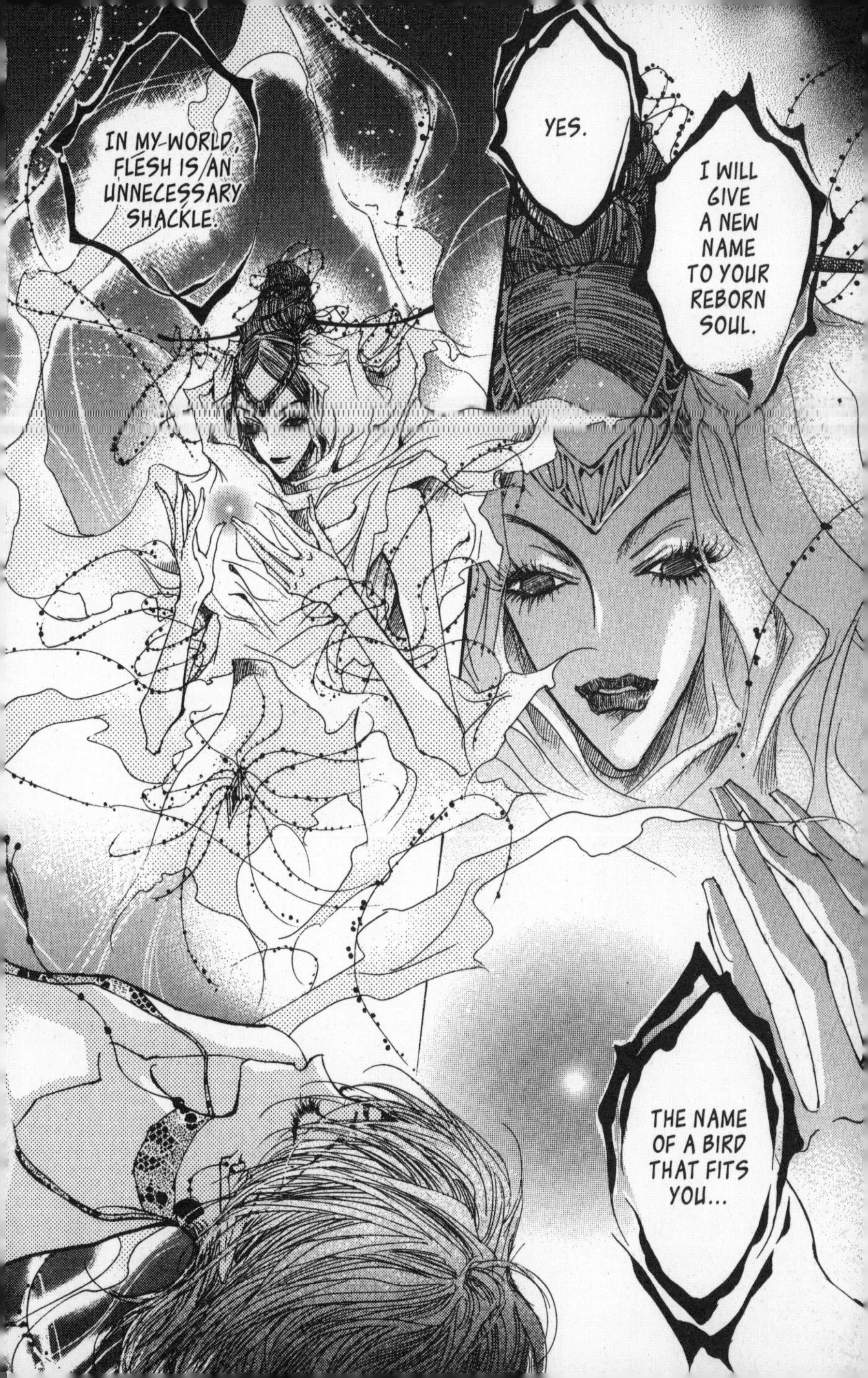
IN MY WORLD, FLESH IS AN UNNECESSARY SHACKLE.
YES.
I WILL GIVE A NEW NAME TO YOUR REBORN SOUL.
THE NAME OF A BIRD THAT FITS YOU...

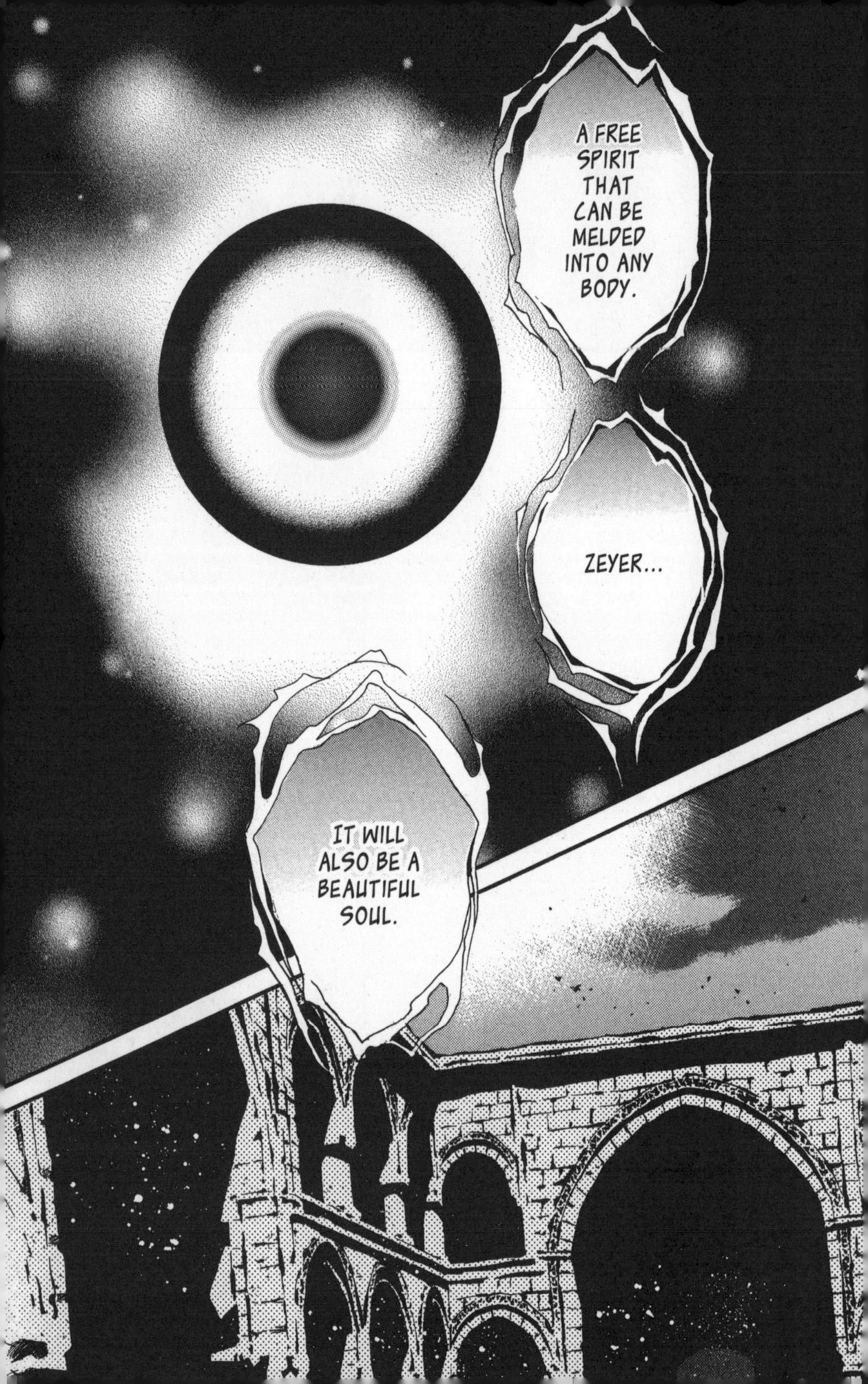
A FREE SPIRIT THAT CAN BE MELDED INTO ANY BODY.
ZEYER...
IT WILL ALSO BE A BEAUTIFUL SOUL.

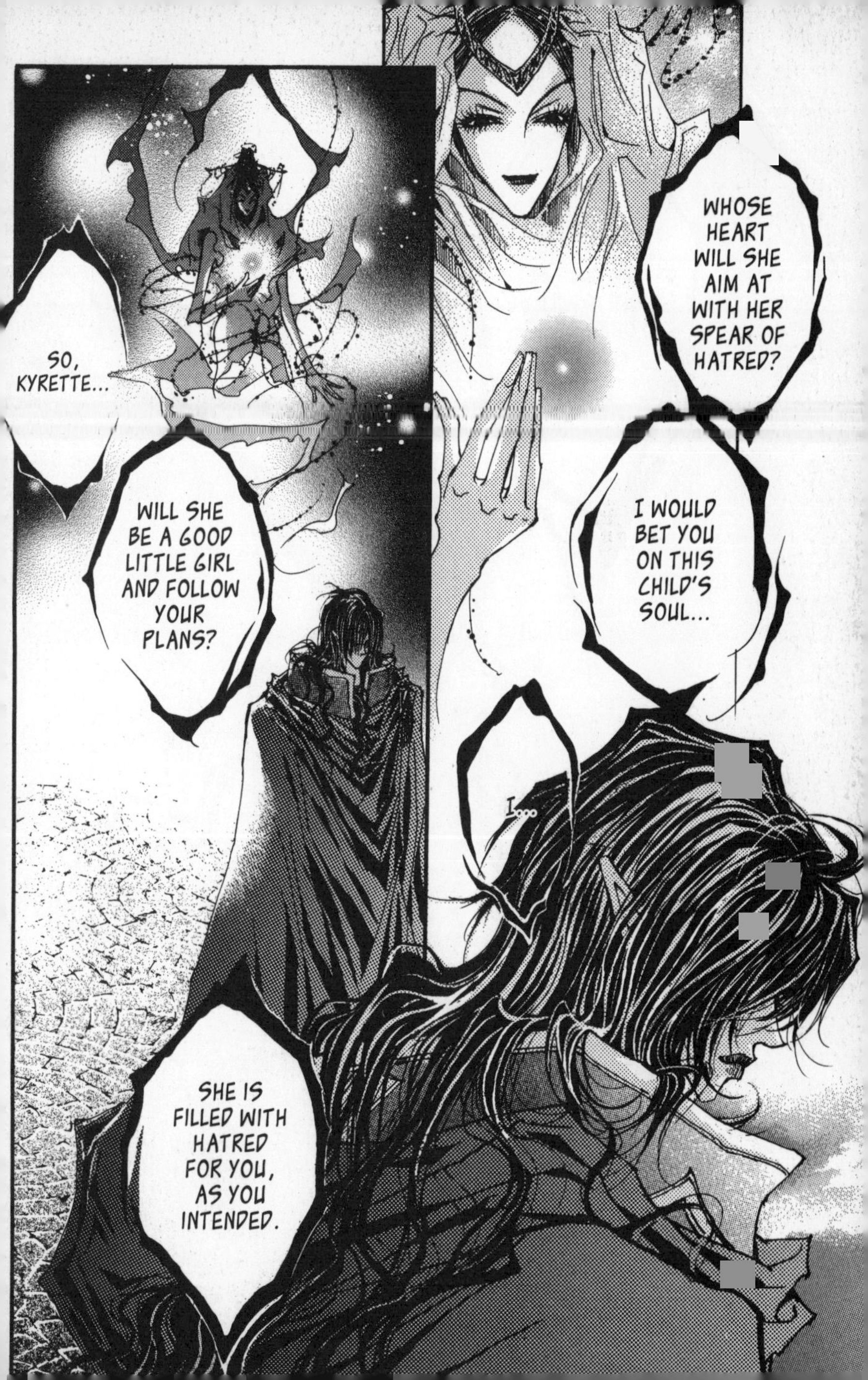
SO, KYRETTE...
WILL SHE BE A GOOD LITTLE GIRL AND FOLLOW YOUR PLANS?
WHOSE HEART WILL SHE AIM AT WITH HER SPEAR OF HATRED?
I WOULD BET YOU ON THIS CHILD'S SOUL...
I...
SHE IS FILLED WITH HATRED FOR YOU, AS YOU INTENDED.

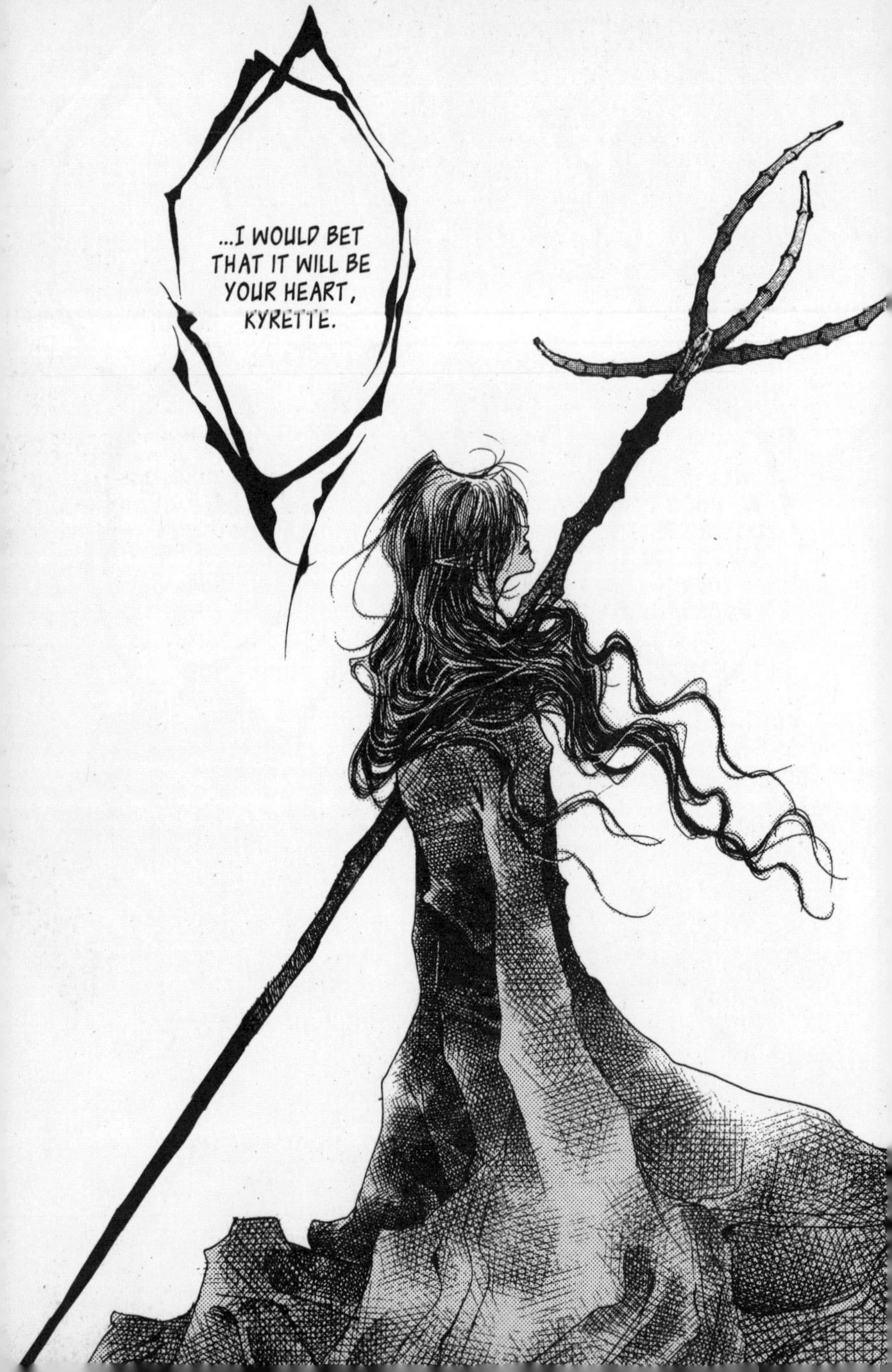
...I WOULD BET THAT IT WILL BE YOUR HEART, KYRETTE.

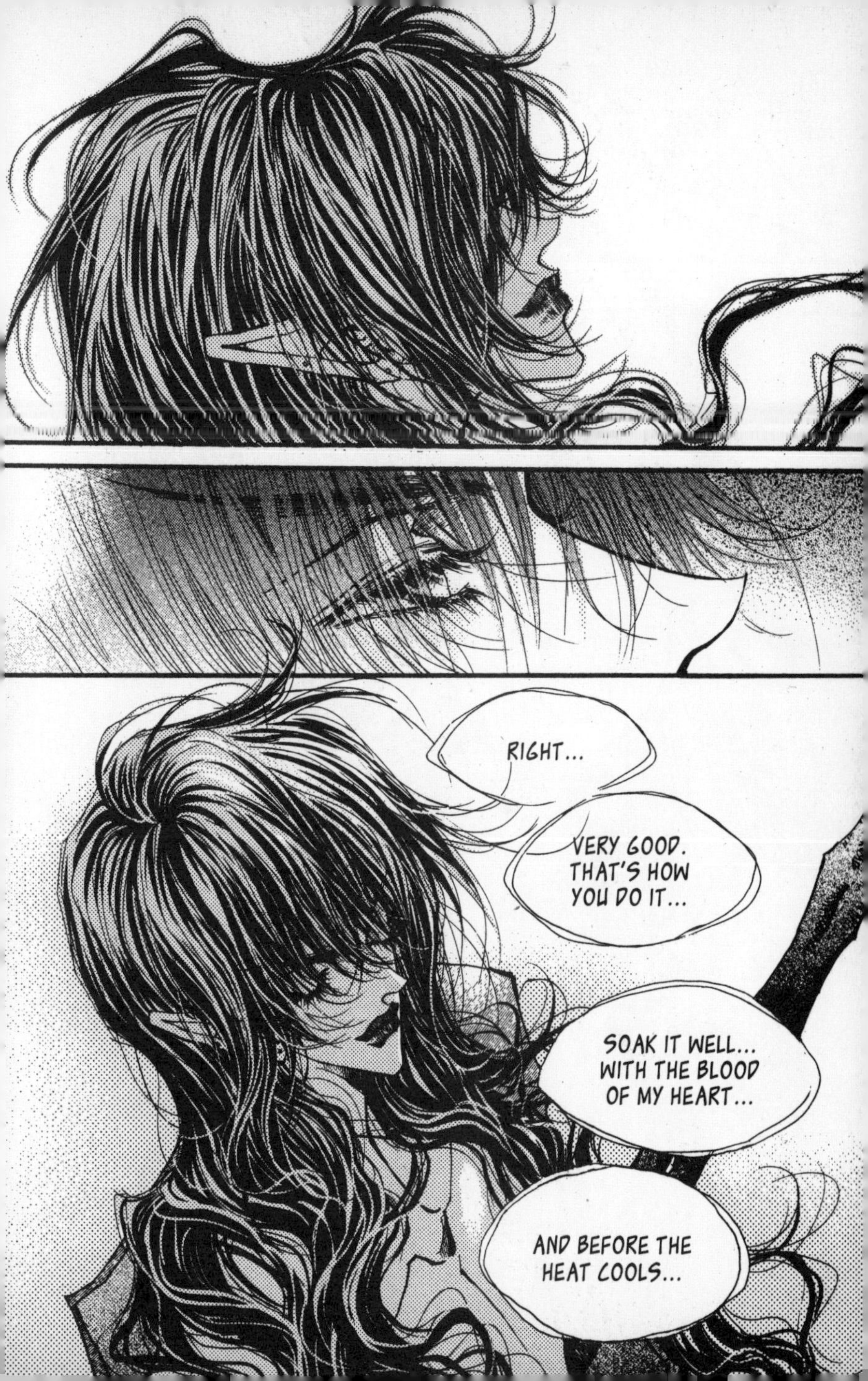
RIGHT...
VERY GOOD. THAT'S HOW YOU DO IT...
SOAK IT WELL... WITH THE BLOOD OF MY HEART...
AND BEFORE THE HEAT COOLS...

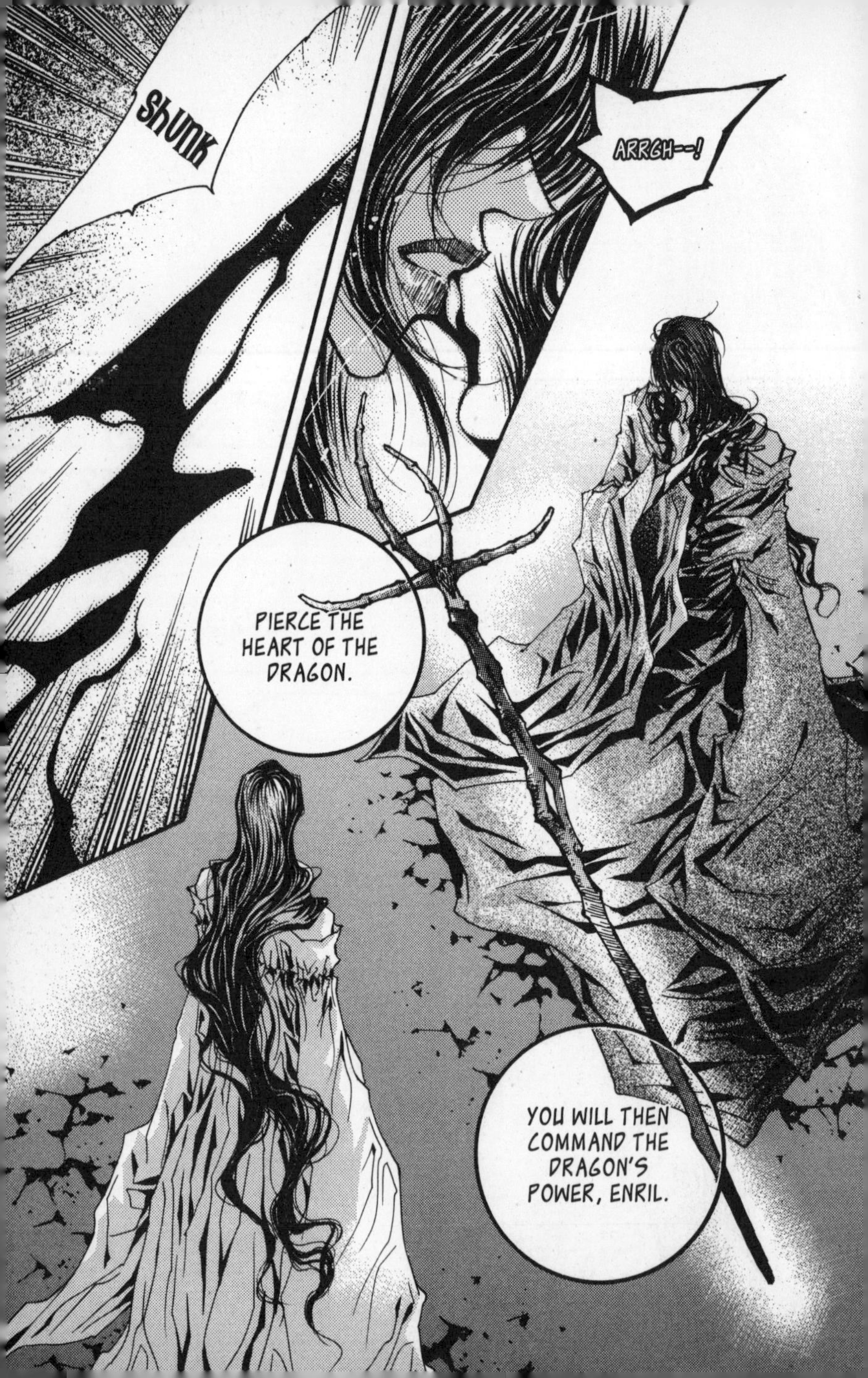
SHUNK
ARRGH--!
PIERCE THE HEART OF THE DRAGON.
YOU WILL THEN COMMAND THE DRAGON'S POWER, ENRIL.

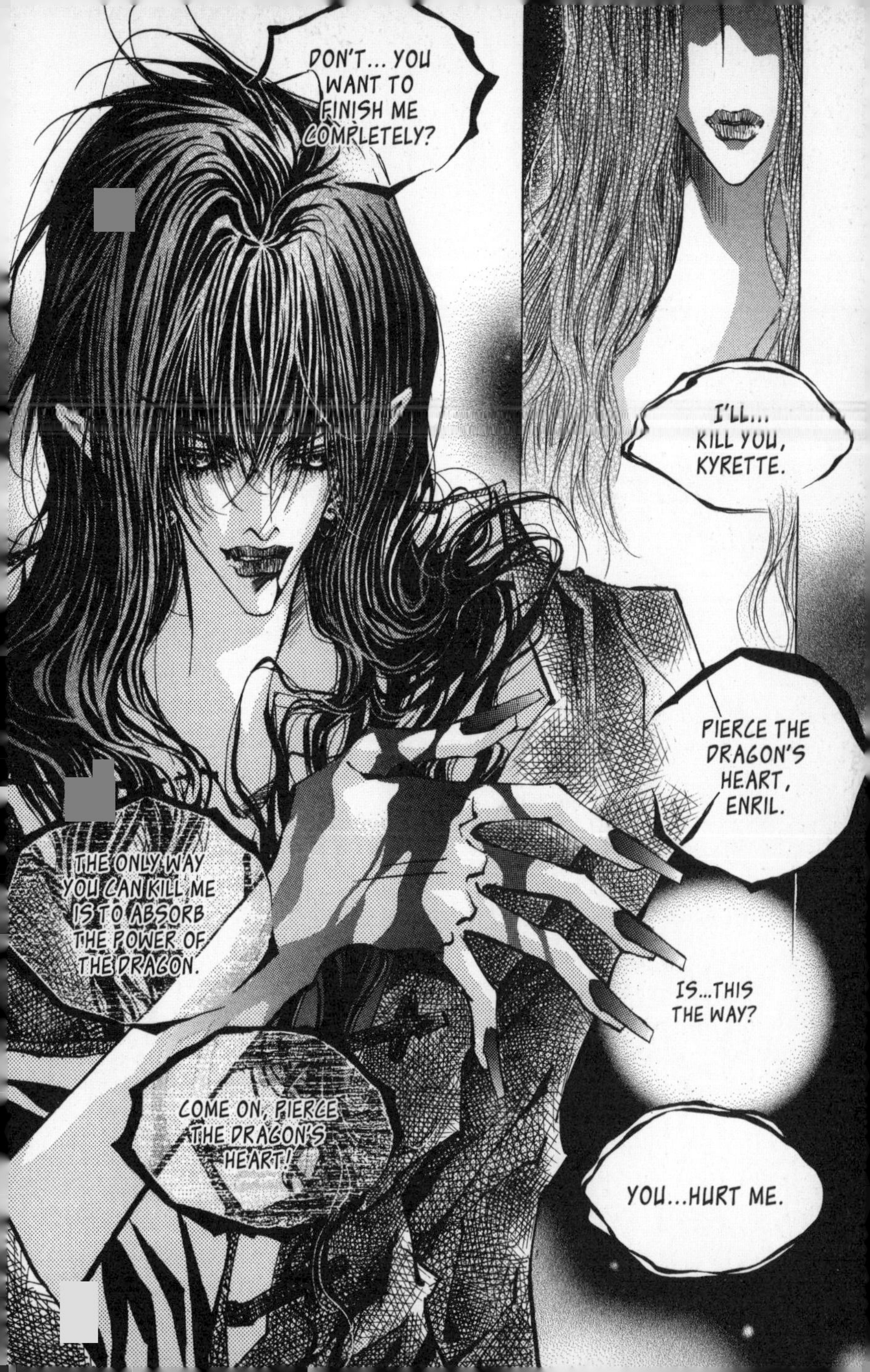
DON'T... YOU WANT TO FINISH ME COMPLETELY?
THE ONLY WAY YOU CAN KILL ME IS TO ABSORB THE POWER OF THE DRAGON.
COME ON, PIERCE THE DRAGON'S HEART!
I'LL... KILL YOU, KYRETTE.
PIERCE THE DRAGON'S HEART, ENRIL.
IS...THIS THE WAY?
YOU...HURT ME.

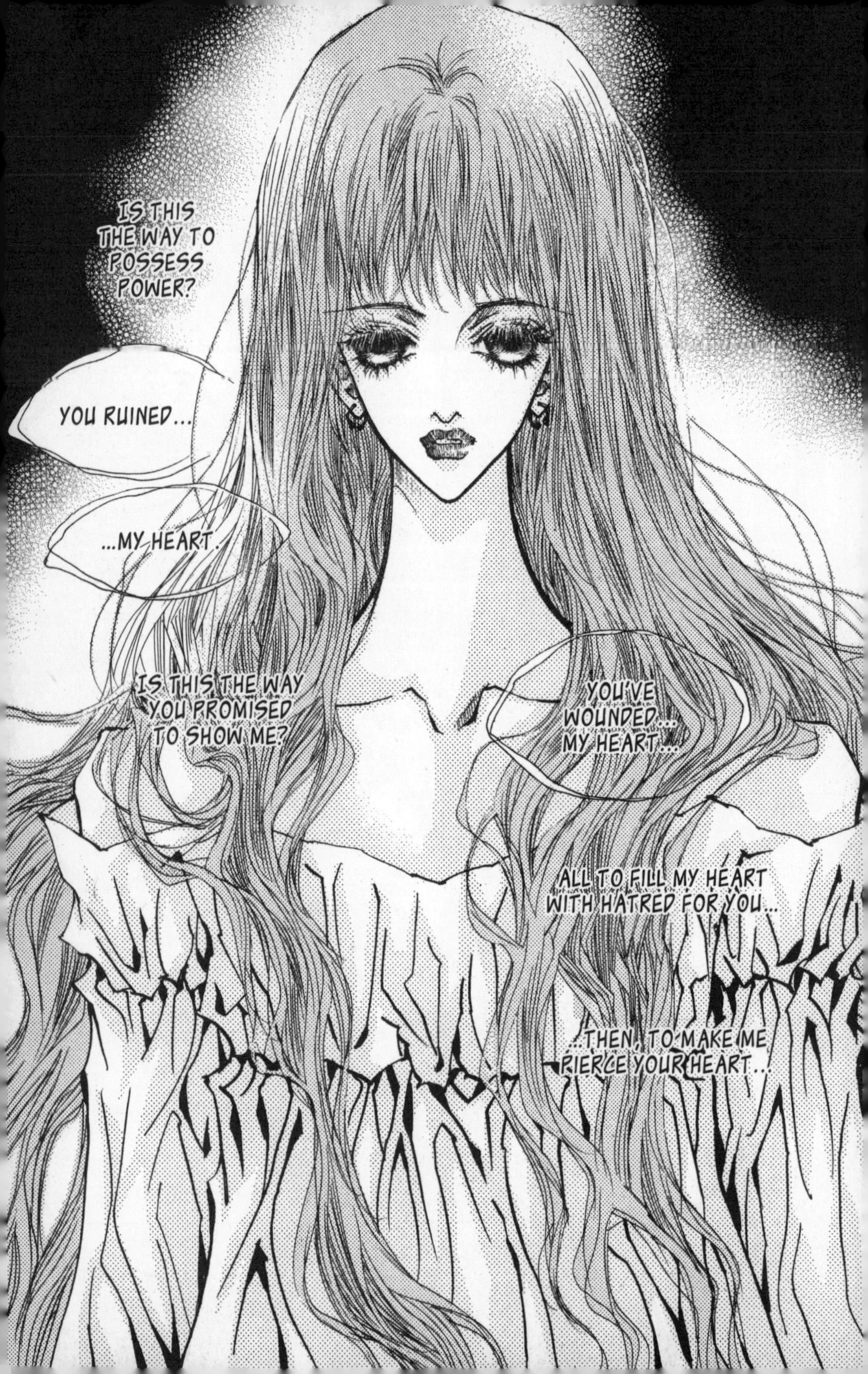
IS THIS THE WAY TO POSSESS POWER?
YOU RUINED...
...MY HEART.
IS THIS THE WAY YOU PROMISED TO SHOW ME?
YOU'VE WOUNDED... MY HEART...
ALL TO FILL MY HEART WITH HATRED FOR YOU...
...THEN, TO MAKE ME PIERCE YOUR HEART...

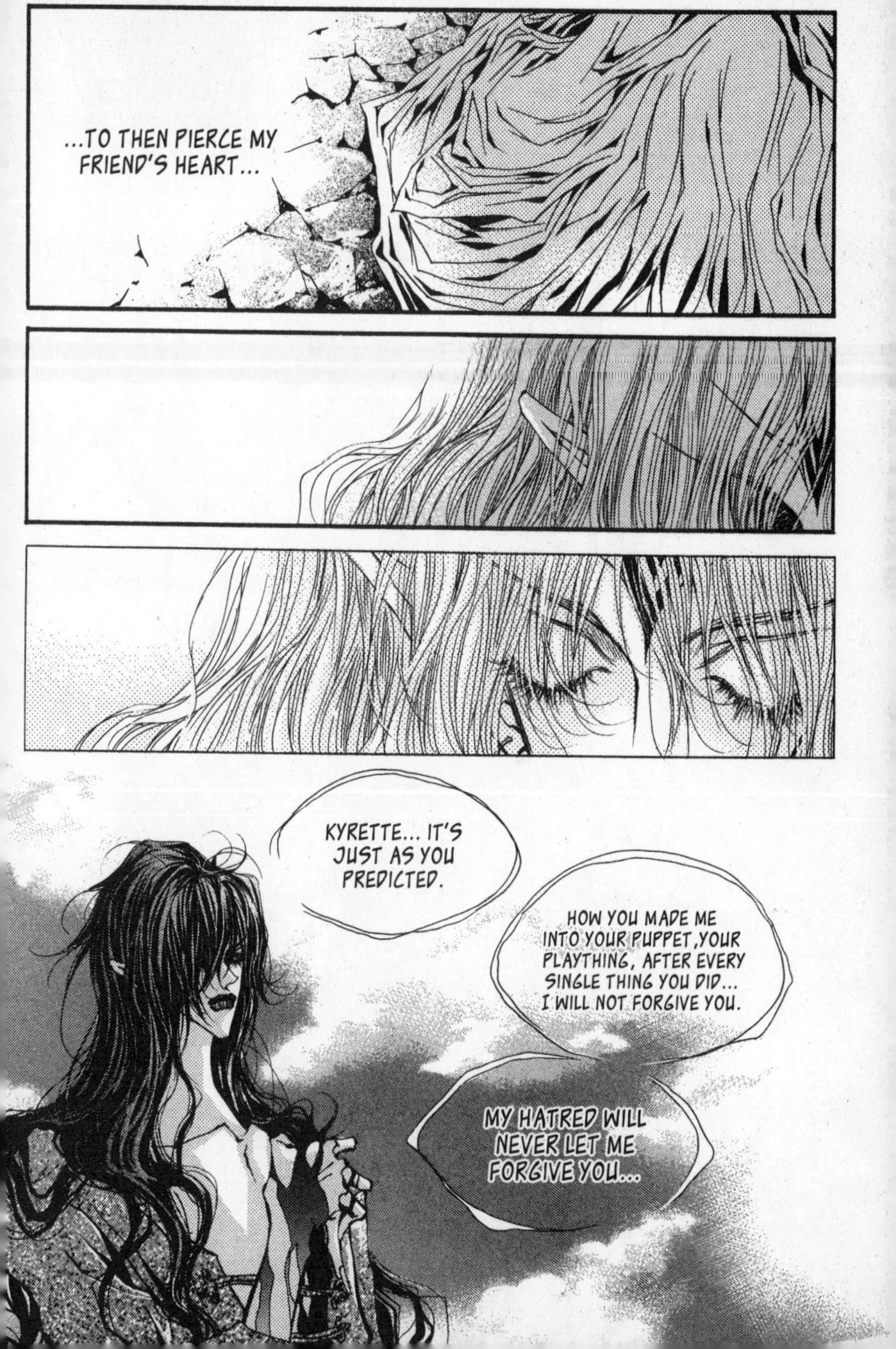
...TO THEN PIERCE MY FRIEND'S HEART...
KYRETTE... IT'S JUST AS YOU PREDICTED.
HOW YOU MADE ME INTO YOUR PUPPET, YOUR PLAYTHING, AFTER EVERY SINGLE THING YOU DID... I WILL NOT FORGIVE YOU.
MY HATRED WILL NEVER LET ME FORGIVE YOU...

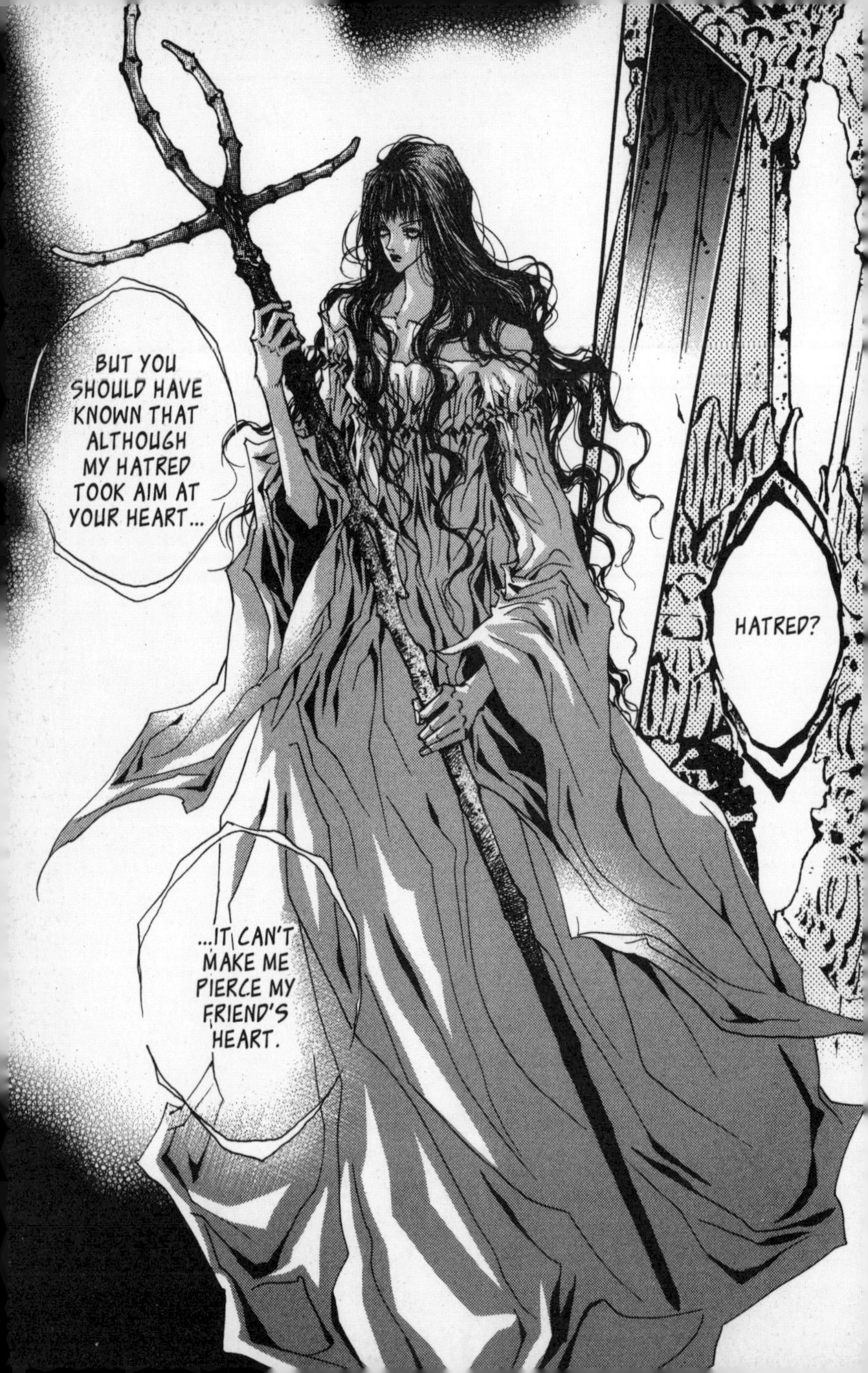
BUT YOU SHOULD HAVE KNOWN THAT ALTHOUGH MY HATRED TOOK AIM AT YOUR HEART...
HATRED?
...IT CAN'T MAKE ME PIERCE MY FRIEND'S HEART.

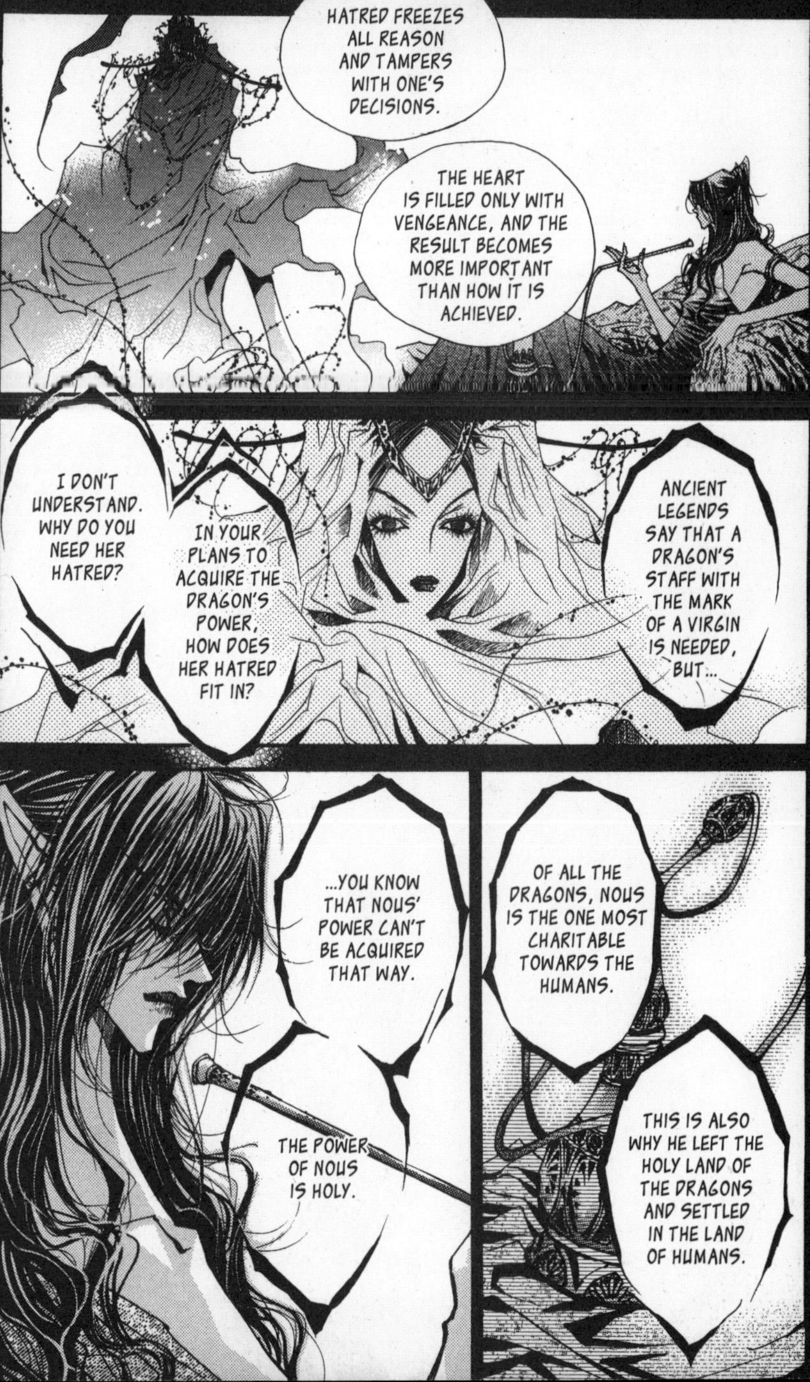
HATRED FREEZES ALL REASON AND TAMPERS WITH ONE'S DECISIONS.
THE HEART IS FILLED ONLY WITH VENGEANCE, AND THE RESULT BECOMES MORE IMPORTANT THAN HOW IT IS ACHIEVED.
I DON'T UNDERSTAND. WHY DO YOU NEED HER HATRED?
IN YOUR PLANS TO ACQUIRE THE DRAGON'S POWER, HOW DOES HER HATRED FIT IN?
ANCIENT LEGENDS SAY THAT A DRAGON'S STAFF WITH THE MARK OF A VIRGIN IS NEEDED, BUT...
...YOU KNOW THAT NOUS' POWER CAN'T BE ACQUIRED THAT WAY.
THE POWER OF NOUS IS HOLY.
OF ALL THE DRAGONS, NOUS IS THE ONE MOST CHARITABLE TOWARDS THE HUMANS.
THIS IS ALSO WHY HE LEFT THE HOLY LAND OF THE DRAGONS AND SETTLED IN THE LAND OF HUMANS.

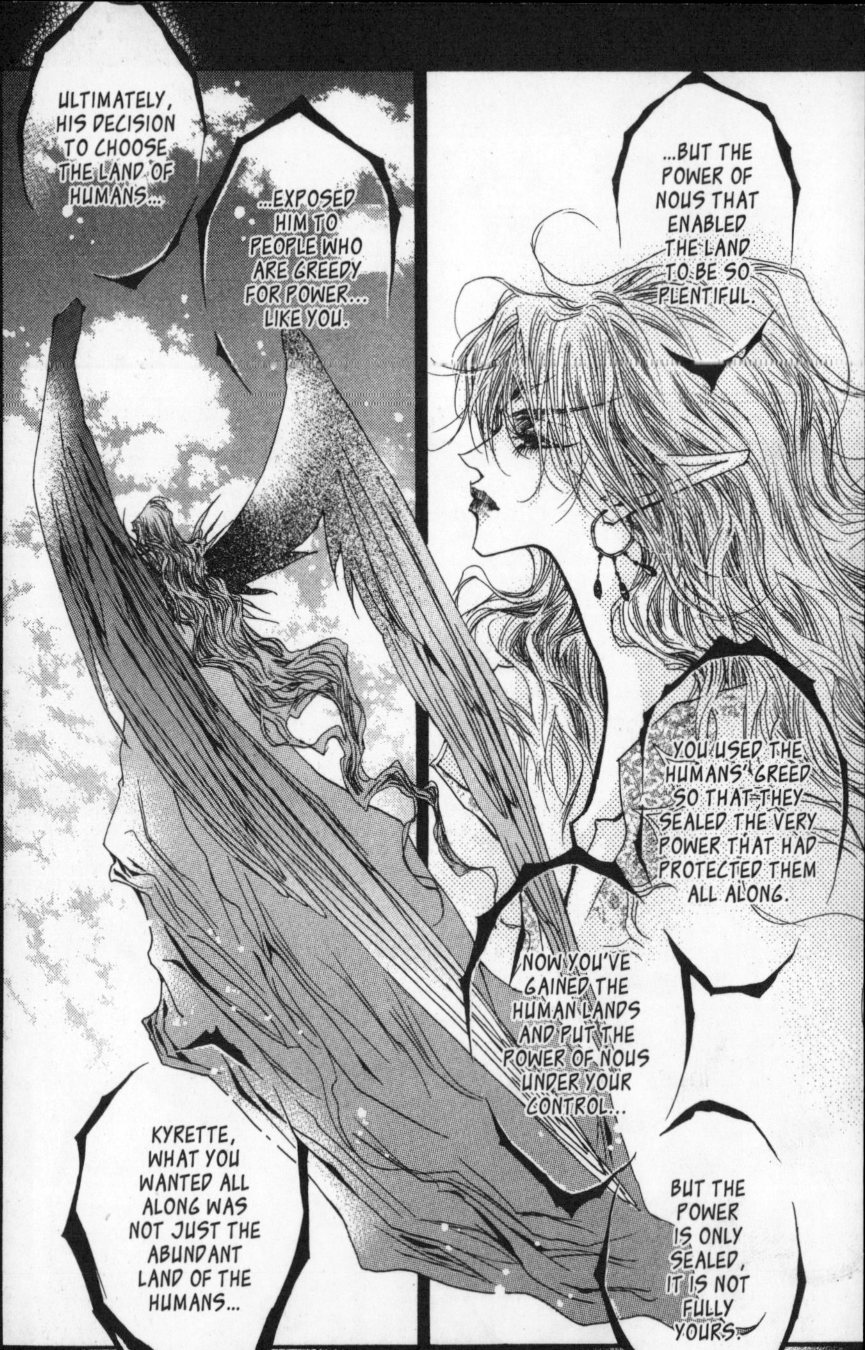
ULTIMATELY, HIS DECISION TO CHOOSE THE LAND OF HUMANS...
...EXPOSED HIM TO PEOPLE WHO ARE GREEDY FOR POWER... LIKE YOU.
KYRETTE, WHAT YOU WANTED ALL ALONG WAS NOT JUST THE ABUNDANT LAND OF THE HUMANS...
...BUT THE POWER OF NOUS THAT ENABLED THE LAND TO BE SO PLENTIFUL.
YOU USED THE HUMANS' GREED SO THAT THEY SEALED THE VERY POWER THAT HAD PROTECTED THEM ALL ALONG.
NOW YOU'VE GAINED THE HUMAN LANDS AND PUT THE POWER OF NOUS UNDER YOUR CONTROL...
BUT THE POWER IS ONLY SEALED, IT IS NOT FULLY YOURS.

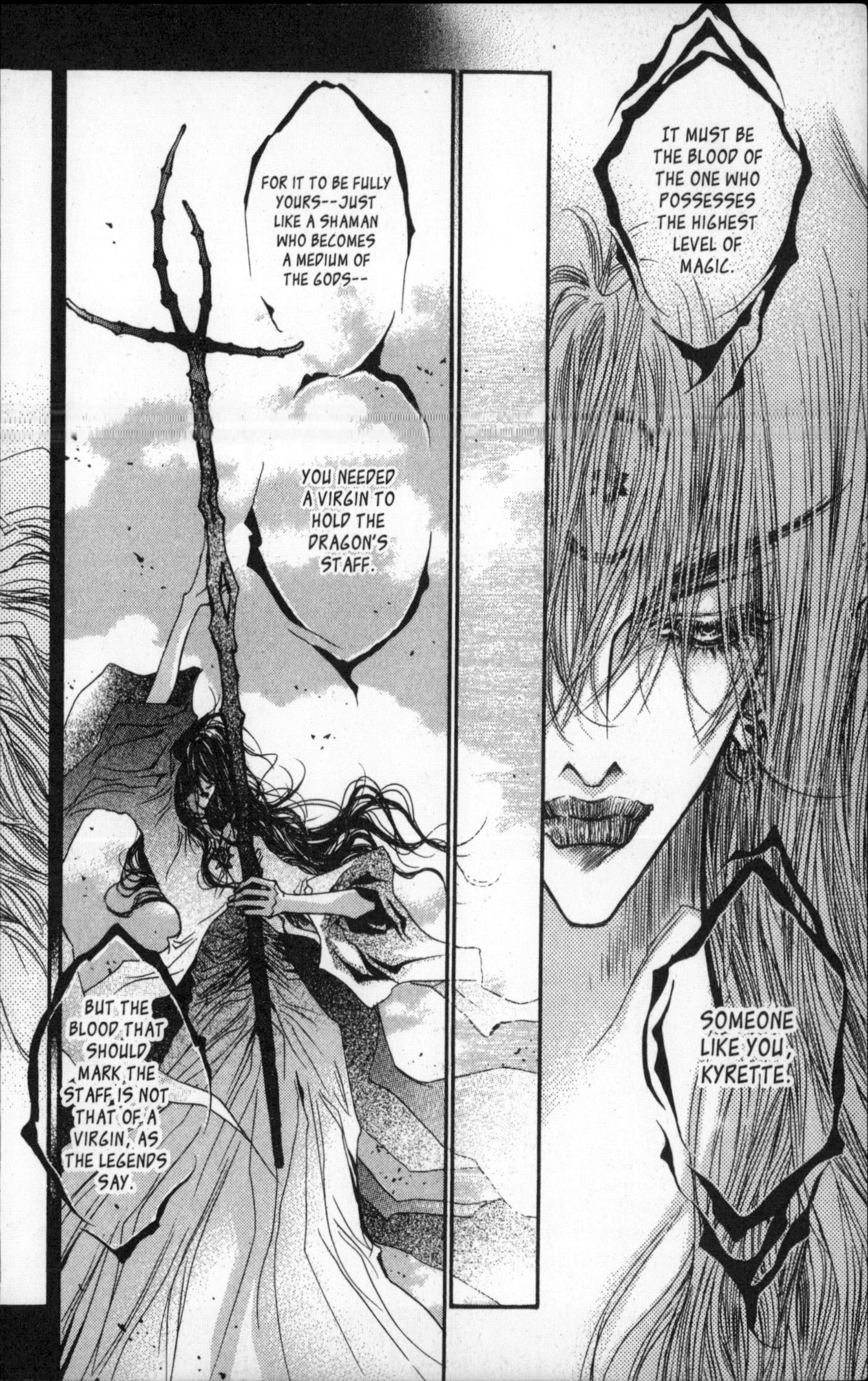
FOR IT TO BE FULLY YOURS--JUST LIKE A SHAMAN WHO BECOMES A MEDIUM OF THE GODS--
YOU NEEDED A VIRGIN TO HOLD THE DRAGON'S STAFF.
BUT THE BLOOD THAT SHOULD MARK THE STAFF IS NOT THAT OF A VIRGIN, AS THE LEGENDS SAY.
IT MUST BE THE BLOOD OF THE ONE WHO POSSESSES THE HIGHEST LEVEL OF MAGIC.
SOMEONE LIKE YOU, KYRETTE.

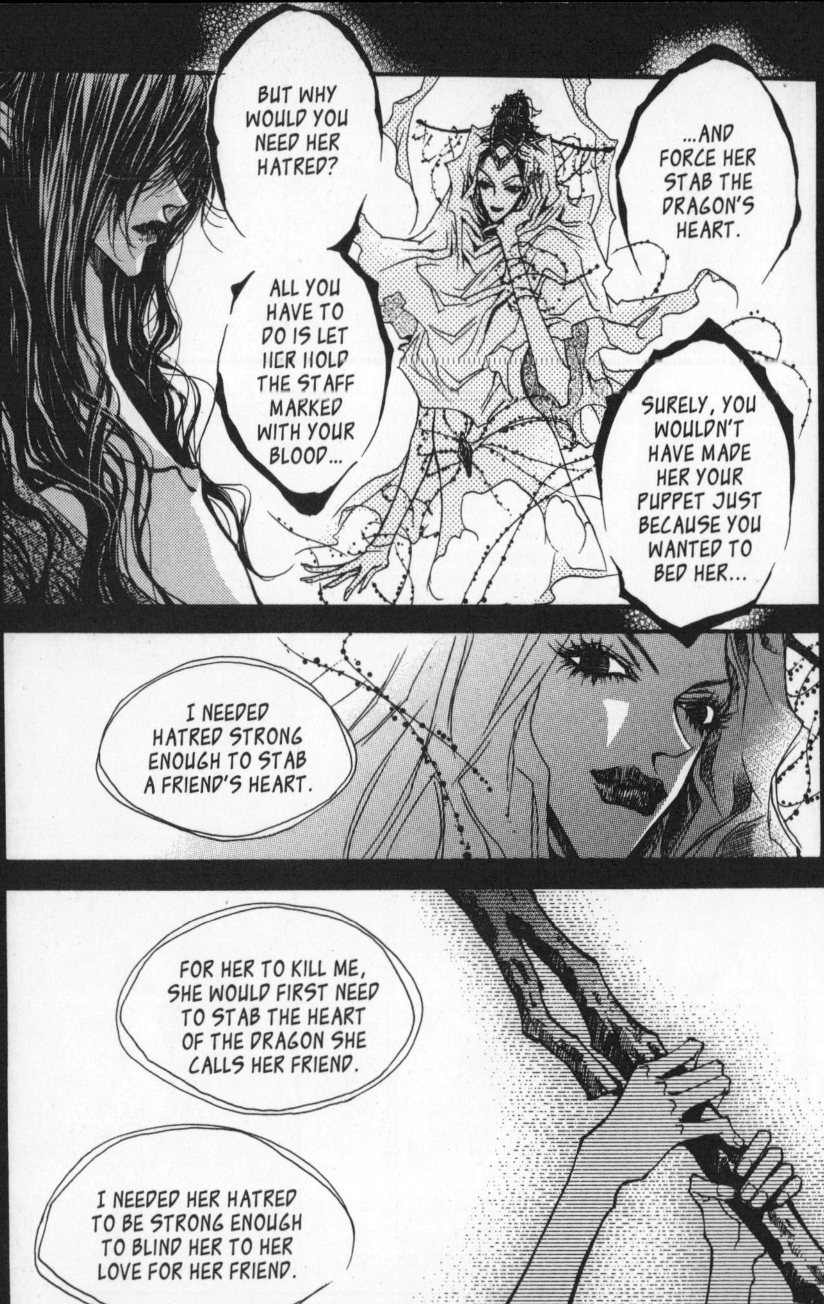
BUT WHY WOULD YOU NEED HER HATRED?
ALL YOU HAVE TO DO IS LET HER HOLD THE STAFF MARKED WITH YOUR BLOOD...
...AND FORCE HER STAB THE DRAGON'S HEART.
SURELY, YOU WOULDN'T HAVE MADE HER YOUR PUPPET JUST BECAUSE YOU WANTED TO BED HER...
I NEEDED HATRED STRONG ENOUGH TO STAB A FRIEND'S HEART.
FOR HER TO KILL ME, SHE WOULD FIRST NEED TO STAB THE HEART OF THE DRAGON SHE CALLS HER FRIEND.
I NEEDED HER HATRED TO BE STRONG ENOUGH TO BLIND HER TO HER LOVE FOR HER FRIEND.

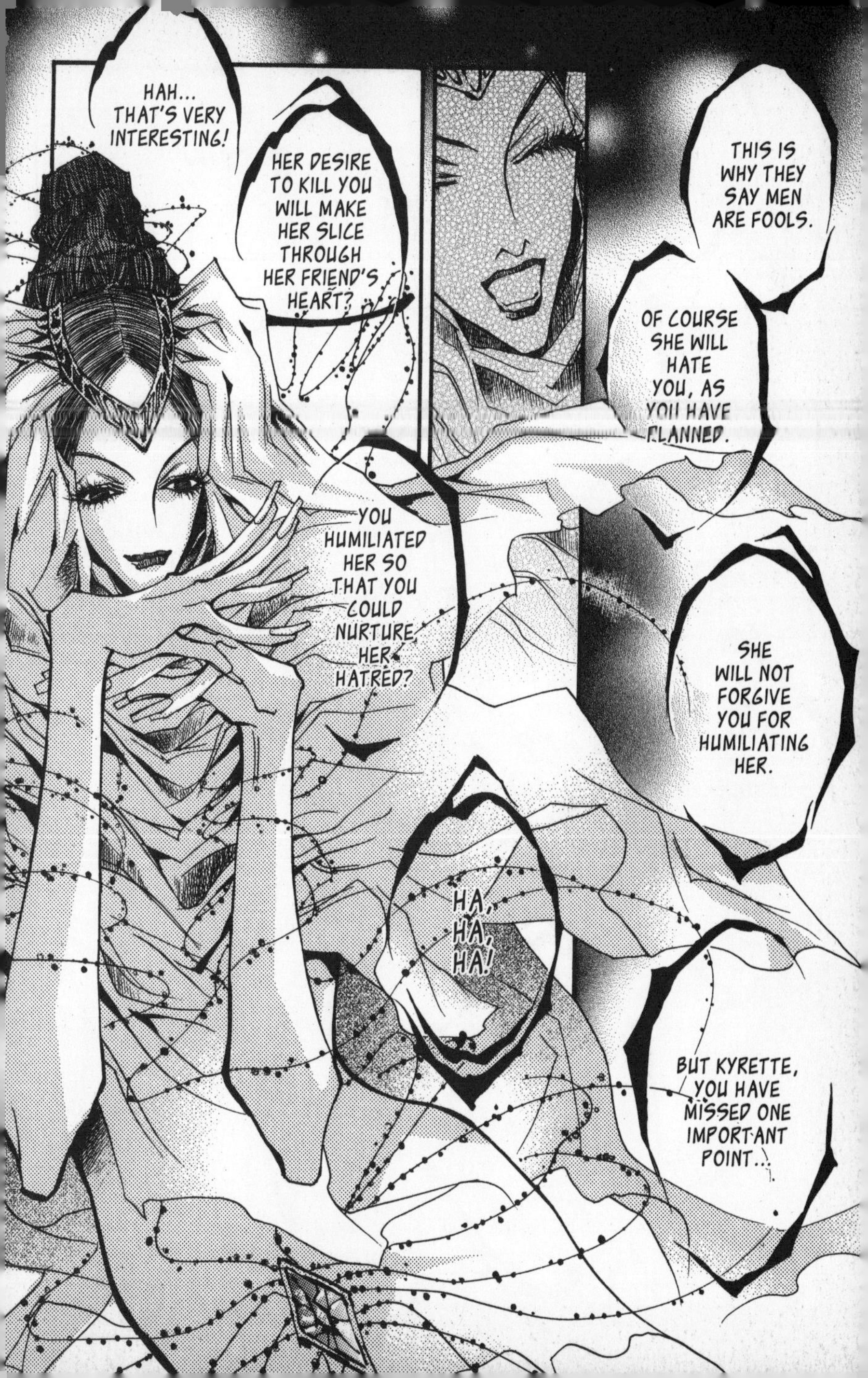
HAH... THAT'S VERY INTERESTING!
HER DESIRE TO KILL YOU WILL MAKE HER SLICE THROUGH HER FRIEND'S HEART?
THIS IS WHY THEY SAY MEN ARE FOOLS.
OF COURSE SHE WILL HATE YOU, AS YOU HAVE PLANNED.
YOU HUMILIATED HER SO THAT YOU COULD NURTURE HER HATRED?
SHE WILL NOT FORGIVE YOU FOR HUMILIATING HER.
HA, HA, HA!
BUT KYRETTE, YOU HAVE MISSED ONE IMPORTANT POINT...

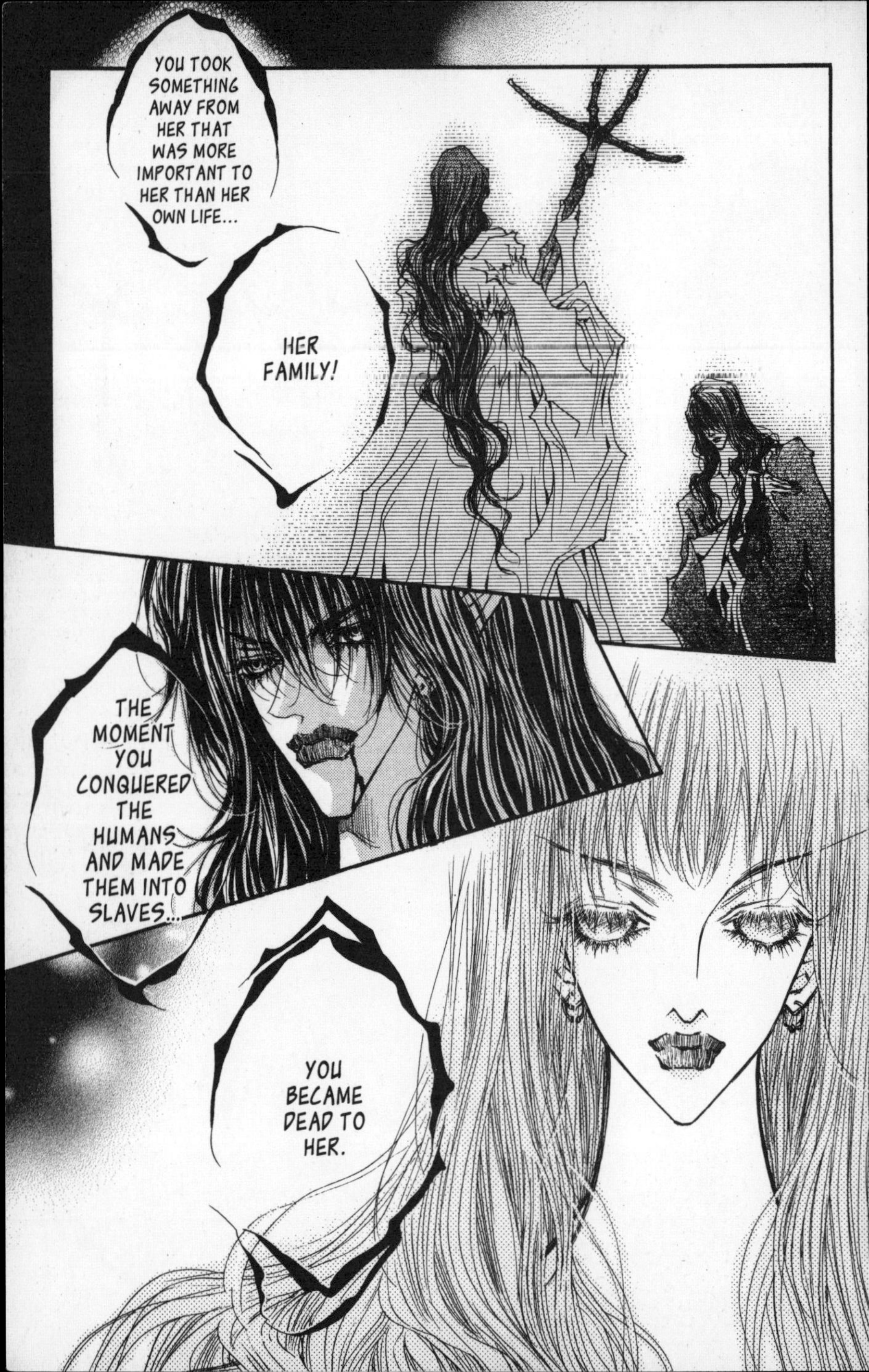
YOU TOOK SOMETHING AWAY FROM HER THAT WAS MORE IMPORTANT TO HER THAN HER OWN LIFE...
HER FAMILY!
THE MOMENT YOU CONQUERED THE HUMANS AND MADE THEM INTO SLAVES...
YOU BECAME DEAD TO HER.

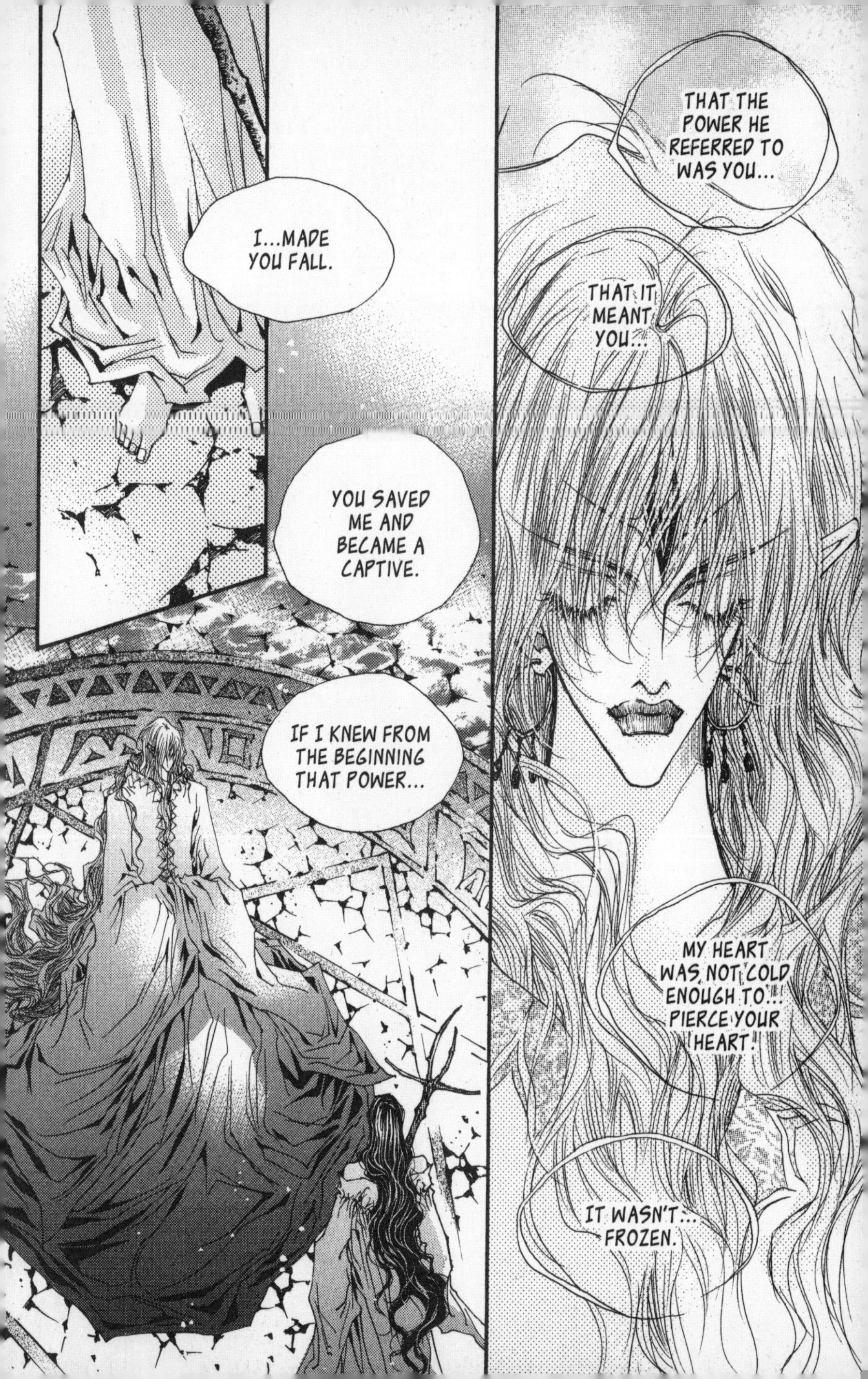
I...MADE YOU FALL.
YOU SAVED ME AND BECAME A CAPTIVE.
IF I KNEW FROM THE BEGINNING THAT POWER...
THAT THE POWER HE REFERRED TO WAS YOU...
THAT IT MEANT YOU...
MY HEART WAS NOT COLD ENOUGH TO... PIERCE YOUR HEART!
IT WASN'T... FROZEN.

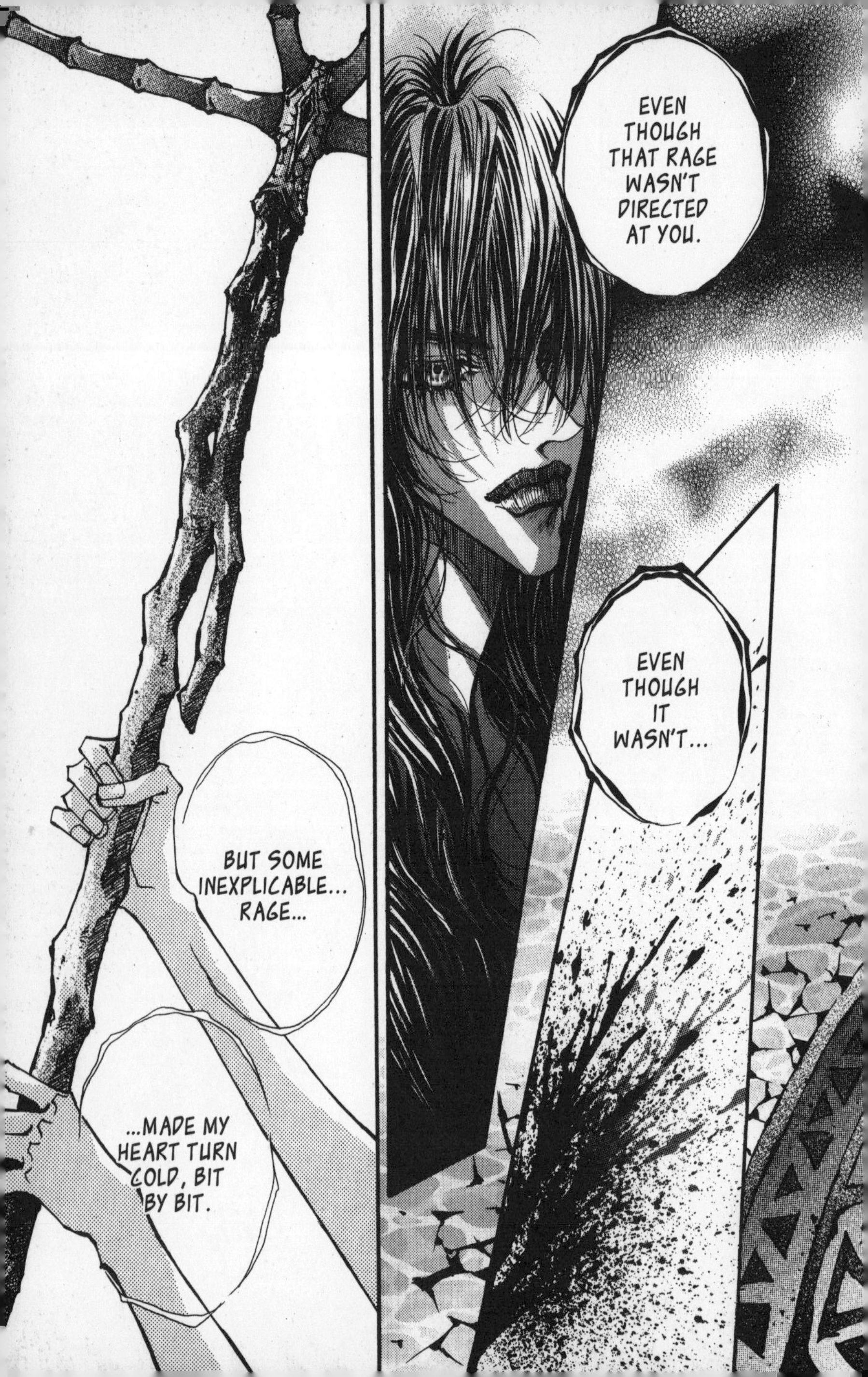
BUT SOME INEXPLICABLE... RAGE...
...MADE MY HEART TURN COLD, BIT BY BIT.
EVEN THOUGH THAT RAGE WASN'T DIRECTED AT YOU.
EVEN THOUGH IT WASN'T...

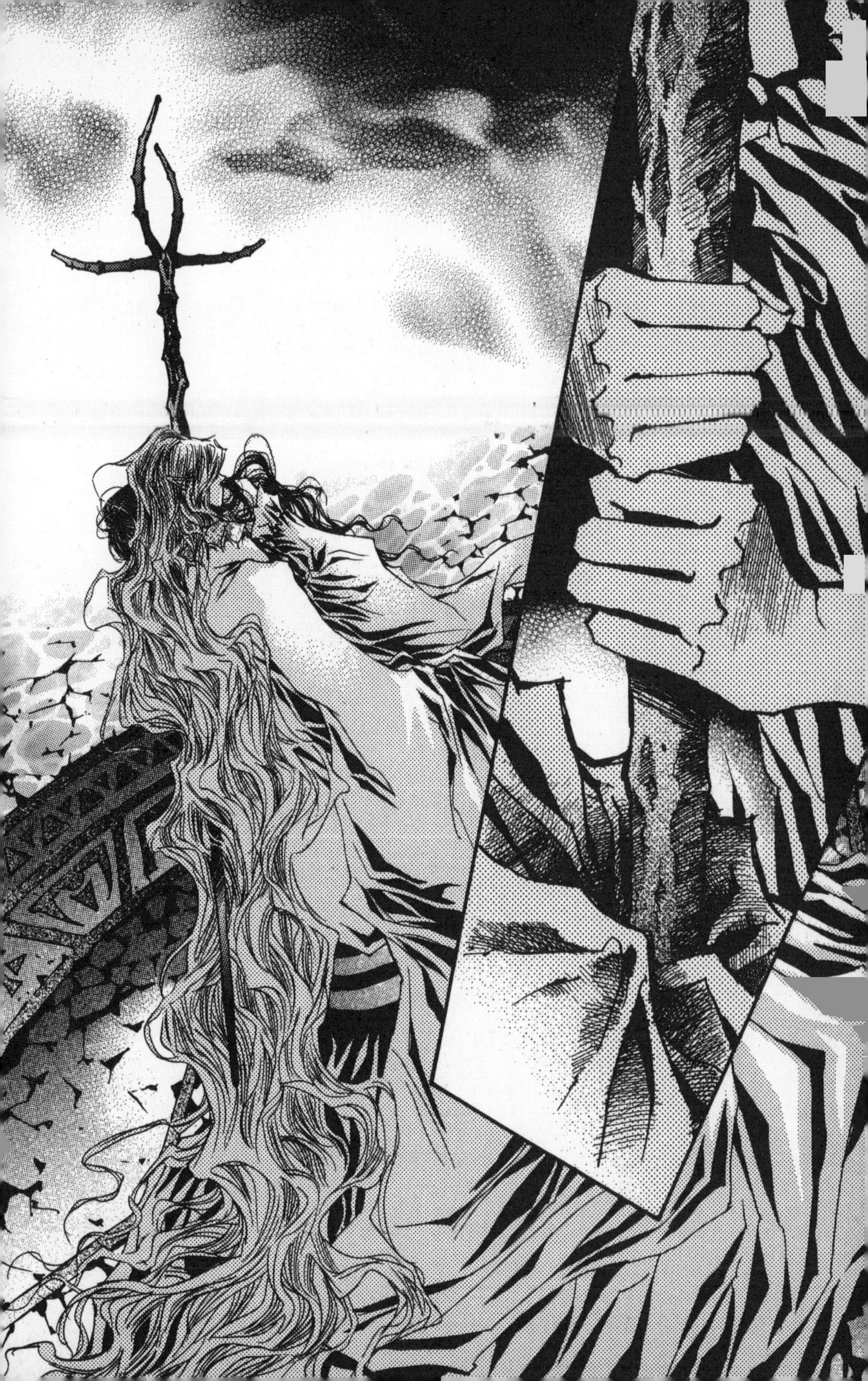

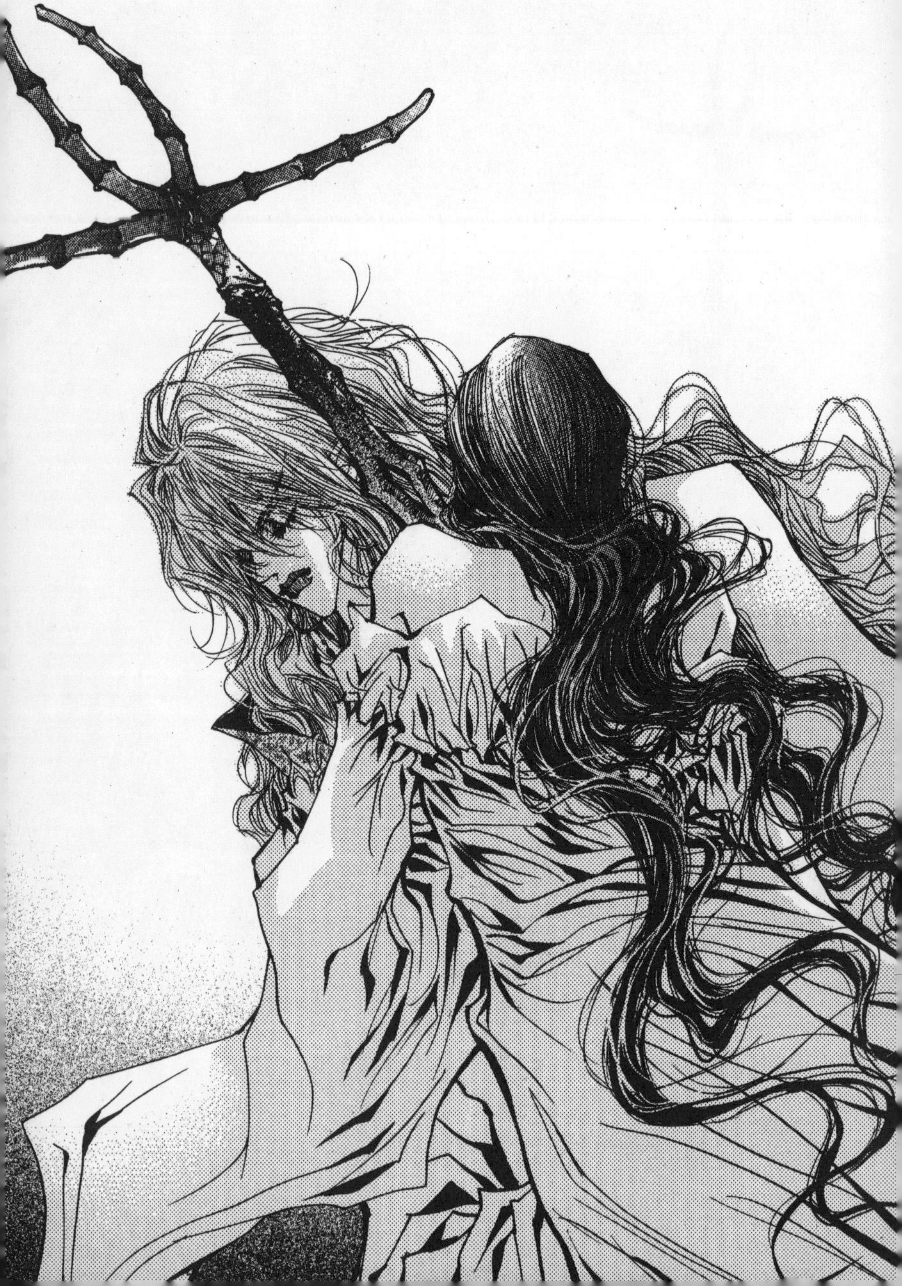

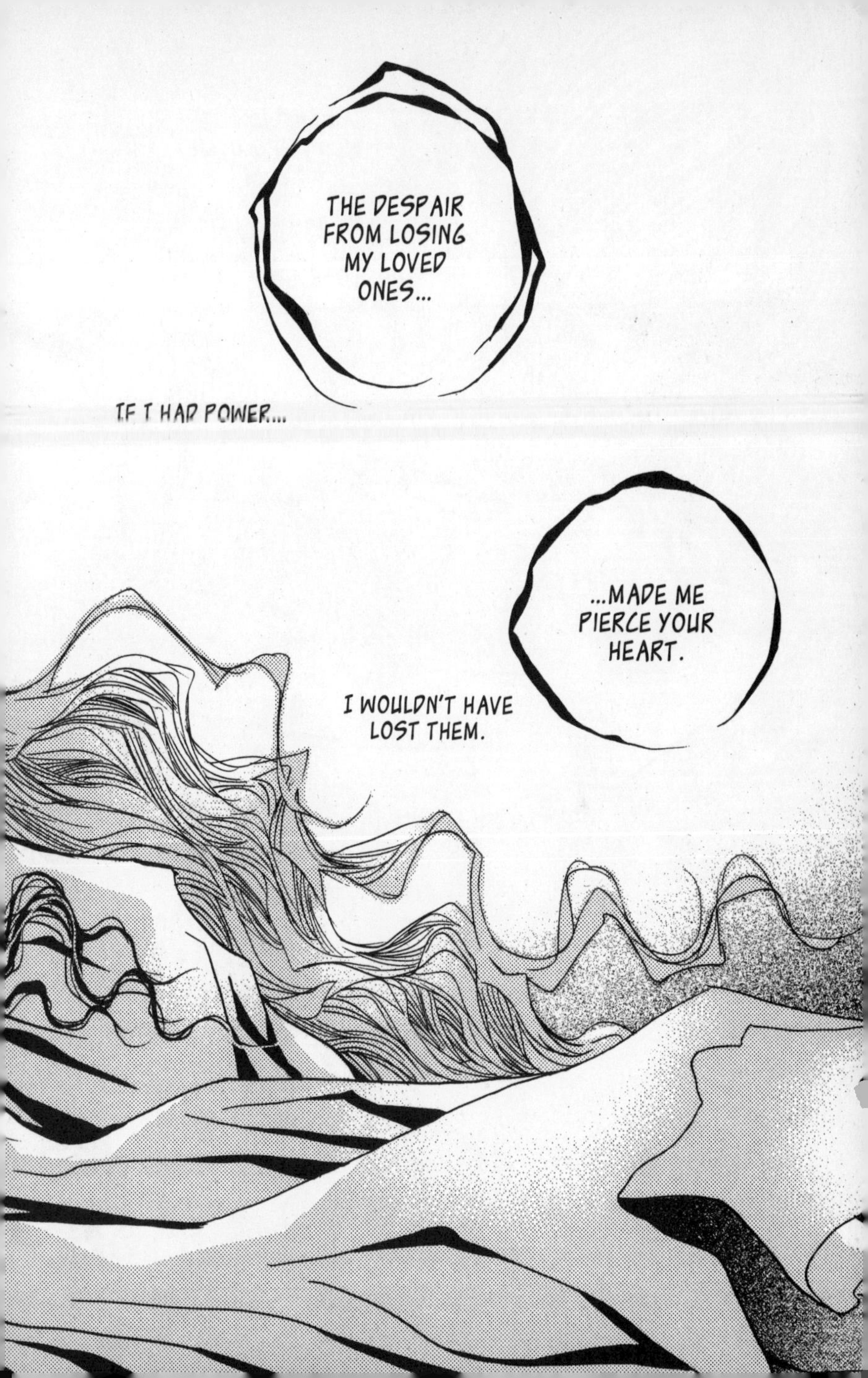
THE DESPAIR FROM LOSING MY LOVED ONES...
IF I HAD POWER...
...MADE ME PIERCE YOUR HEART.
I WOULDN'T HAVE LOST THEM.

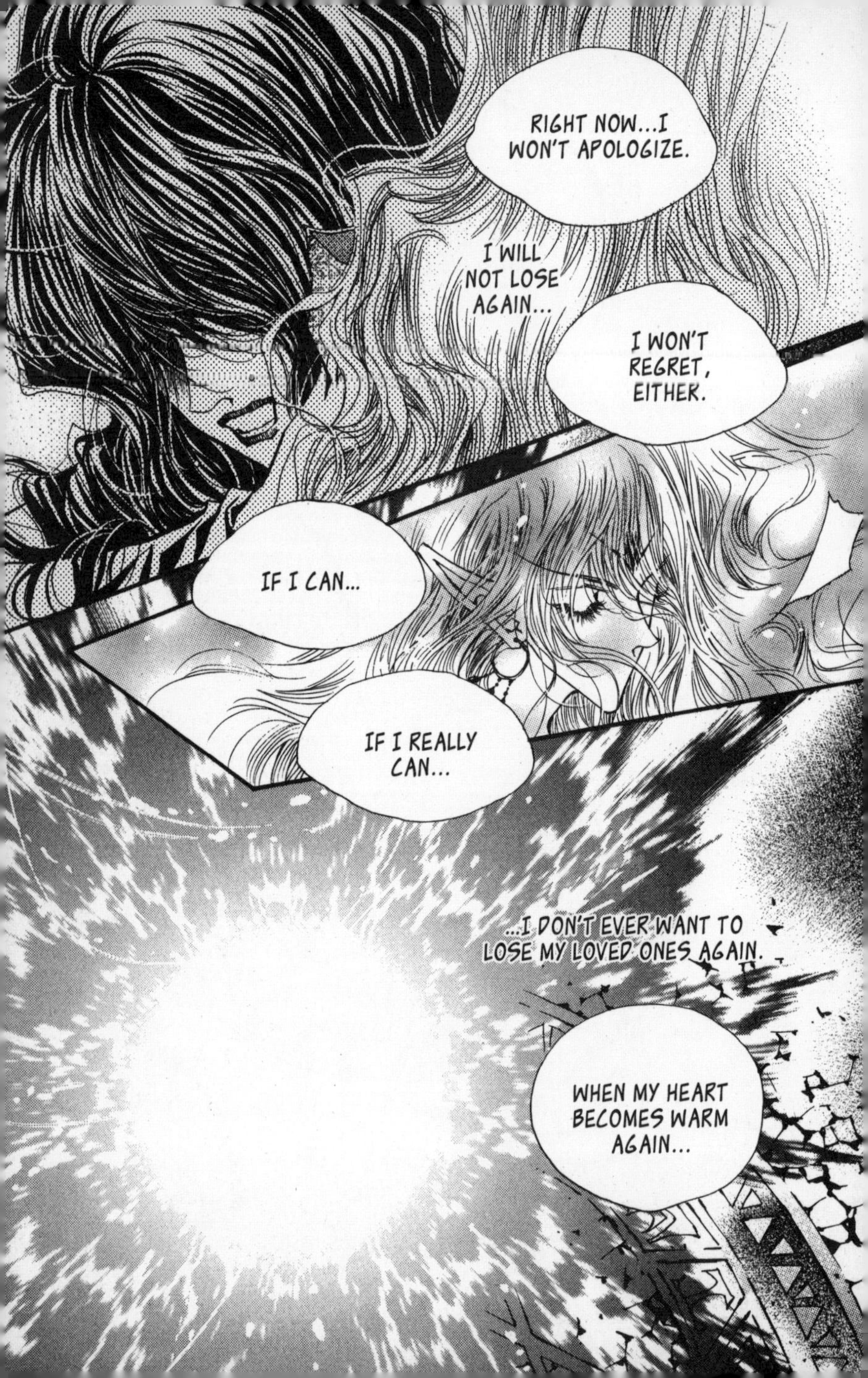
RIGHT NOW...I WON'T APOLOGIZE.
I WILL NOT LOSE AGAIN...
I WON'T REGRET, EITHER.
IF I CAN...
IF I REALLY CAN...
...I DON'T EVER WANT TO LOSE MY LOVED ONES AGAIN.
WHEN MY HEART BECOMES WARM AGAIN...

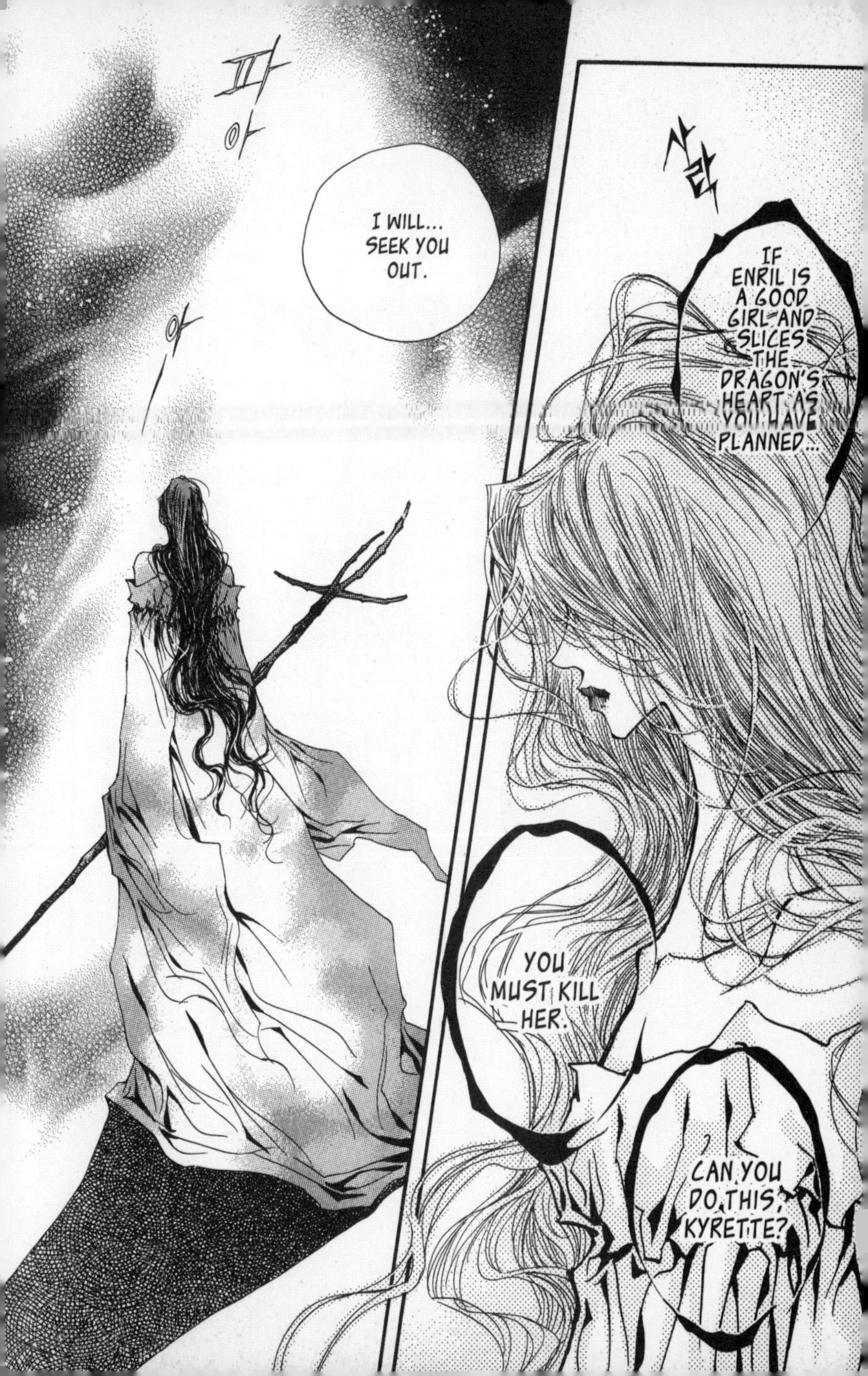
I WILL... SEEK YOU OUT.
IF ENRIL IS A GOOD GIRL AND SLICES THE DRAGON'S HEART AS YOU HAVE PLANNED...
YOU MUST KILL HER.
CAN YOU DO THIS, KYRETTE?

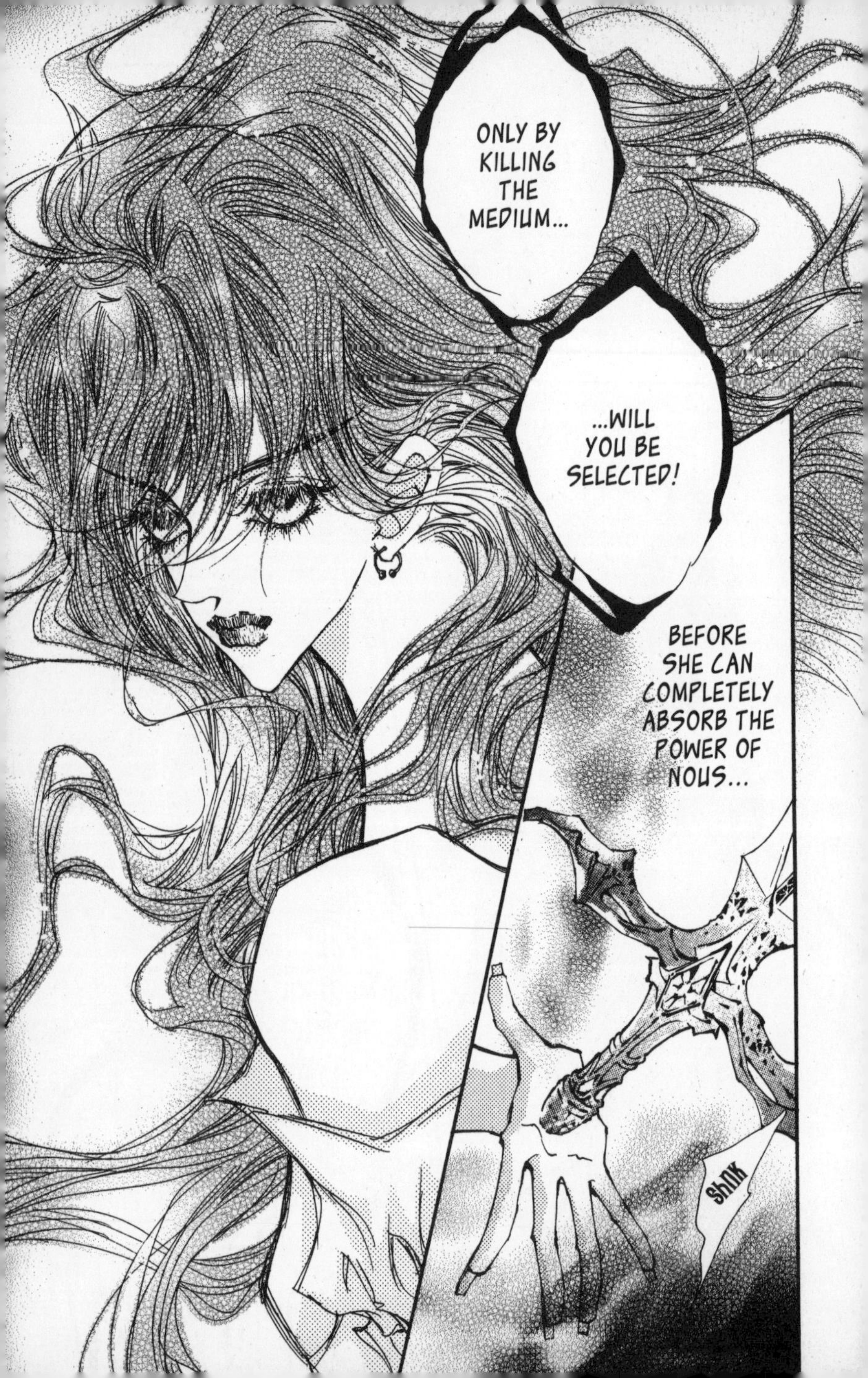

ONLY BY KILLING THE MEDIUM...
...WILL YOU BE SELECTED!
BEFORE SHE CAN COMPLETELY ABSORB THE POWER OF NOUS...
ShNK

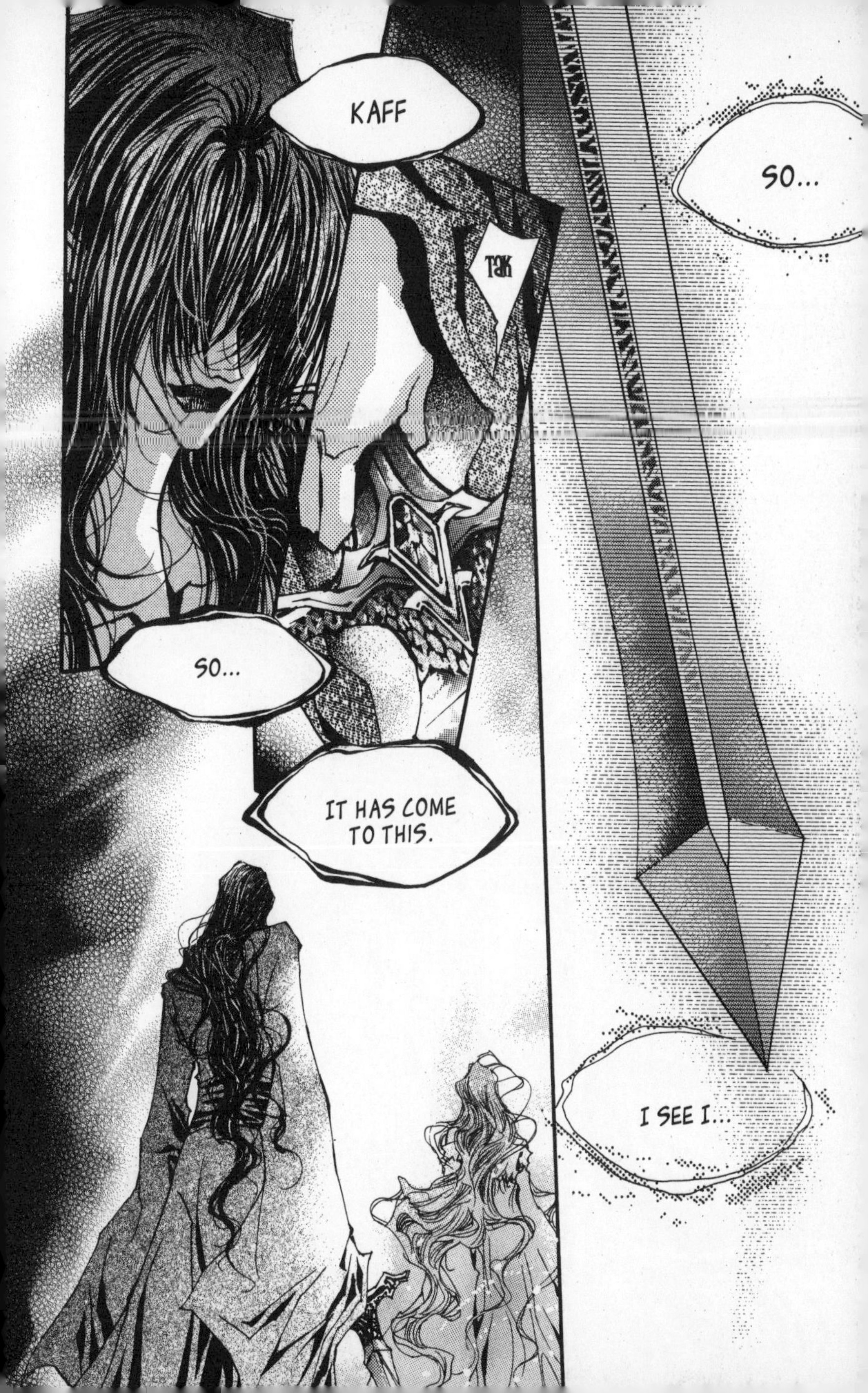
KAFF
TAK
SO...
IT HAS COME TO THIS.
SO...
I SEE I...

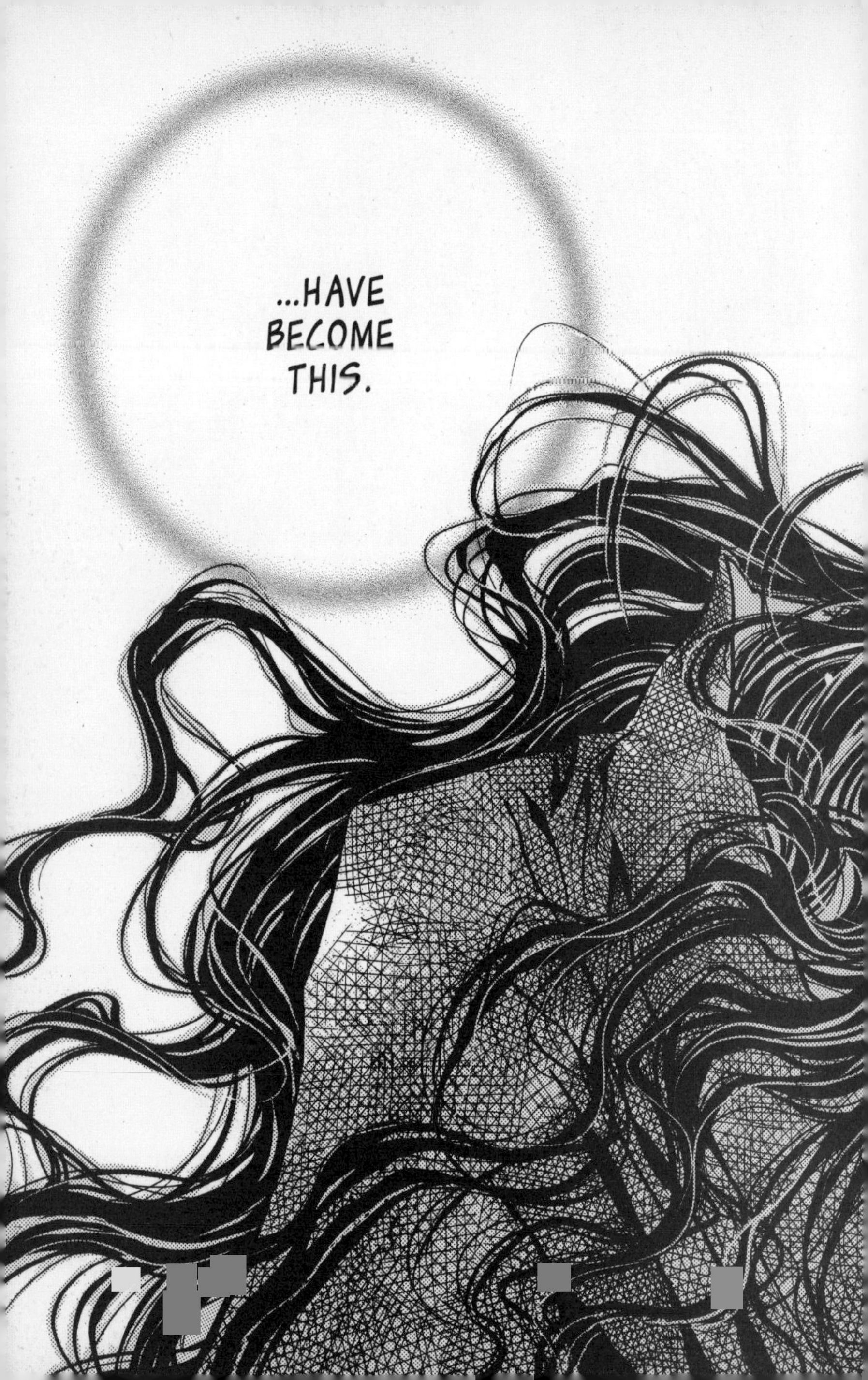
...HAVE
BECOME
THIS.

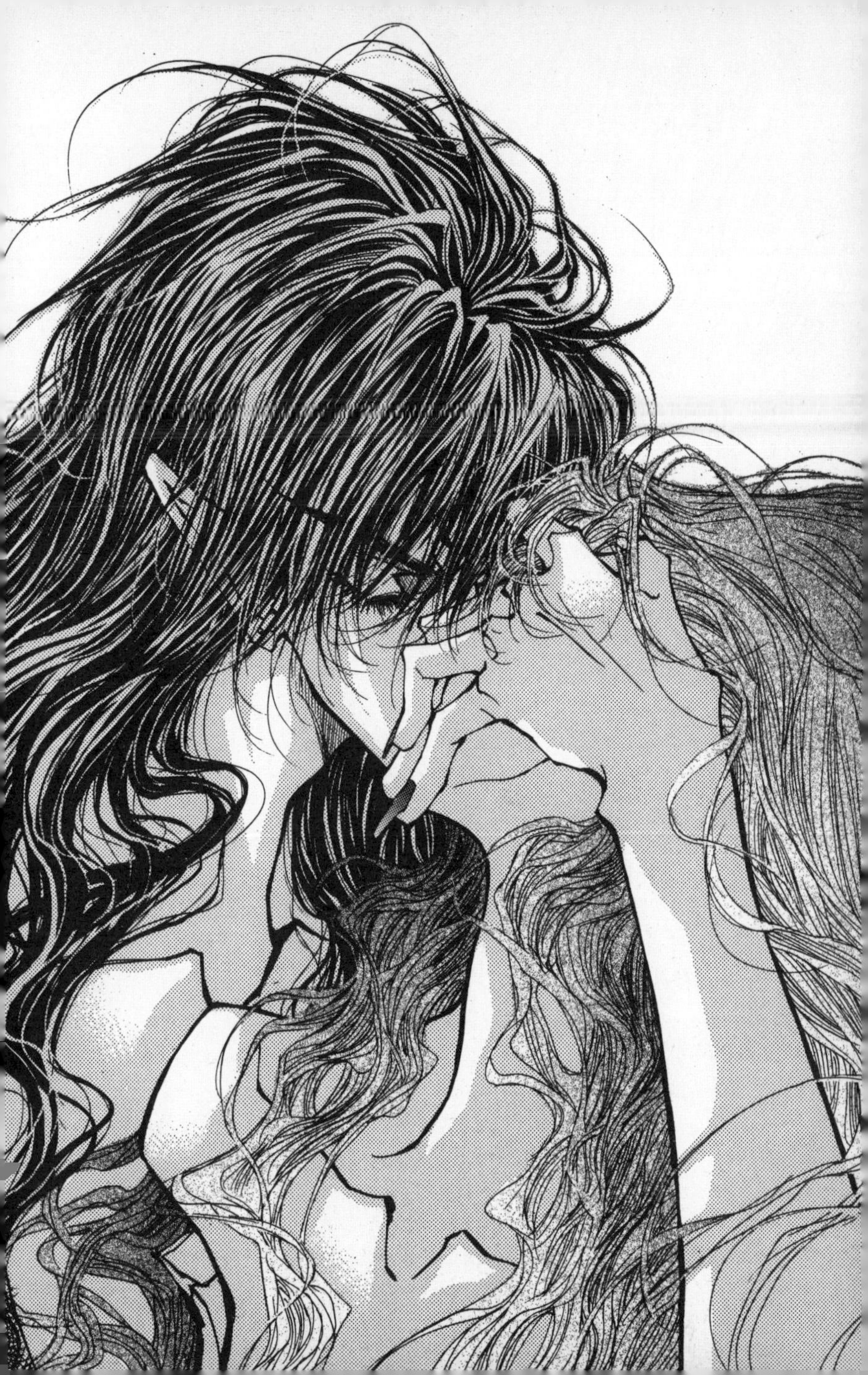

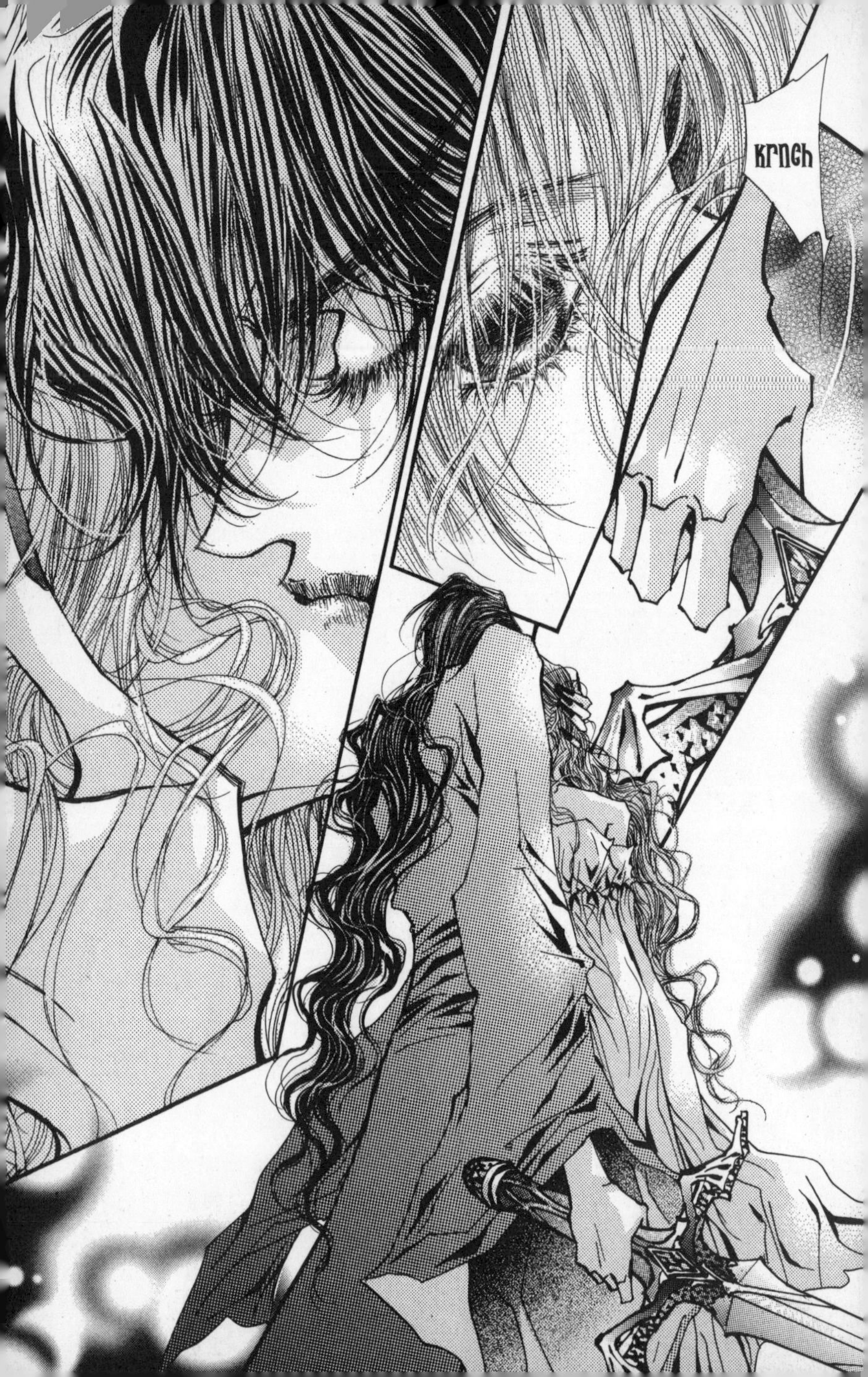
KRNCH

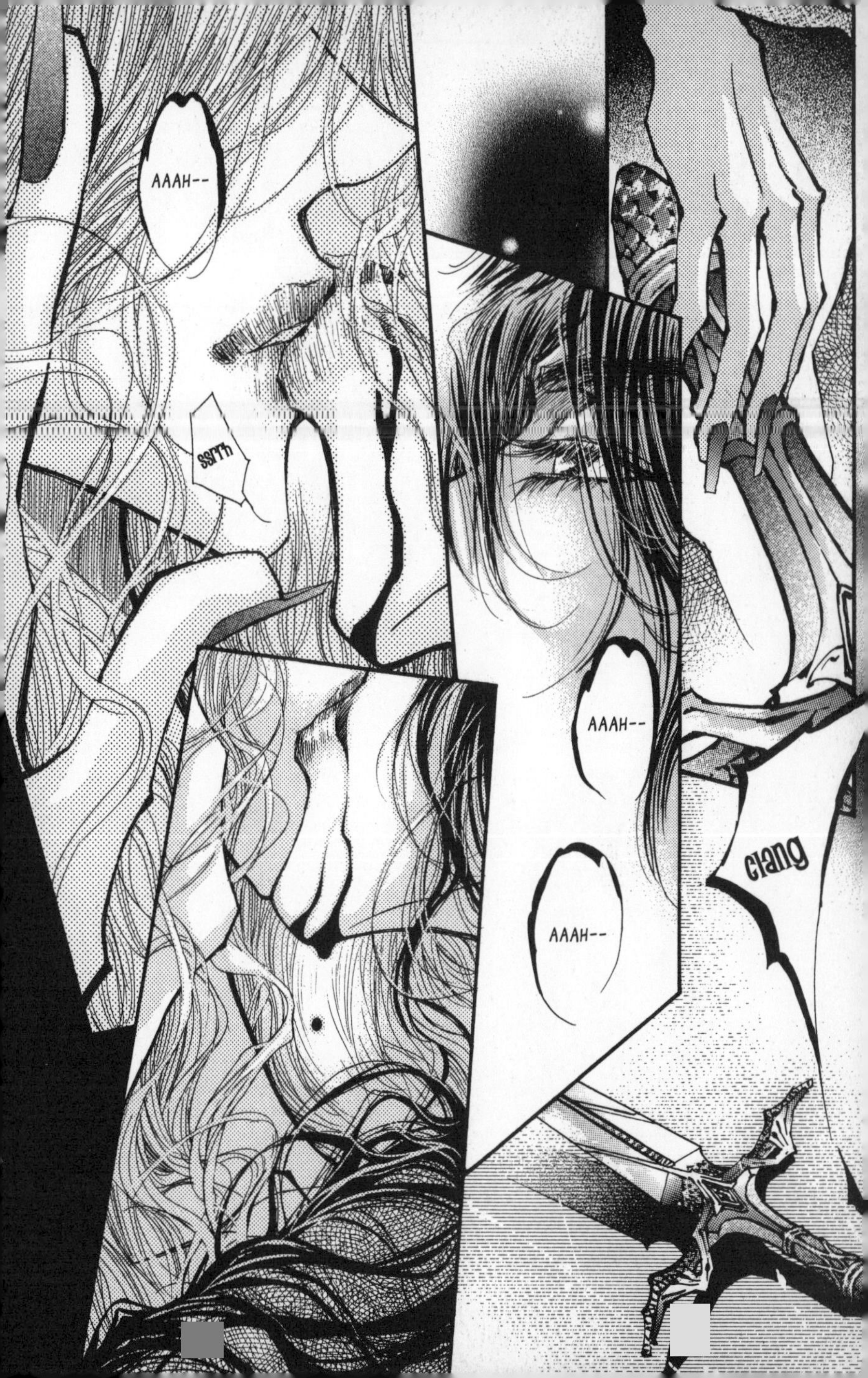
AAAH--
SSrrh
AAAH--
AAAH--
clang

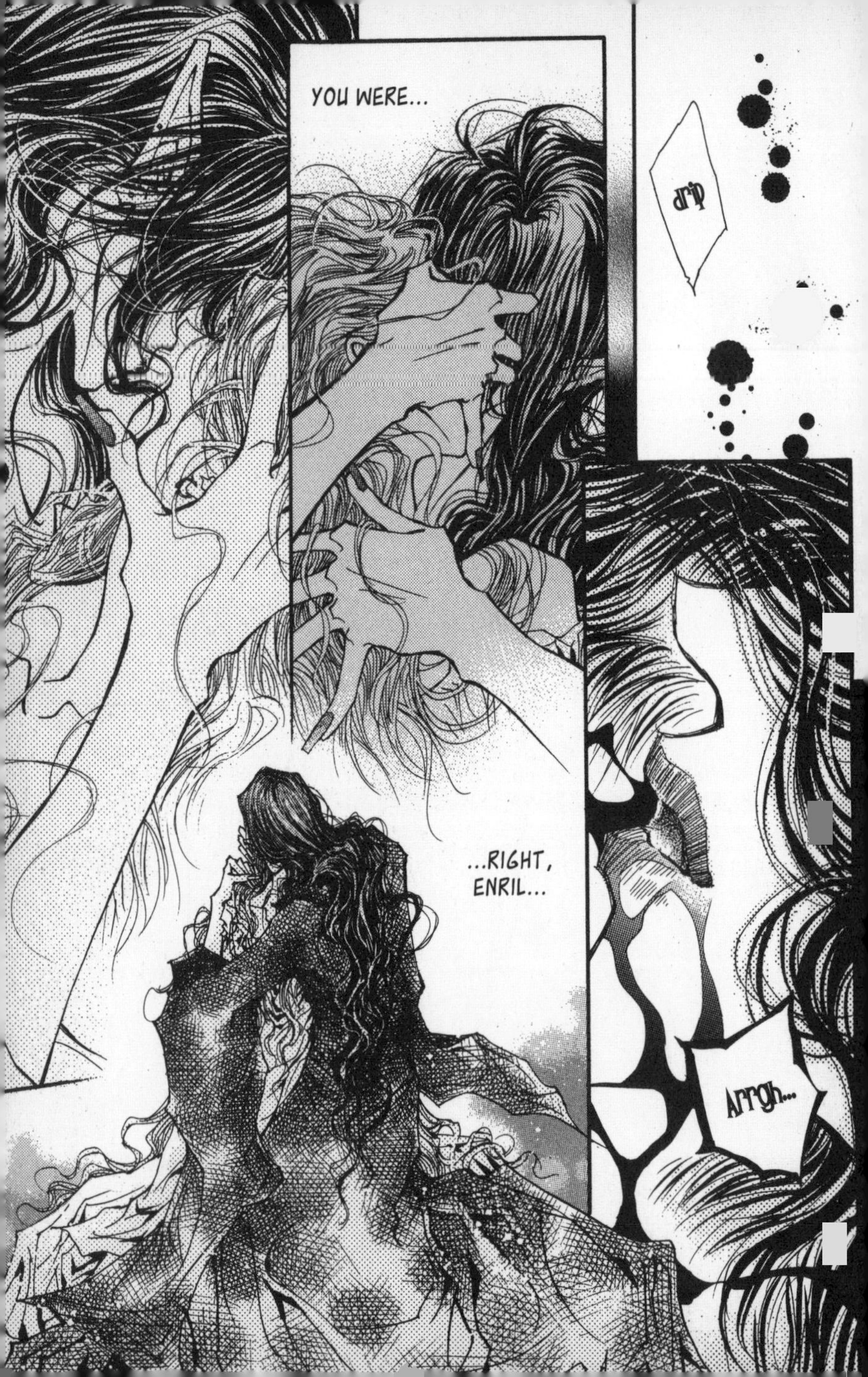
YOU WERE...
drip
...RIGHT, ENRIL...
Arrgh...

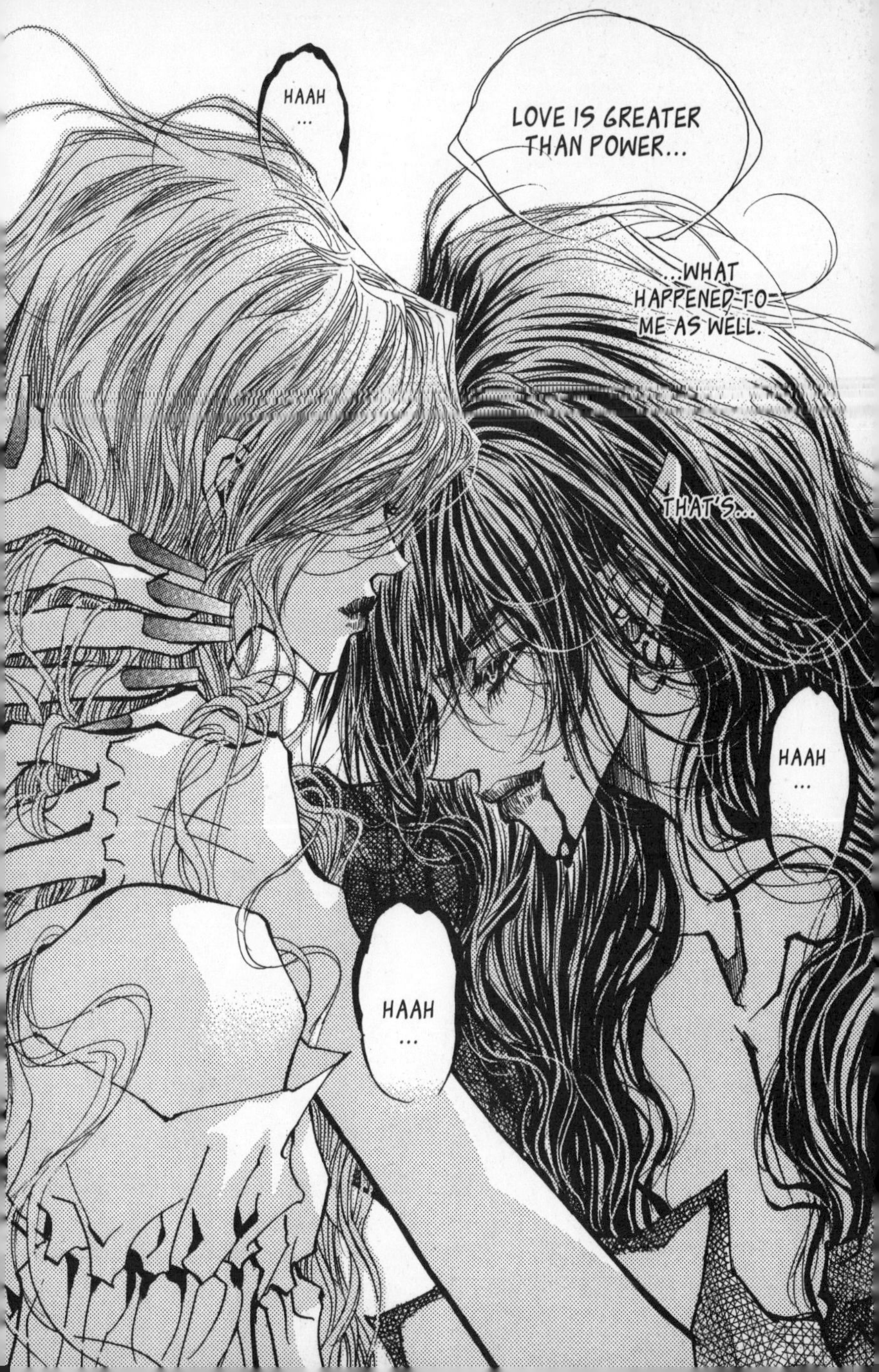
HAAH ...
LOVE IS GREATER THAN POWER...
...WHAT HAPPENED TO ME AS WELL.
THAT'S...
HAAH ...
HAAH ...

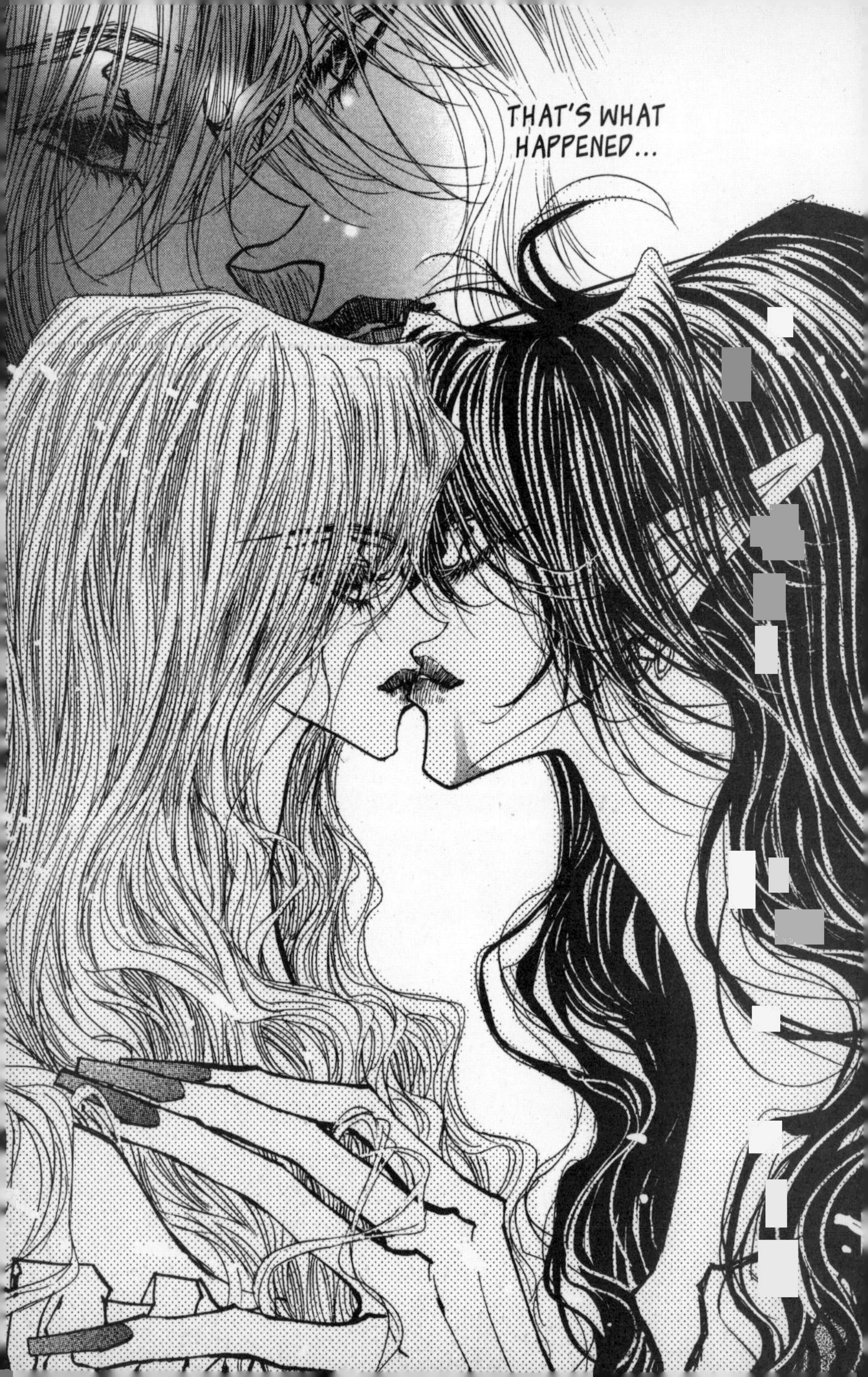
THAT'S WHAT HAPPENED...

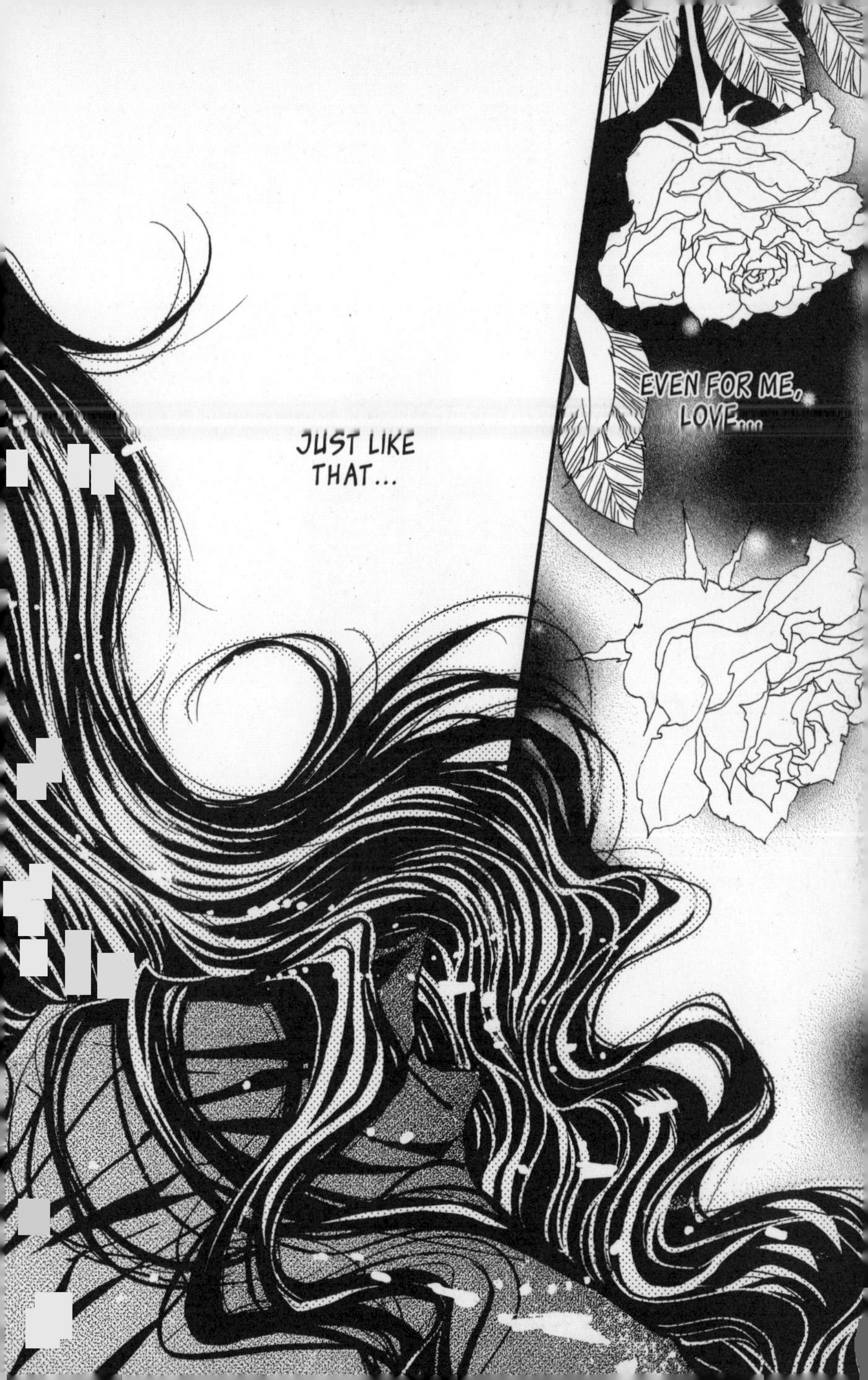
JUST LIKE THAT...
EVEN FOR ME, LOVE...

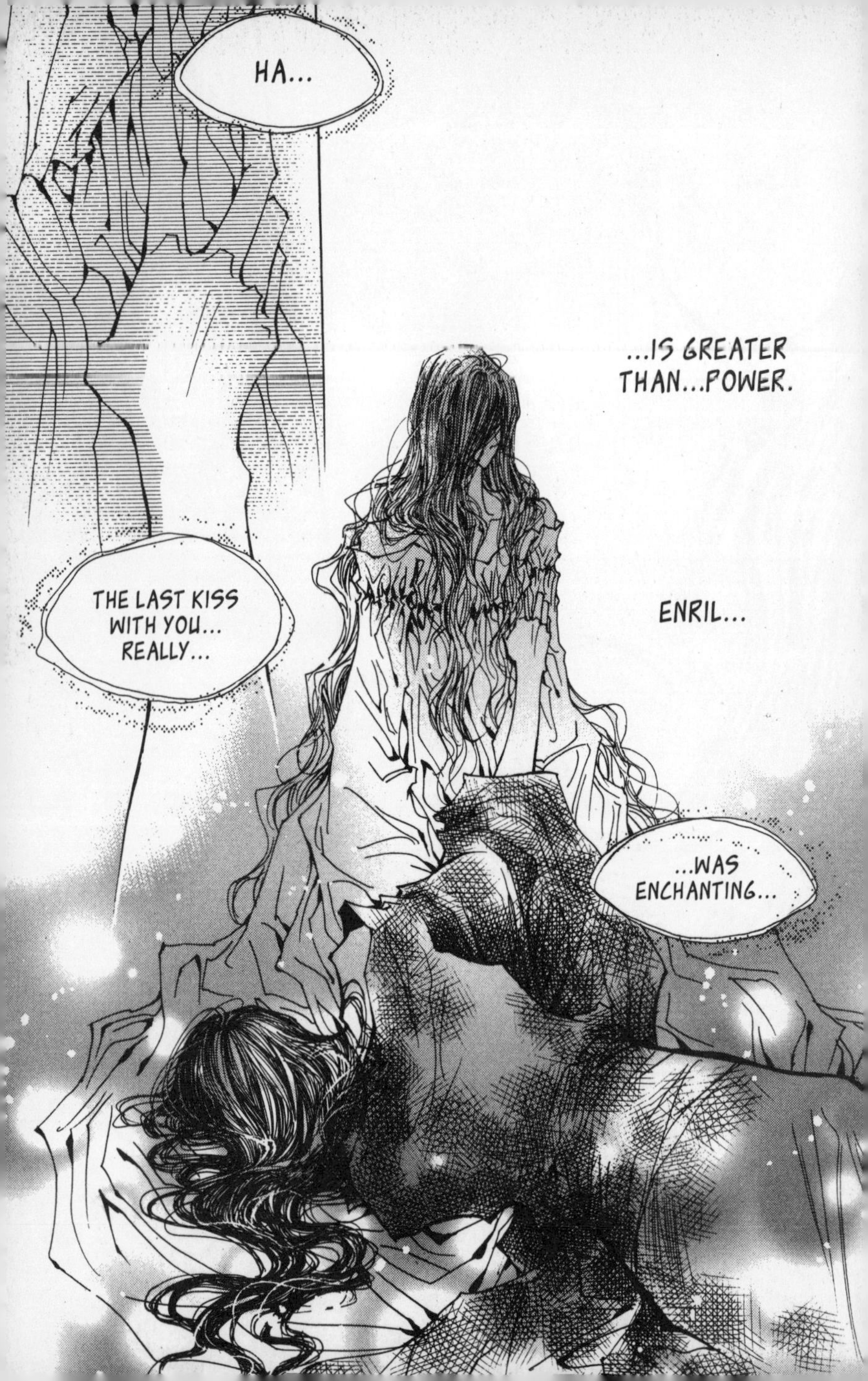
HA...
...IS GREATER THAN...POWER.
THE LAST KISS WITH YOU... REALLY...
ENRIL...
...WAS ENCHANTING...

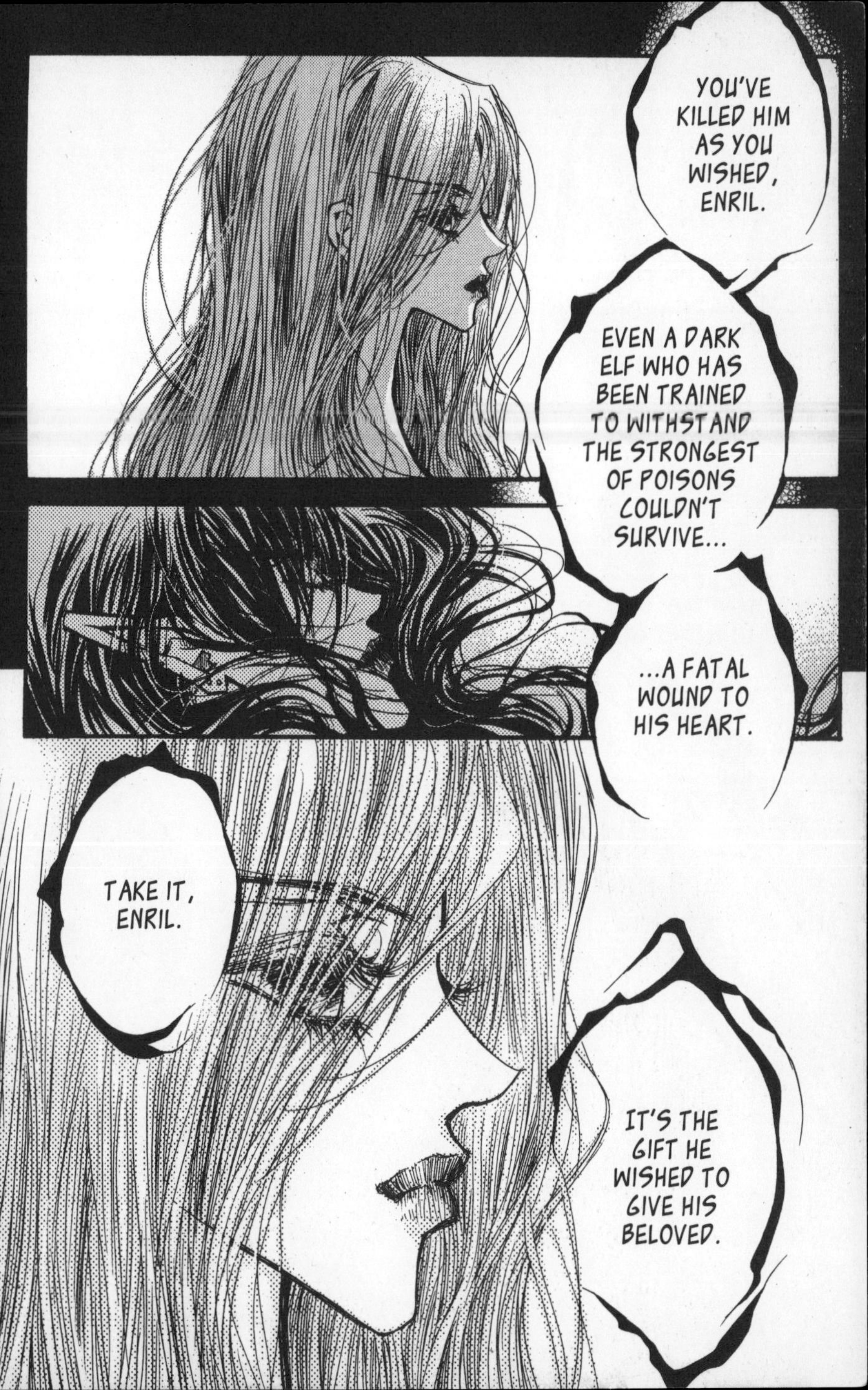
YOU'VE KILLED HIM AS YOU WISHED, ENRIL.
EVEN A DARK ELF WHO HAS BEEN TRAINED TO WITHSTAND THE STRONGEST OF POISONS COULDN'T SURVIVE...
...A FATAL WOUND TO HIS HEART.
TAKE IT, ENRIL.
IT'S THE GIFT HE WISHED TO GIVE HIS BELOVED.

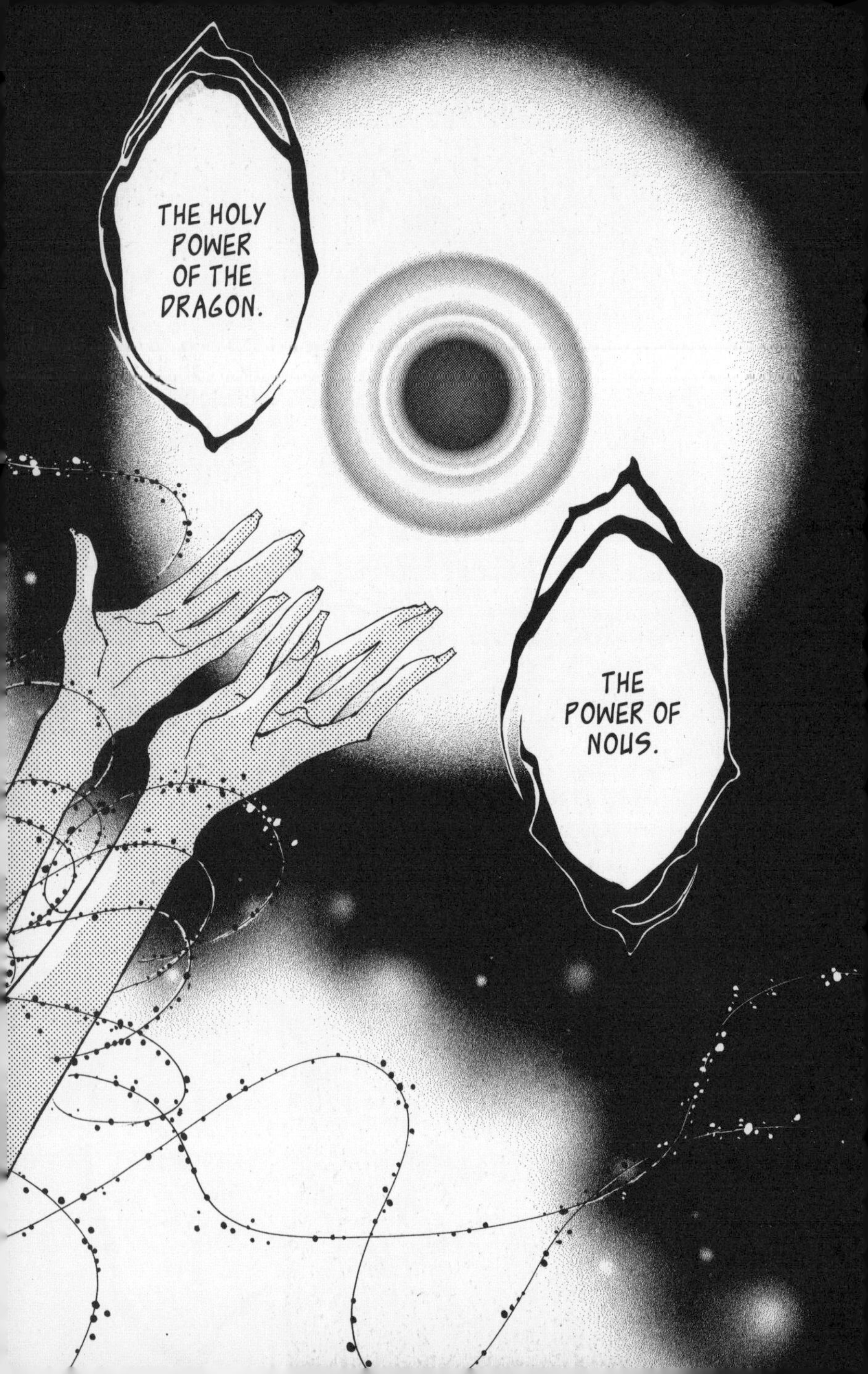
THE HOLY POWER OF THE DRAGON.
THE POWER OF NOUS.

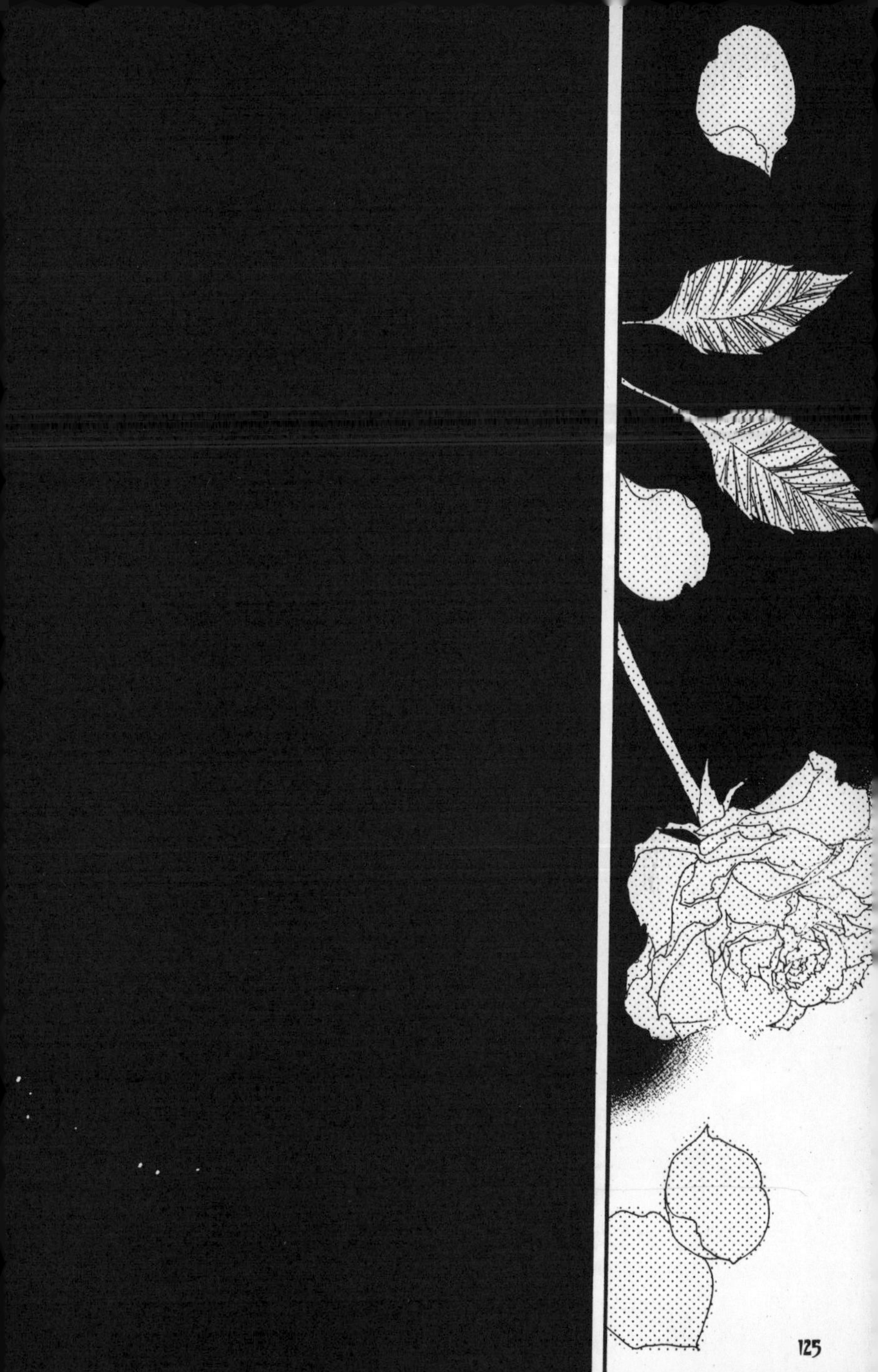

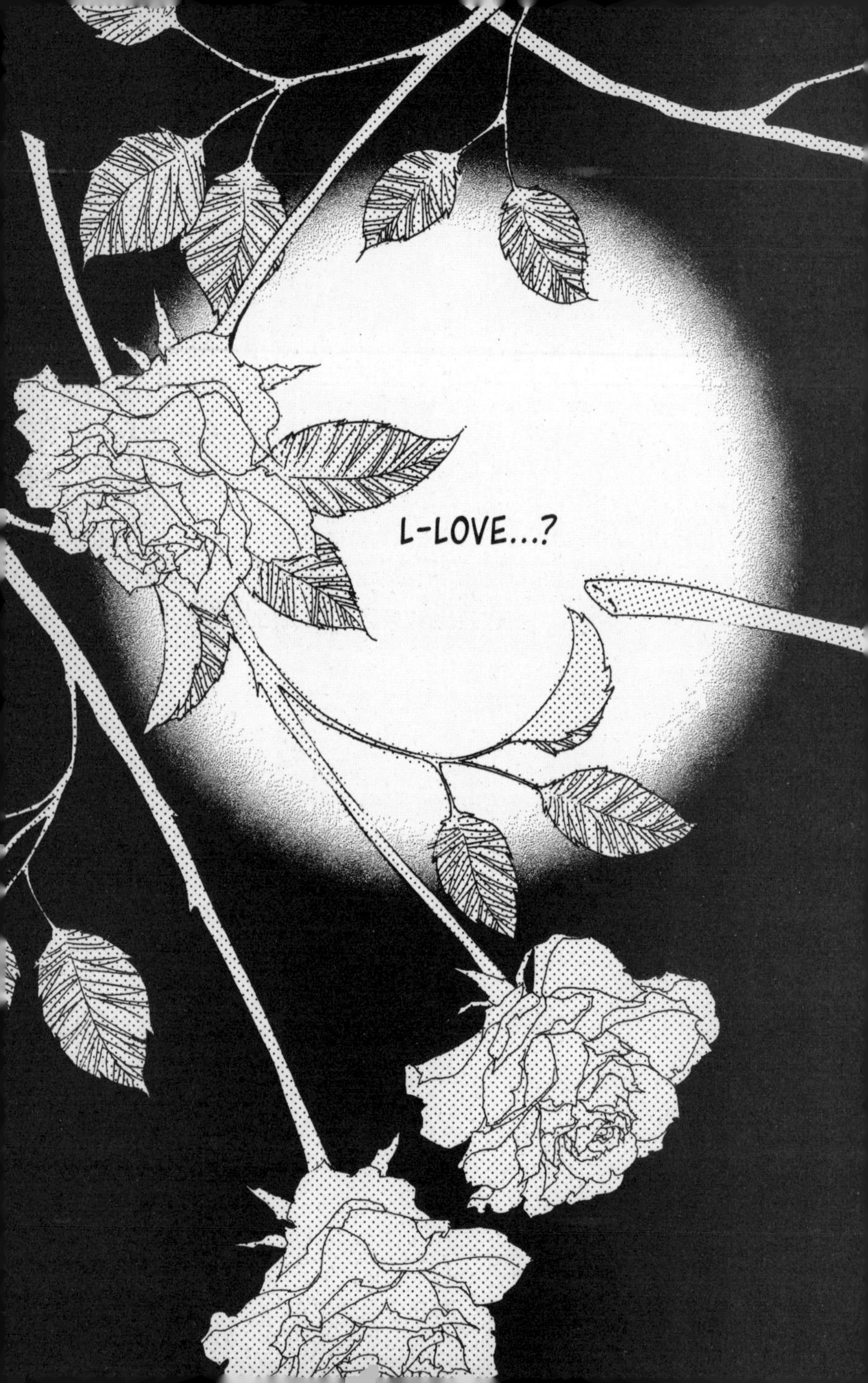
L-LOVE...?

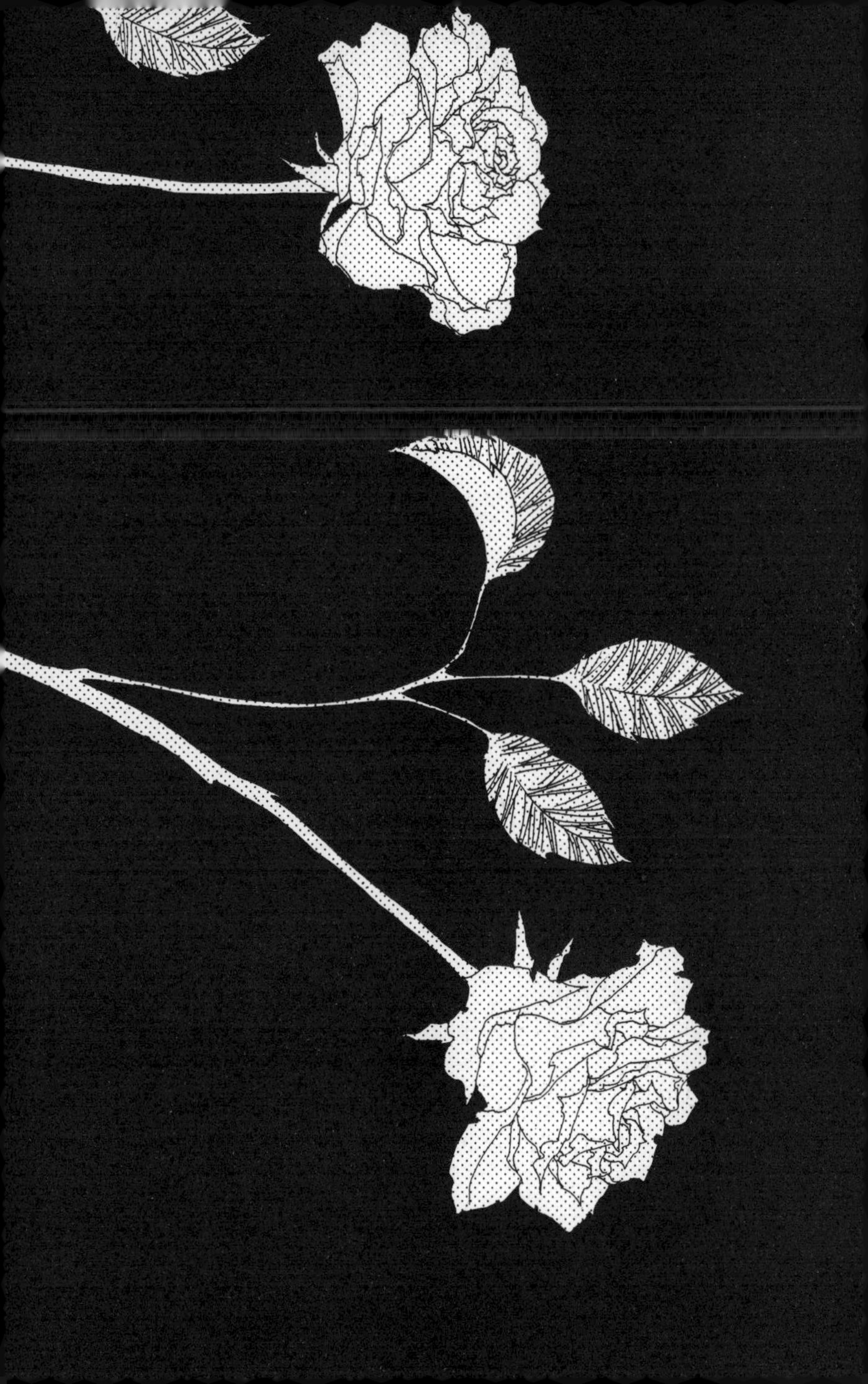

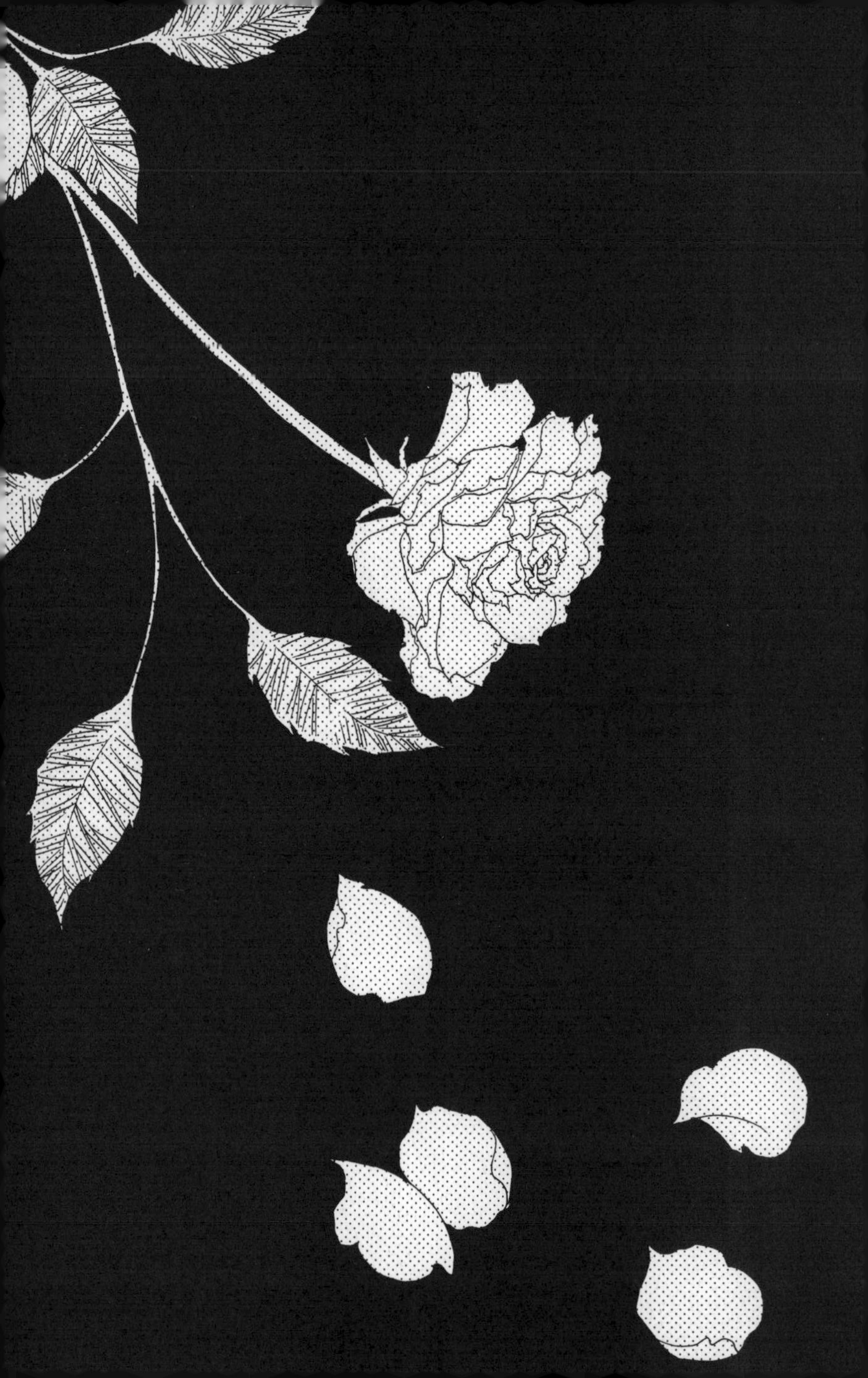

EPISODE 15
ARCANA

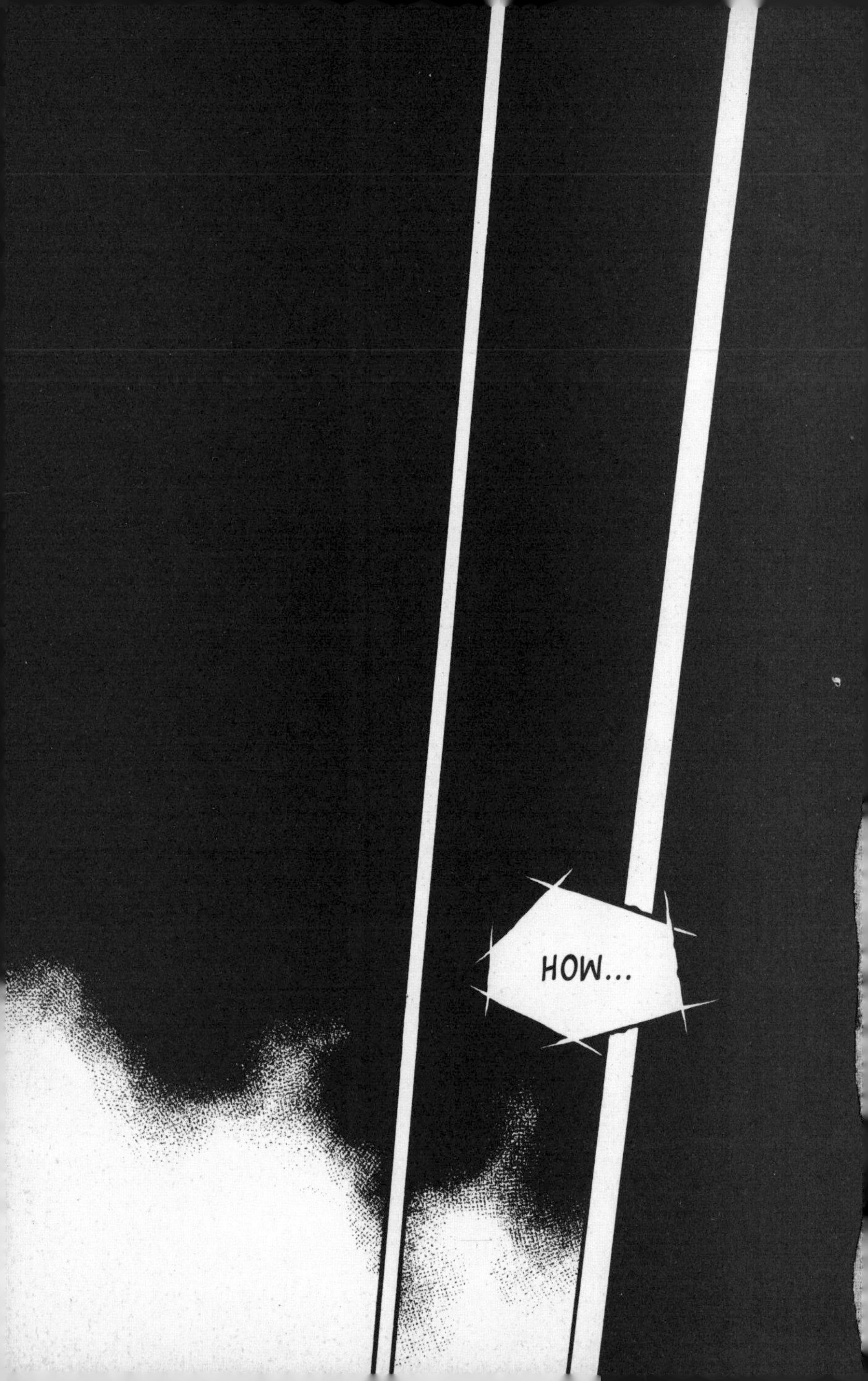
HOW...

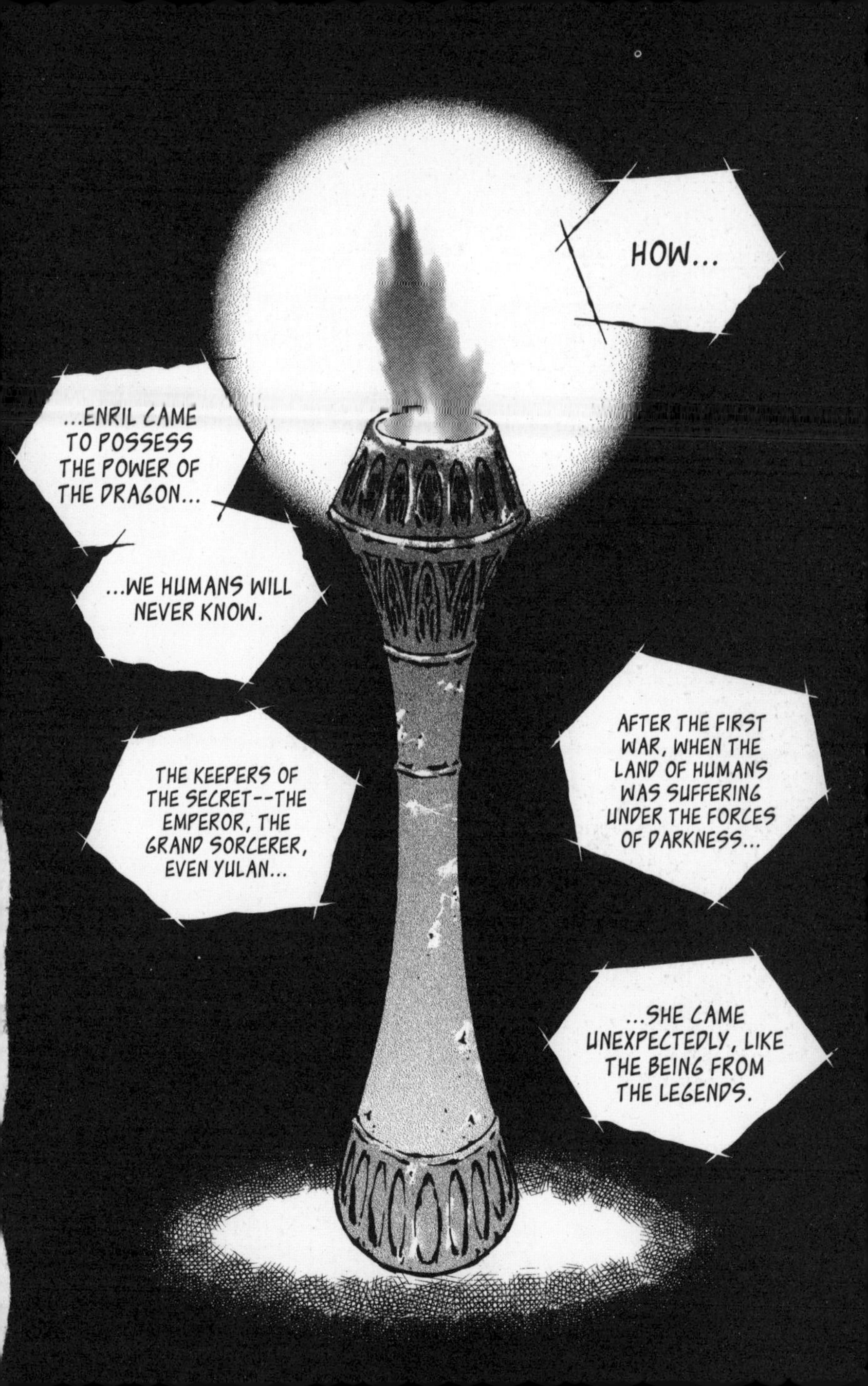
HOW...
...ENRIL CAME TO POSSESS THE POWER OF THE DRAGON...
...WE HUMANS WILL NEVER KNOW.
THE KEEPERS OF THE SECRET--THE EMPEROR, THE GRAND SORCERER, EVEN YULAN...
AFTER THE FIRST WAR, WHEN THE LAND OF HUMANS WAS SUFFERING UNDER THE FORCES OF DARKNESS...
...SHE CAME UNEXPECTEDLY, LIKE THE BEING FROM THE LEGENDS.

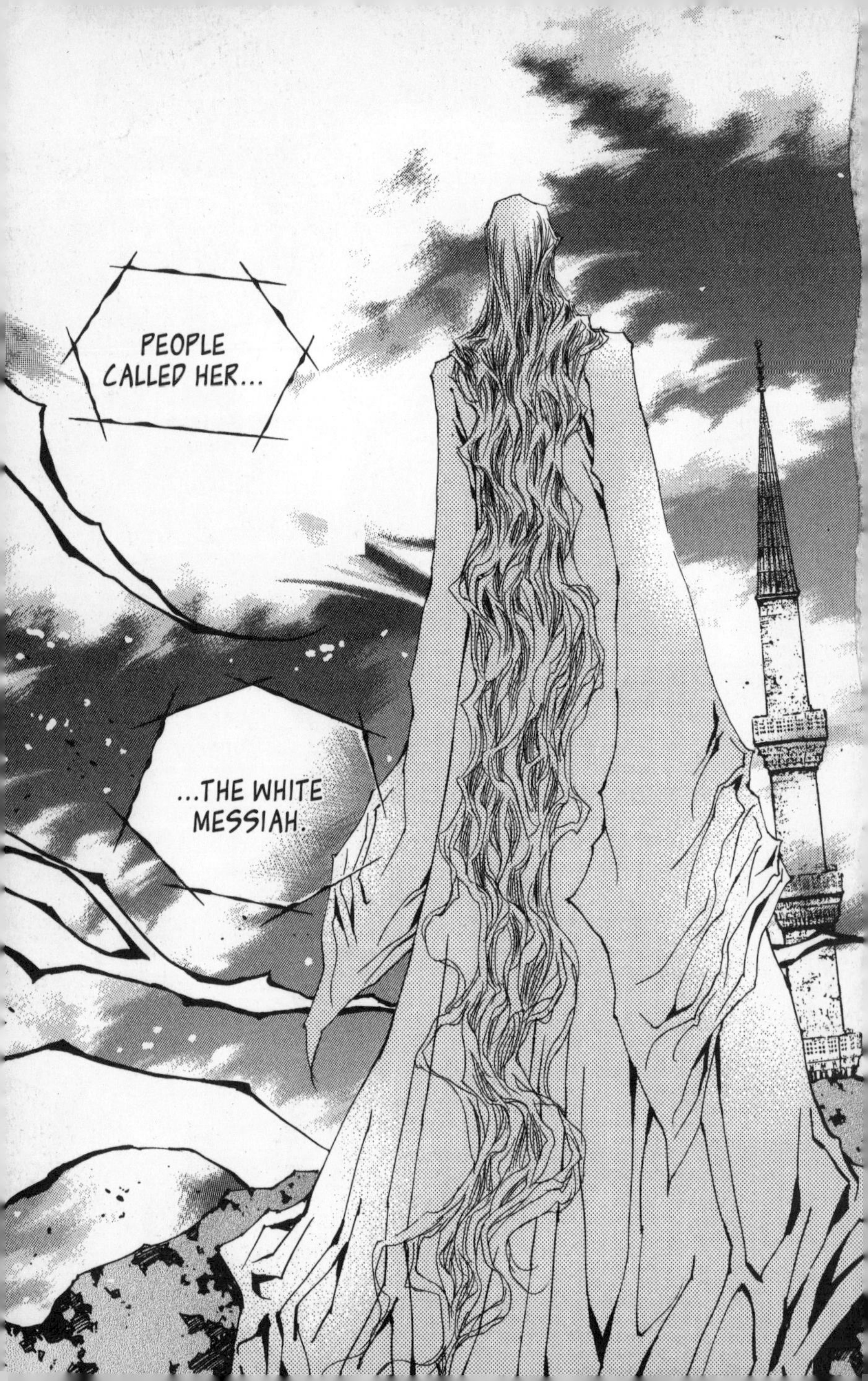
PEOPLE CALLED HER...
...THE WHITE MESSIAH.

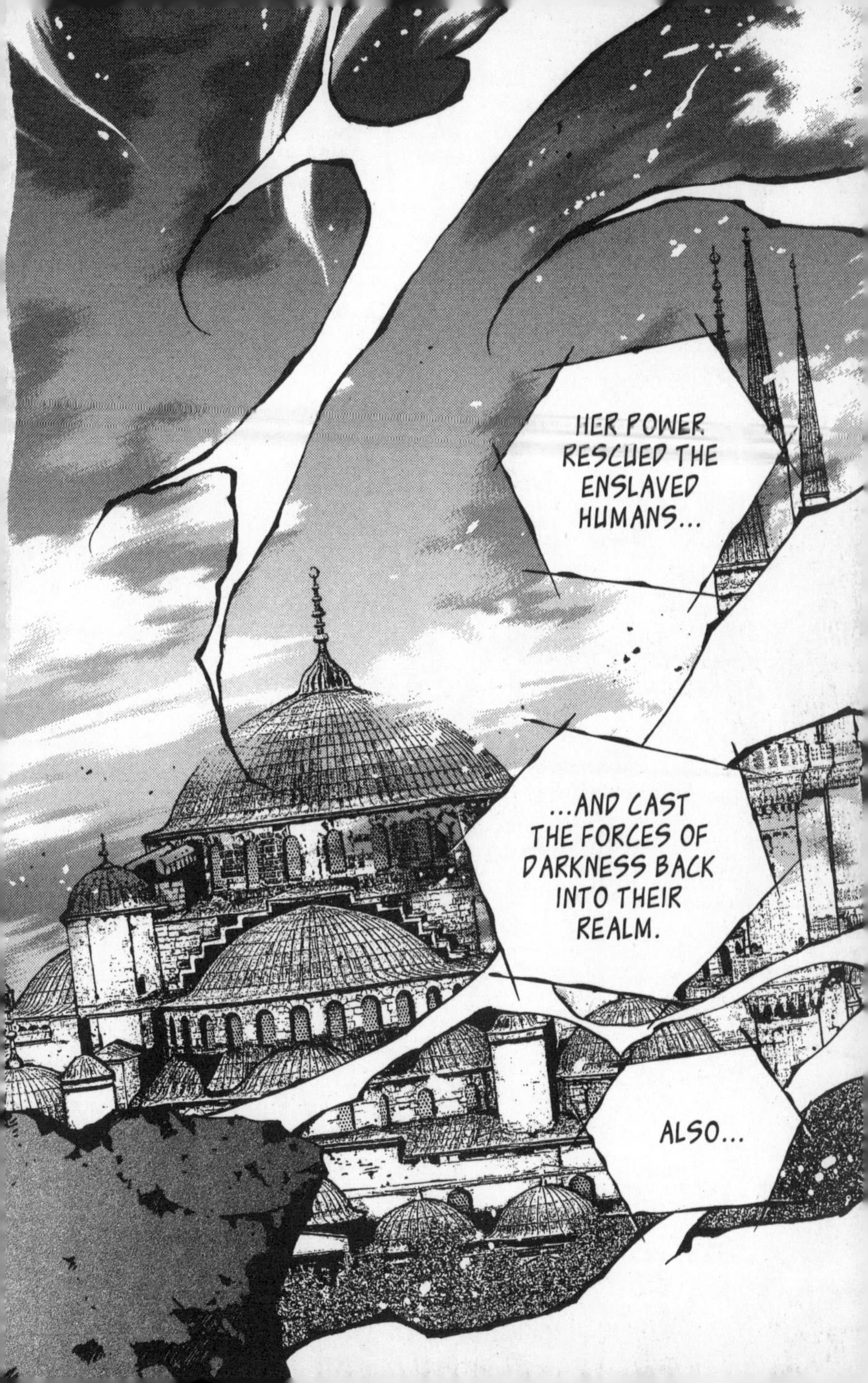
HER POWER RESCUED THE ENSLAVED HUMANS...
...AND CAST THE FORCES OF DARKNESS BACK INTO THEIR REALM.
ALSO...

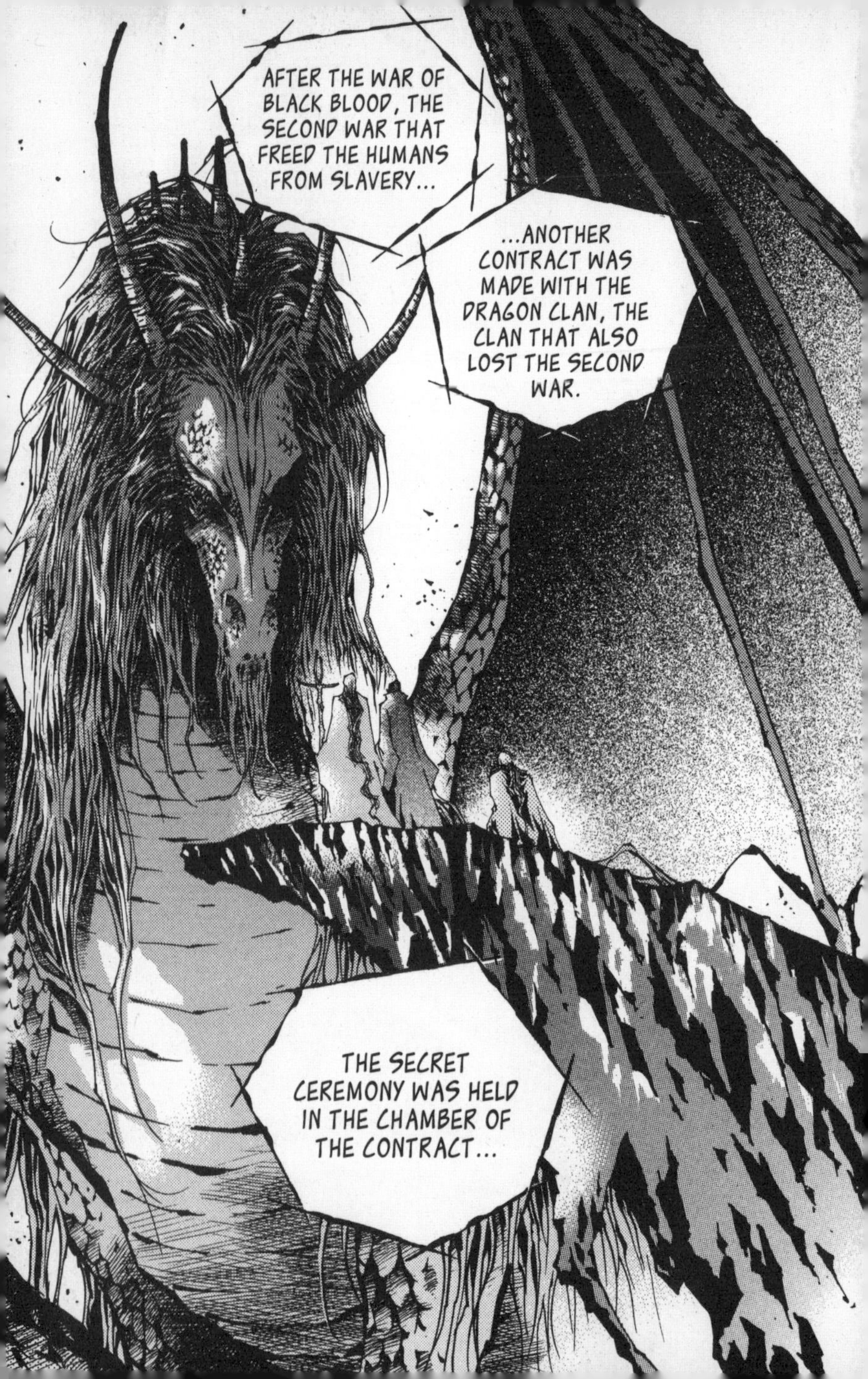
AFTER THE WAR OF BLACK BLOOD, THE SECOND WAR THAT FREED THE HUMANS FROM SLAVERY...
...ANOTHER CONTRACT WAS MADE WITH THE DRAGON CLAN, THE CLAN THAT ALSO LOST THE SECOND WAR.
THE SECRET CEREMONY WAS HELD IN THE CHAMBER OF THE CONTRACT...

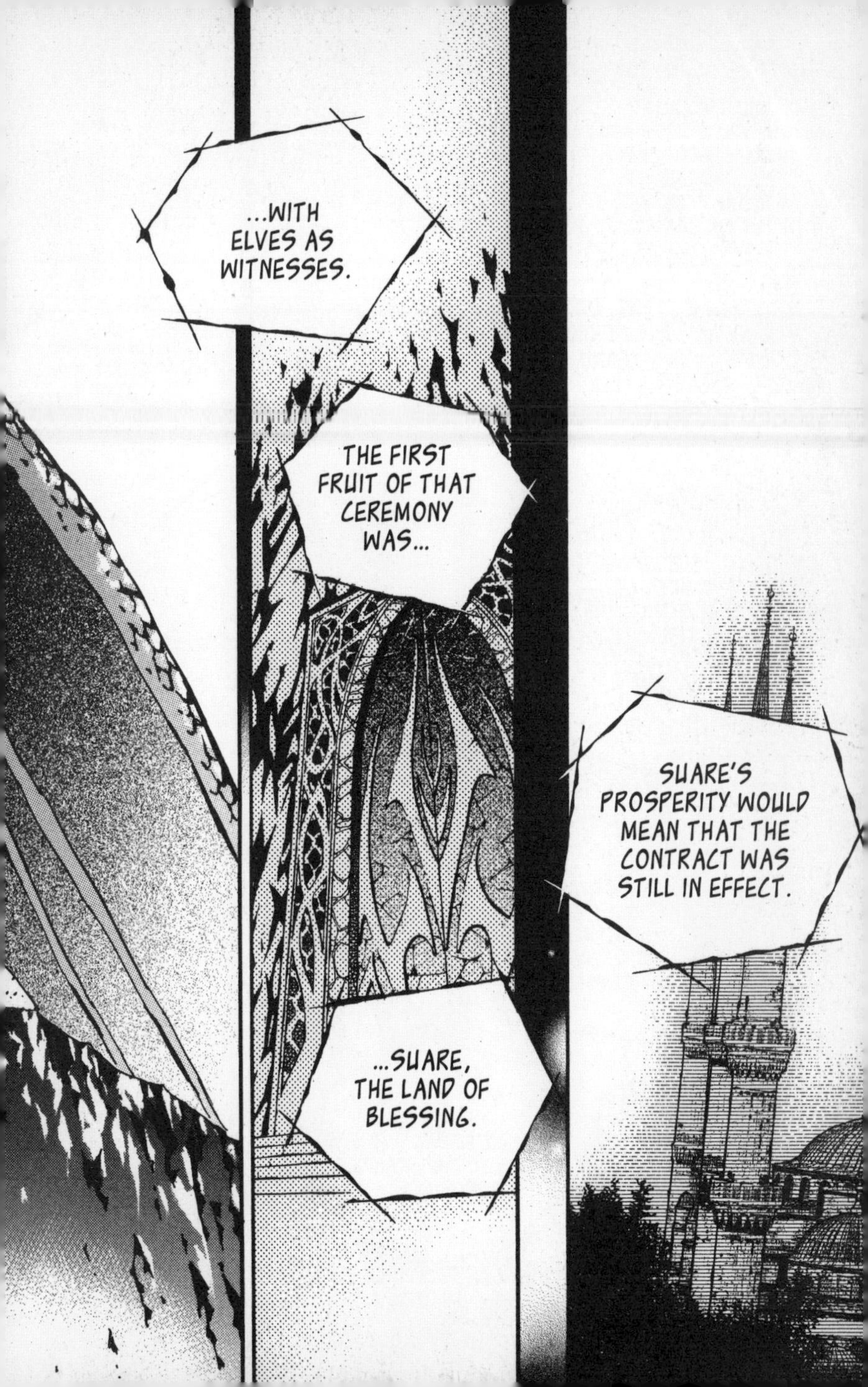
...WITH ELVES AS WITNESSES.
THE FIRST FRUIT OF THAT CEREMONY WAS...
...SUARE, THE LAND OF BLESSING.
SUARE'S PROSPERITY WOULD MEAN THAT THE CONTRACT WAS STILL IN EFFECT.

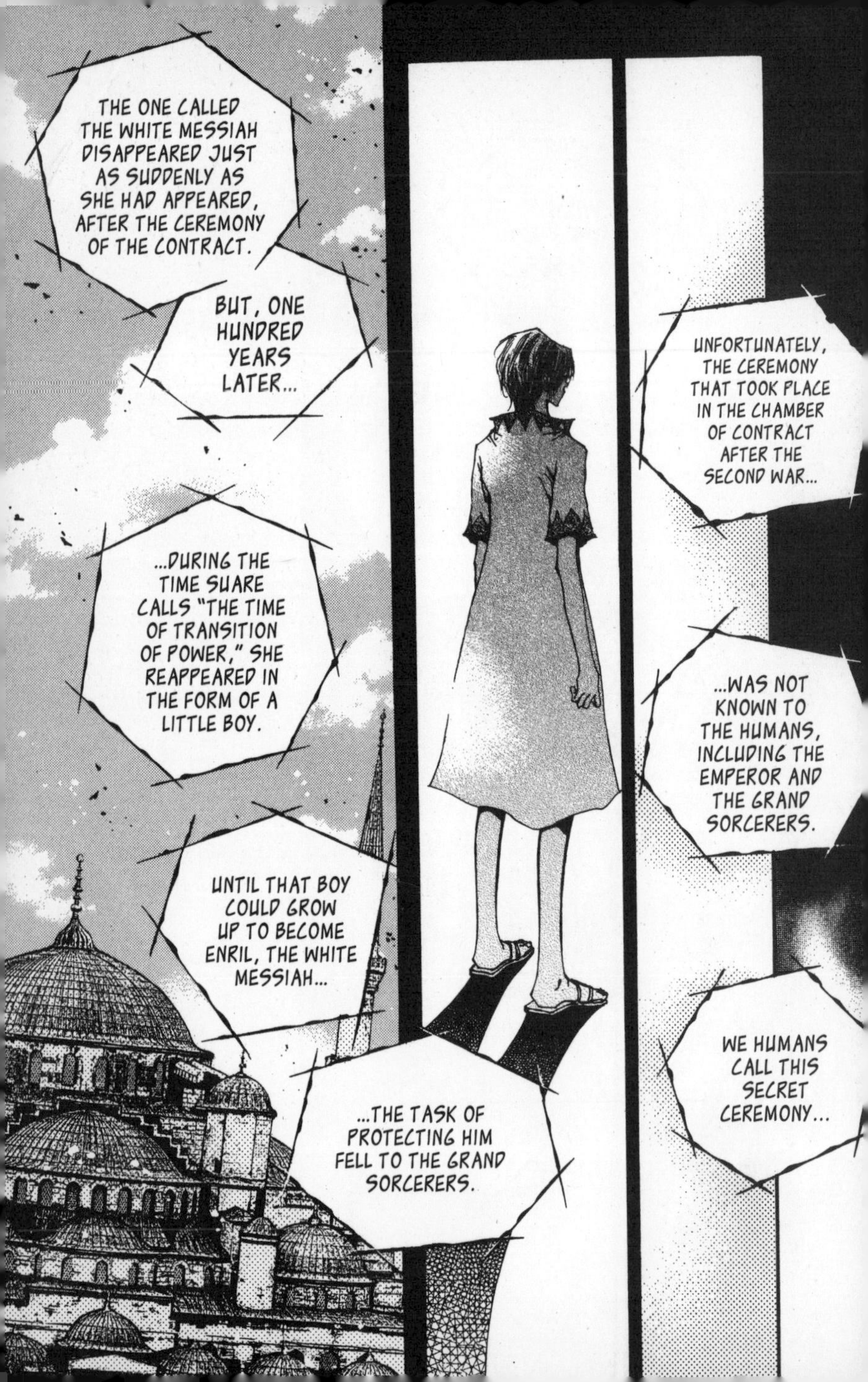
THE ONE CALLED THE WHITE MESSIAH DISAPPEARED JUST AS SUDDENLY AS SHE HAD APPEARED, AFTER THE CEREMONY OF THE CONTRACT.
BUT, ONE HUNDRED YEARS LATER...
...DURING THE TIME SUARE CALLS "THE TIME OF TRANSITION OF POWER," SHE REAPPEARED IN THE FORM OF A LITTLE BOY.
UNTIL THAT BOY COULD GROW UP TO BECOME ENRIL, THE WHITE MESSIAH...
...THE TASK OF PROTECTING HIM FELL TO THE GRAND SORCERERS.
UNFORTUNATELY, THE CEREMONY THAT TOOK PLACE IN THE CHAMBER OF CONTRACT AFTER THE SECOND WAR...
...WAS NOT KNOWN TO THE HUMANS, INCLUDING THE EMPEROR AND THE GRAND SORCERERS.
WE HUMANS CALL THIS SECRET CEREMONY...

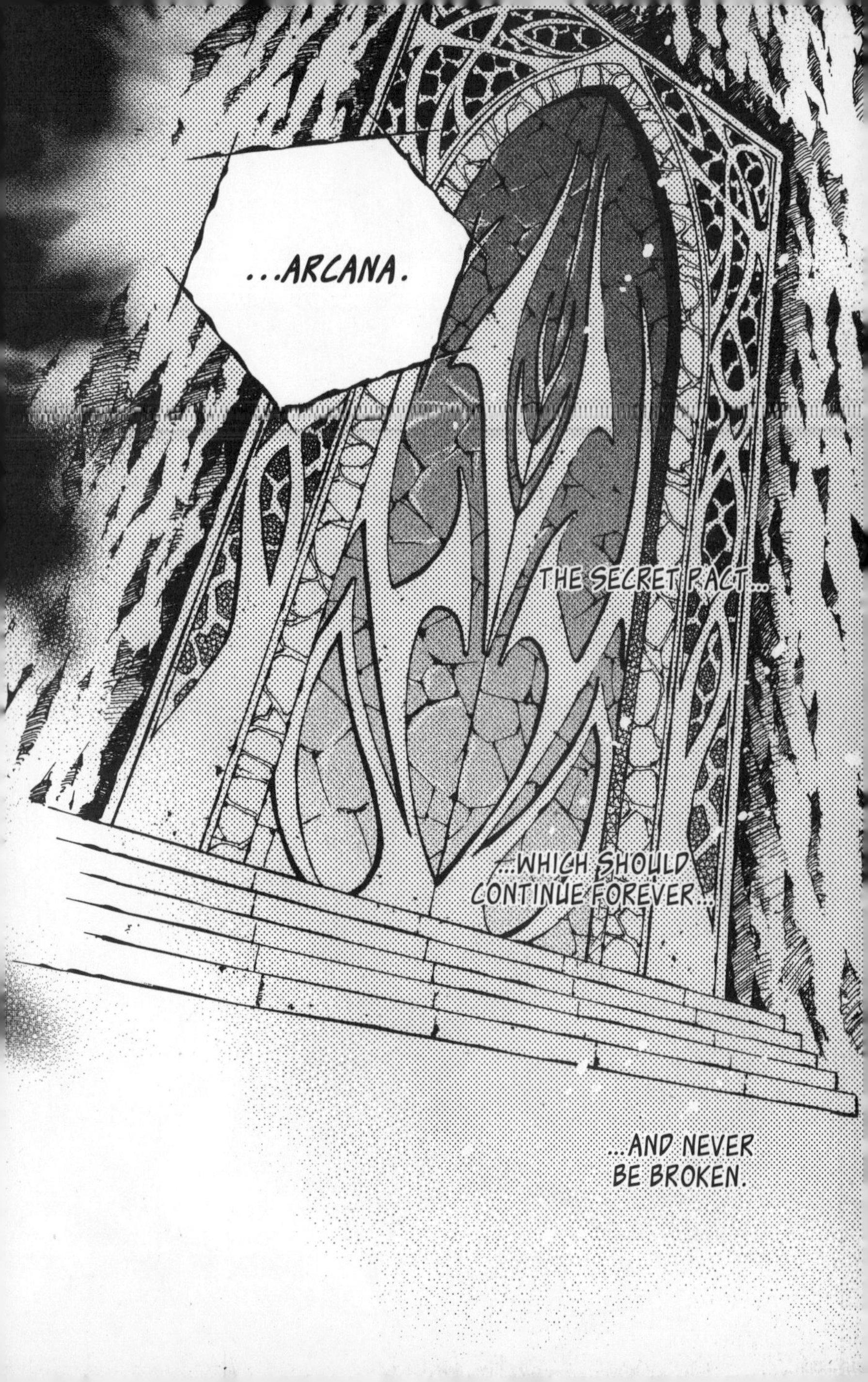
...ARCANA.
THE SECRET PACT...
...WHICH SHOULD CONTINUE FOREVER...
...AND NEVER BE BROKEN.

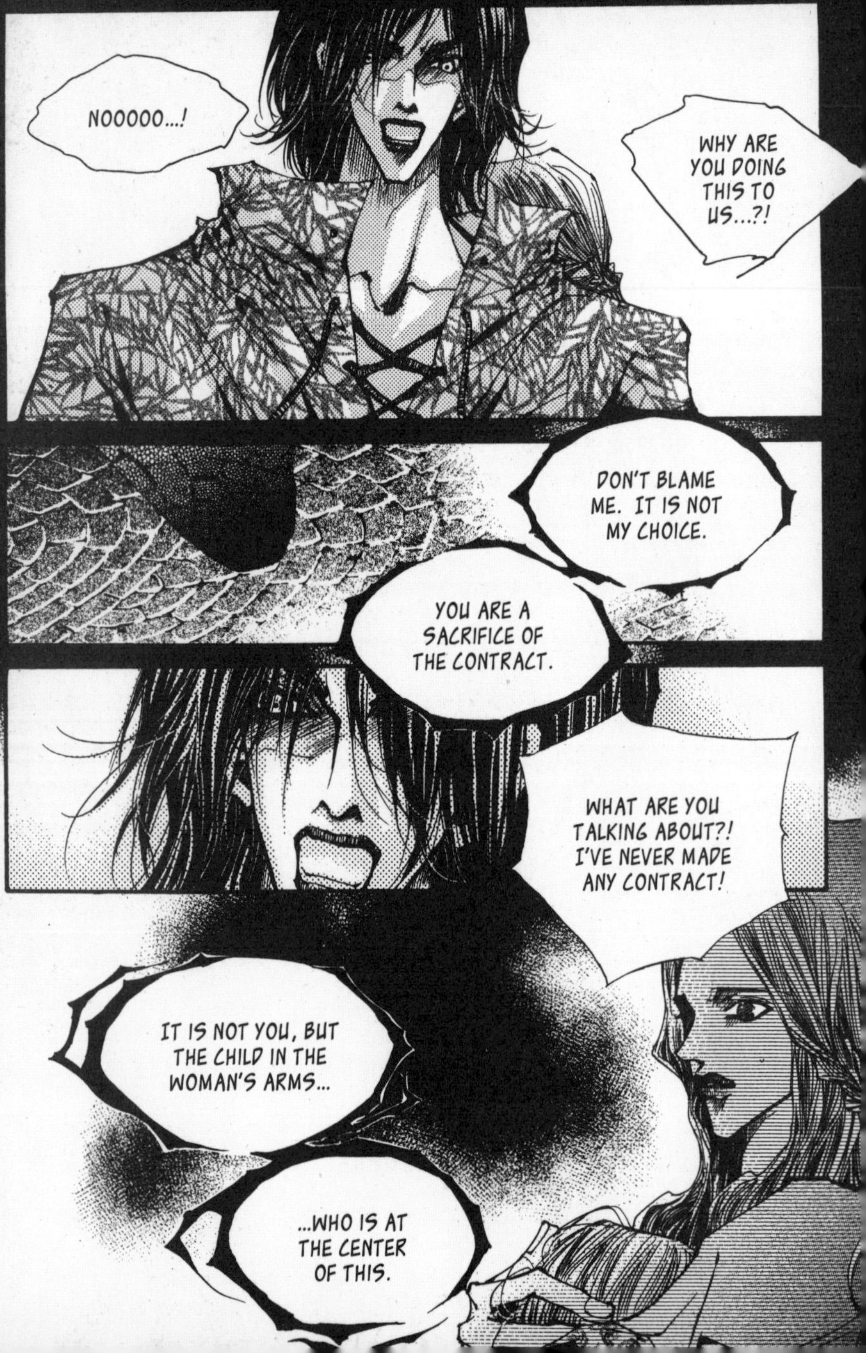
NOOOOO...!
WHY ARE YOU DOING THIS TO US...?!
DON'T BLAME ME. IT IS NOT MY CHOICE.
YOU ARE A SACRIFICE OF THE CONTRACT.
WHAT ARE YOU TALKING ABOUT?! I'VE NEVER MADE ANY CONTRACT!
IT IS NOT YOU, BUT THE CHILD IN THE WOMAN'S ARMS...
...WHO IS AT THE CENTER OF THIS.

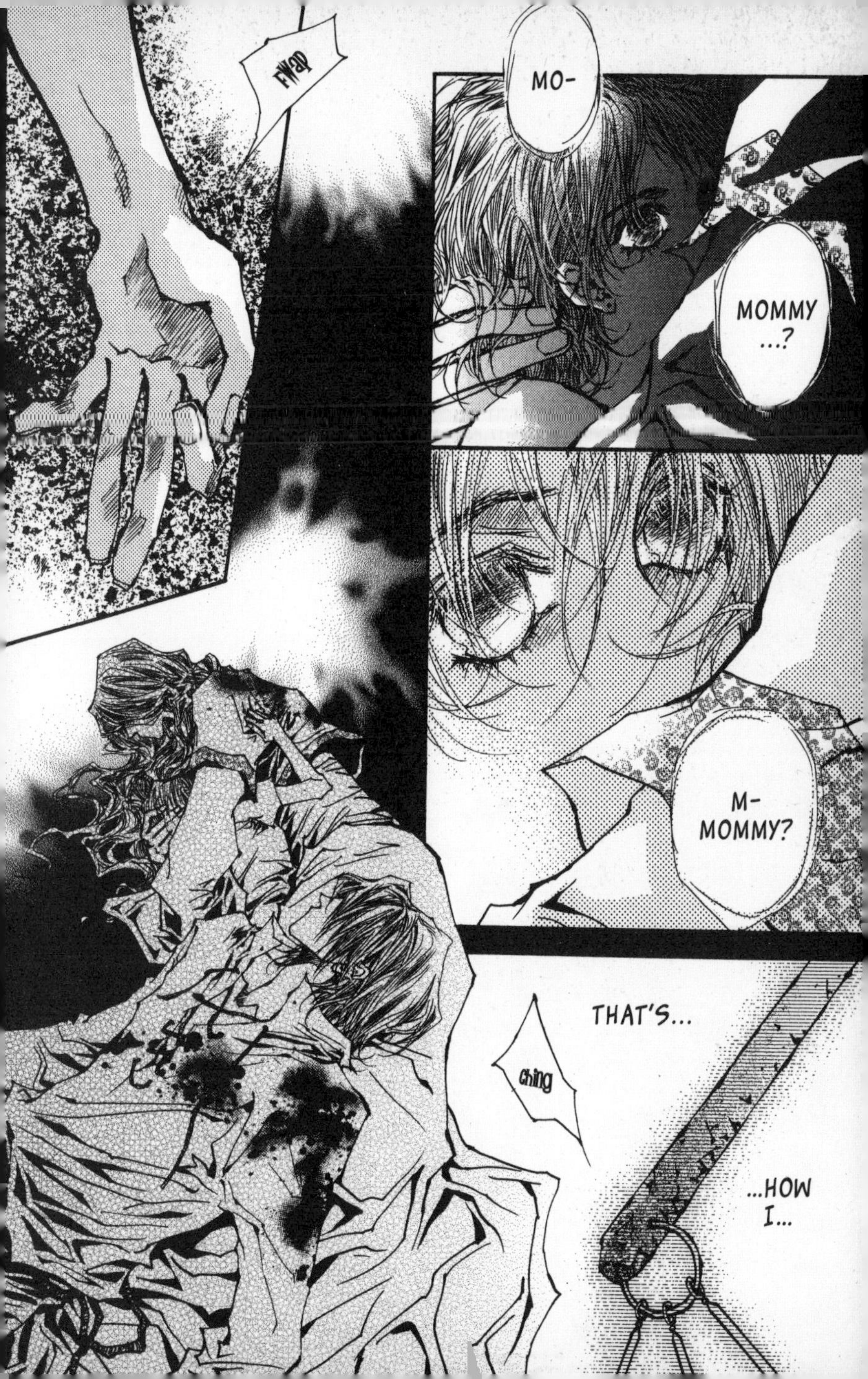
FWAP
MO-
MOMMY ...?
M-MOMMY?
ching
THAT'S...
...HOW I...

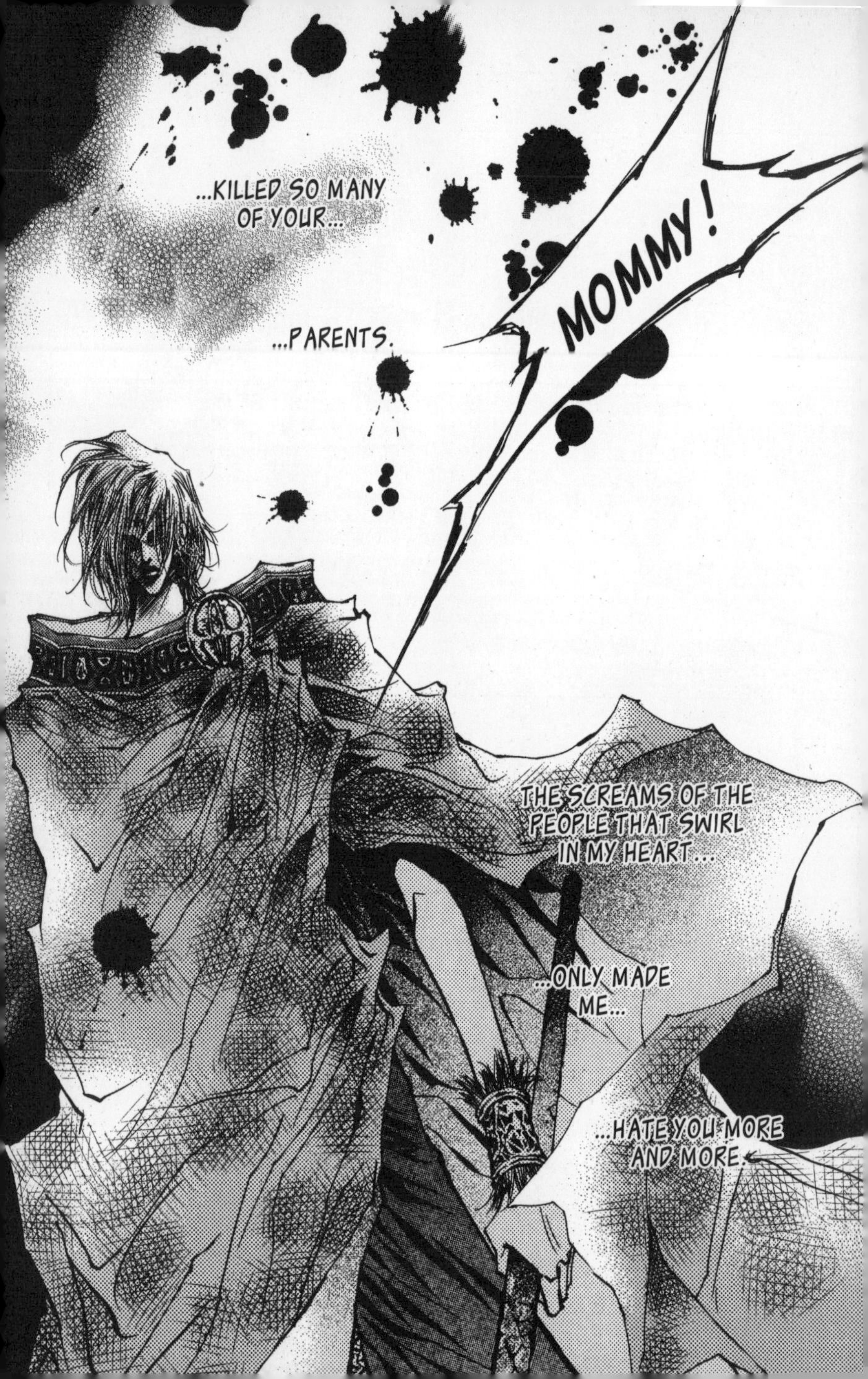
...KILLED SO MANY OF YOUR...
...PARENTS.
MOMMY!
THE SCREAMS OF THE PEOPLE THAT SWIRL IN MY HEART...
...ONLY MADE ME...
...HATE YOU MORE AND MORE.

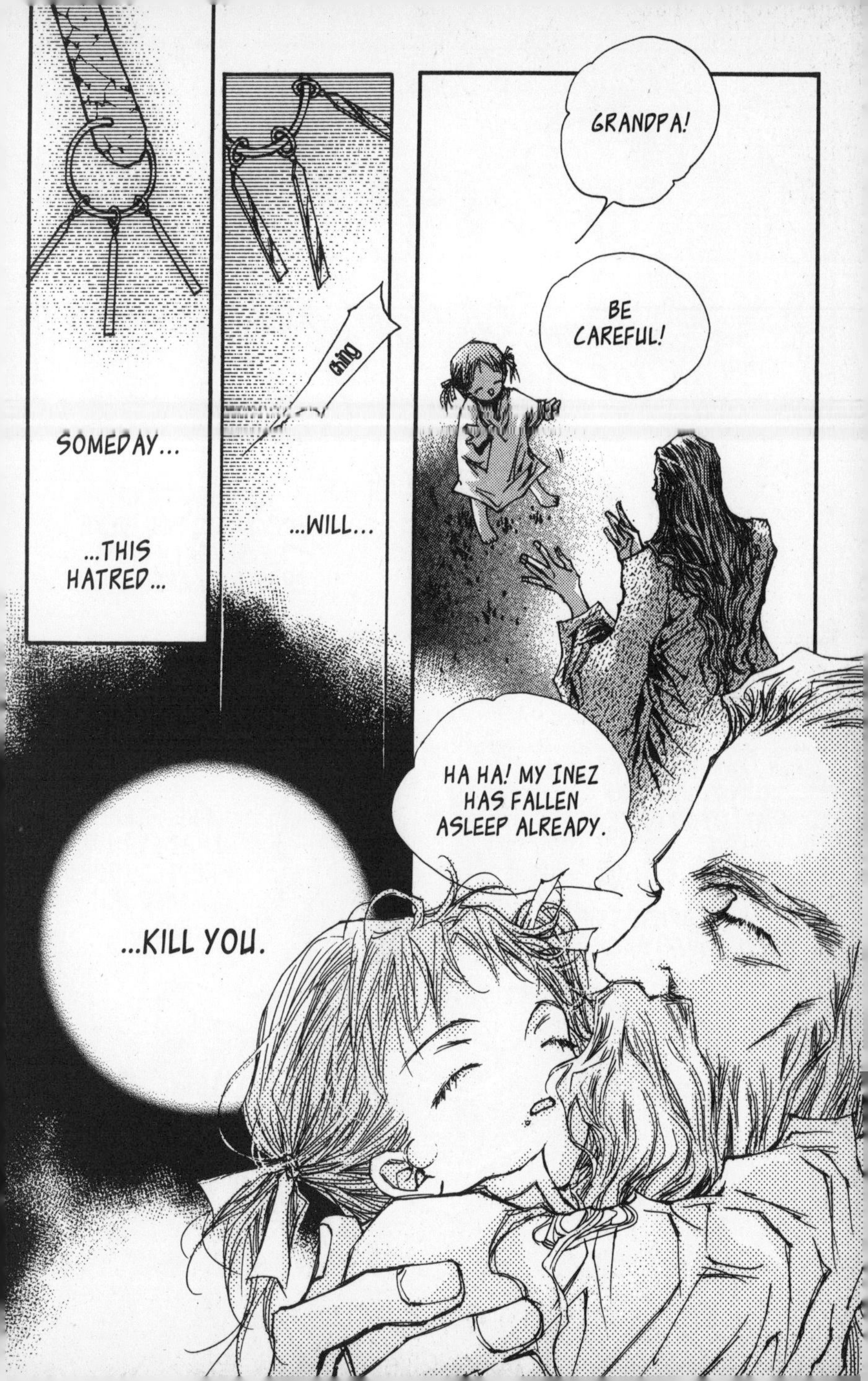
SOMEDAY...
...THIS HATRED...
ching
...WILL...
GRANDPA!
BE CAREFUL!
...KILL YOU.
HA HA! MY INEZ HAS FALLEN ASLEEP ALREADY.

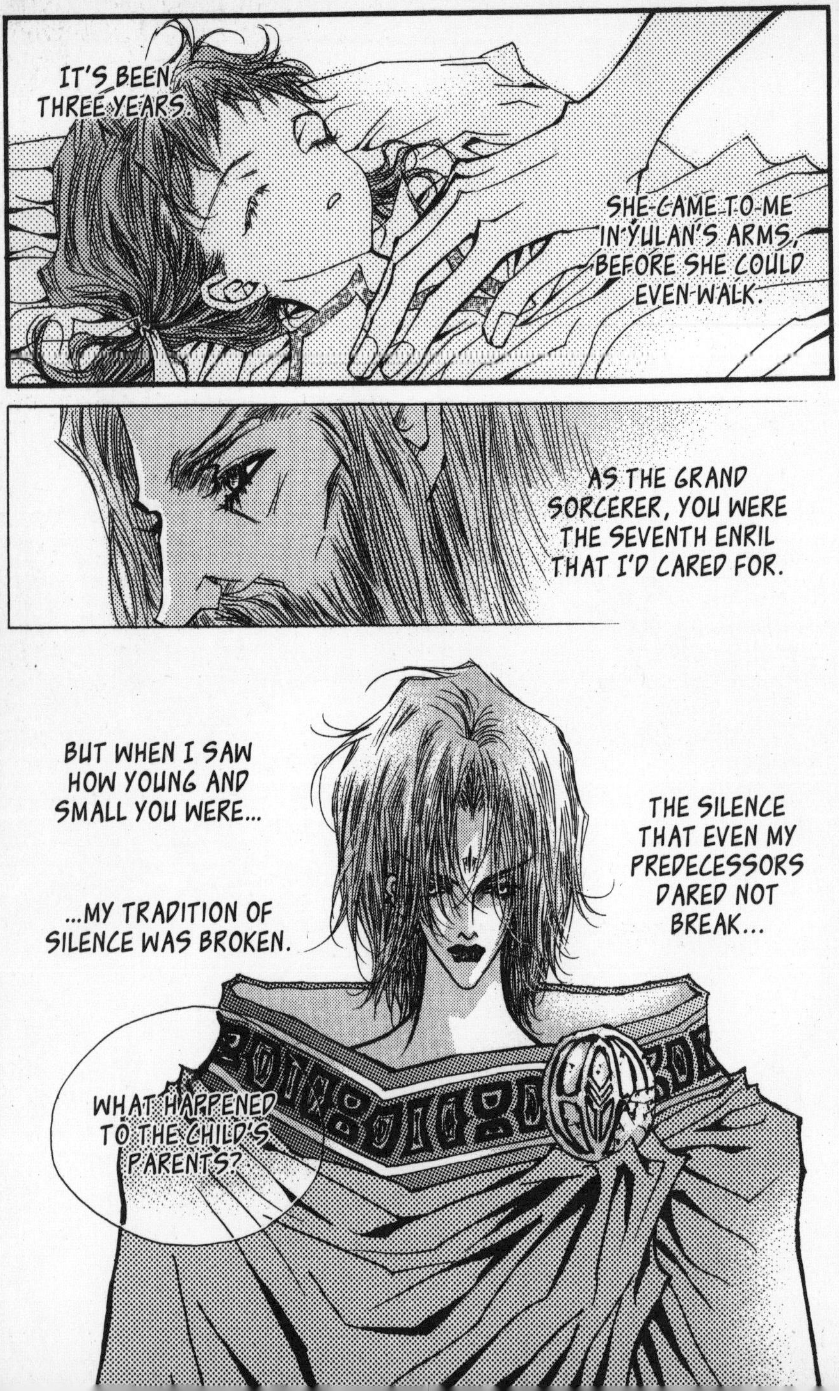
IT'S BEEN THREE YEARS.
SHE CAME TO ME IN YULAN'S ARMS, BEFORE SHE COULD EVEN WALK.
AS THE GRAND SORCERER, YOU WERE THE SEVENTH ENRIL THAT I'D CARED FOR.
BUT WHEN I SAW HOW YOUNG AND SMALL YOU WERE...
...MY TRADITION OF SILENCE WAS BROKEN.
THE SILENCE THAT EVEN MY PREDECESSORS DARED NOT BREAK...
WHAT HAPPENED TO THE CHILD'S PARENTS?

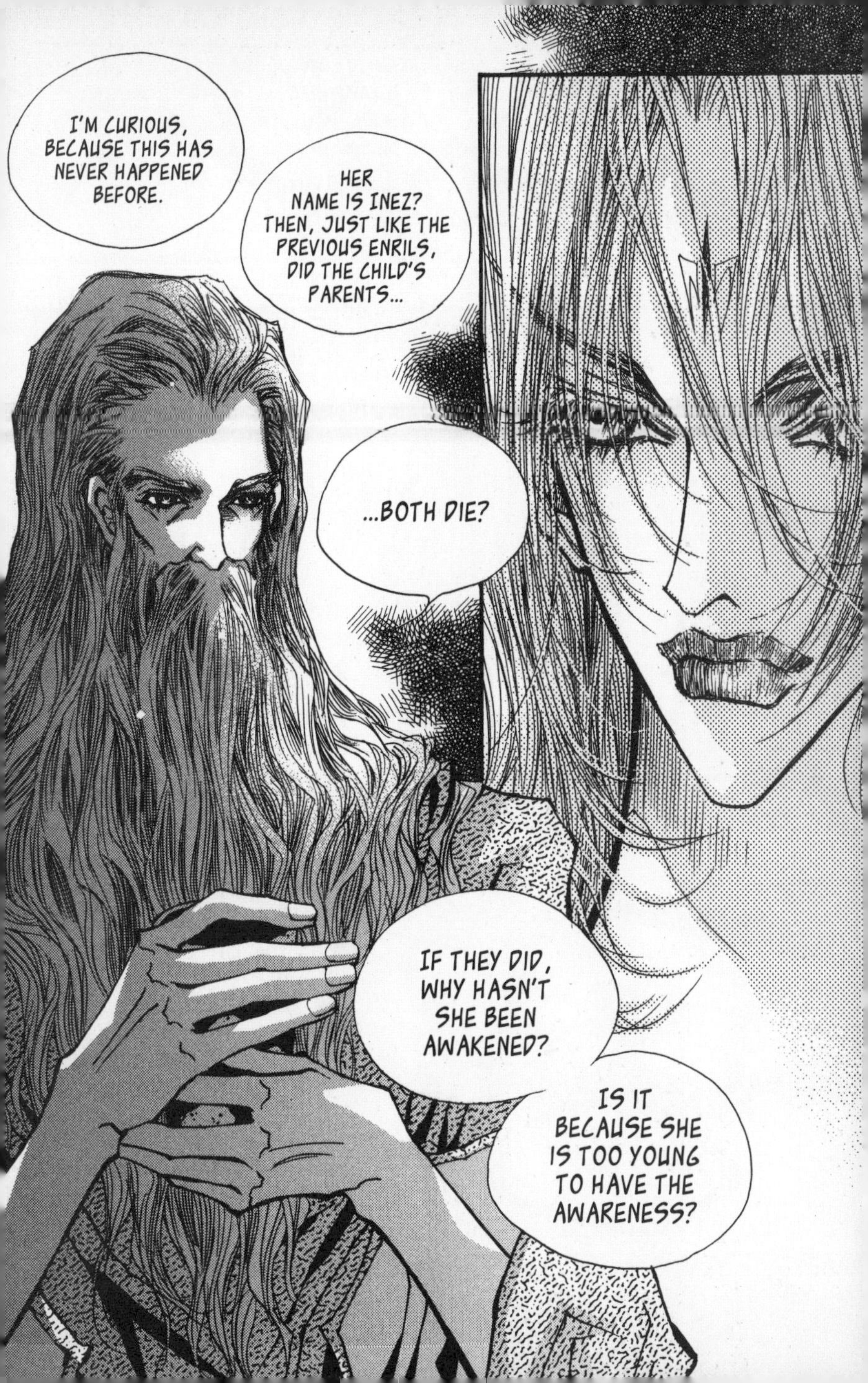
I'M CURIOUS, BECAUSE THIS HAS NEVER HAPPENED BEFORE.
HER NAME IS INEZ? THEN, JUST LIKE THE PREVIOUS ENRILS, DID THE CHILD'S PARENTS...
...BOTH DIE?
IF THEY DID, WHY HASN'T SHE BEEN AWAKENED?
IS IT BECAUSE SHE IS TOO YOUNG TO HAVE THE AWARENESS?

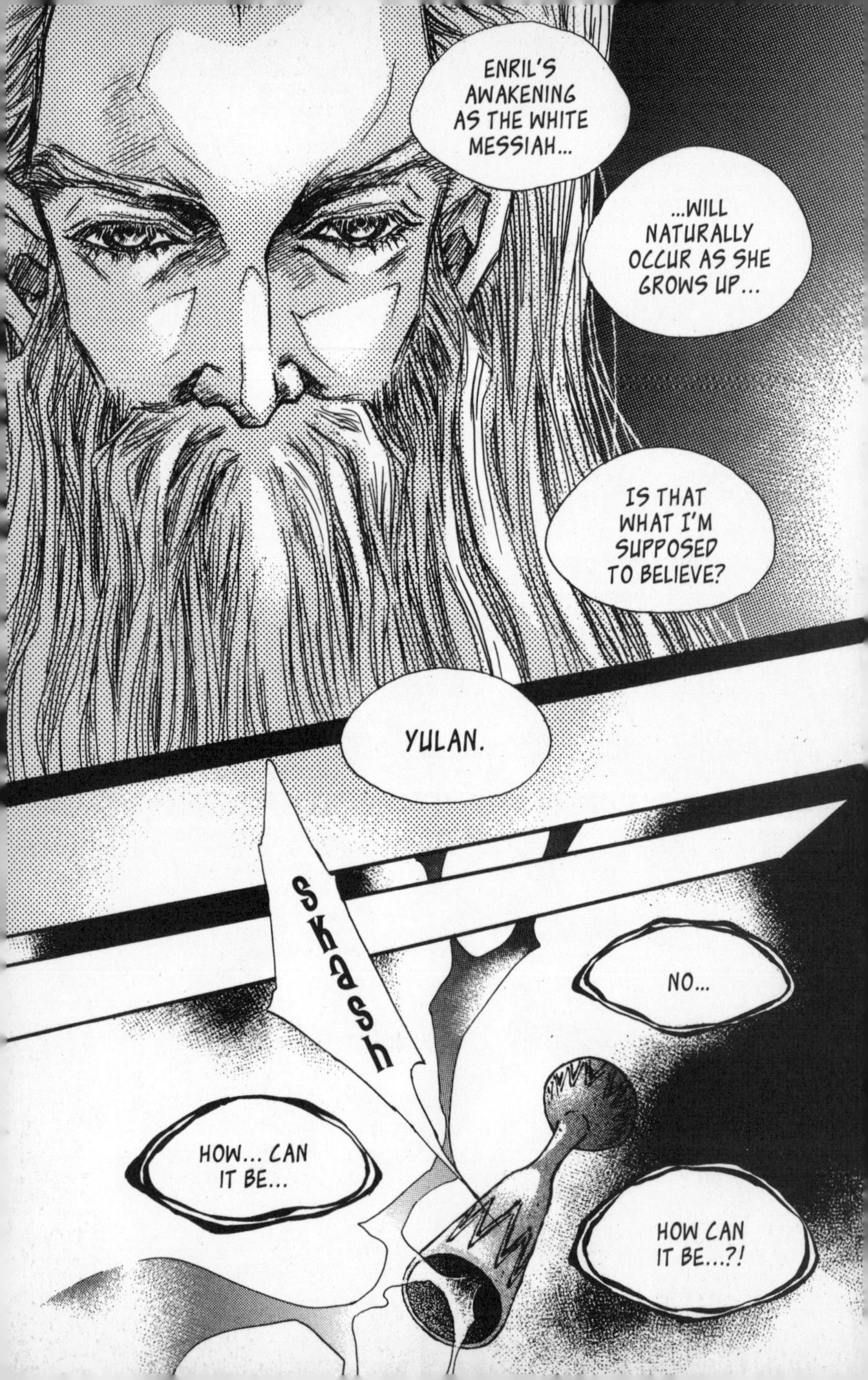

ENRIL'S AWAKENING AS THE WHITE MESSIAH...
...WILL NATURALLY OCCUR AS SHE GROWS UP...
IS THAT WHAT I'M SUPPOSED TO BELIEVE?
YULAN.
SKASH
NO...
HOW... CAN IT BE...
HOW CAN IT BE...?!

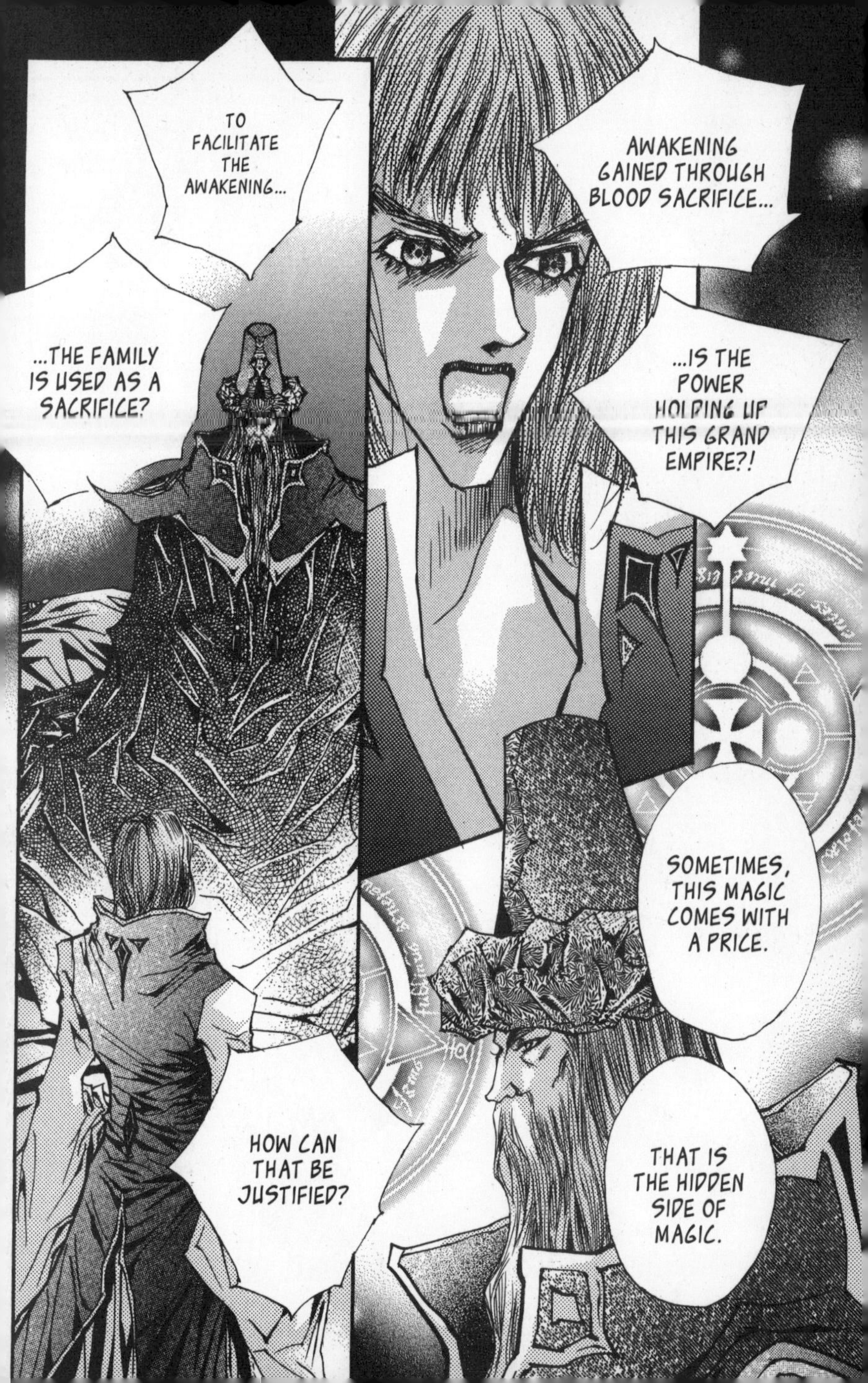
TO FACILITATE THE AWAKENING...
...THE FAMILY IS USED AS A SACRIFICE?
HOW CAN THAT BE JUSTIFIED?
AWAKENING GAINED THROUGH BLOOD SACRIFICE...
...IS THE POWER HOLDING UP THIS GRAND EMPIRE?!
SOMETIMES, THIS MAGIC COMES WITH A PRICE.
THAT IS THE HIDDEN SIDE OF MAGIC.

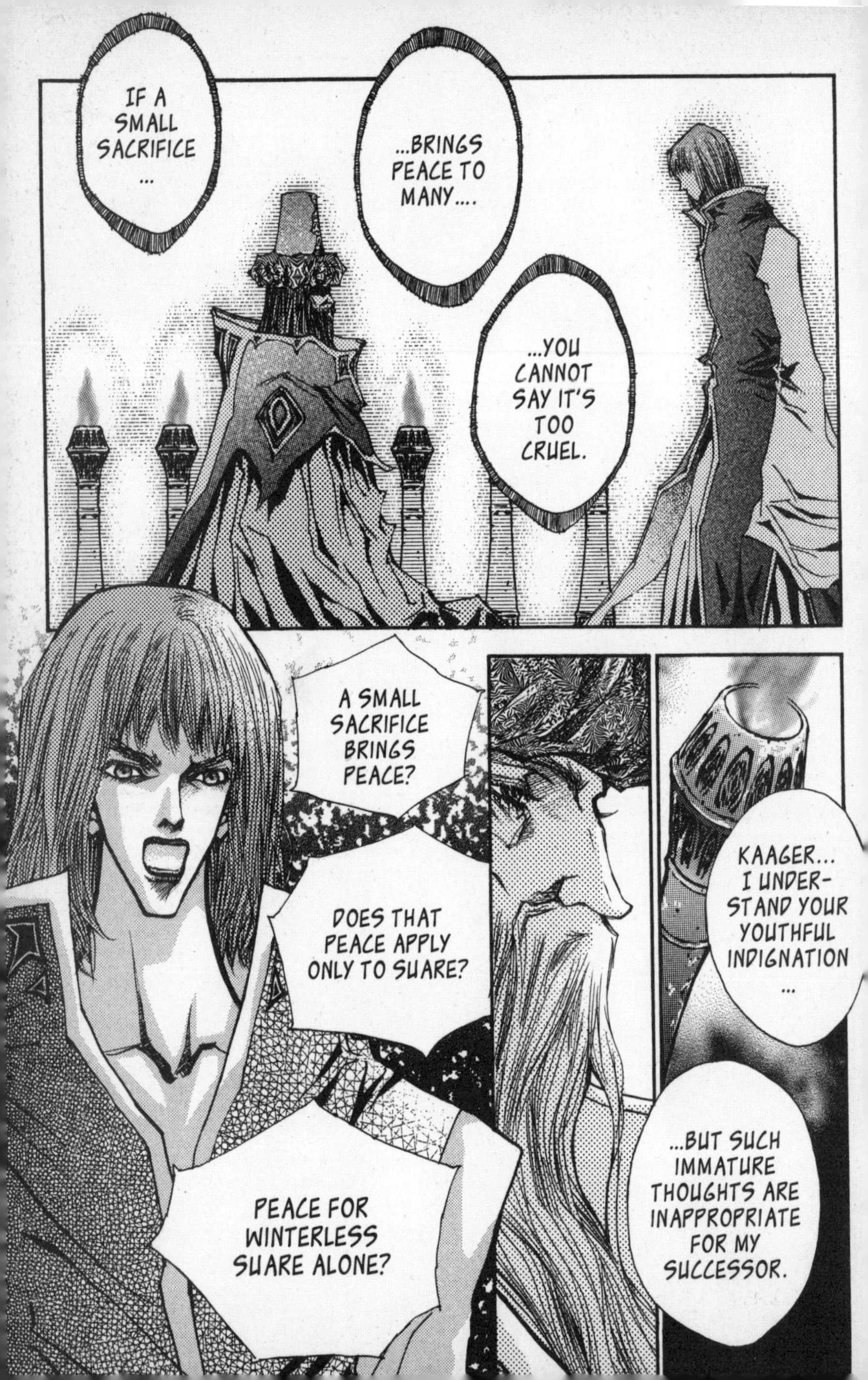
IF A SMALL SACRIFICE ...
...BRINGS PEACE TO MANY....
...YOU CANNOT SAY IT'S TOO CRUEL.
A SMALL SACRIFICE BRINGS PEACE?
DOES THAT PEACE APPLY ONLY TO SUARE?
PEACE FOR WINTERLESS SUARE ALONE?
KAAGER... I UNDER-STAND YOUR YOUTHFUL INDIGNATION ...
...BUT SUCH IMMATURE THOUGHTS ARE INAPPROPRIATE FOR MY SUCCESSOR.

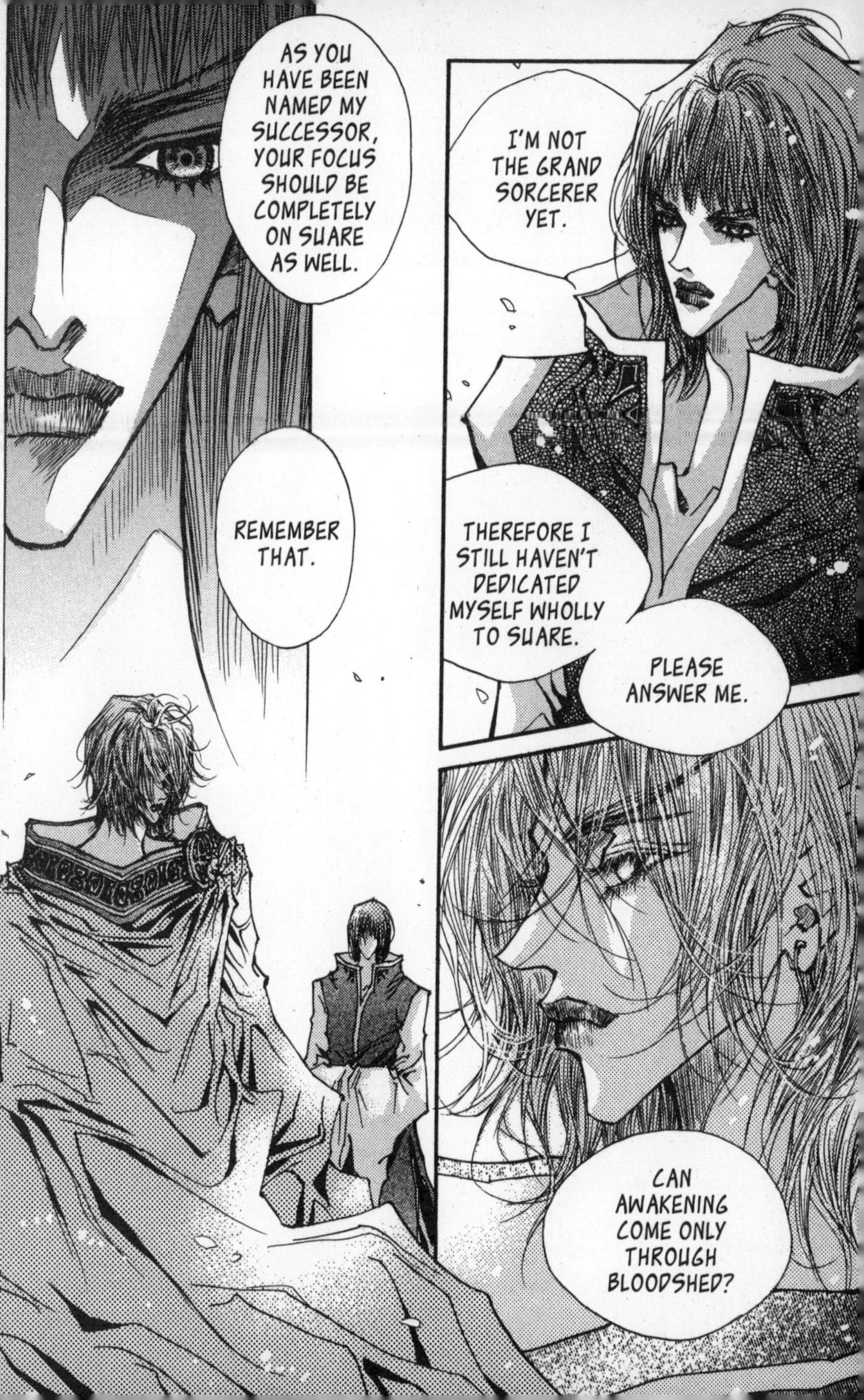
AS YOU HAVE BEEN NAMED MY SUCCESSOR, YOUR FOCUS SHOULD BE COMPLETELY ON SUARE AS WELL.
REMEMBER THAT.
I'M NOT THE GRAND SORCERER YET.
THEREFORE I STILL HAVEN'T DEDICATED MYSELF WHOLLY TO SUARE.
PLEASE ANSWER ME.
CAN AWAKENING COME ONLY THROUGH BLOODSHED?

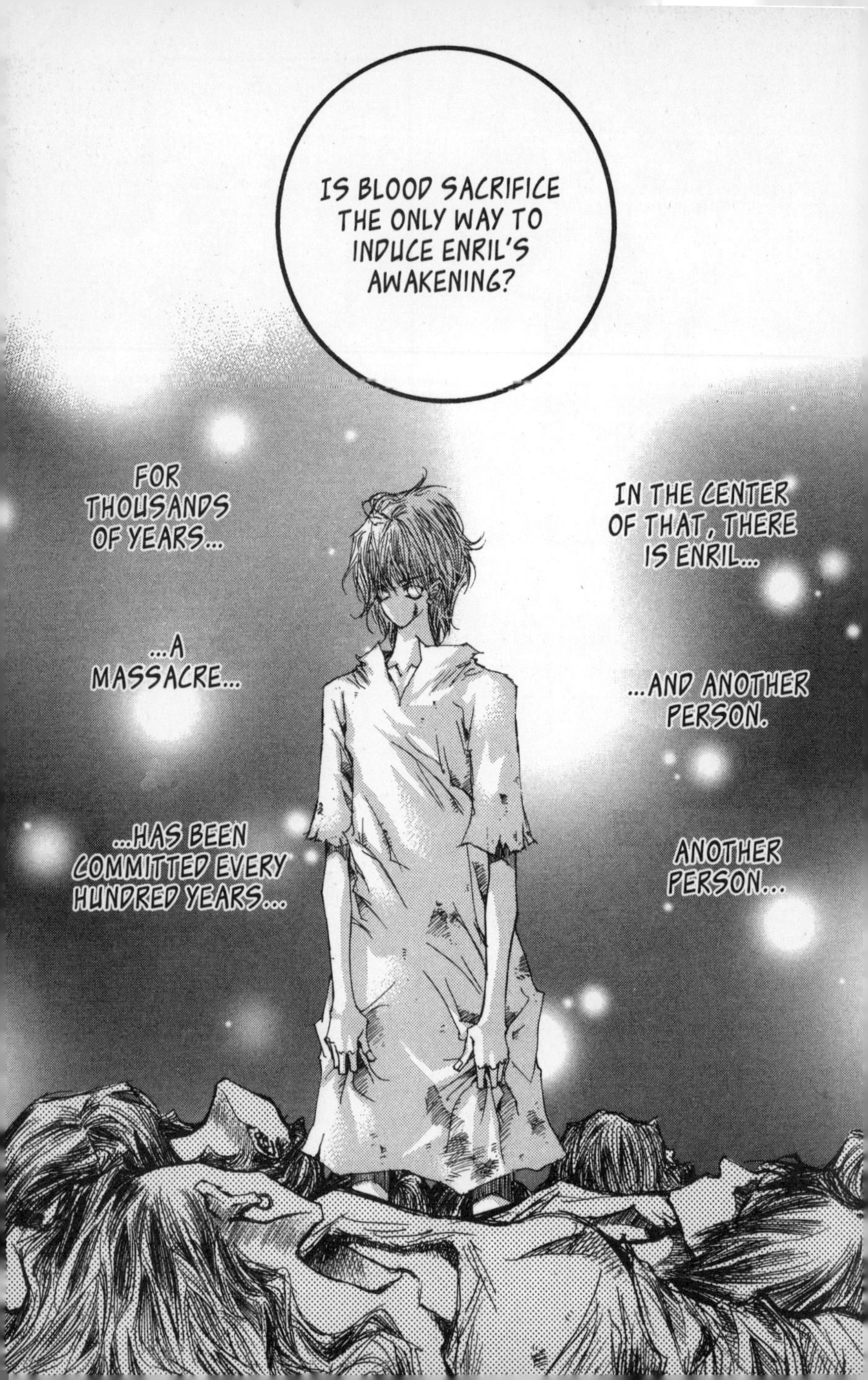
IS BLOOD SACRIFICE THE ONLY WAY TO INDUCE ENRIL'S AWAKENING?
IN THE CENTER OF THAT, THERE IS ENRIL...
...AND ANOTHER PERSON.
ANOTHER PERSON...
FOR THOUSANDS OF YEARS...
...A MASSACRE...
...HAS BEEN COMMITTED EVERY HUNDRED YEARS...

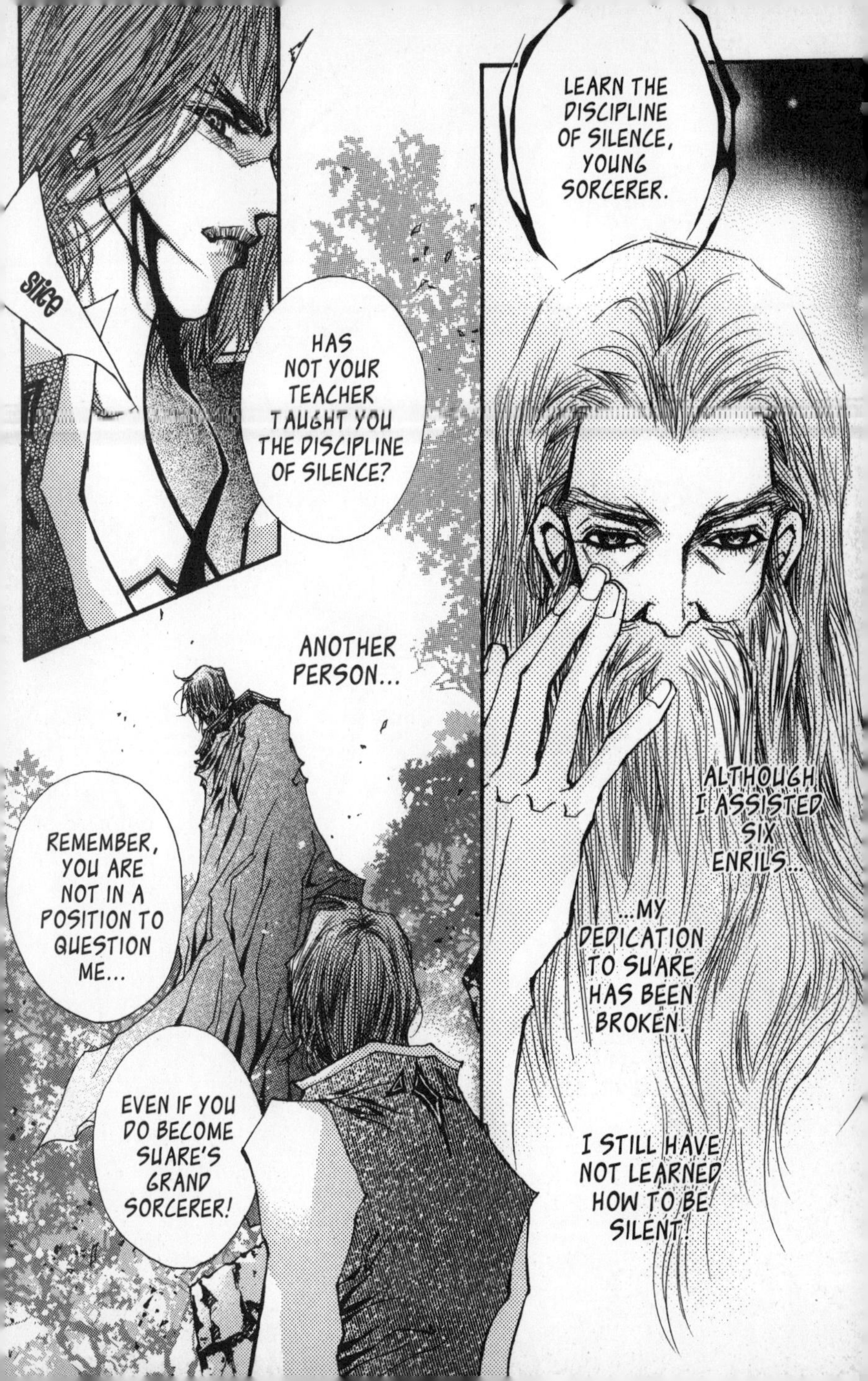
Slice
HAS NOT YOUR TEACHER TAUGHT YOU THE DISCIPLINE OF SILENCE?
ANOTHER PERSON...
REMEMBER, YOU ARE NOT IN A POSITION TO QUESTION ME...
EVEN IF YOU DO BECOME SUARE'S GRAND SORCERER!
LEARN THE DISCIPLINE OF SILENCE, YOUNG SORCERER.
ALTHOUGH I ASSISTED SIX ENRILS...
...MY DEDICATION TO SUARE HAS BEEN BROKEN!
I STILL HAVE NOT LEARNED HOW TO BE SILENT!

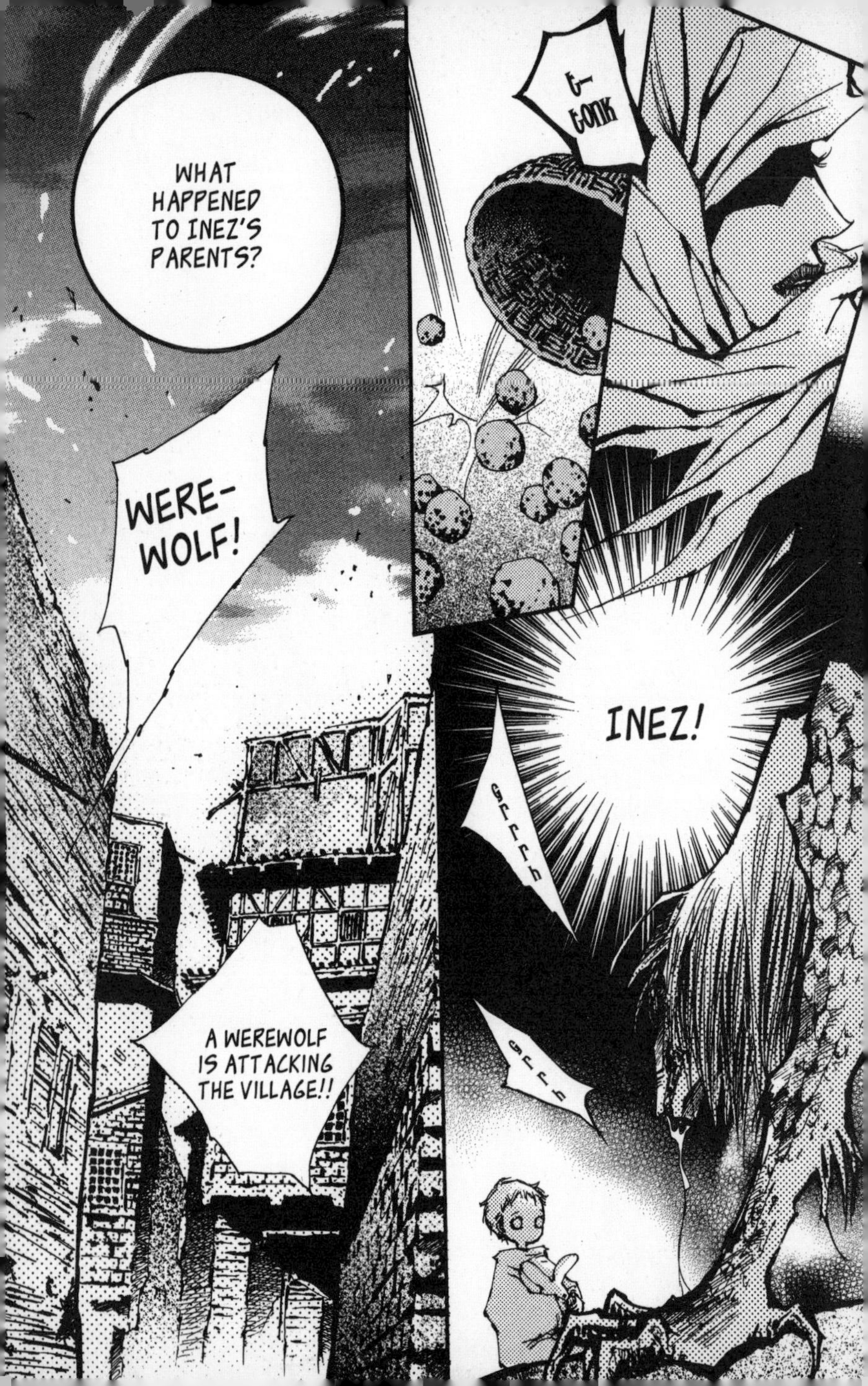

WHAT HAPPENED TO INEZ'S PARENTS?
WERE-WOLF!
A WEREWOLF IS ATTACKING THE VILLAGE!!
T-TONK
INEZ!
Grrrh
Grrh

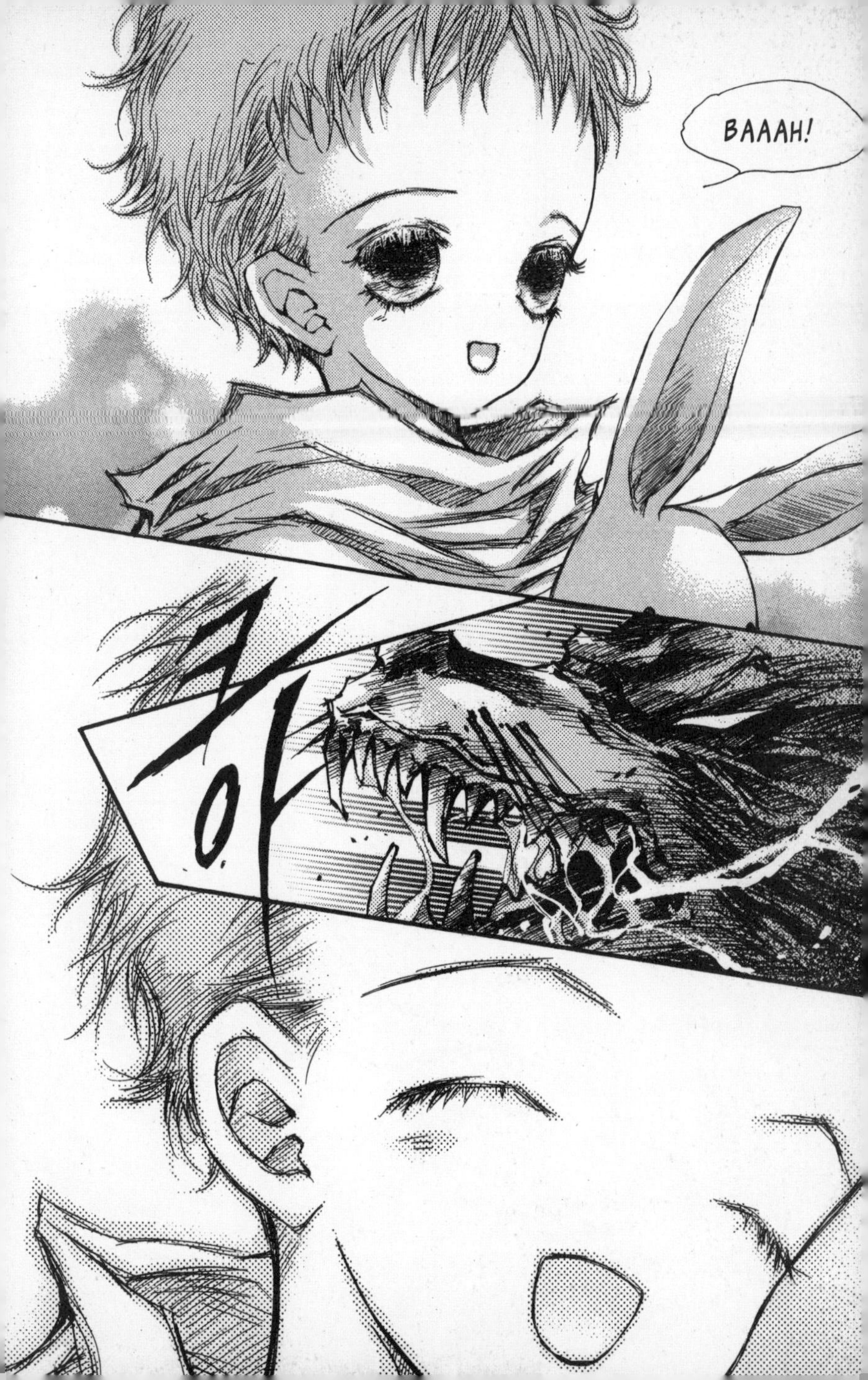
BAAAH!

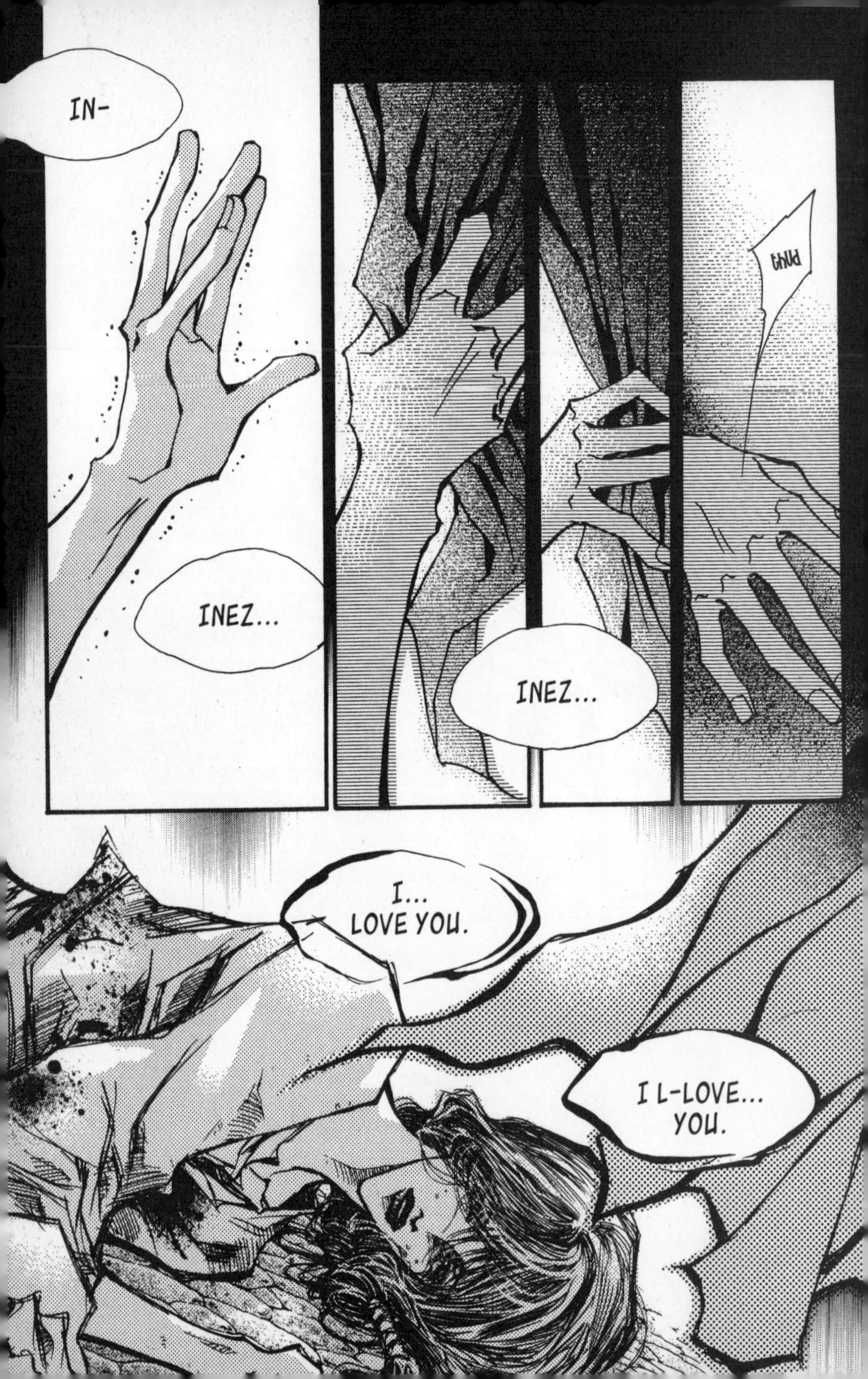
IN-
INEZ...
INEZ...
THUD
I... LOVE YOU.
I L-LOVE... YOU.

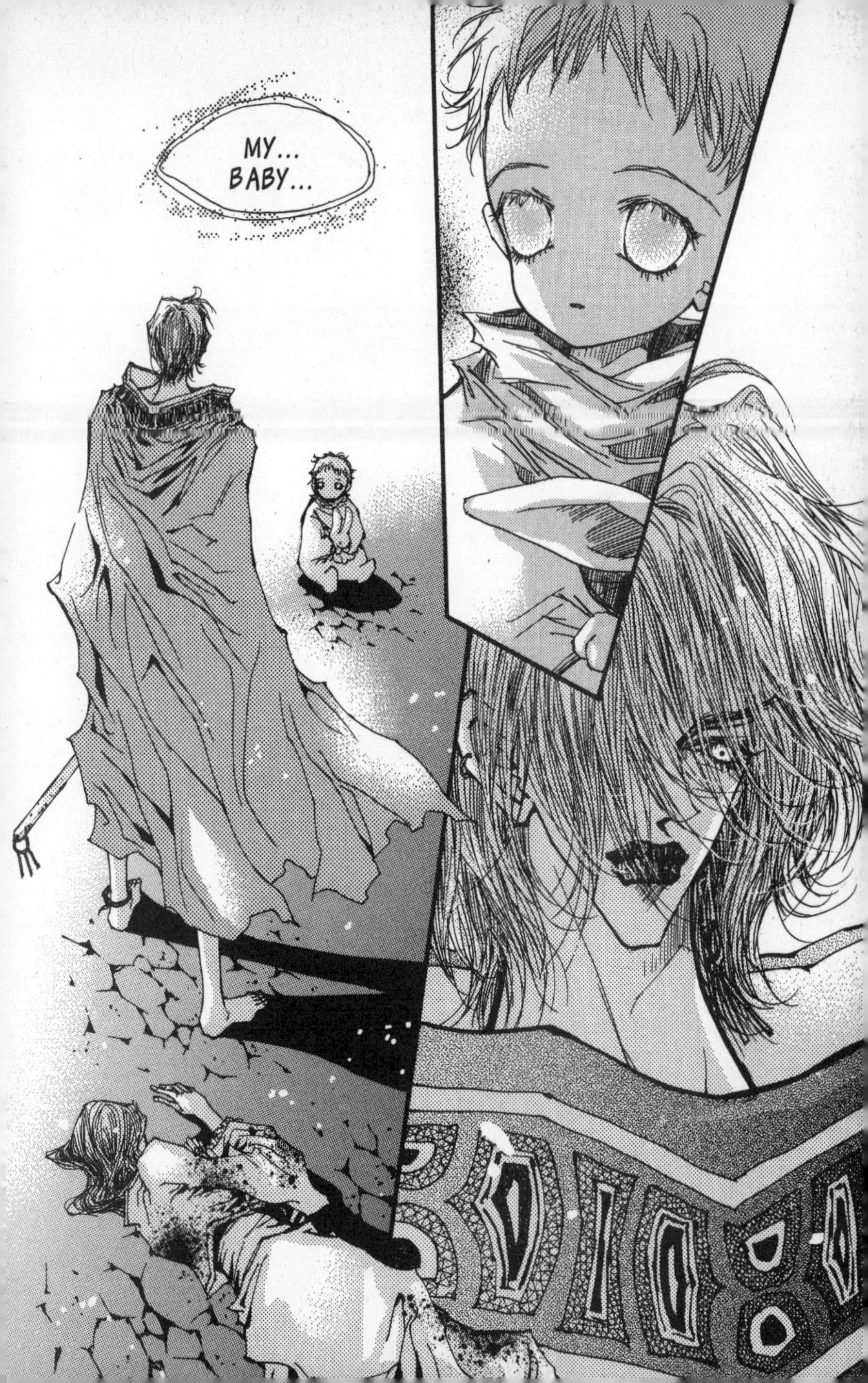
MY...
BABY...

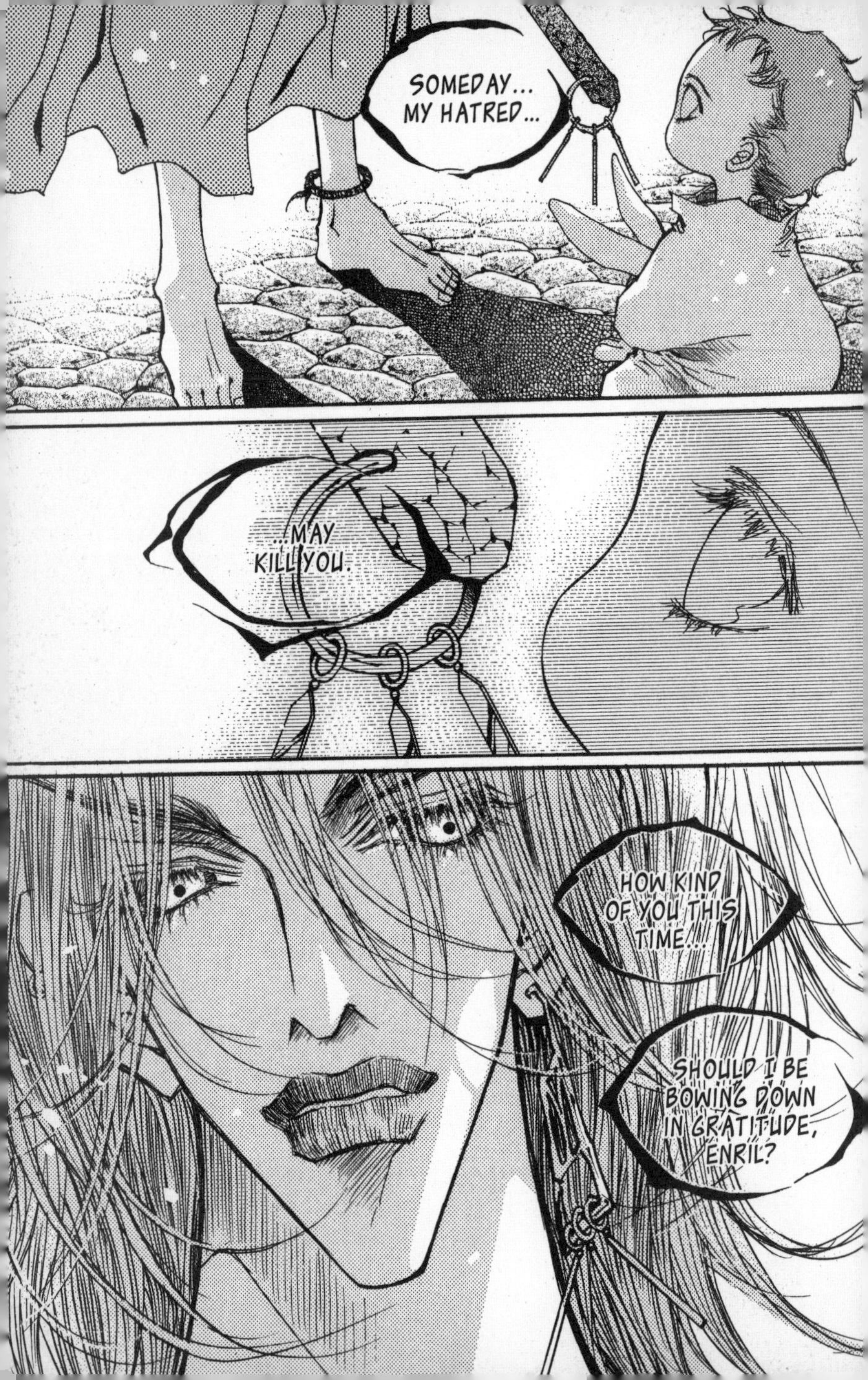
SOMEDAY... MY HATRED...
...MAY KILL YOU.
HOW KIND OF YOU THIS TIME...
SHOULD I BE BOWING DOWN IN GRATITUDE, ENRIL?

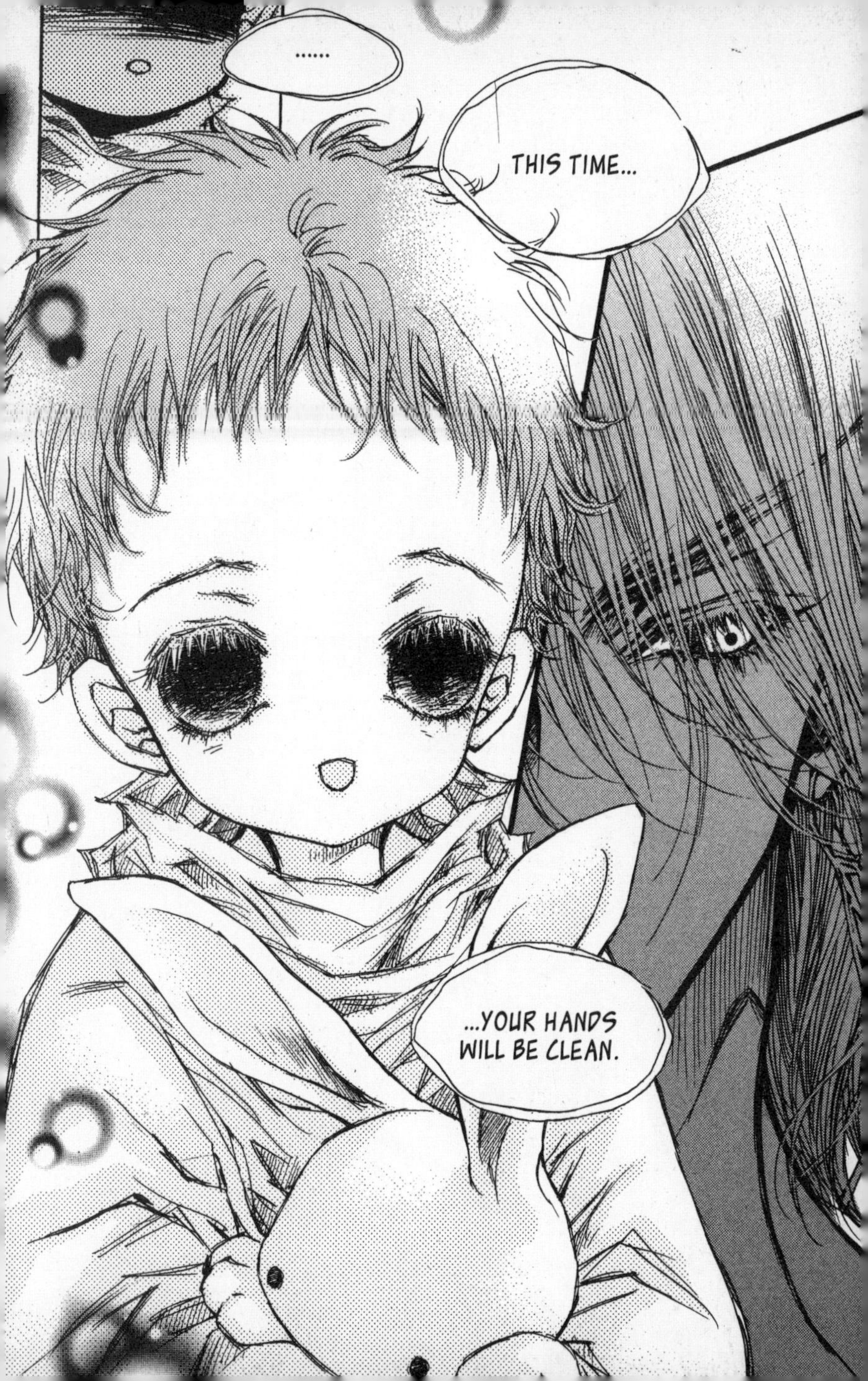
......
THIS TIME...
...YOUR HANDS WILL BE CLEAN.

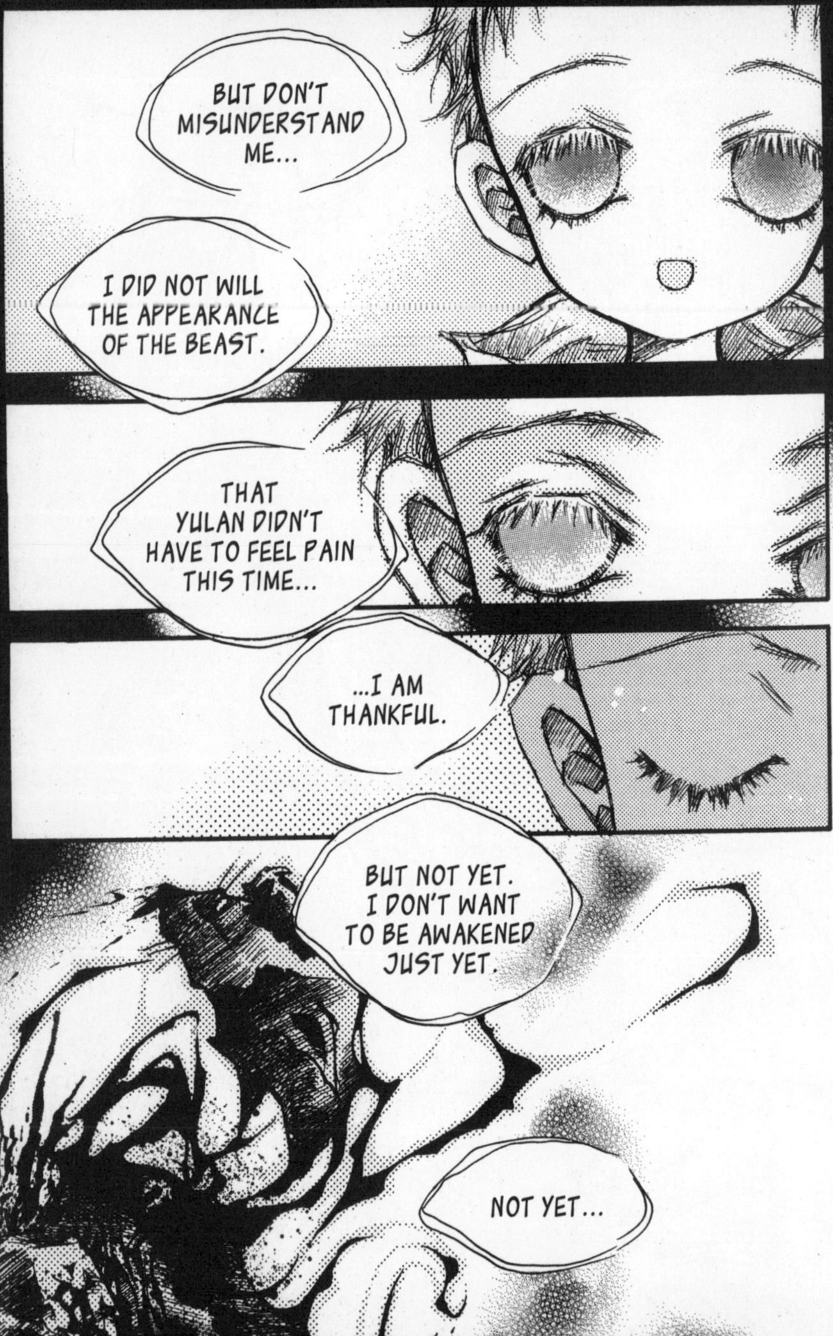
BUT DON'T MISUNDERSTAND ME...
I DID NOT WILL THE APPEARANCE OF THE BEAST.
THAT YULAN DIDN'T HAVE TO FEEL PAIN THIS TIME...
...I AM THANKFUL.
BUT NOT YET. I DON'T WANT TO BE AWAKENED JUST YET.
NOT YET...

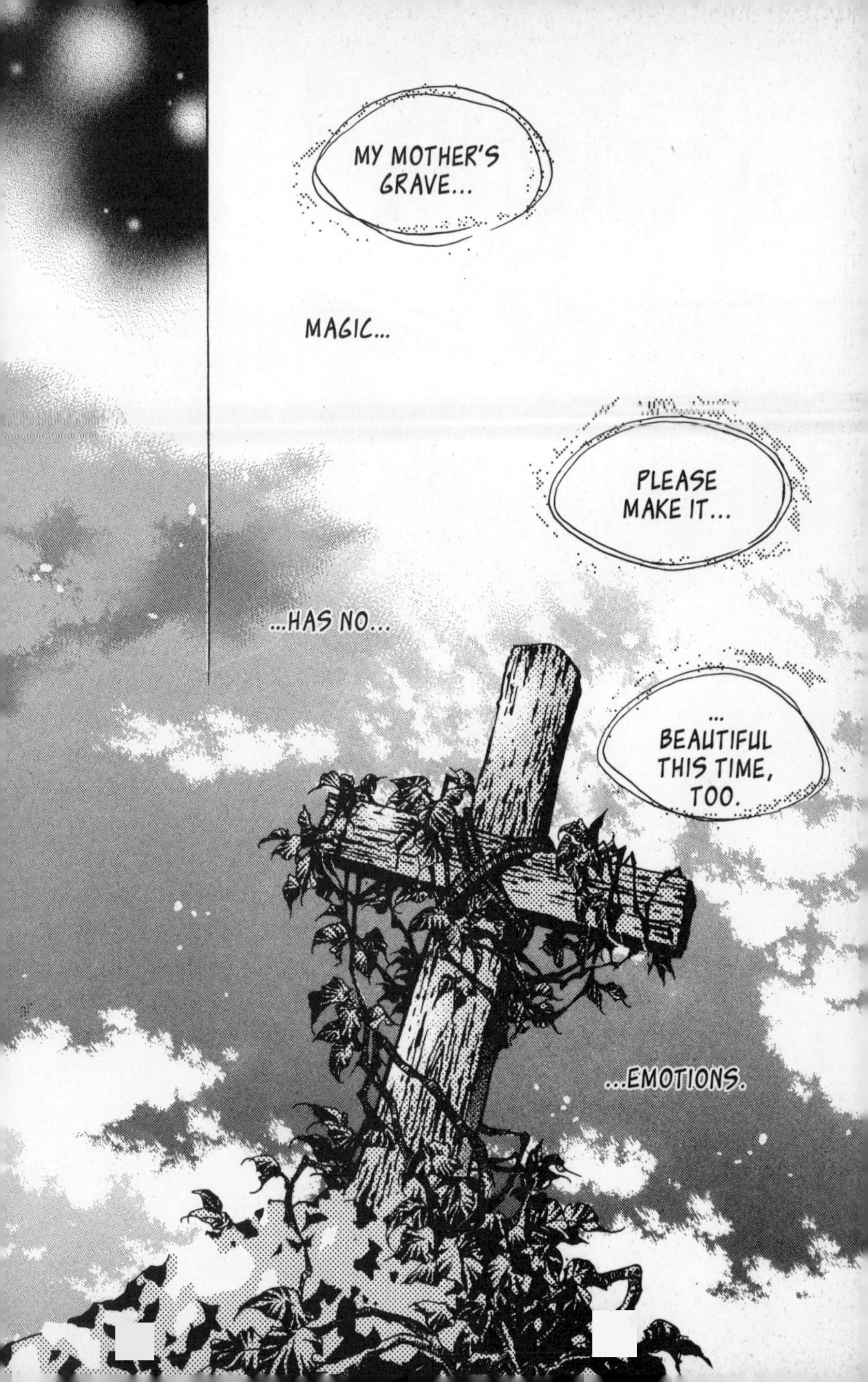
MY MOTHER'S GRAVE...
MAGIC...
PLEASE MAKE IT...
...HAS NO...
... BEAUTIFUL THIS TIME, TOO.
...EMOTIONS.

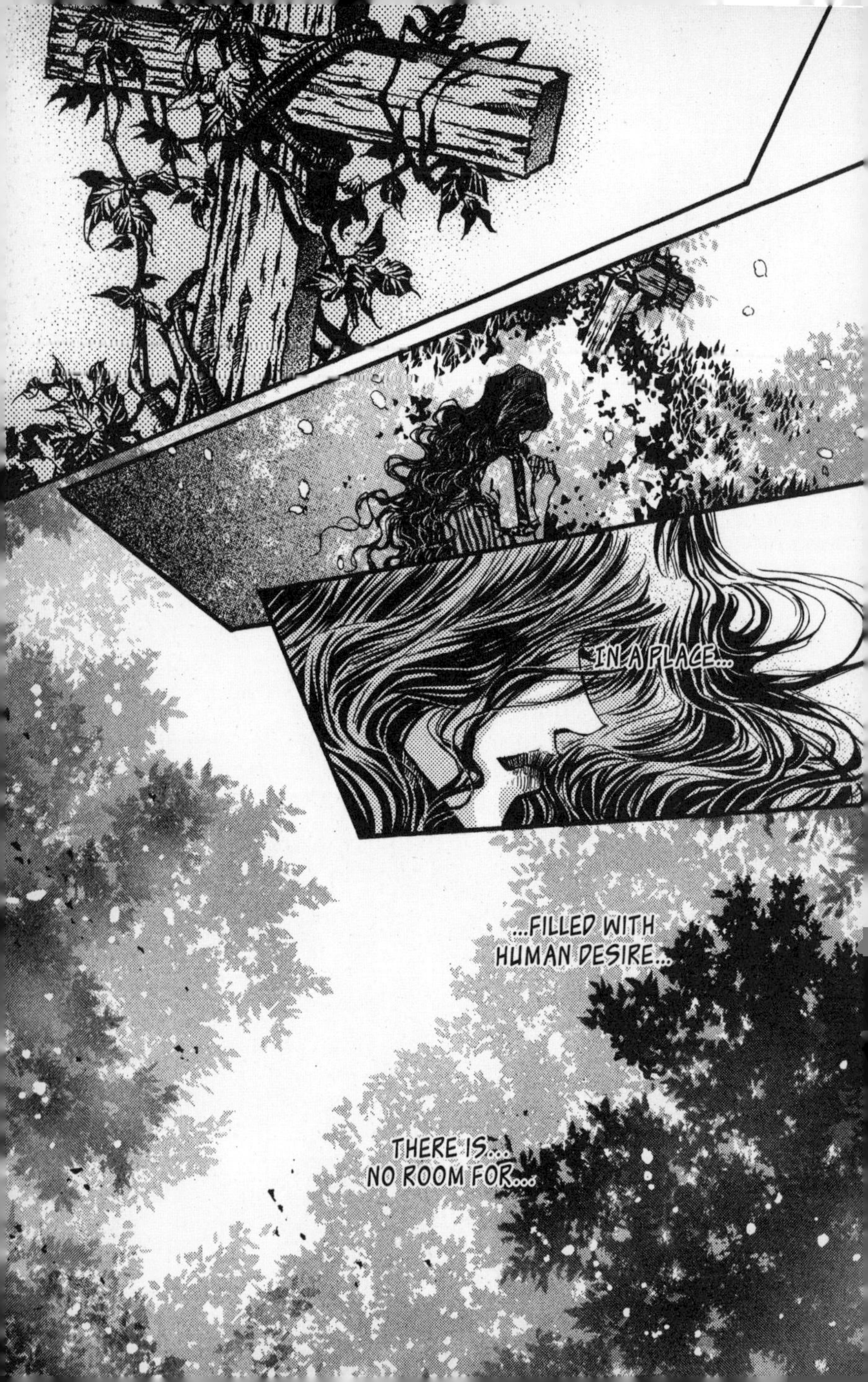
IN A PLACE...
...FILLED WITH
HUMAN DESIRE...
THERE IS...
NO ROOM FOR...

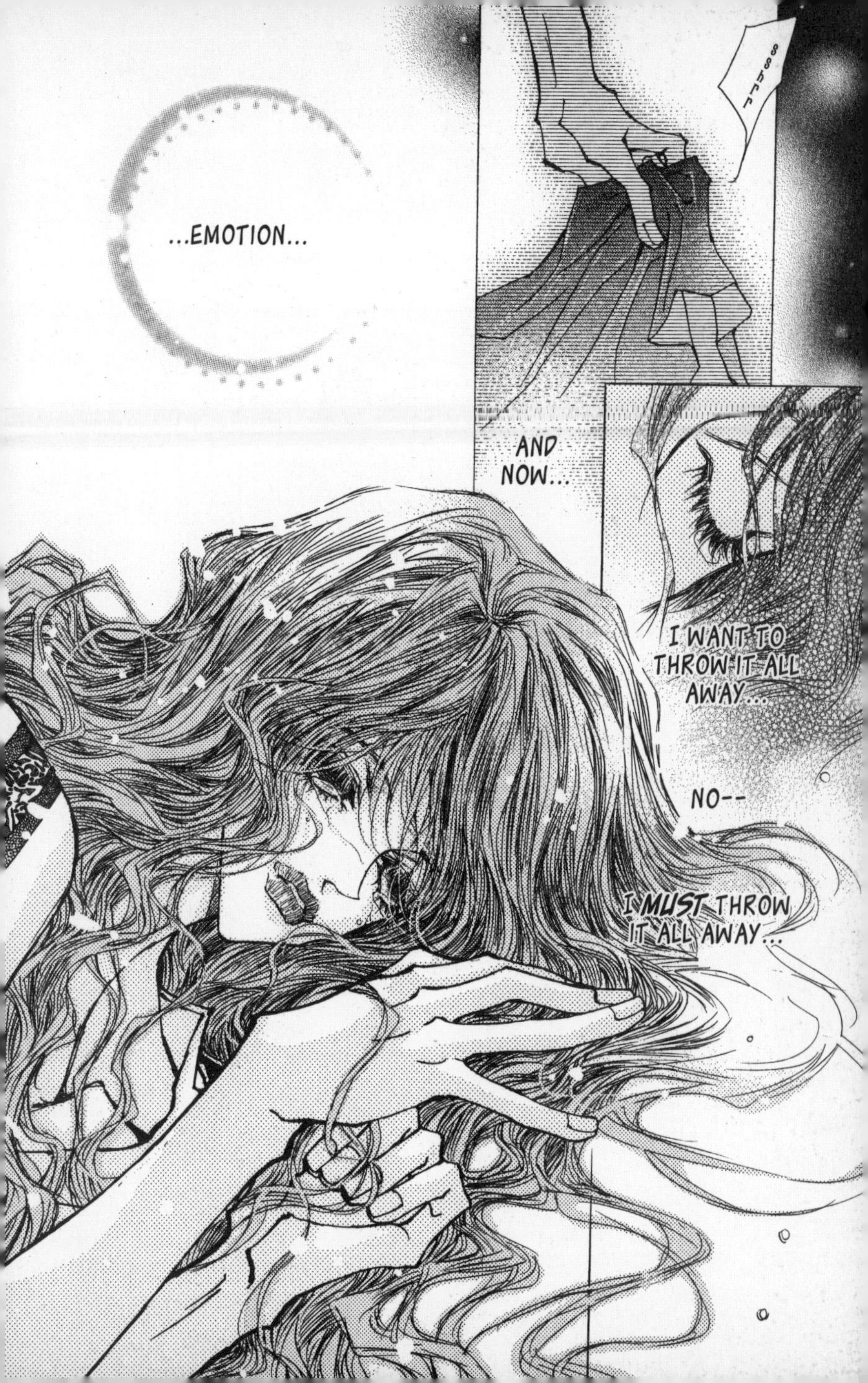
...EMOTION...
sshrr
AND NOW...
I WANT TO THROW IT ALL AWAY...
NO--
I **MUST** THROW IT ALL AWAY...

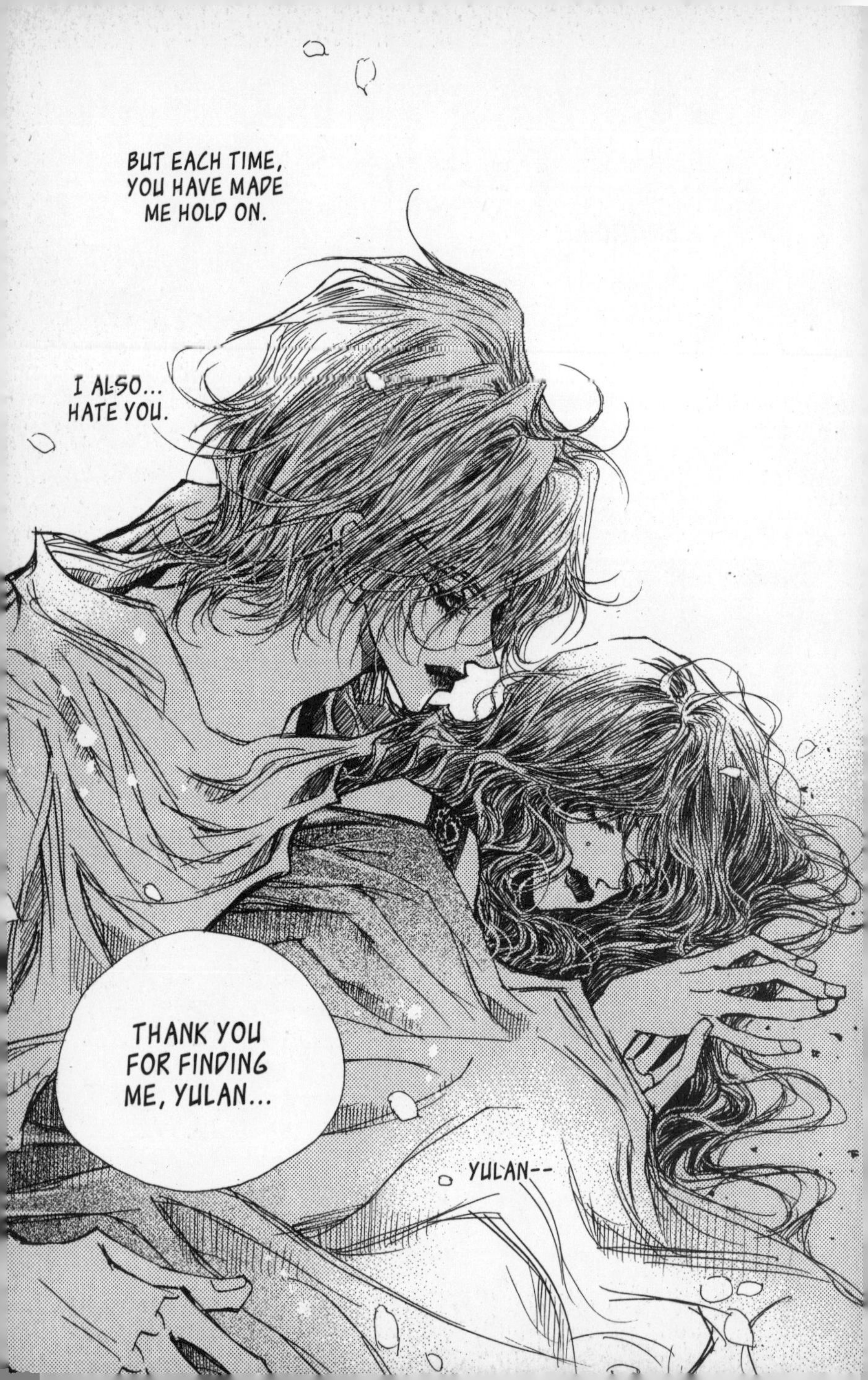
BUT EACH TIME, YOU HAVE MADE ME HOLD ON.
I ALSO... HATE YOU.
THANK YOU FOR FINDING ME, YULAN...
YULAN--

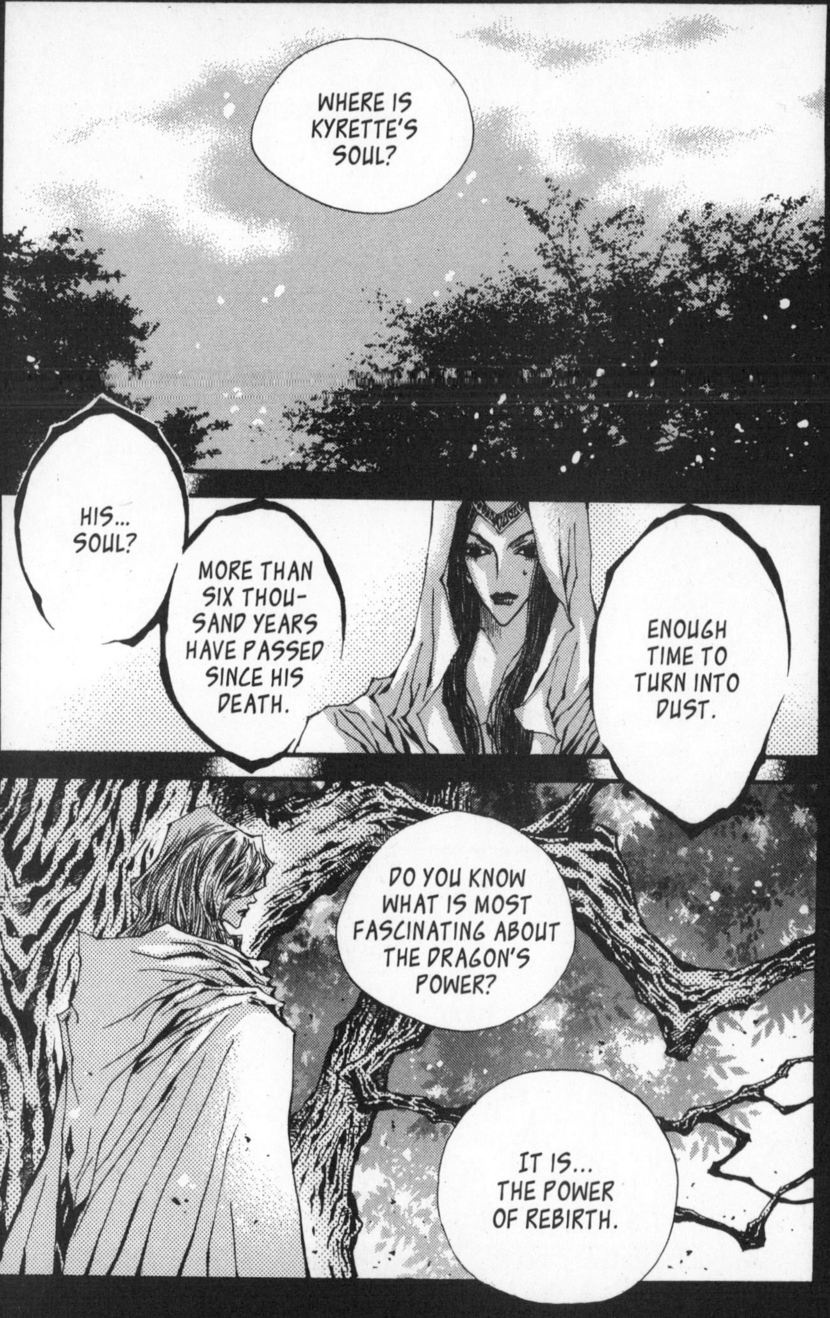
WHERE IS KYRETTE'S SOUL?
HIS... SOUL?
MORE THAN SIX THOU-SAND YEARS HAVE PASSED SINCE HIS DEATH.
ENOUGH TIME TO TURN INTO DUST.
DO YOU KNOW WHAT IS MOST FASCINATING ABOUT THE DRAGON'S POWER?
IT IS... THE POWER OF REBIRTH.

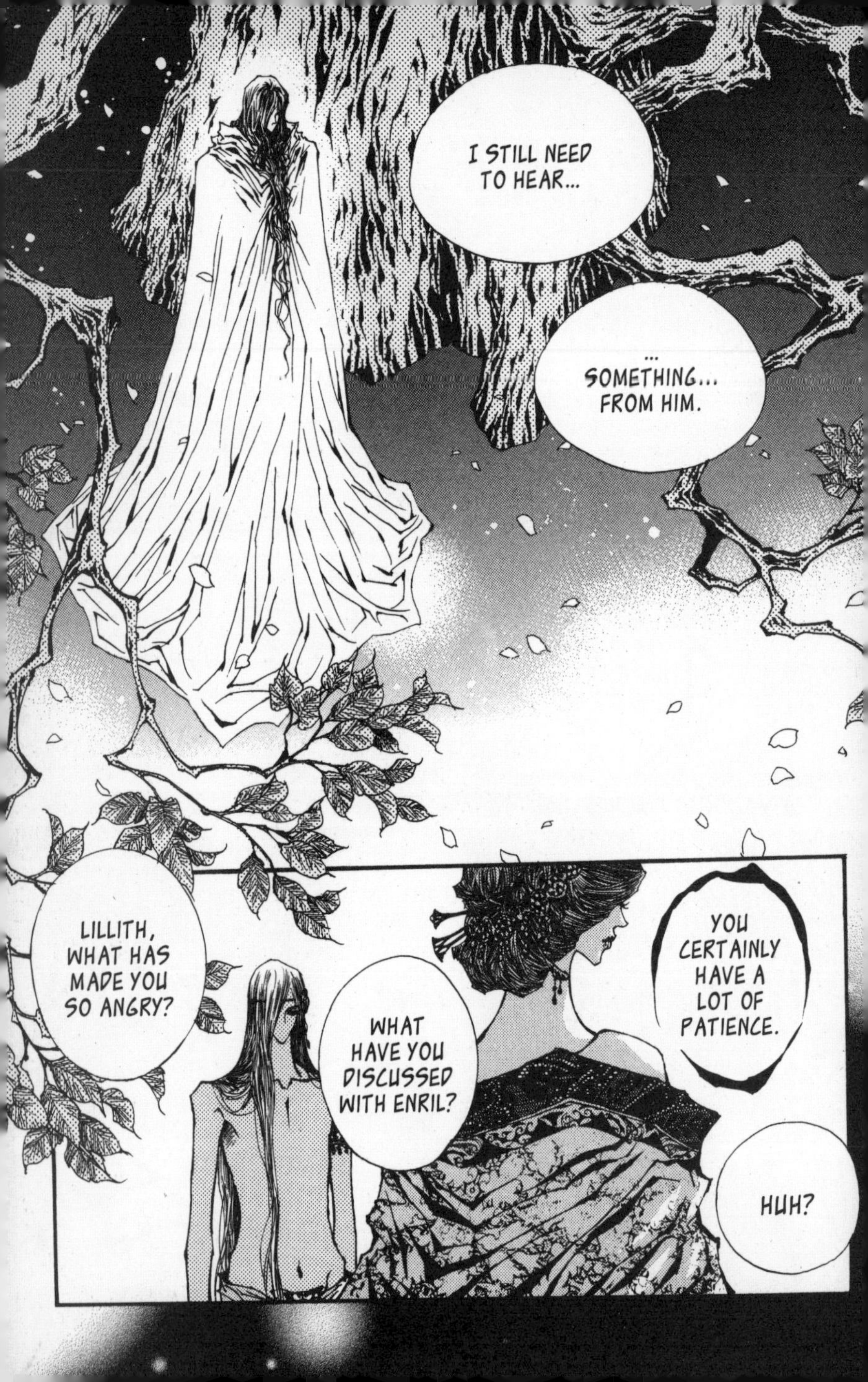
I STILL NEED TO HEAR...
... SOMETHING... FROM HIM.
LILLITH, WHAT HAS MADE YOU SO ANGRY?
WHAT HAVE YOU DISCUSSED WITH ENRIL?
YOU CERTAINLY HAVE A LOT OF PATIENCE.
HUH?

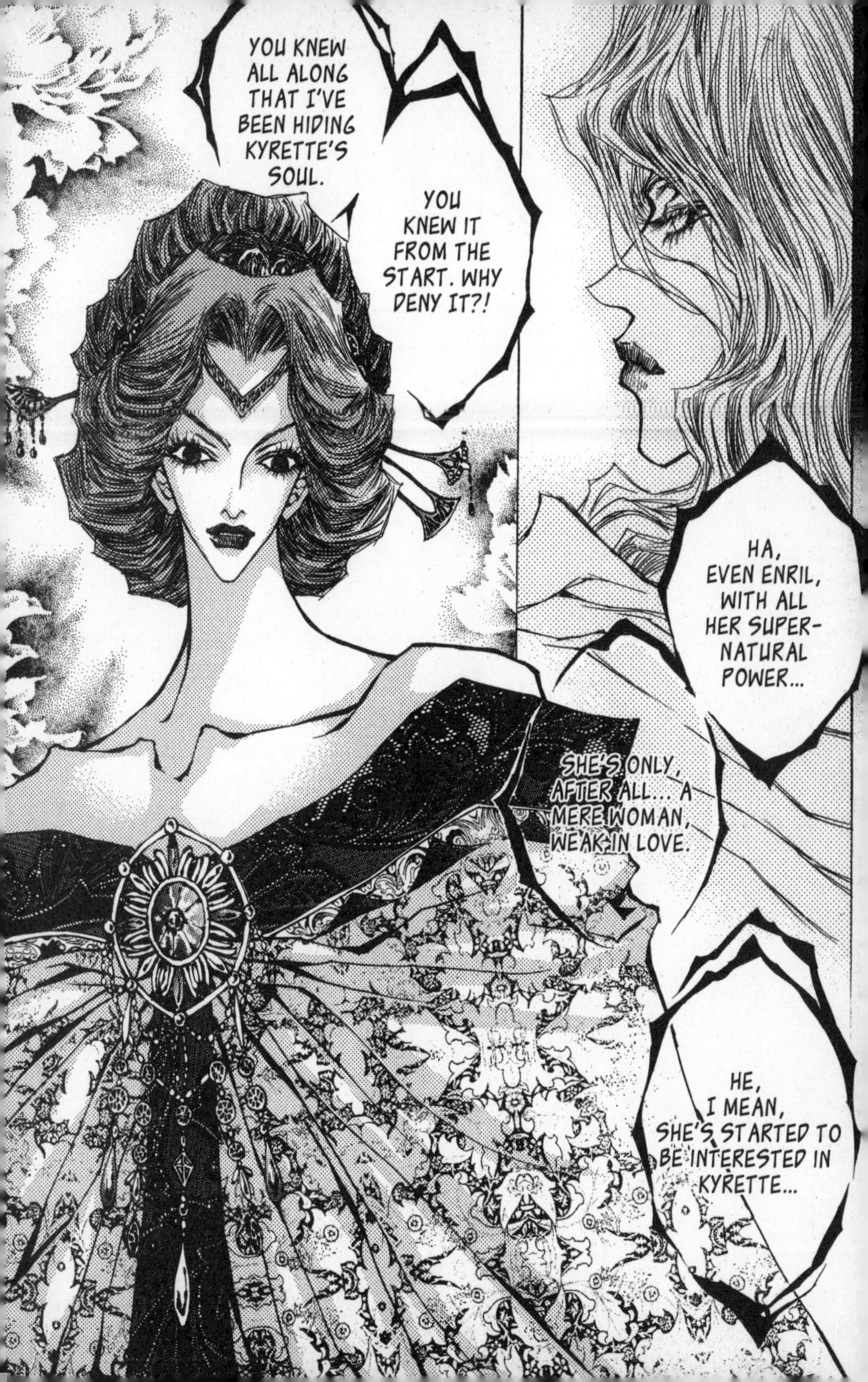
YOU KNEW ALL ALONG THAT I'VE BEEN HIDING KYRETTE'S SOUL.
YOU KNEW IT FROM THE START. WHY DENY IT?!
HA, EVEN ENRIL, WITH ALL HER SUPER-NATURAL POWER...
SHE'S ONLY, AFTER ALL... A MERE WOMAN, WEAK IN LOVE.
HE, I MEAN, SHE'S STARTED TO BE INTERESTED IN KYRETTE...

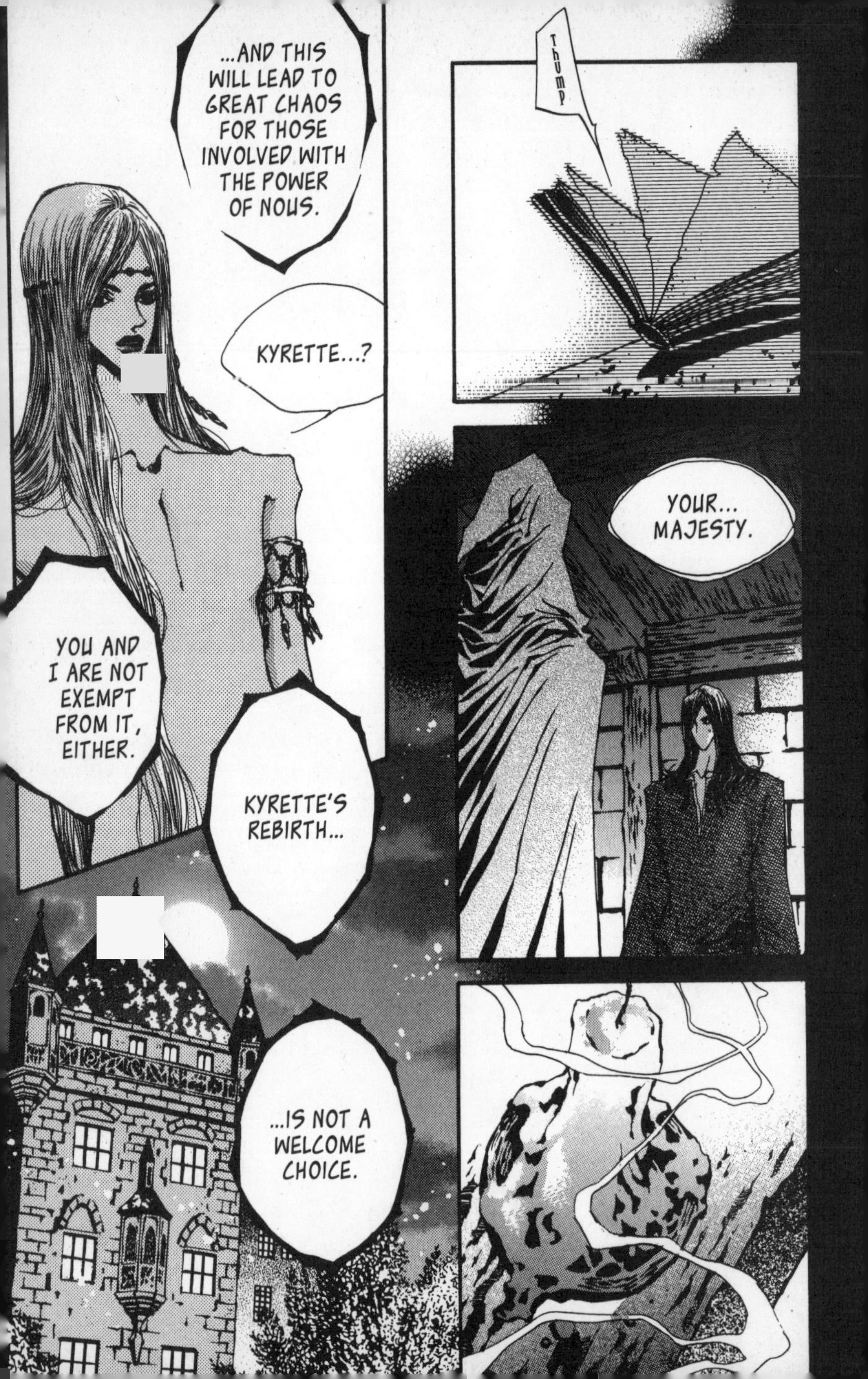
...AND THIS WILL LEAD TO GREAT CHAOS FOR THOSE INVOLVED WITH THE POWER OF NOUS.
KYRETTE...?
YOU AND I ARE NOT EXEMPT FROM IT, EITHER.
KYRETTE'S REBIRTH...
...IS NOT A WELCOME CHOICE.
THUMP
YOUR... MAJESTY.

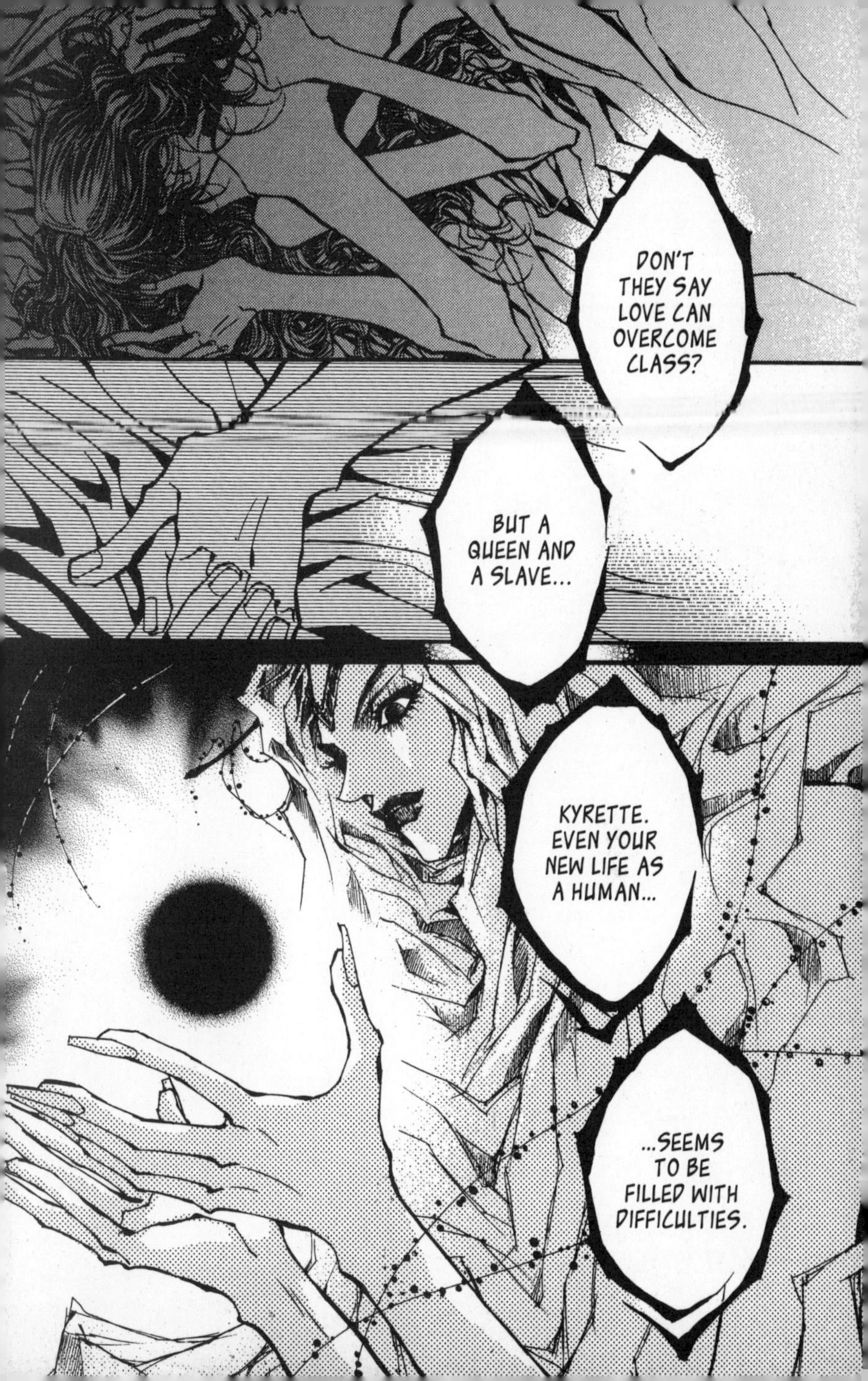
DON'T THEY SAY LOVE CAN OVERCOME CLASS?
BUT A QUEEN AND A SLAVE...
KYRETTE. EVEN YOUR NEW LIFE AS A HUMAN...
...SEEMS TO BE FILLED WITH DIFFICULTIES.

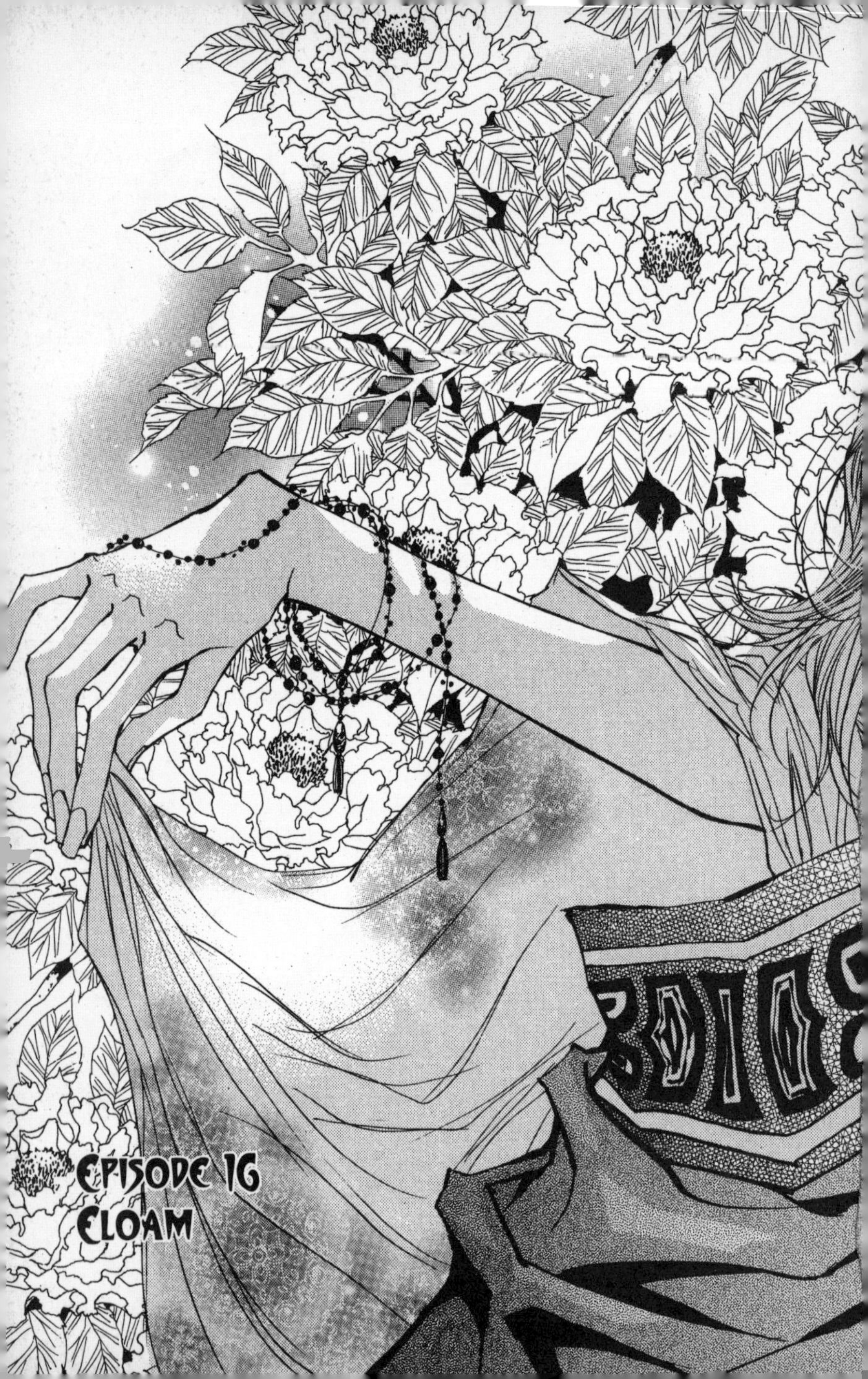
Episode 16
Cloam

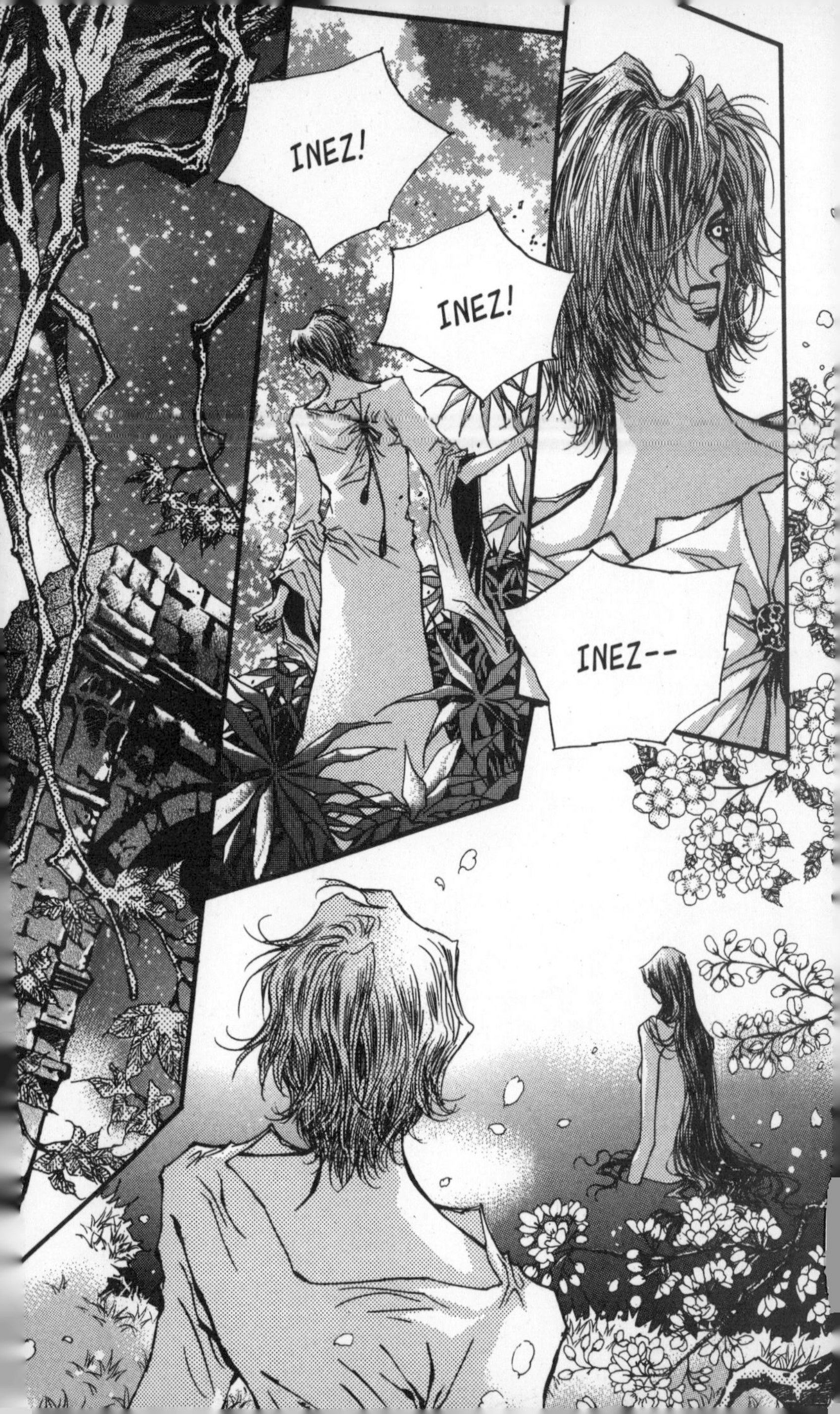
INEZ!
INEZ!
INEZ--

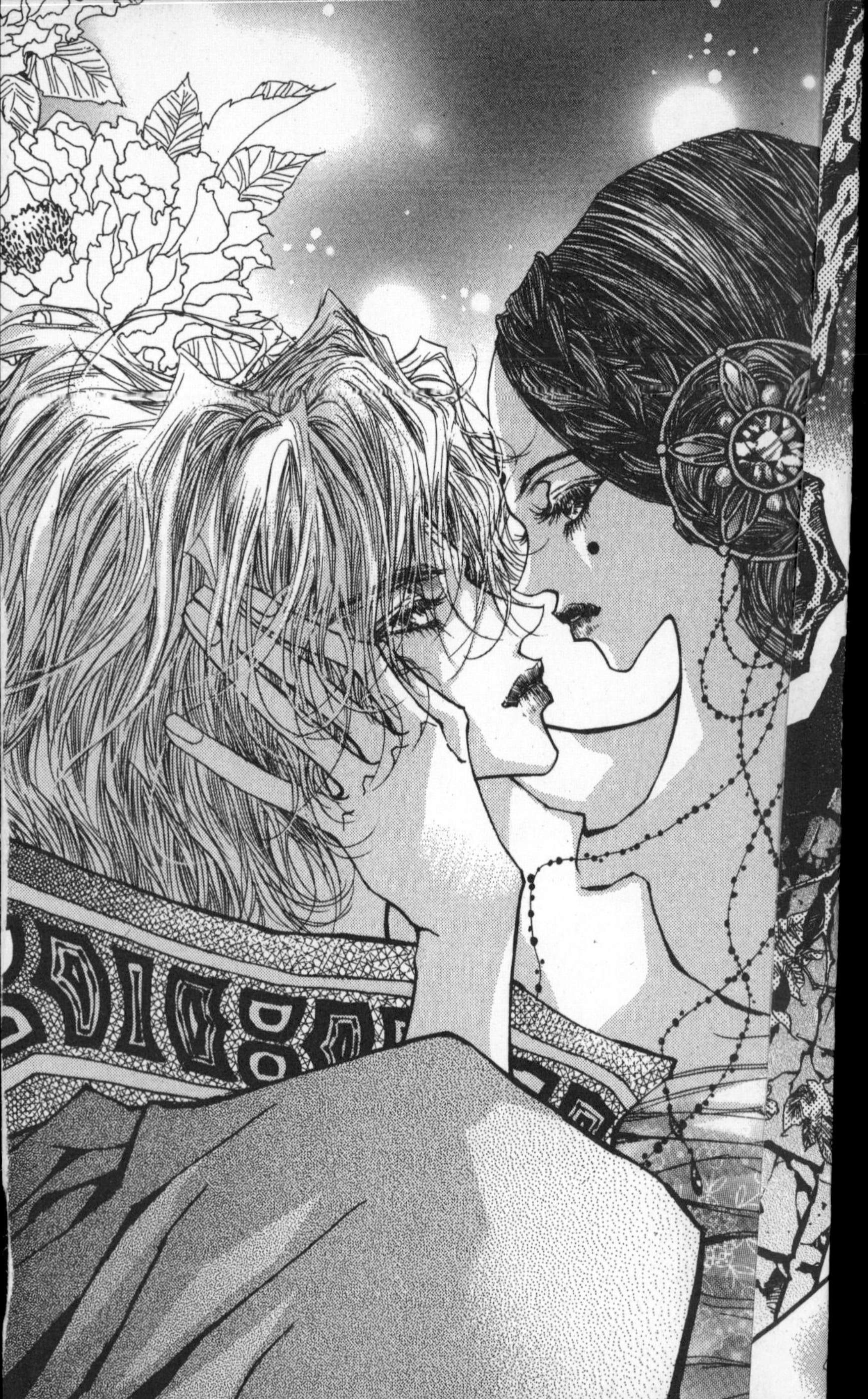

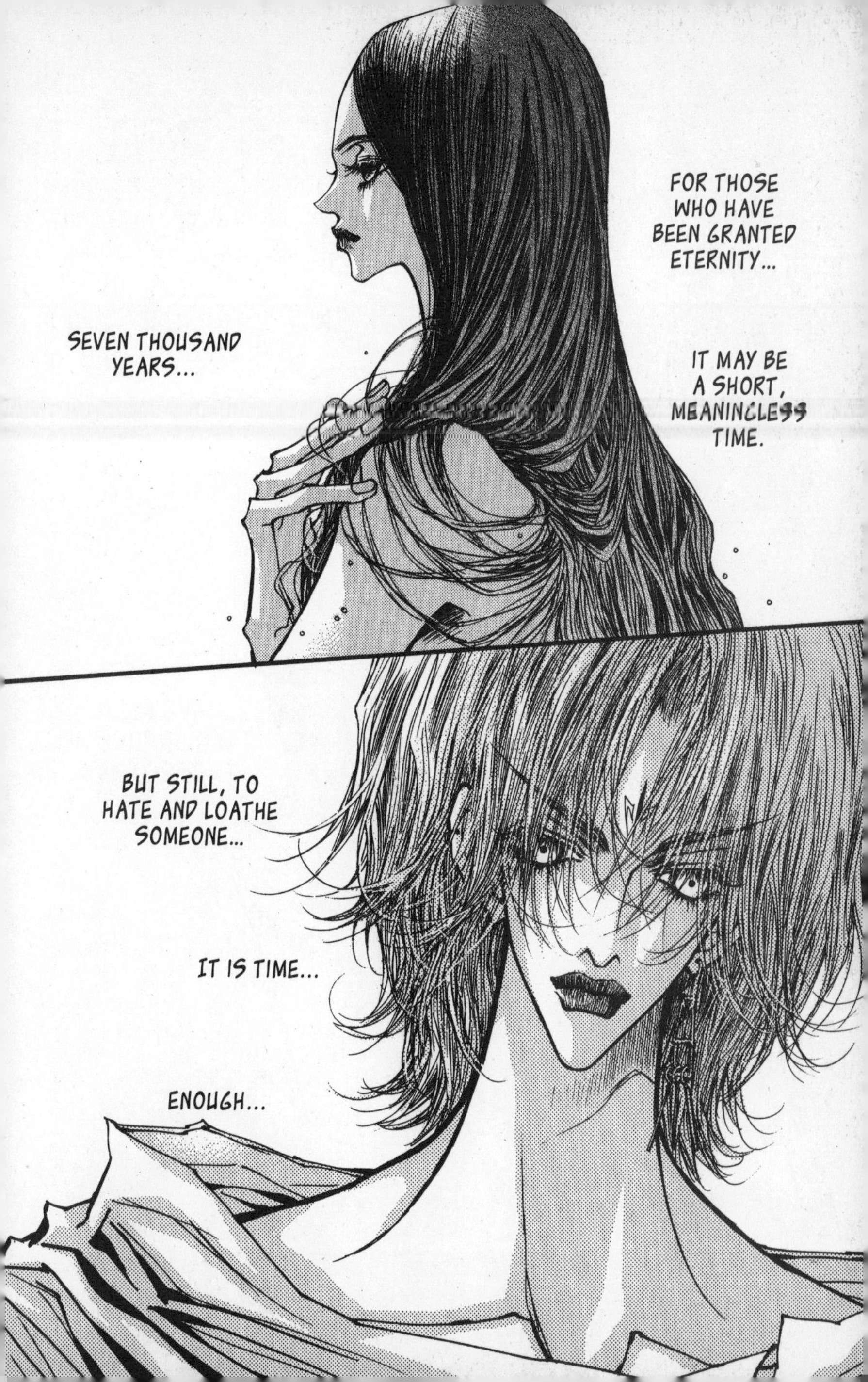
SEVEN THOUSAND YEARS...
FOR THOSE WHO HAVE BEEN GRANTED ETERNITY...
IT MAY BE A SHORT, MEANINGLESS TIME.
BUT STILL, TO HATE AND LOATHE SOMEONE...
IT IS TIME...
ENOUGH...

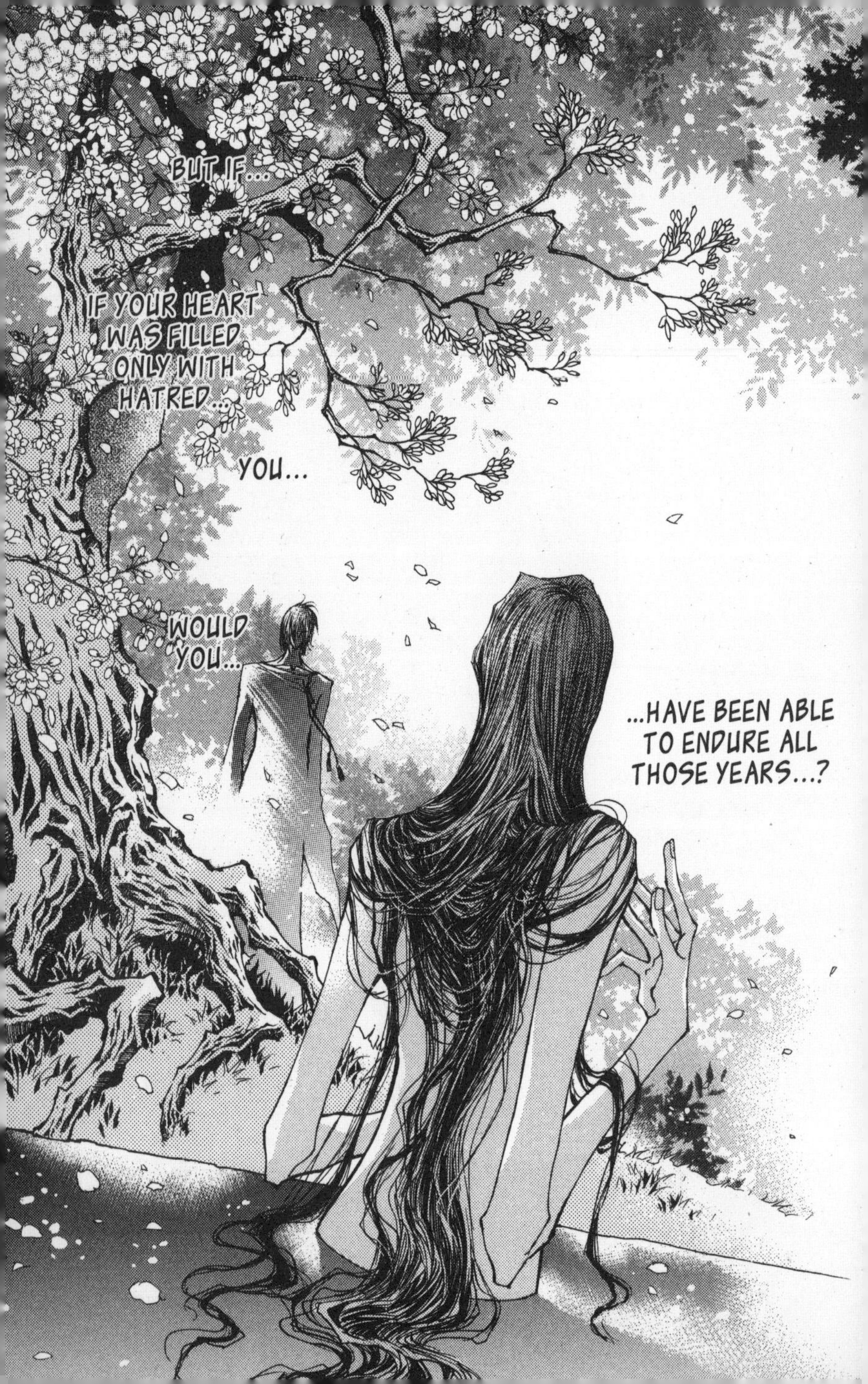
BUT IF...
IF YOUR HEART WAS FILLED ONLY WITH HATRED...
YOU...
WOULD YOU...
...HAVE BEEN ABLE TO ENDURE ALL THOSE YEARS...?

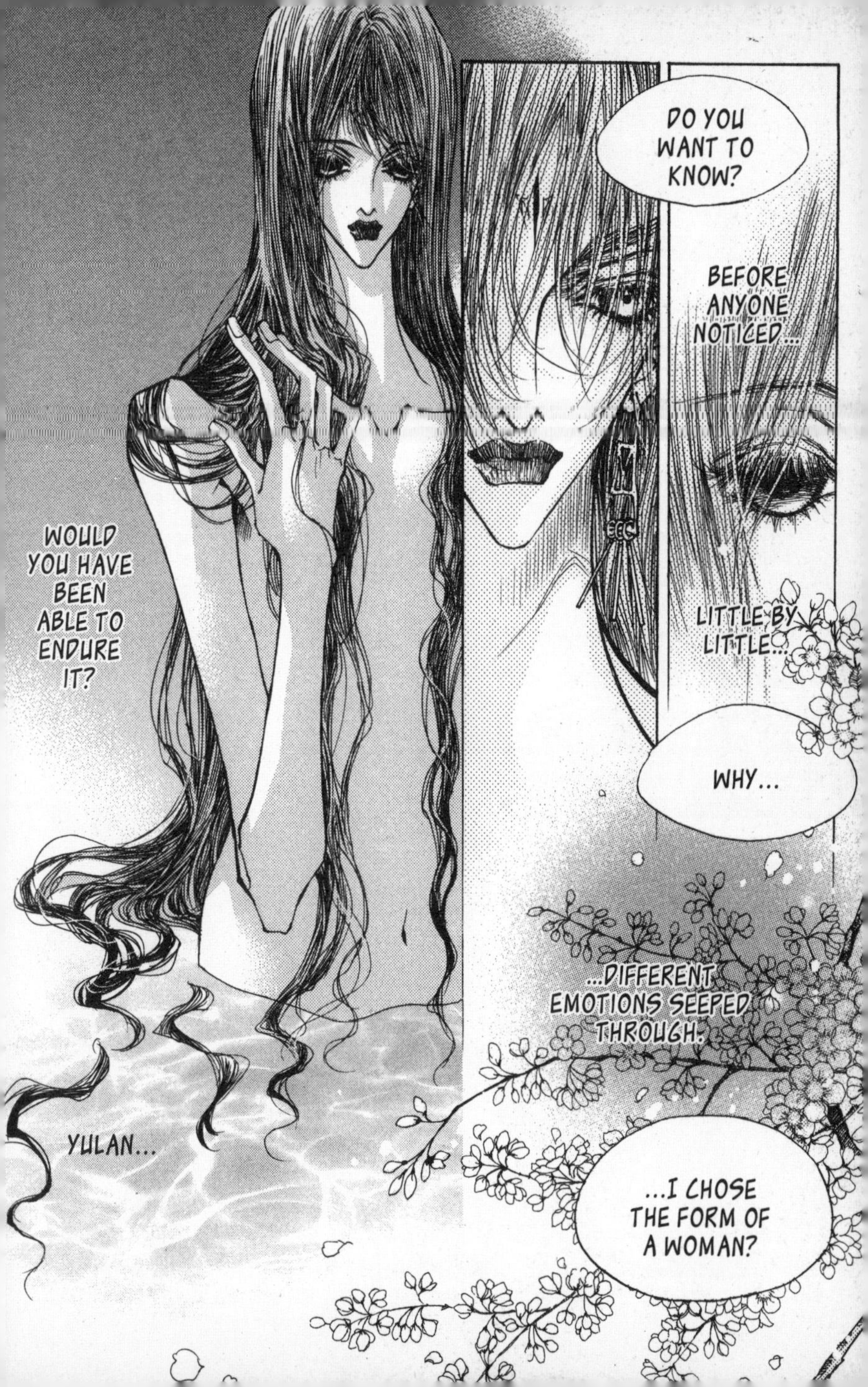
WOULD YOU HAVE BEEN ABLE TO ENDURE IT?
YULAN...
DO YOU WANT TO KNOW?
BEFORE ANYONE NOTICED...
LITTLE BY LITTLE...
WHY...
...DIFFERENT EMOTIONS SEEPED THROUGH.
...I CHOSE THE FORM OF A WOMAN?

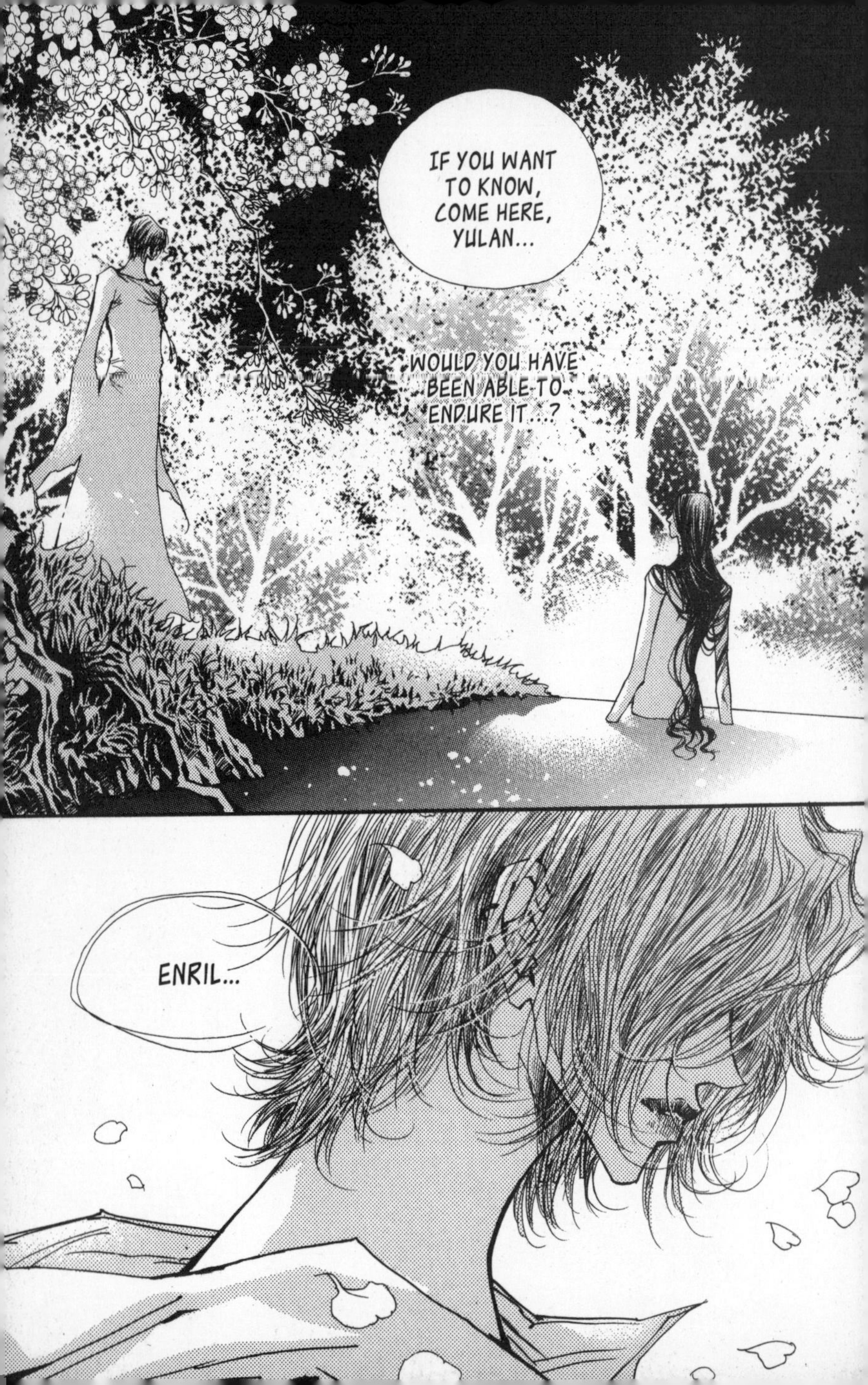
IF YOU WANT TO KNOW, COME HERE, YULAN...
WOULD YOU HAVE BEEN ABLE TO ENDURE IT...?
ENRIL...

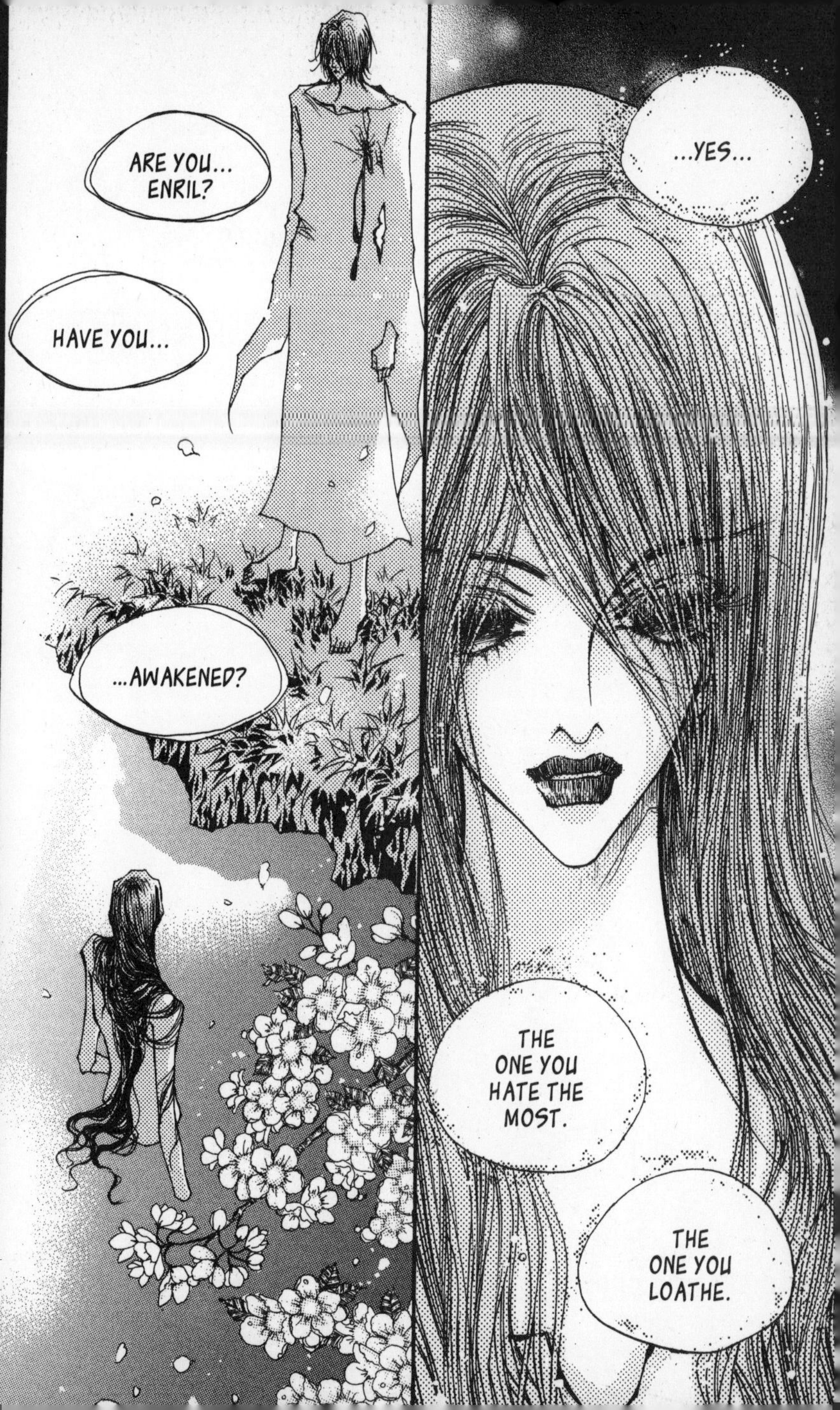
ARE YOU... ENRIL?
HAVE YOU...
...AWAKENED?
...YES...
THE ONE YOU HATE THE MOST.
THE ONE YOU LOATHE.

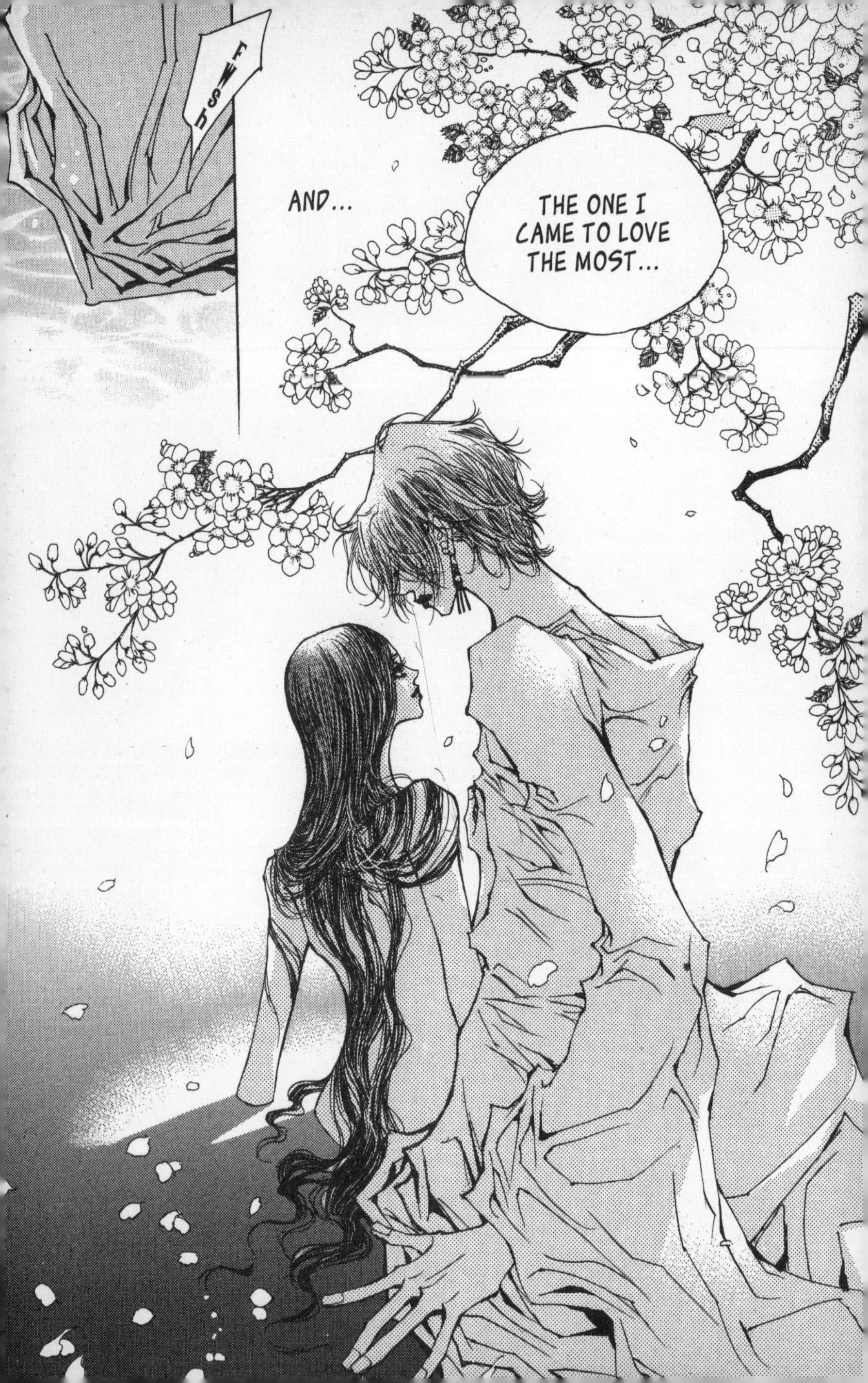
FWSH
AND...
THE ONE I CAME TO LOVE THE MOST...

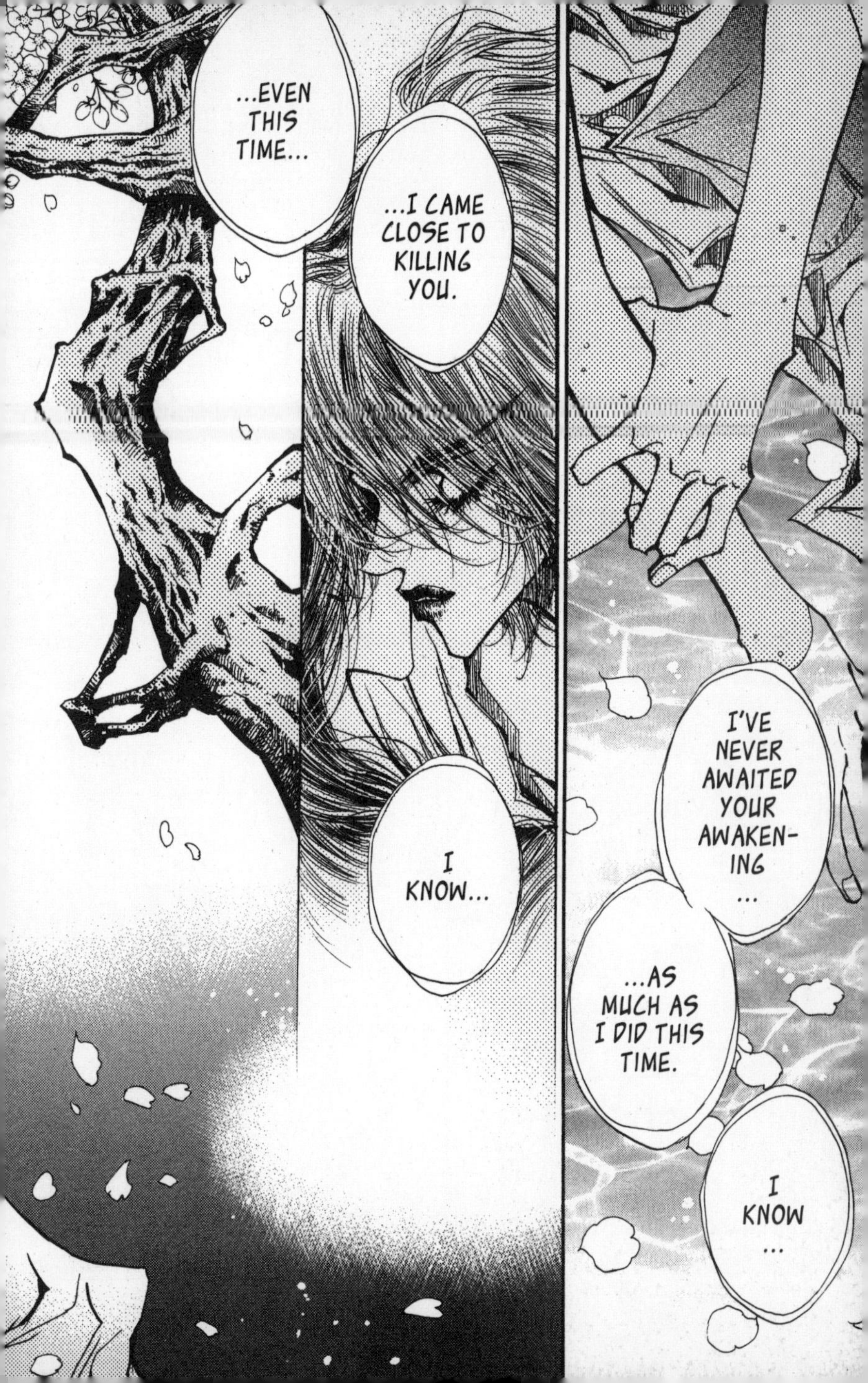
...EVEN THIS TIME...
...I CAME CLOSE TO KILLING YOU.
I KNOW...
I'VE NEVER AWAITED YOUR AWAKEN-ING ...
...AS MUCH AS I DID THIS TIME.
I KNOW ...

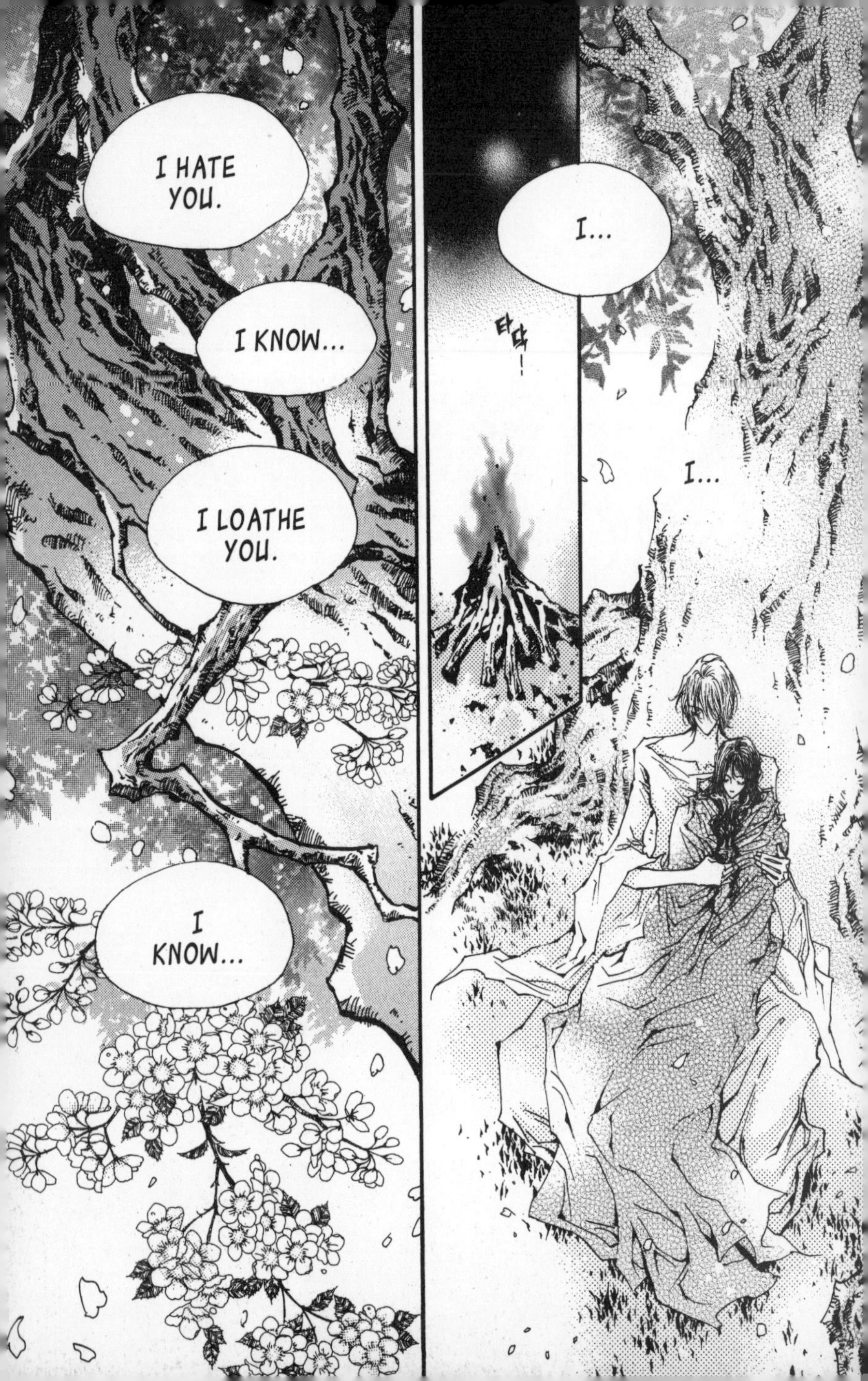
I HATE YOU.
I KNOW...
I LOATHE YOU.
I KNOW...
I...
타닥!
I...

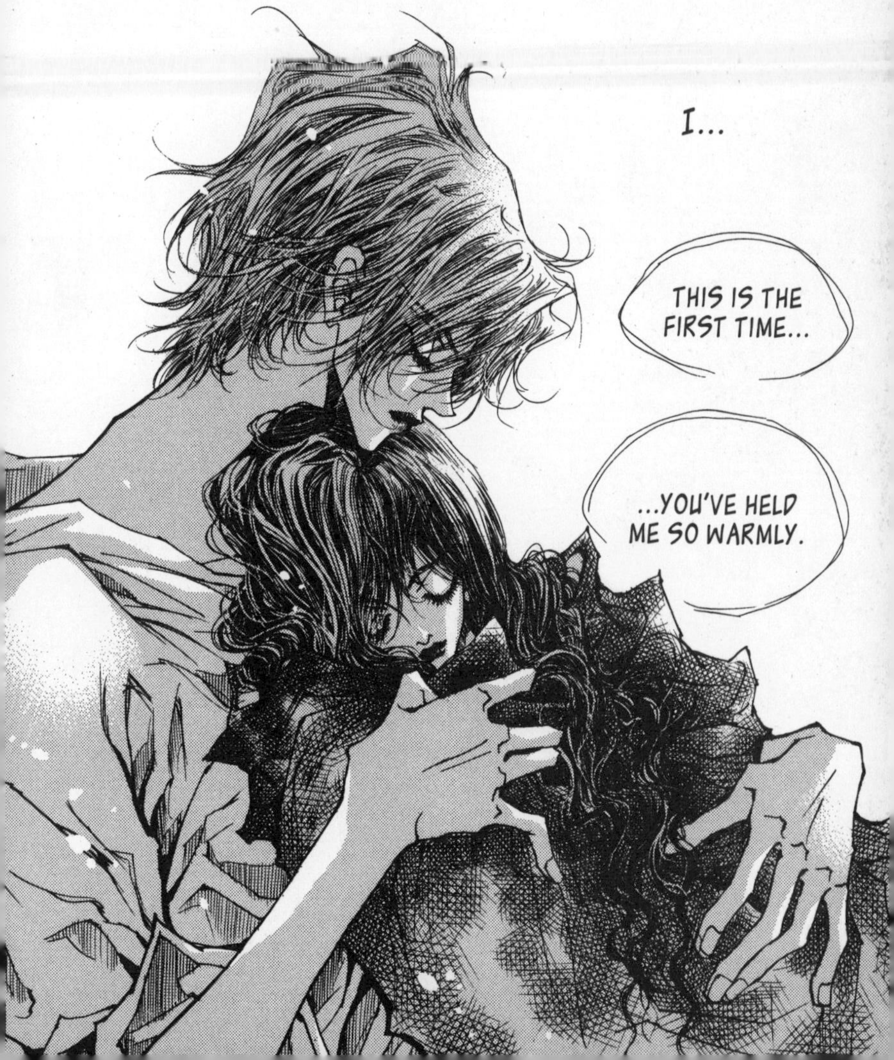
I...
THIS IS THE FIRST TIME...
...YOU'VE HELD ME SO WARMLY.

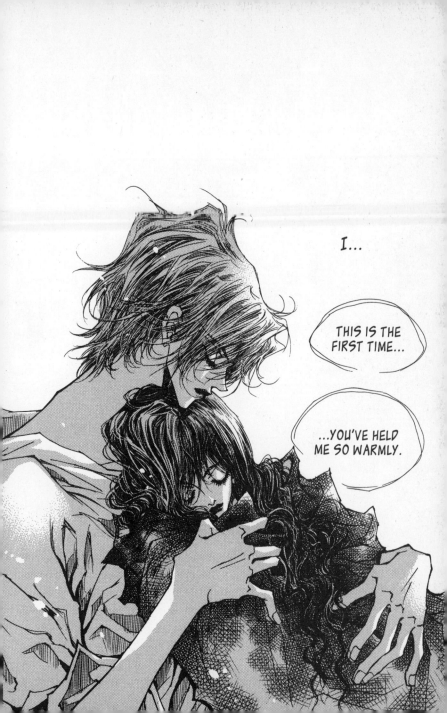

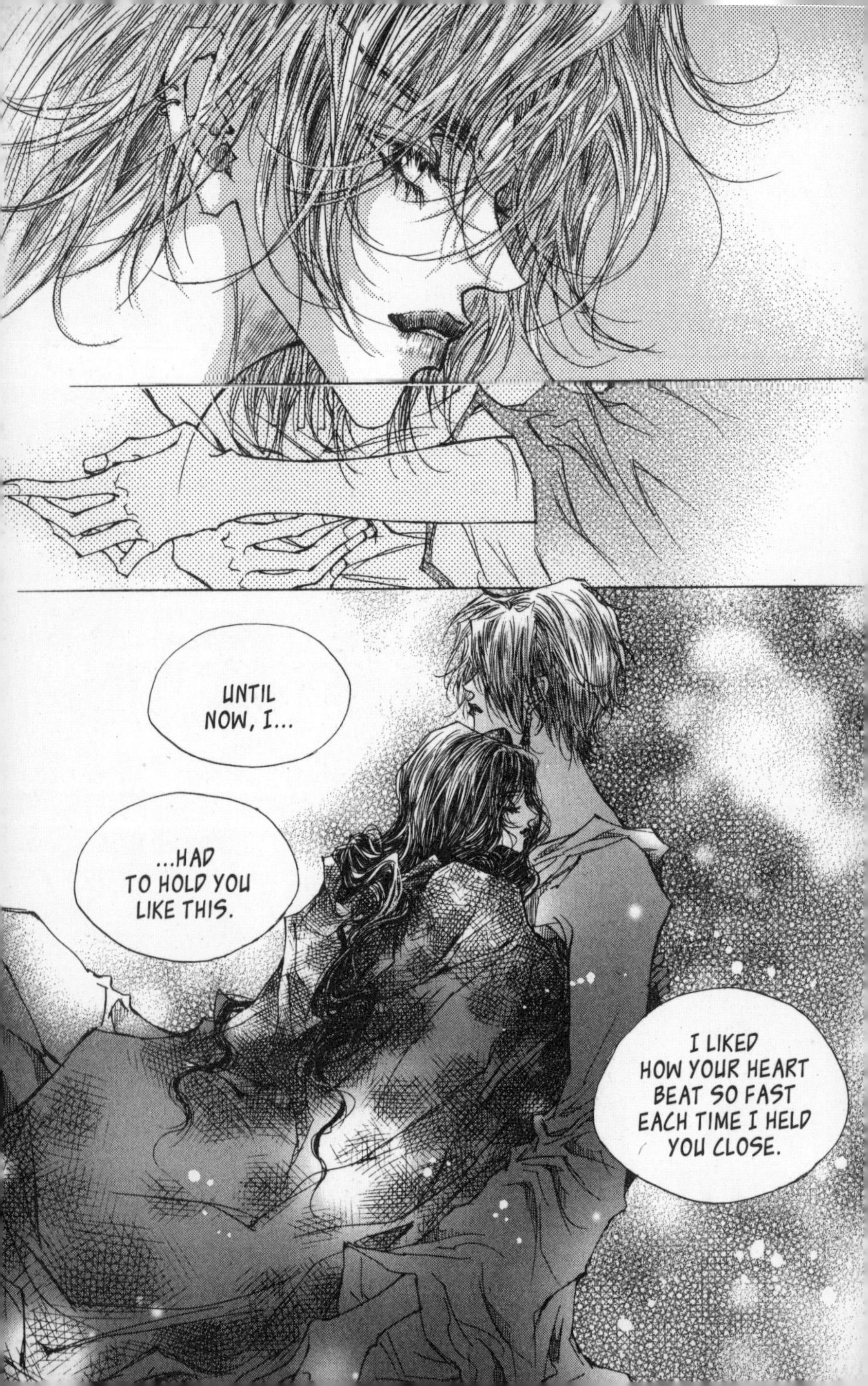
UNTIL NOW, I...
...HAD TO HOLD YOU LIKE THIS.
I LIKED HOW YOUR HEART BEAT SO FAST EACH TIME I HELD YOU CLOSE.

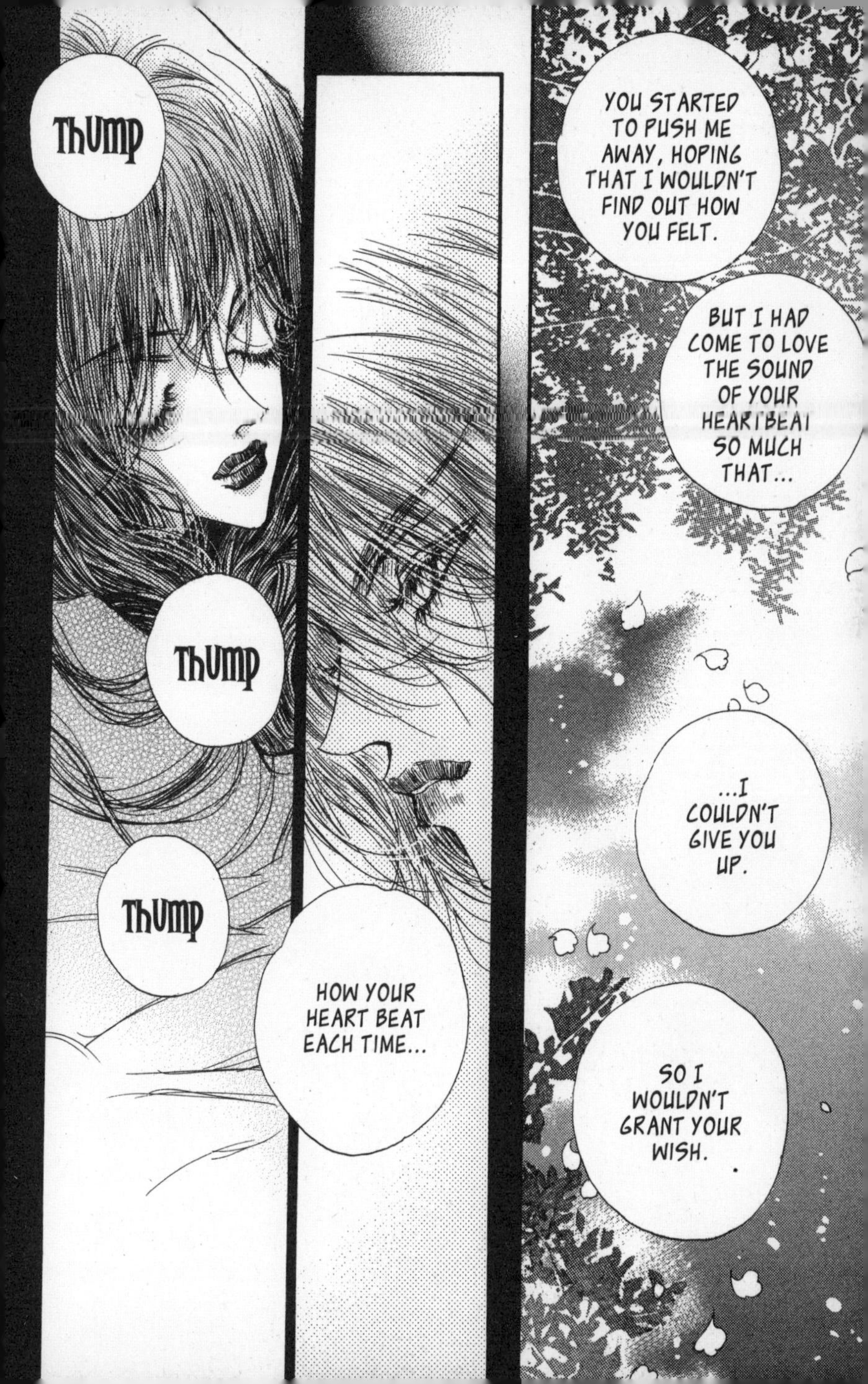
THUMP
THUMP
THUMP
HOW YOUR HEART BEAT EACH TIME...
YOU STARTED TO PUSH ME AWAY, HOPING THAT I WOULDN'T FIND OUT HOW YOU FELT.
BUT I HAD COME TO LOVE THE SOUND OF YOUR HEARTBEAT SO MUCH THAT...
...I COULDN'T GIVE YOU UP.
SO I WOULDN'T GRANT YOUR WISH.

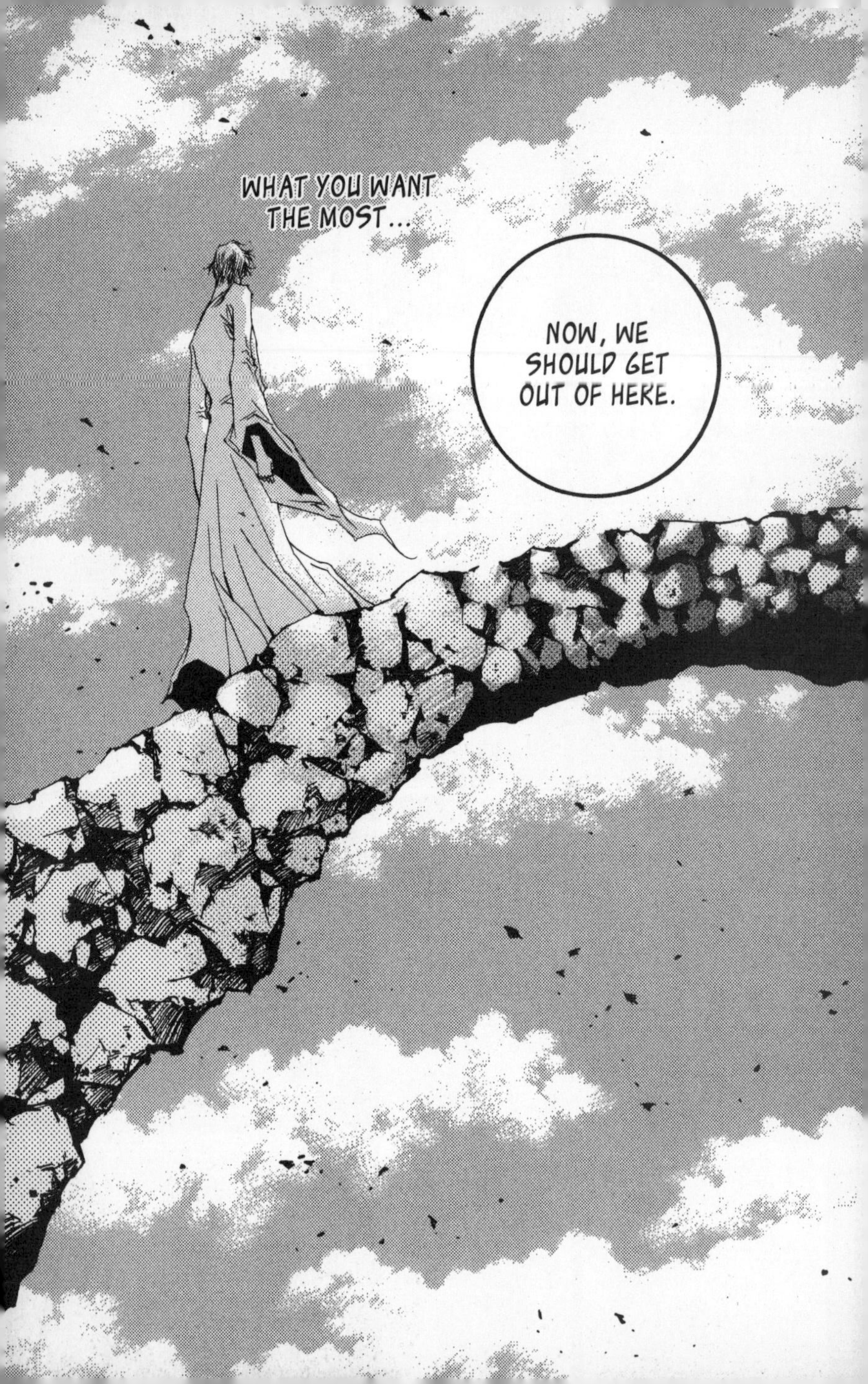
WHAT YOU WANT THE MOST...
NOW, WE SHOULD GET OUT OF HERE.

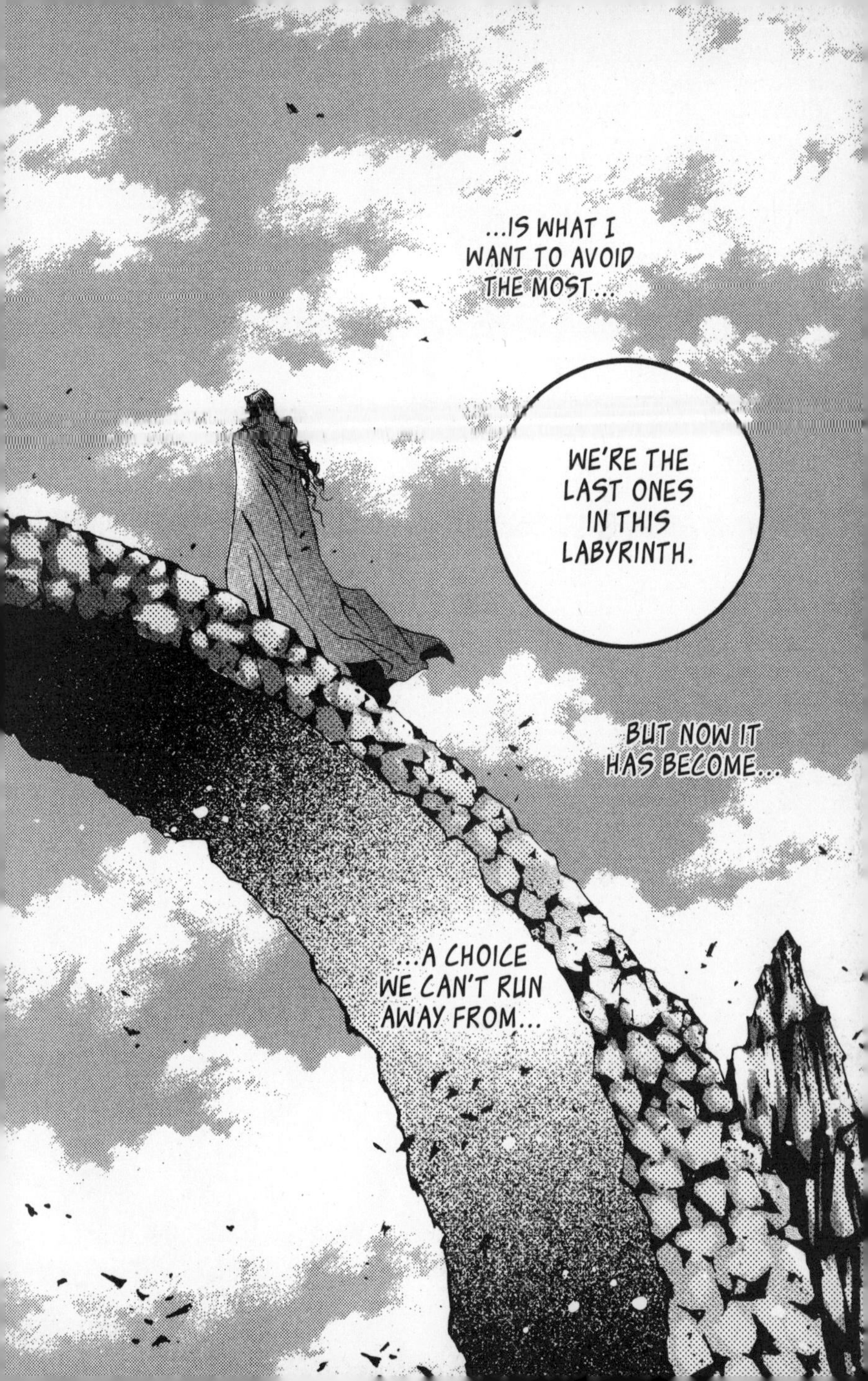
...IS WHAT I WANT TO AVOID THE MOST...
WE'RE THE LAST ONES IN THIS LABYRINTH.
BUT NOW IT HAS BECOME...
...A CHOICE WE CAN'T RUN AWAY FROM...

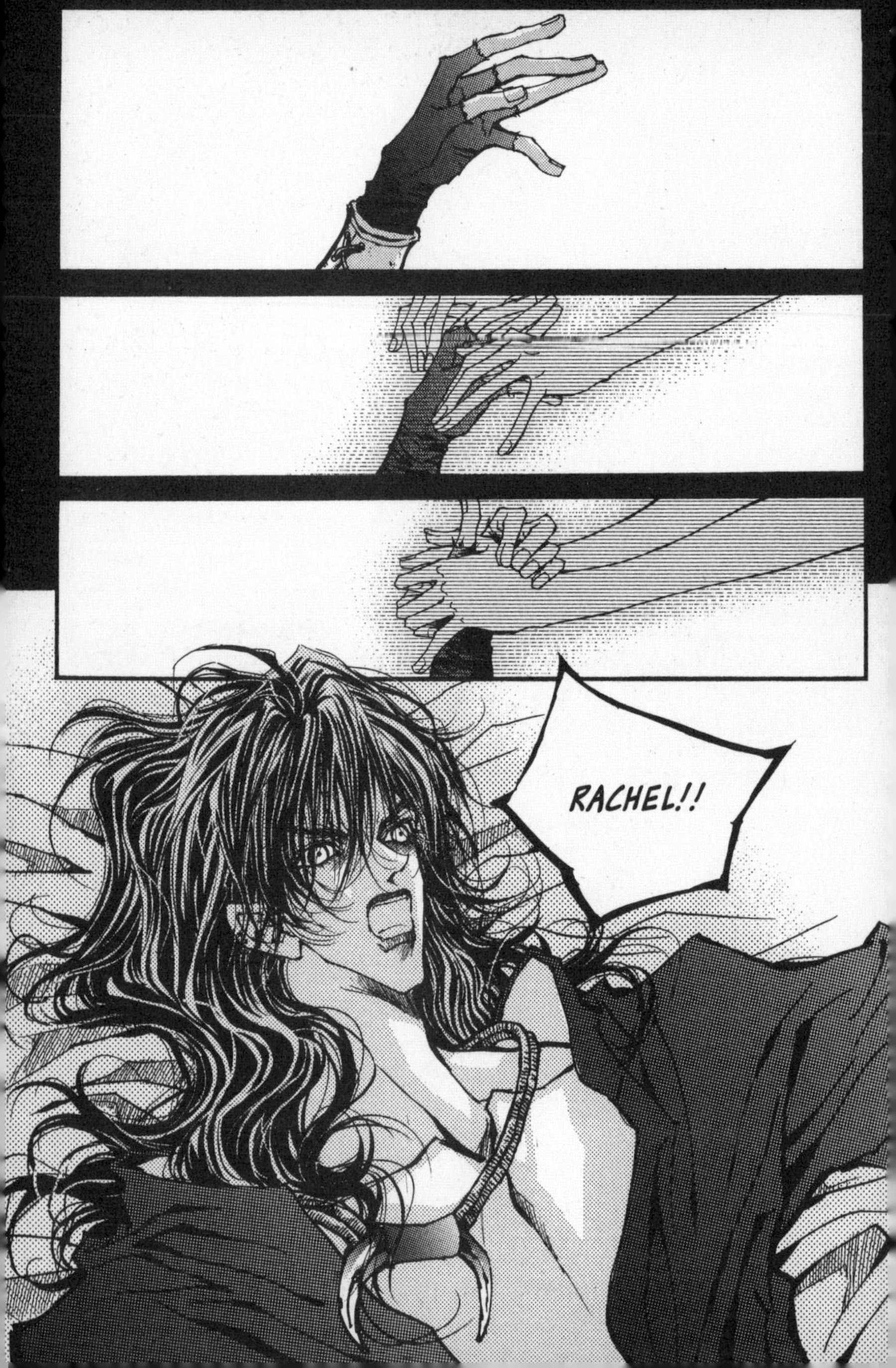
RACHEL!!

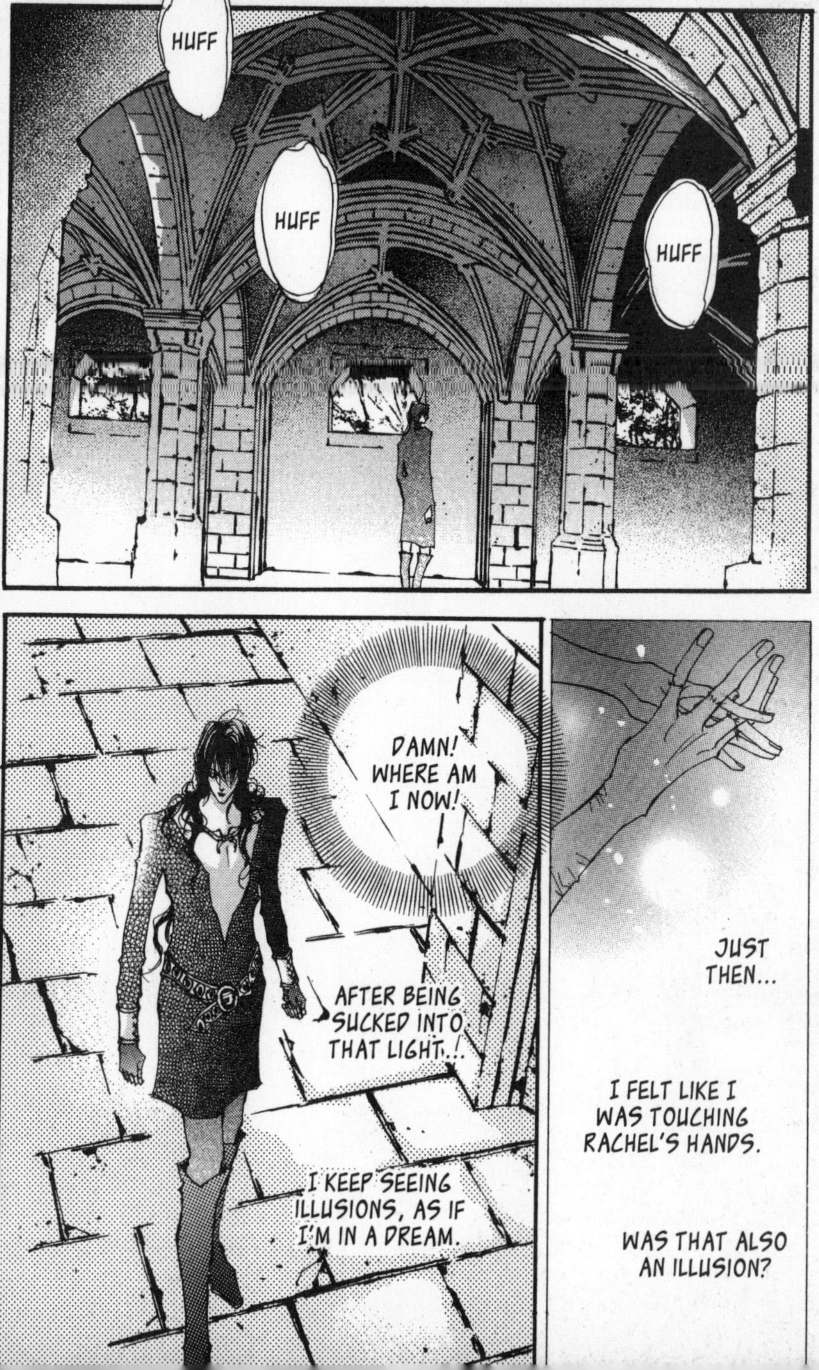
HUFF
HUFF
HUFF
DAMN! WHERE AM I NOW!
AFTER BEING SUCKED INTO THAT LIGHT...!
I KEEP SEEING ILLUSIONS, AS IF I'M IN A DREAM.
JUST THEN...
I FELT LIKE I WAS TOUCHING RACHEL'S HANDS.
WAS THAT ALSO AN ILLUSION?

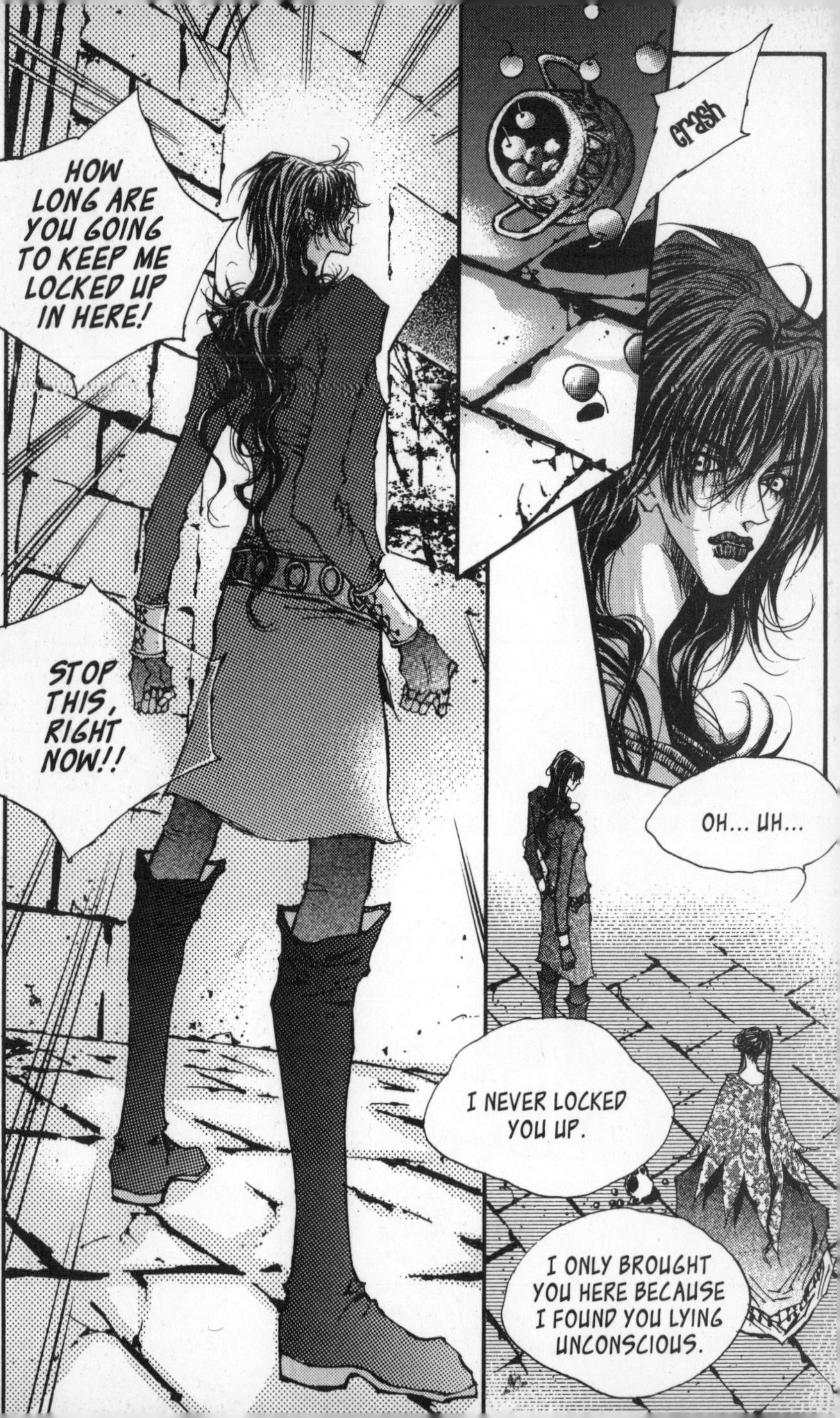
HOW LONG ARE YOU GOING TO KEEP ME LOCKED UP IN HERE!
STOP THIS, RIGHT NOW!!
CRASH
OH... UH...
I NEVER LOCKED YOU UP.
I ONLY BROUGHT YOU HERE BECAUSE I FOUND YOU LYING UNCONSCIOUS.

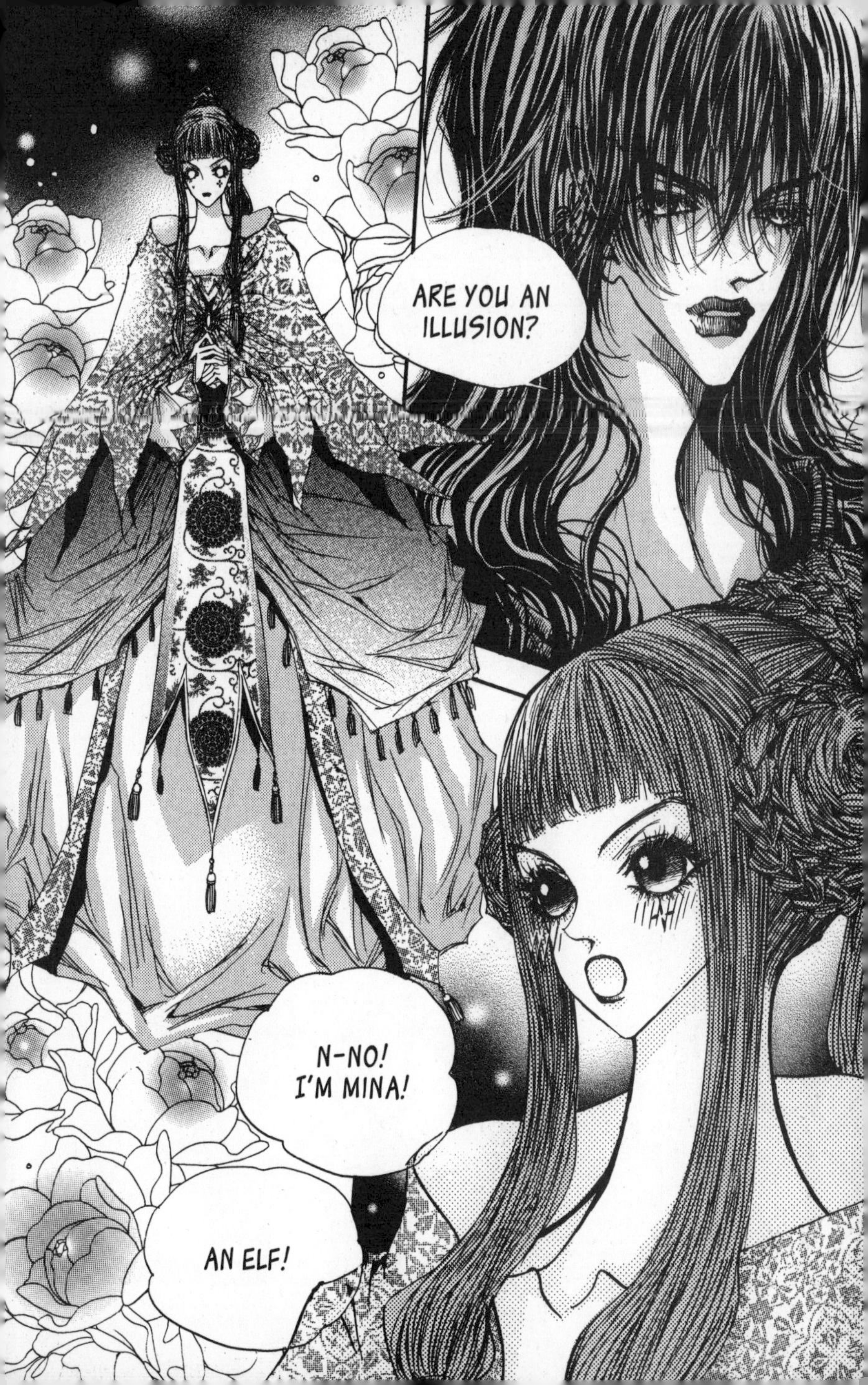
ARE YOU AN ILLUSION?
N-NO! I'M MINA!
AN ELF!

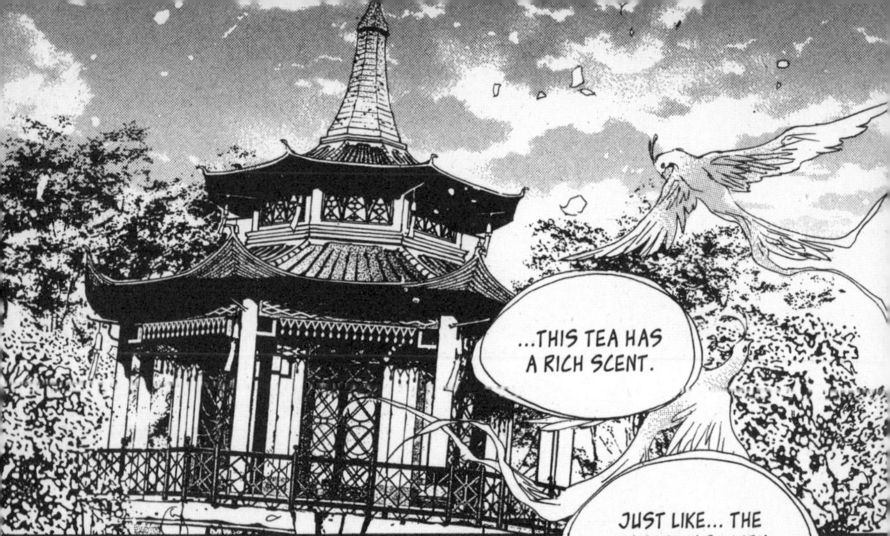
...THIS TEA HAS A RICH SCENT.
JUST LIKE... THE WAY IT WAS WHEN WE SHARED TEA HERE LONG AGO.

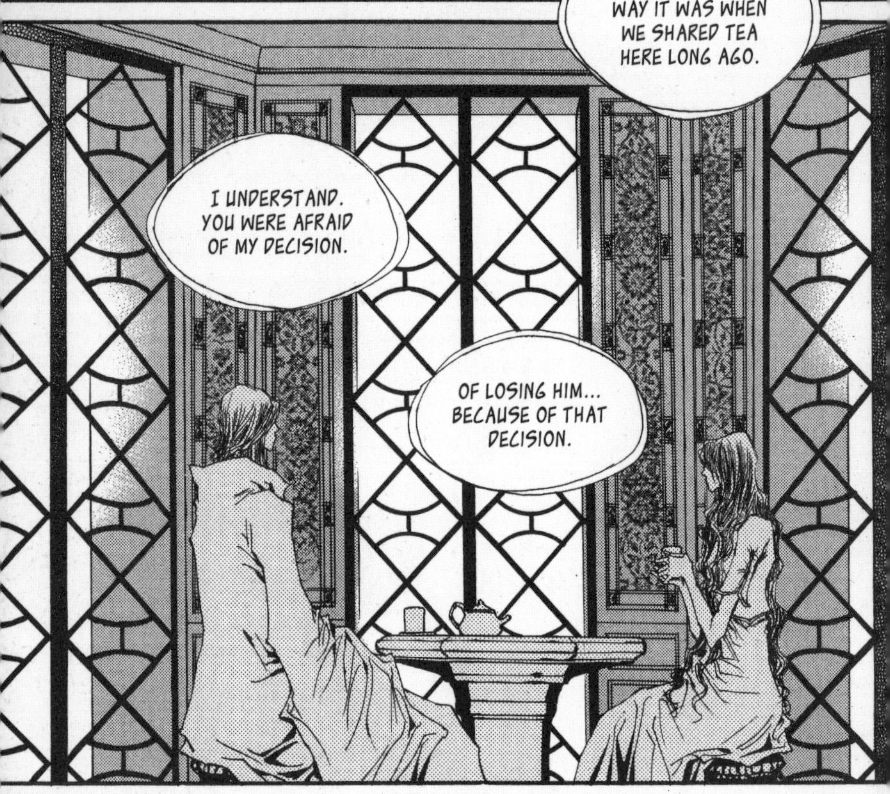
I UNDERSTAND. YOU WERE AFRAID OF MY DECISION.
OF LOSING HIM... BECAUSE OF THAT DECISION.

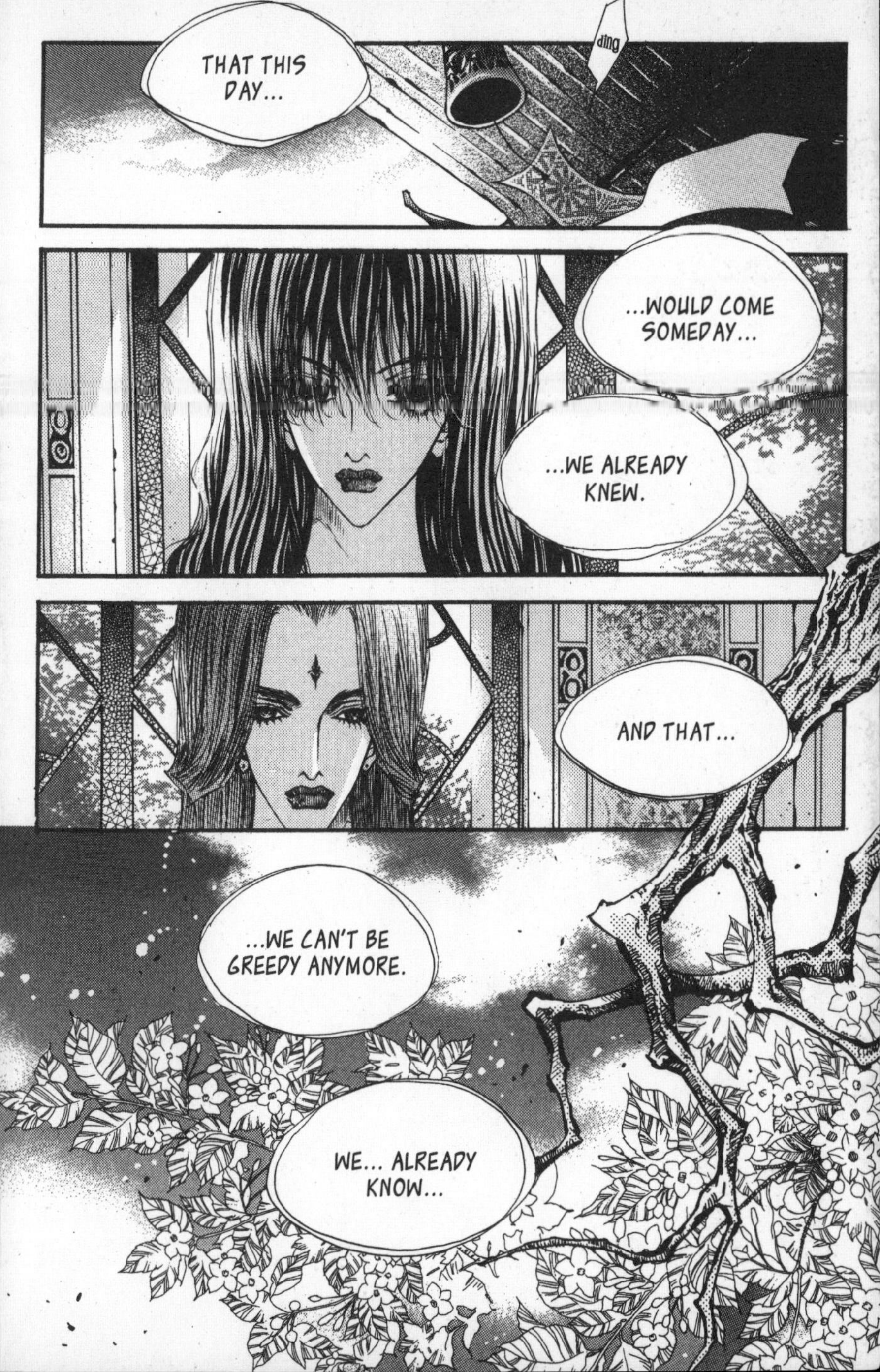
THAT THIS DAY...
ding
...WOULD COME SOMEDAY...
...WE ALREADY KNEW.
AND THAT...
...WE CAN'T BE GREEDY ANYMORE.
WE... ALREADY KNOW...

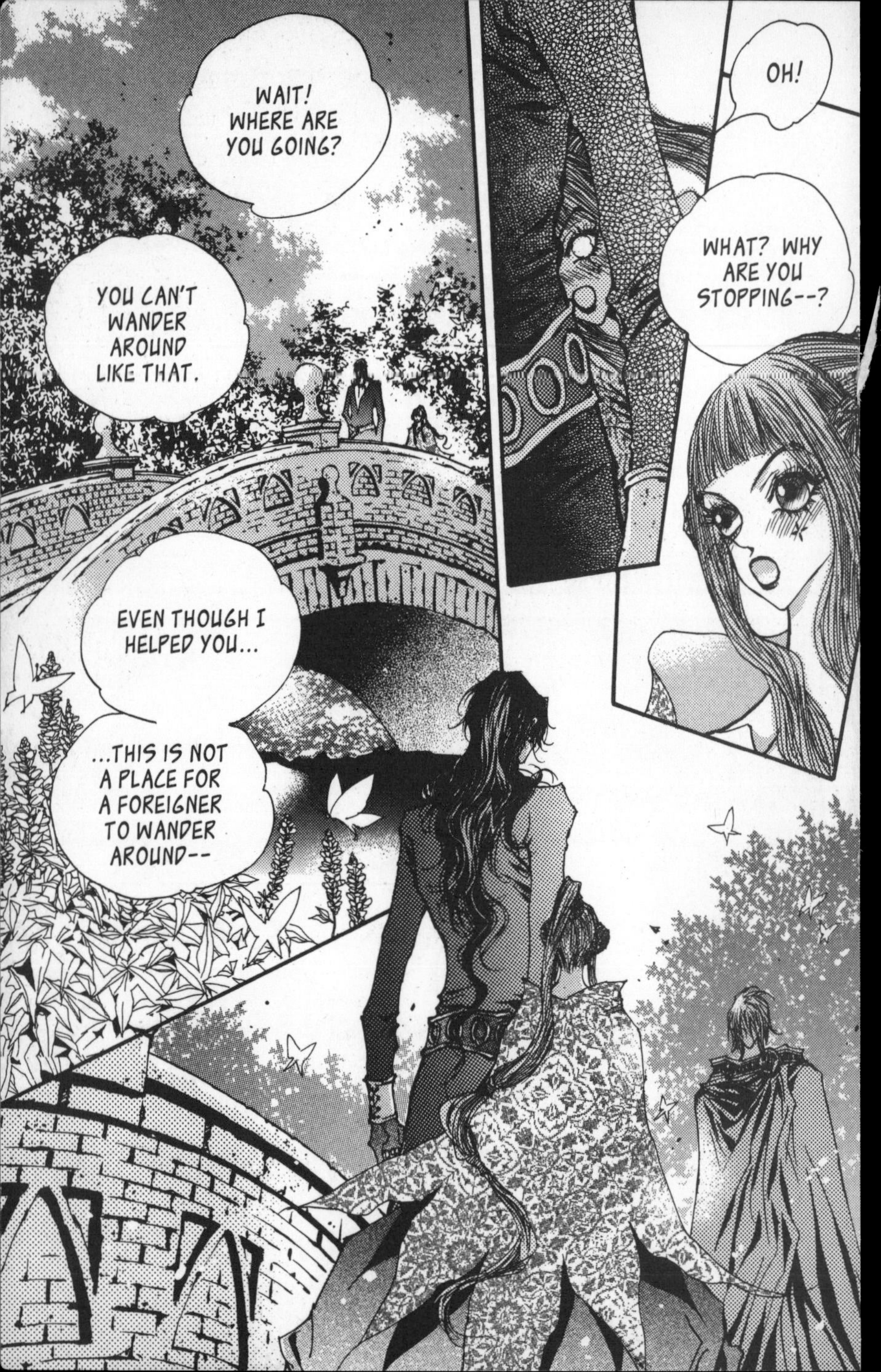
WAIT! WHERE ARE YOU GOING?
YOU CAN'T WANDER AROUND LIKE THAT.
EVEN THOUGH I HELPED YOU...
...THIS IS NOT A PLACE FOR A FOREIGNER TO WANDER AROUND--
OH!
WHAT? WHY ARE YOU STOPPING--?

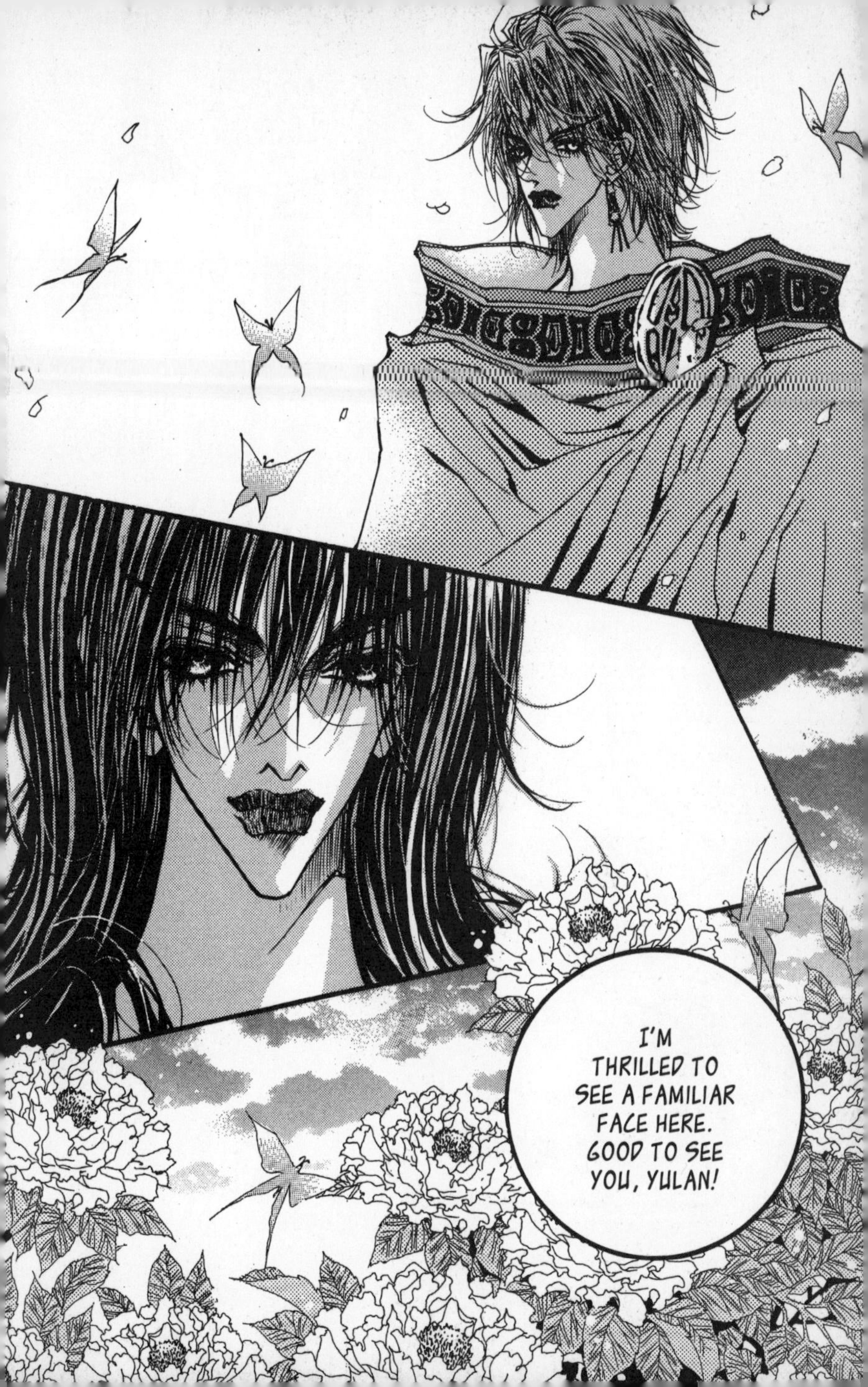
I'M THRILLED TO SEE A FAMILIAR FACE HERE. GOOD TO SEE YOU, YULAN!

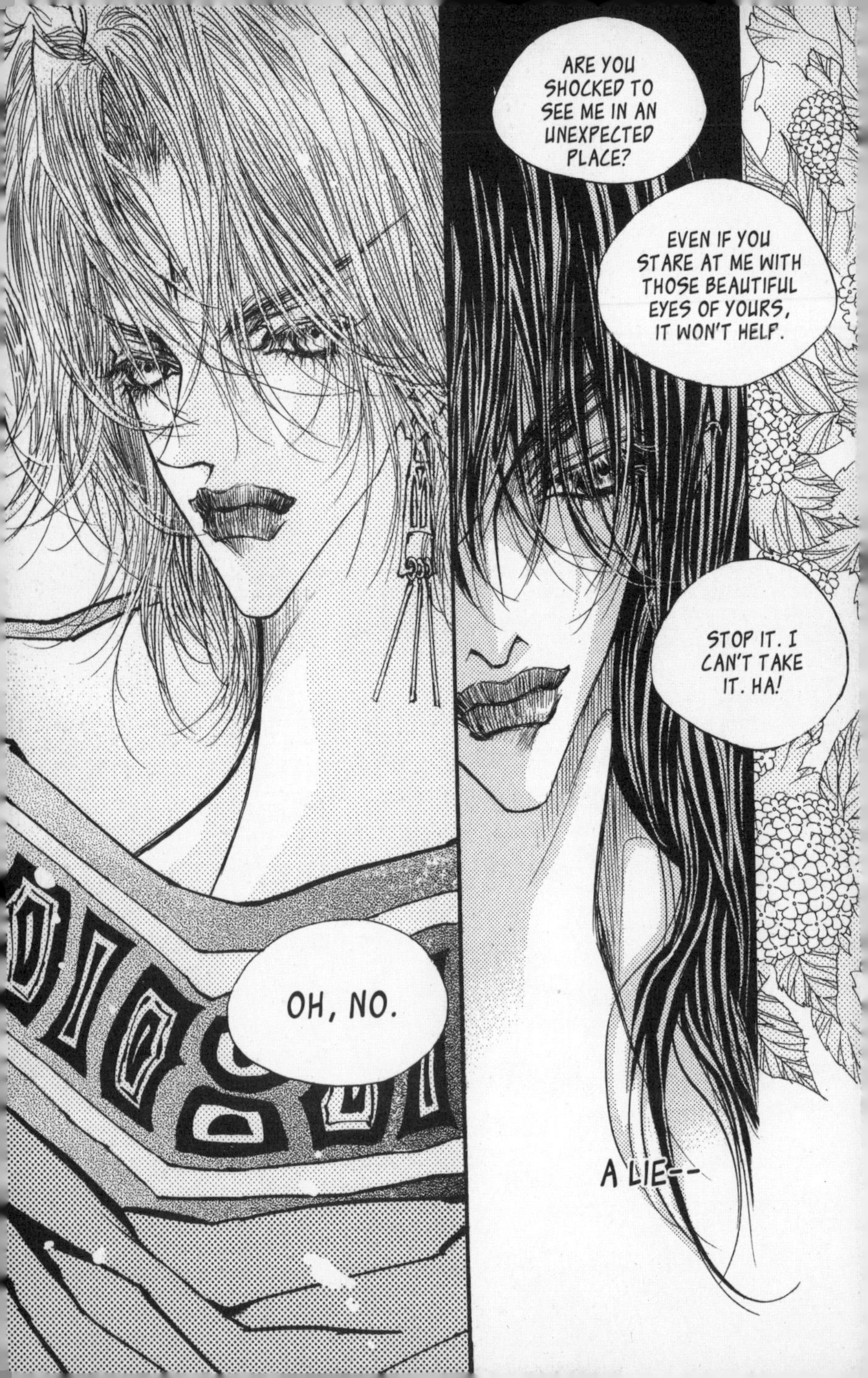
OH, NO.
ARE YOU SHOCKED TO SEE ME IN AN UNEXPECTED PLACE?
EVEN IF YOU STARE AT ME WITH THOSE BEAUTIFUL EYES OF YOURS, IT WON'T HELP.
STOP IT. I CAN'T TAKE IT. HA!
A LIE--

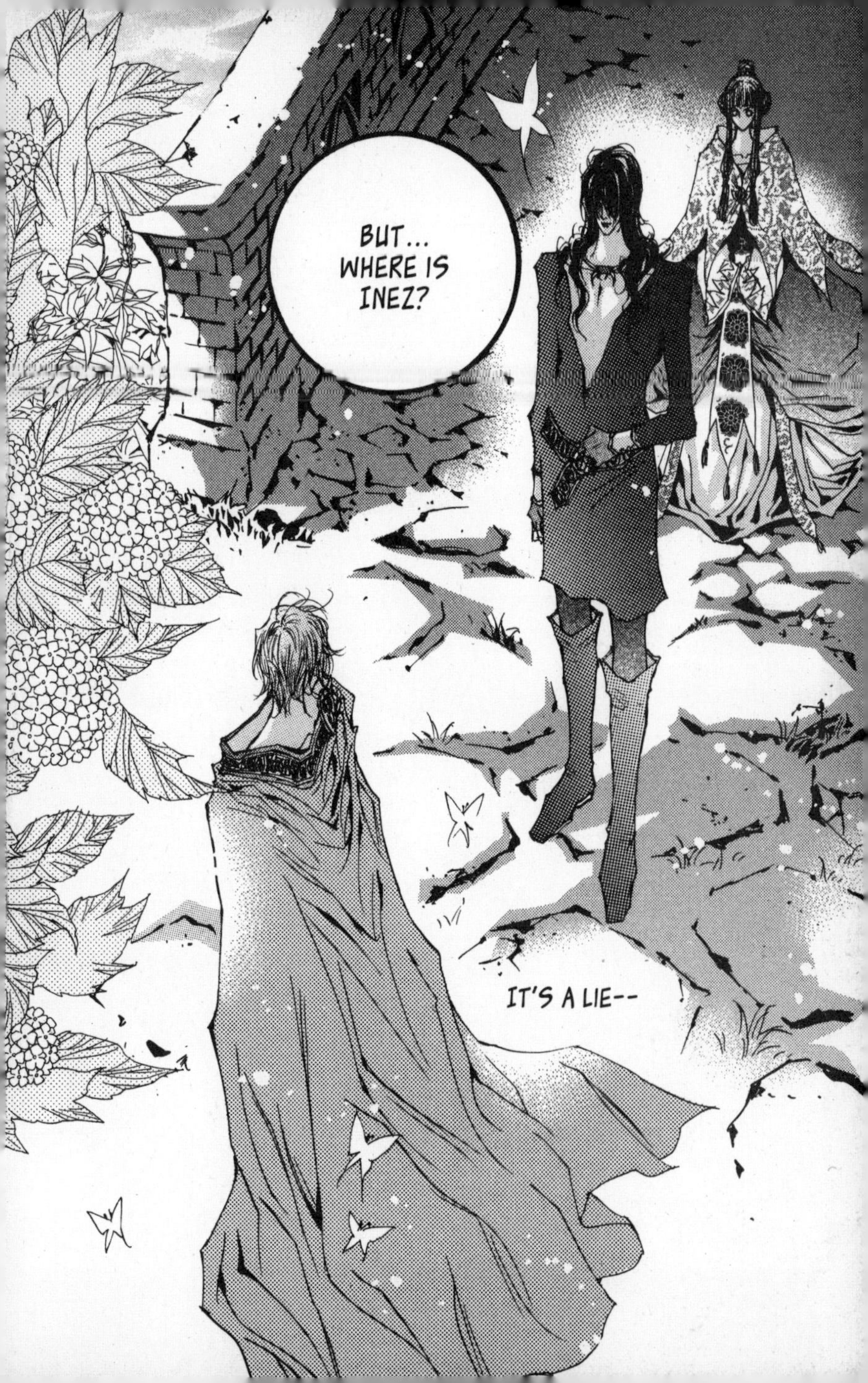
BUT... WHERE IS INEZ?
IT'S A LIE--

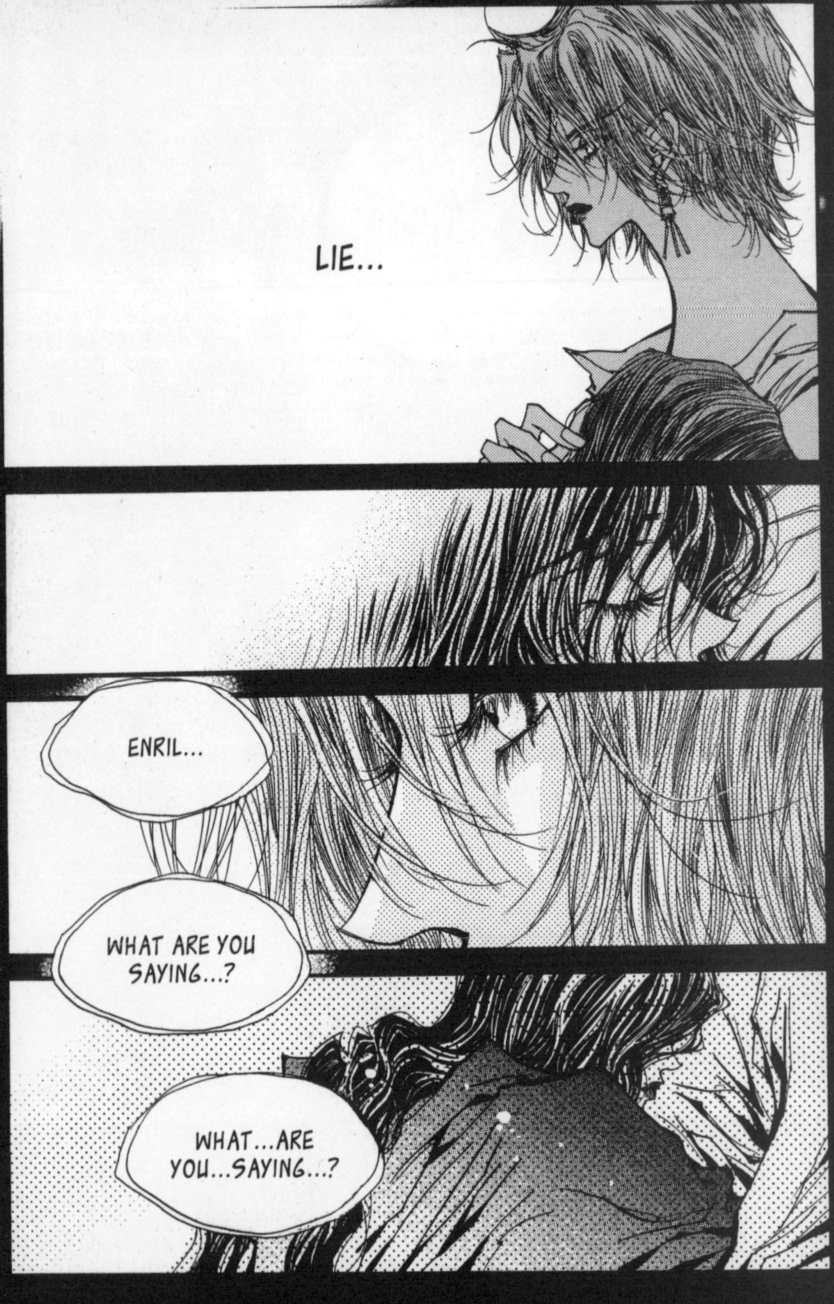
LIE...
ENRIL...
WHAT ARE YOU SAYING...?
WHAT...ARE YOU...SAYING...?

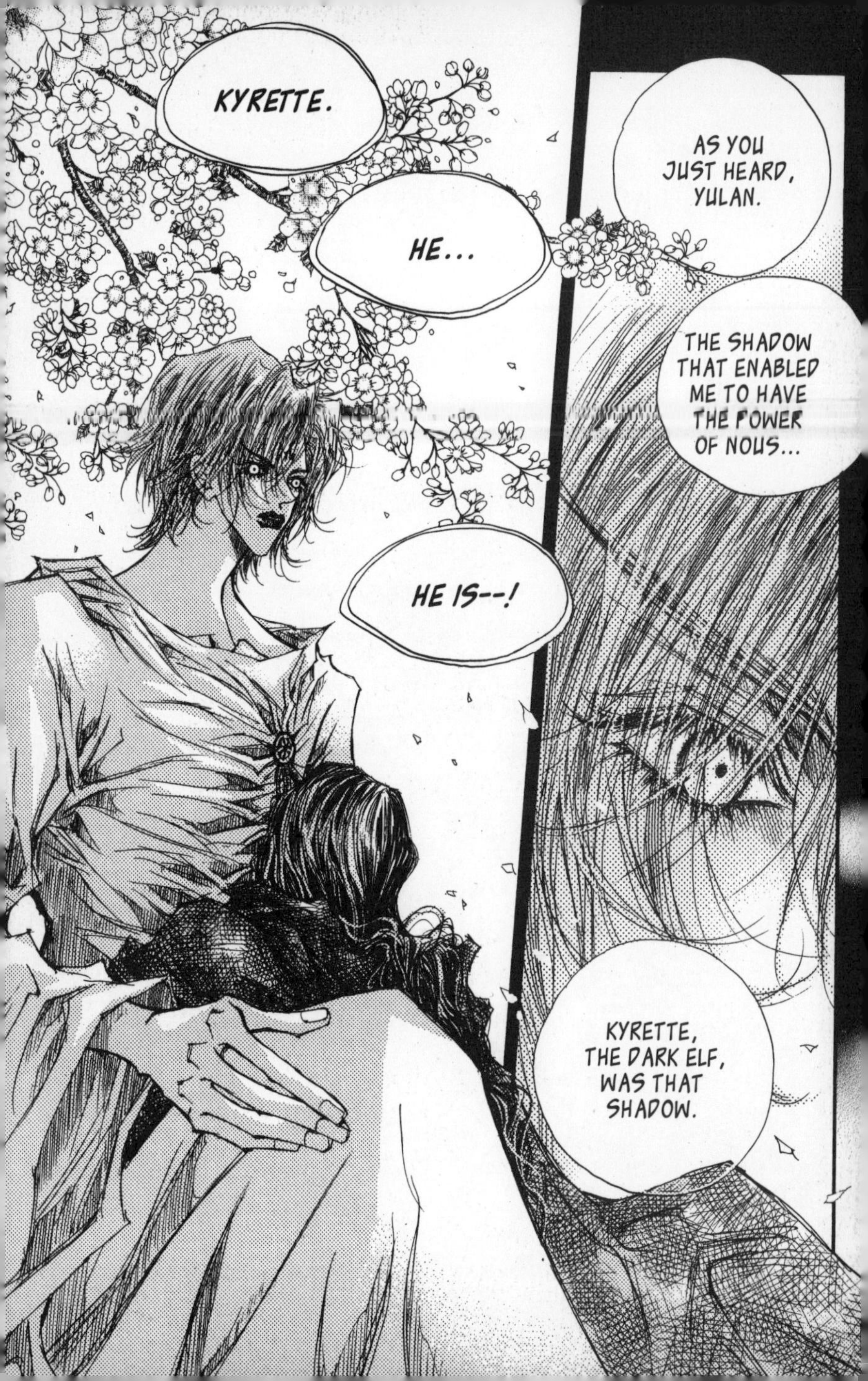
KYRETTE.
HE...
HE IS--!
AS YOU JUST HEARD, YULAN.
THE SHADOW THAT ENABLED ME TO HAVE THE POWER OF NOUS...
KYRETTE, THE DARK ELF, WAS THAT SHADOW.

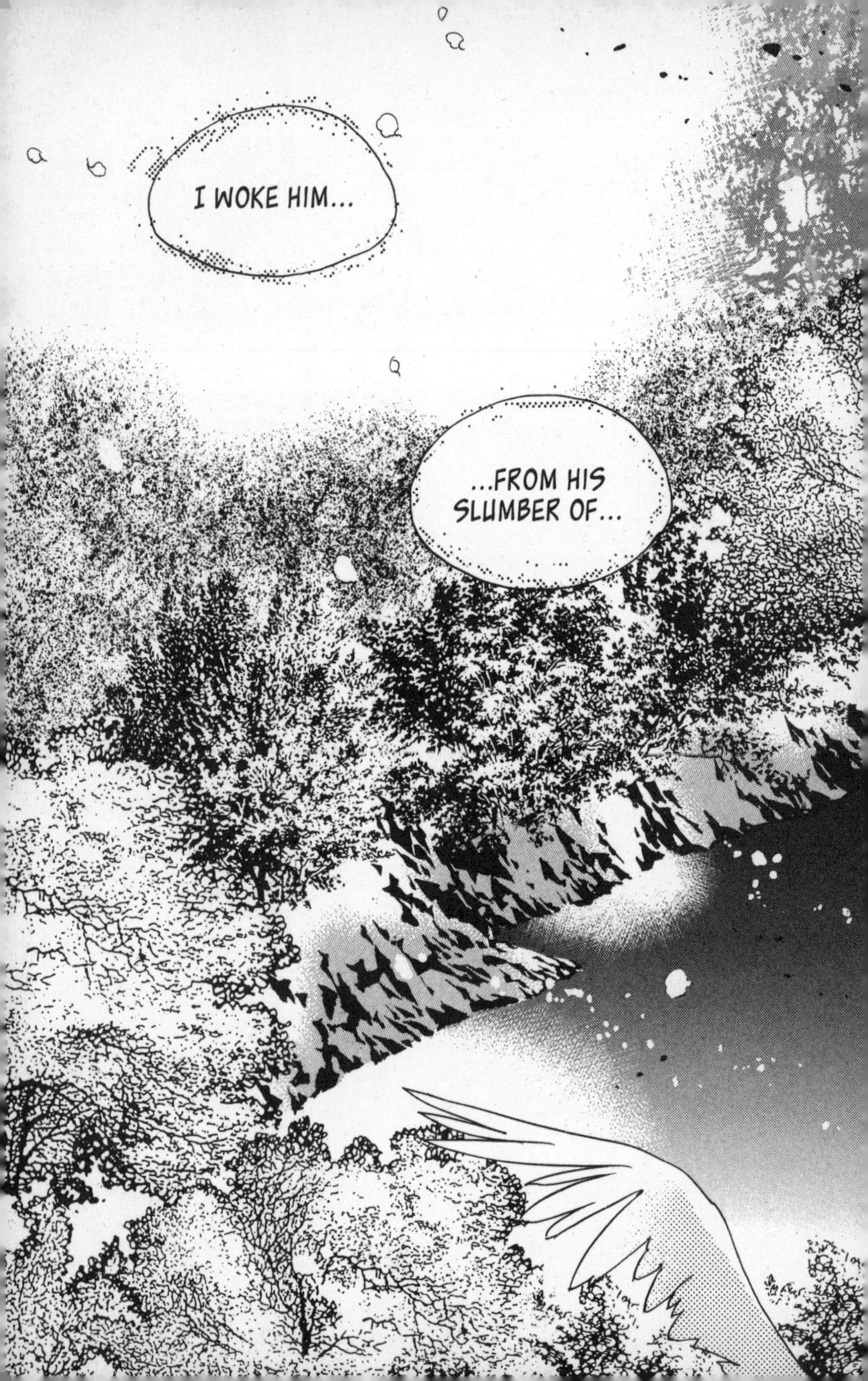
I WOKE HIM...
...FROM HIS SLUMBER OF...

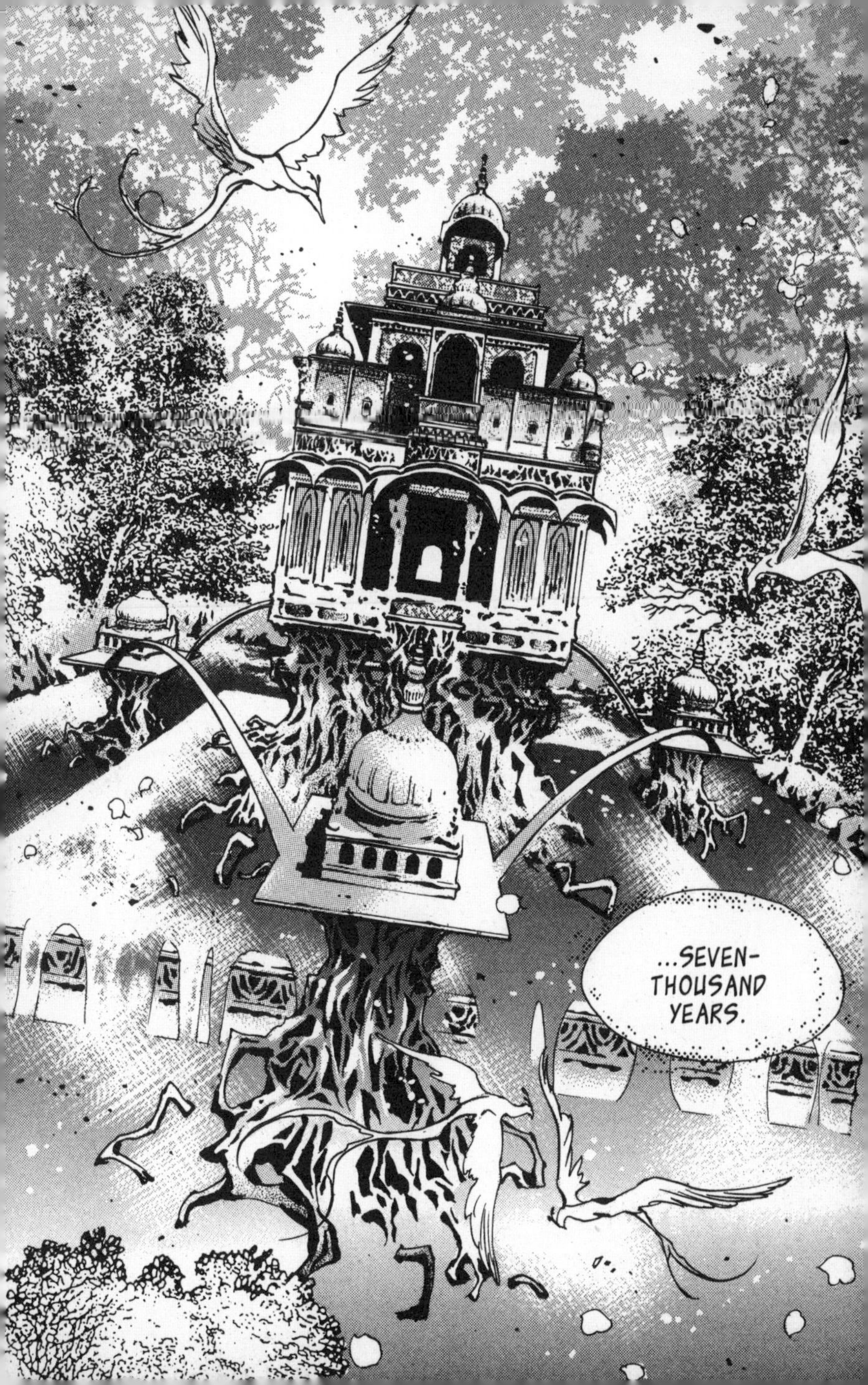
...SEVEN-THOUSAND YEARS.

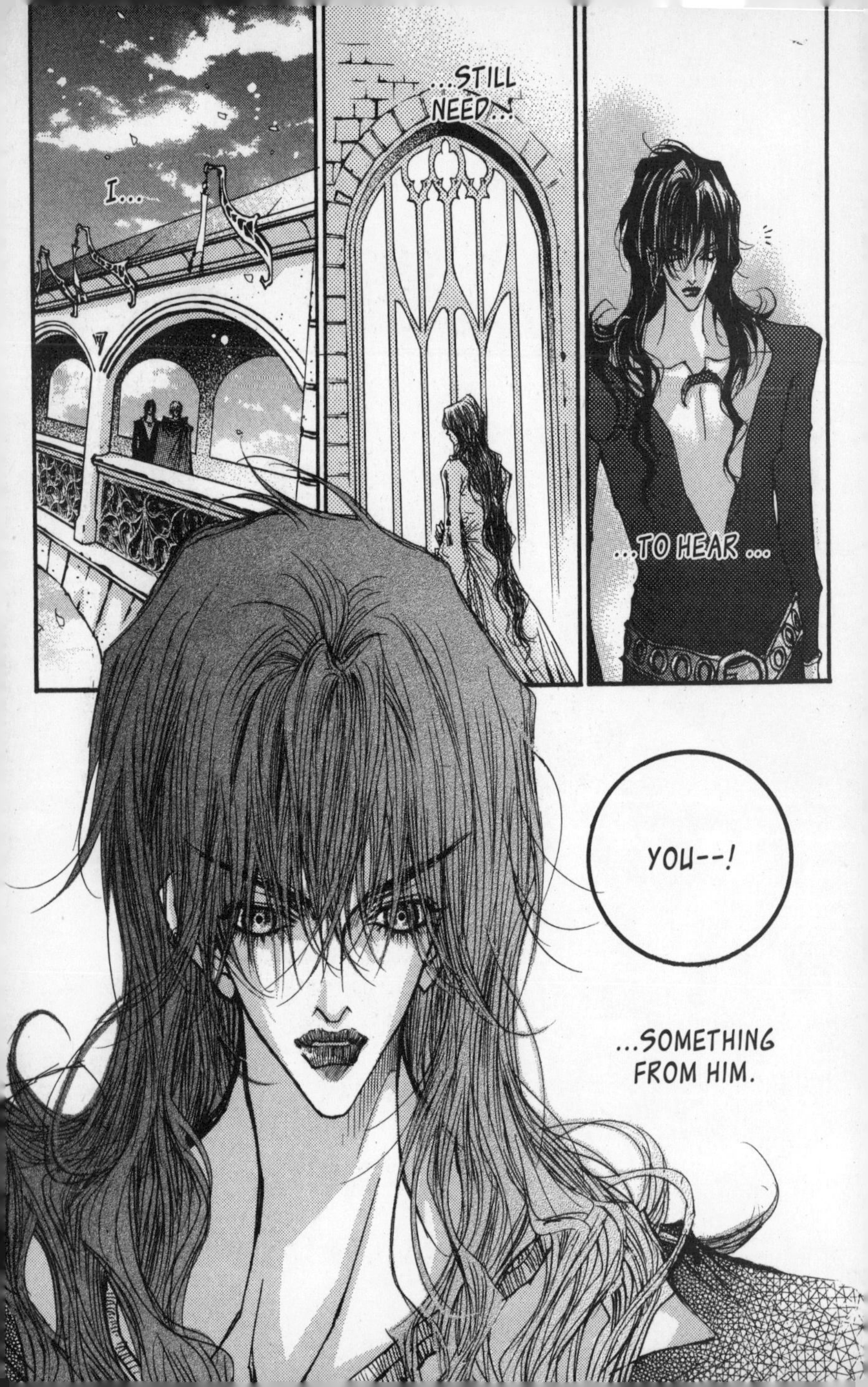
I...
...STILL NEED...
...TO HEAR ...
YOU--!
...SOMETHING FROM HIM.

TO BE CONTINUED IN ARCANA VOLUME 9!

THE QUEST CONTINUES IN

VOLUME 9

IN THE CONTINUING STORY OF ARCANA'S
PAST -- THE TALE OF ENRIL -- YULAN
BECOMES ENRIL'S UNWITTING PAWN IN HER
MYSTERIOUS PLAN. ALTHOUGH HER GOALS
SEEM NOBLE, ENRIL'S METHODS BECOME
INCREASINGLY PAINFUL FOR THE CONFUSED
AND IRATE YULAN, SENDING HIM INTO A
NEARLY CATATONIC STATE...

THERE'S INTRIGUE AND ADVENTURE IN
EVERY PAGE OF THE NEXT VOLUME OF
ARCANA!